PECULIAR PROPHETS

PECULIAR PROPHETS

A Biographical Dictionary
of New Religions

by

James R. Lewis

PARAGON HOUSE
St. Paul, Minnesota

First Edition, 1999

Published in the United States by
Paragon House
2700 University Avenue West
St. Paul, MN 55114

Manufactured in the United States of America.

Library of Congress Cataloging-in-Publishing data

Lewis, James R.,
     Peculiar prophets: a biographical dictionary of new religions /
by James R. Lewis.—1st ed.
        p.   cm.
     ISBN 1-55778-768-9 (alk. paper)
     1. Religions biography Dictionaries.   2. Cults—Dictionaries.
3. Sects—Dictionaries.   I. Title
BL72.L48   1999
200' .92'2 — dc21
[B]   99-21563
                                                                          CIP

10 9 8 7 6 5 4 3 2 1

For current information about all releases from Paragon House,
visit the web site at http://www.paragonhouse.com

CONTENTS

Contents

Contents

Contents

INTRODUCTION

The special promise of the study of religion is to nurture [our] resources of tolerance for difference, our capacity to learn from the other and to respect the other.
　　　　　　　　　　　　　　　　　　　　　　　—Jacob Neusner

In North America, historians have noted a recurring pattern of religious awakenings, beginning with the Great Awakening of the late colonial period. Such periods of renewed spiritual activity typically occur in the wake of disruptive social and economic changes: The established vision of reality no longer seems to apply, and people begin searching for new visions. In previous cycles of American religious experimentation, innovative forms of Protestantism most often formed the basis for these new visions.

The most recent period of religious innovation took place in the decades following the decline of the 1960s counterculture. However, unlike previous cycles of revival, the religious explosion that occurred in the 1970s and 1980s has served to push American spirituality in a number of new directions, thus shattering the traditional hegemony of Protestant Christianity. Lacking the power to generate a new basis for cultural synthesis, the current proliferation of new religions can strike the casual observer as a negative phase of contemporary life—a factor contributing to the disintegration of modern society.

An earlier generation of social scientists also pronounced negative judgments on new religious movements, though for very different reasons. Older scholars used adjustment to modern, secular society as the standard for judging rationality and mental health because of an implicit evolutionary paradigm that influenced them to view contemporary society as an evolutionary stage beyond traditional societies, and secularism as a step above religion. It was assumed that traditional society and religion represented an earlier, child-like stage of development and that the contemporaneous secular social order embodied humanity's emergence into mature adulthood. Any movement contrary to this hypothetical evolutionary current, such as an individual's conversion from a secular to a religious world view, was thus judged as regressive—a retreat from maturity to childhood. As the twentieth century draws to a close, these assumptions of our "academic ancestors" might strike us as quaint and näive, but their formulations continue to influence us.

In many ways, religions partially re-establish the world of traditional communities—arguably the "natural" environment for human beings. What this means for the present discussion is that, far from being symptomatic of social pathology, perhaps the emergence of new religious movements represent a *healthy* (or at least a health-seeking) response to the dislocations of modern secular society. To people confused by a complex, rapidly changing social environment—forced to make morally ambiguous choices in a world without ultimate meaning—it is not so self-evident that becoming an alienated cog in mass society is the most life-affirming option. Rather, for many individuals, it is the world view, values and community one finds in a religious fellowship that provides the context for a humanly meaningful life.

The present reference work focusses attention on the founders and other important leaders of groups normally regarded as outside the pale of the American religious mainstream. Not unlike most new businesses, new religions almost always embody the vision of a single, influential prophet. This comparison with the business world is *not*, of course, meant to imply that the motive for creating new religions is personal gain. Rather, given the secular orientation of contemporary society, it is not difficult to understand why new businesses require the dynamism of unusually talented and motivated entrepreneurs. (By way of contrast, How many successful new businesses have been created by committees?) This understanding can then be transfered to the religious realm where, as in the business world, new enterprises are usually built around the vision of a single leader.

While the majority of new religions are innocuous, many have been involved in social conflicts. A handful of these conflicts have made national and even international headlines, from the siege of the Branch Davidian community to the group suicide of Heaven's Gate members. One consequence of these highly publicized incidents is that they have served to reinforce unreflective stereotypes about "cults" and "cult leaders" that are appropriate for some—but certainly not the majority of—newer minority religions. Unfortunately, such stereotyped information is often the only "data" readily available to the media and law enforcement at the onset of such conflicts. One of the goals of the present volume is to address this lack of objective information.

At one time, "cult" was a neutral, descriptive label. However, by the middle of the 1970s, it had become a pejorative term, applied to any unpopular religious group. In ordinary language people talk as if there is an objective category of groups called "cults" that can be distinguished from genuine religions. In this commonly accepted view, cults are by definition socially-dangerous, false religions, led by cynical cult leaders who exploit followers for their own gain. This portrayal is, however, deeply flawed. While a handful of religious groups may at least partially fit the stereotype, "cult" is best understood as a socially-negotiated label that frequently means little more than a religion one personally dislikes.

Because of its negative connotations, mainstream scholars working in the field now tend to avoid the term, preferring the label "new religion" or "new religious movement." This term appears to have been taken from Japanese scholars of religion, who coined the term "new religion" to refer to the many groups that exploded onto the Japanese religious scene in the years following the war. Even this term, however, is problematic because the great majority of religious organizations—even new organizations—view themselves as embodying a much older religious tradition. There is thus no truly adequate term currently in common usage.

The following pages contain information on the leaders and/or founders of 350 religious or spiritual groups. These groups run the gamut from tiny churches with less than a hundred members to organizations like Rissho Kosei Kai that number into the millions. Many of these leaders make extraordinary claims. To avoid stylistic awkwardness, most entries make selective use of qualifiers like, "the leader *asserts* that...." or "the founder *claims* that...." In other words, the absence of these qualifiers should NOT be interpreted as implying that the author of the relevant entry necessarily accepts such statements on face value.

Finally note that we sent copies of entries on leader-founders of extant organizations to the relevant organizational headquarters with a request for corrections and/or updated information. The response to our mailing was tremendous. However, because so many churches have moved their HQ, and because the postal service refuses to forward mail beyond six months after an address change, many of our letters were returned. For those churches which did not receive our original mailing, we would appreciate receiving updated information and a current address for possible future editions of the present work. Please write: James R. Lewis, P.O. Box 5097, Stanford, CA 94309.

A

Abdu'l-Baha: Abdu'l-Baha (May 23, 1844-November 28, 1921), a major figure in the beginnings of the Baha'i Faith, was born in Persia (today's Iran). His birth name was Abbas Effendi, son of Mirza Husayn Ali, better known as Baha'u'llah (Glory of God). Baha'u'llah had come to believe that he was the promised messenger of God spoken of by Siyyad Ali Muhammad of Shiraz (1819-1850), known as the Bab. The Bab had preached that the successor of the prophet Muhammad, founder of Islam, was coming. In 1863 Baha'u'llah, Effendi's father, first announced that he was that holy figure.

From the beginning, Abdu'l-Baha (Effendi) was a devoted follower of his father, even though it meant a life of hardship, at least at the beginning. Followers of the Bab in general were persecuted and Baha'u'llah lived in a Palestine prison from 1868 to 1879, when he was allowed to live under house arrest with his family. Abdu'l-Baha helped write his books in prison and otherwise assisted with the organizational work. When Baha'u'llah died in 1892, Abdu'l-Baha was the designated successor. At that time he took the name Abdu'l-Baha, meaning Slave of Baha.

For a long time his life was almost as restricted by authorities as his father's life, and not until 1911 was he free to travel. He directed the international growth of the Baha'i Faith and made a world tour in 1912. On that tour he visited the United States and dedicated the grounds for the Baha'i temple in Wilmette, Illinois. His writings are considered holy by the Baha'i and are included in the two major faith books, *Baha'i Scriptures* and *Baha'i World Faith*. He emphasized the Baha'i Faith as compatible with all religions and aware of their unity. He summarized the faith into a number of principles, including such social goals as the establishment of a world court, compulsory education, a universal language, and equal opportunity to the means of existence.

George Adamski (with a picture of a "space brother")
Courtesy: American Religion Collection

Adamski, George: George Adamski (April 17, 1891-April 23, 1965), America's first well-known reporter of UFO contact, was born in Poland and moved to the United States with his family at the age of two. Little other information is available about his life from that point until he settled with his wife in southern California and in 1936 founded the Royal Order of Tibet. He actually claimed to represent the Royal Order and lecture on their behalf. He also briefly associated with the Order of Loving Service, a metaphysical group in Laguna Beach, California.

His day job was in a cafe near Mt. Palomar and its observatory. In the early 1940s he became interested in Unidentified Flying Objects (UFOs), long before they were much discussed by the public. On October 9, 1946, he reported seeing a UFO for the first time and in 1949 published *Pioneers of Space* to generate interest in the subject. On November 20, 1952, he reported telepathic contact with a human-like Venusian and the following month reported another contact in which a hieroglyphic message was given. These encounters were reported in his second book (written with Leslie Desmond), *Flying Saucers Have Landed* (1953). This became one of the most popular flying saucer books ever written. He gained a broad following and was a sought-after lecturer.

Adamski's following was gained, not just from those interested in UFOs, but from those interested in the knowledge, advice, and wisdom Adamski claimed to receive from the space people. In 1957 he organized the International Get Acquainted Club to bring his followers together. The pinnacle of his career was reached with a world tour in 1959, the publication of *Cosmic Philosophy* (1961), and the establishment of *Science Publications Newsletter* in 1962.

Adamski's work was discredited in the eyes of many people when UFO researcher James Moseley in 1957 stated that Adamski had faked his photographs, taken the "hieroglyphs" from an obscure scholarly work, and plagiarized old science fiction as space messages. Adamski's close associate C. A. Honey broke away in 1963 after confirming for himself apparent fraudulent activity. Despite these setbacks, Adamski's work continued and is currently maintained by the George Adamski Foundation and the UFO Education Center.

Adi Da and Devotees
Courtesy: Adi Dham

Adi Da: Adi Da, or Avatar Adi Da Samraj (aka: Franklin Jones, Da Free John, etc.): Franklin Jones (b. November 3, 1939), founder of the religion of Adidam, was born in Jamaica, New York. He claims that he knew enlightenment at birth, but that he voluntarily chose to submit to a condition of ordinary consciousness in order to discover what is necessary for human beings to realize enlightenment. In 1960, while studying at Columbia University in New York City, he had a "crisis of despair" that began a long period of spiritual searching.

After receiving his B.A. from Columbia University in 1961 he did further work in English literature at Stanford University in 1961-62. During that time he participated in drug experiments conducted at the Veterans Administration Hospital in Mountain View, California. In 1964 he began studying with Swami Rudrananda, a disciple of Swami Muktananda. In 1966-67, at Rudrananda's suggestion, he spent a year at the Lutheran Theological Seminary in Philadelphia. In 1968-70 he spent periods of time at Swami Muktananda's ashram in India. After settling in Los Angeles, an event occurred on September 10, 1970, while he was at the Vedanta Society Temple in Hollywood, which he claims was his entrance into a permanent state of enlightenment, or "seventh stage Sahaj Samadhi."

In 1972, after writing his autobiography, *The Knee Of Listening* (first published in 1973), he began his public ministry in Hollywood through the Dawn Horse Fellowship (later going through several name changes, eventually becoming the Adidam Pan-Communion). In 1973 he made a pilgrimage to India, formally ended his devotional relationship to Swami Muktananda, and changed his name to Bubba Free John ("Bubba" meaning "brother"). When he returned from India, he began what he described as a "crazy" manner of working with his devotees, dealing very directly with their preoccupations, especially relative to sexuality and spiritual experience. He states that he adopted the "crazy" manner in order to demonstrate the futility of all forms of seeking and also to give instruction in how sex and all other realms of experience can be rightly integrated with spiritual life. After several years of such work with large numbers of his devotees, Adi Da began in the late 70s to concentrate in continuing the same kind of work with small groups of those who were most serious. In 1979 he changed his name to Da Free John ("Da" meaning "giver"). In 1983 he moved to a South Pacific island, where he established his principal ashram (Adidam Samrajashram). In 1986 his name changed again to Heart-Master Da Love-Ananda ("Ananda" meaning "bliss"), and then again in the mid-1990s to Adi Da Samraj. He remained primarily at Adidam Samrajashram for about ten years; the years 1994-1998 he spent traveling between the communities of his devotees in Adidam Samrajashram, the U.S., and Europe.

Adi Da's work has not been without controversy. Some have objected to his "crazy" manner of teaching; Adi Da has said in response that his work is inevitably unacceptable from the conventional point of view, because his purpose is to completely undermine the ego and turn his devotees entirely to the Divine Reality. In 1997-98, Adi Da created a series of twenty-three books (or "source-texts") which he intends to stand as his authoritative summaries of his teaching and the practice of Adidam.

Adler, Felix: Felix Adler (August 13, 1851-April 24, 1933) founded the Ethical Culture Society in New York City on May 15, 1876, a group devoted to a nontheistic, ethical way of life. Adler was born in Alzey, Germany and traveled to the United States at age six with his family when his father accepted the prestigious position of rabbi of Temple Emanu-El in New York. Adler seemed destined to follow in his father's footsteps, but during graduate studies in Berlin and Heidelberg his faith was shaken by the new waves of biblical criticism and philosophy. He completed his education, but was not ordained a rabbi.

After returning to the United States, Adler became professor of Hebrew and Oriental Literature at Cornell University (1874-76) in Ithaca, New York, and struggled with the further implications of his religious journey. He wanted to establish a strong philosophical basis for a moral life without dependence on a divinity. He found some like-minded people in the Free Religious Association, led by Octavius Brooks Frothingham in New York City. By 1878 Adler's own formulations had gained sufficient support that he was able to leave the university and found the Ethical Culture Society.

Adler shaped the Ethical Culture Society into a well-known center for serious reflection and social concern, following the society's motto, "Deed Before Creed." Over the years he founded a visiting nurse program for the poor, a tenement house committee, the Manhattan Trade School for Girls, the first free kindergarten, and was active in many other arenas. He was often called upon to speak on behalf of the garment workers of New York City and from 1894 to 1921 he was chair of the National Child Labor Committee.

Adler returned to teaching in 1902, serving as professor of political and social ethics at Columbia University until 1921, and was the author of a number of books. By the time of his death, there were at least six branches of the society in the United States and several abroad. The society is currently federated in the United States as the American Ethical Union and internationally as part of the International Humanist and Ethical Union.

Adler, Margot: Margot Adler (b. April 16, 1946), well-known journalist and spokesperson for the Neo-Pagan movement, was born in Little Rock, Arkansas. Her grandfather was the famous psychiatrist Alfred Adler and her father was also a psychiatrist. She received her B.A. in political science in 1968 from the University of California at Berkeley and began working for WBAI-FM in New York. Deciding to stay with broadcast journalism, she received her M.S. in 1970 from the Columbia University Graduate School of Journalism.

About 1972 Adler joined a study group of the New York Coven of Welsh Traditional Witches. From 1973 to 1975 she was a leader of the Manhattan Pagan Way, of the Gardnerian tradition, and from 1976 to 1981 was priestess of the Gardnerian coven Largalon. By this time she was a known figure in national Neo-Pagan circles, assisted by her move in 1978 to a prominent broadcast position with National Public Radio, where she has since remained.

In 1979 she published *Drawing Down the Moon*, an important book that has introduced many thousands to the beliefs and practices of contemporary wiccan Neo-Paganism. Since 1982 she has not associated with any particular coven, but travels extensively as a popular workshop leader and speaker. In 1988 Selena Fox, priestess of Circle Wicca, officiated in the hand-fasting (marriage) ceremony of Adler and John Gliedman, the first such ceremony to be recognized in the society pages of the *New York Times*.

Aglipay, Gregorio: Gregorio Aglipay (1860-September 1, 1940), founder of the Iglesia Filipina Católica Independiente (Philippine Independent Catholic Church), was born in the Philippines. In his youth he was houseboy at the Augustinian friary in Manila and was determined to become a priest. He was ordained a Roman Catholic priest in 1889, during a time of revolutionary struggle against Spanish rule. In 1890 he and others formed an anti-Spanish Catholic church and sought protection from an ambivalent Rome.

The Philippines gained independence from Spain in 1898, but soon another struggle began against American colonialism, with Aglipay's church again siding with the revolutionaries. The following year Rome excommunicated Aglipay, and the church reorganized as the Philippine Independent Catholic Church. Because of his courage and patriotism, Aglipay gained a hero's status among much of the population. After the revolutionary leader Emilio Aguinaldo surrendered to the Americans in March 1901, Aglipay's church sought renewed ties with the Vatican, but with no success. In need of an episcopal consecration to maintain the church's activities, Aglipay unsuccessfully approached both the Episcopalians and Old Catholics. On January 18, 1903 he and a colleague were consecrated bishops presbyterial style by twelve of the church's priests.

Aglipay led the church as head bishop for the rest of his life. He became strongly attracted to Unitarianism and attended a number of Unitarian conferences, but did not ask the church to move in that direction. A Unitarian minister performed the wedding for Aglipay and his common-law wife. Seven years after his death the church achieved communion with and a line of episcopal succession from the Protestant Episcopal Church in the United States.

Ahmad, Mirza Ghulam Hazrat: Mirza Ghulam Hazrat Admad (February 13, 1835-May 26, 1908), founder of the Ahmadiyya Movement in Islam, was born in Qadian, Pakistan. According to custom, he married a cousin in 1852, and reared two children. In 1865 he began working for the government, but left three years later to oversee the family estate.

Ahmad was concerned about what he considered the declining state of Islam. In 1880 he published *Barahin-i-Ahmadiyah*, in which he defended Islam against its critics, particularly Christian critics. This gained Ahmad an initial following. In 1891 he declared himself to be the Messiah of Christianity and the Mahdi, the long-awaited reformer of Islam. He claimed to be the Messiah in the sense that he had the spirit and power of Jesus. Jesus, he said, was not going to be resurrected because he was a prophet only, and not divine. Further, Jesus only fainted on the cross and later escaped to live out a natural life span in India. This gained Ahmad an additional following, and a cautious watch from the religious authorities.

In 1901, Ahmad asserted that he was not just a reformer with the spirit and power of Jesus, but was a full prophet on a par with Muhammad himself. He also declared abolition of the practice of *jihad*, or holy war. These actions earned him the position of heretic in the mainstream Islamic faith, and he and his followers were persecuted. Despite (or because of) the persecution, the Ahmadiyya Movement kept growing and eventually established headquarters in Rabwah, Pakistan.

The movement's growth did not stop with Ahmad's death in 1908, and a particularly successful location for the movement has been the United States, beginning in 1921. There, for various reasons, the movement attracted primarily African American followers. They have been joined, after changes in immigration patterns in the mid-1960s, by large numbers of Middle Eastern and Asian immigrants.

Robert Aitken Rashi, founder Diamond Sangha
© *Tom Haar*

Robert Aitken: Robert Aitken, founder of the Diamond Sangha, began studying Zen in California with Nyogen Senzaki Sensei in 1947. He continued training with Soen Nakagawa Roshi and other teachers in Japan before affiliating himself with Sanbo Kyodan. In 1962, Hakuun Yasutani Roshi, founder of Sanbo Kyodan, began periodic visits to Hawaii to guide the Diamond Sangha in Zen practice. In 1974 Yamada Roshi authorized Robert Aitken to teach.

Robert Aitken began leading annual retreats in Nevada City, California, in 1978. He started annual retreats in Sydney, Australia, the following year. These retreats have resulted in the Ring of Bone Zendo in Nevada City, the Sydney Zen Centre, the Zen Group of Western Australia in Perth and the Zen Desert Sangha in Tucson, Arizona, affiliating with the Diamond Sangha.

Robert Aitken Roshi retired in 1996 and was succeeded by Nelson Foster, who is also the teacher for the Ring of Bone community in Nevada City, CA. Robert Aitken now lives near his son on the island of Hawaii and continues to write and consult with other Buddhist leaders. He has published eight books on buddhism. There are now 20 practice groups around the world officially affiliated with Diamond Sangha. The Diamond Sangha is headquartered in Honolulu, Hawaii, and is affiliated with the Sanbo Kyodan (Order of the Three Treasures) which is headquartered in Kamakura, Japan.

Ali, Noble Drew: Noble Drew Ali (January 8, 1886-July 20, 1929), founder of the Moorish Science Temple of America, was born Timothy Drew in North Carolina. He grew up poor and with little education, but managed as a young man to see much of the world. He was surprised at the small amount of prejudice in the Muslim nations, and came to believe that African Americans were really Moors, descendants of the Moabites of Canaan, and Morocco was their land of origin.

Ali believed it was his duty to re-educate African Americans as to their true roots and heritage, including their history in America. He thought that the Continental Congress conspired to enslave the previously free and Muslim blacks. Once enslaved, the blacks slowly forgot their identity and turned to Christianity, the white people's religion. In 1912 Ali went so far as to request that President Woodrow Wilson release the Moorish flag, which was supposedly hidden in a safe in Independence Hall.

Ali opened the first Moorish Temple (later incorporated as the Moorish Science Temple of America) in 1913 in Newark, New Jersey, and began using the name Noble Drew Ali, claiming that, while on a visit in the Middle East, Sultan Abdul Asis Abn Saud had given him that name. In 1927 Ali published *The Holy Koran*, a small booklet of beliefs drawing upon spiritualism and occult traditions, not to be confused with the similarly-named holy book of mainstream Muslim faith.

By 1928 Ali had almost twenty temples in fifteen states. There were many eager to hear his message of black unity and proud heritage. He said that Jesus was a black man who had tried to redeem the black Moabites, only to be thwarted by the white Romans. Just as Ali's organization was reaching its strength, it was rent by problems stemming from temple leaders, including Ali's own business manager, Claude D. Green, reaping quick profits by selling such items as Old Moorish Healing Oil. As it became known that Ali was going to expel the culprits, Green was killed (March 1929) and Ali arrested for the murder, despite having been out of town. Five months later, awaiting trial, Ali died under rather mysterious circumstances. Ali's organization did not disappear, but continues into the present, and has been the source of several other groups of black Muslims, including the Nation of Islam.

Allen, Asa Alonzo: Asa Alonzo Allen (March 27, 1911-June 11, 1970), famous Pentecostal faith healer and founder of Miracle Life Fellowship International, was born in Sulfur Rock, Arkansas. He had a difficult childhood, contending with his father's alcoholism and his own alcoholism. In 1934 he was converted at a Methodist revival meeting and it turned his life around. Soon he married and in 1936 was licensed to preach by the Assemblies of God.

He spent the next fourteen years alternating between unremarkable pastorates and unsuccessful evangelistic tours. Finally he felt he discovered the 13 requirements for a successful healing ministry and about 1950 associated with William Branham's "Voice of Healing" crusades. He bought a tent and began having spectacular success in healing tours. He established the A. A. Allen Revivals in Dallas, Texas, and began the Allen Revival Hour on the radio. In 1955 he was arrested for driving under the influence of alcohol and he was dropped by the Branham organization.

In 1956 he founded the Miracle Revival Fellowship, composed of independent ministers and congregations, and began touring again. His new *Miracle Magazine* helped tie his followers together. In 1958, thanks to a generous gift of land, he established headquarters near Tombstone, Arizona, and created a community called Miracle Valley. During the 1960s he held integrated revivals in the North and South and gained a significant following among African Americans as a critic of segregation. The last years of his life were marked by both great outward success and great personal difficulties. In 1967 his wife, Lexia, divorced him, and his death in 1970 was reportedly caused by cirrhosis of the liver, suggesting that he was never able to overcome his addiction to alcohol.

Allred, Rulon Clark: Rulon Clark Allred (March 29, 1906-May 10, 1977), leader of the Apostolic United Brethren, was born in Chihuahua, Mexico, the second of ten children. His father, Byron Harvey Allred, was a former Speaker of the House in the state of Idaho, but moved his family to Mexico in 1903 to find a more hospitable environment for his practice of polygamy. The younger Allred did not initially follow his father's polygamous lifestyle, but became part of mainstream Mormonism through the Church of Jesus Christ of Latter-day Saints. He was trained as a chiropractor in Los Angeles, got married, and settled into a respected practice.

In 1933 his father wrote a book defending polygamy and Allred began to write a critical response, but was instead converted to his father's point of view. With this change in belief his marriage dissolved, he was expelled from the church, and his business declined. After a few years he moved to Salt Lake City, Utah, joined the polygamous United Order Effort, and began a new life, with several wives and new chiropractic business. His violation of anti-polygamy laws caught up with him, however, and he was arrested on March 7, 1944. After seven months in jail he was released on parole and tried monogamy for a while. Failing in this effort, in 1947 he went to Mexico, only to return the following year.

In 1954 Allred gained leadership of the United Order Effort and over the next twenty years the group experienced significant growth, including in its ranks a group in Mexico and a colony in Pinesdale, Montana. It incorporated in 1975 as "The Corporation of the Presiding Elder of the Apostolic United Brethren," and has since been known by the shortened, "Apostolic United Brethren." The group's success was marred by the frequent conflicts with similar Mormon fundamentalist groups, particularly one led by Ervil LeBaron. In 1977 two women shot and killed Allred and LeBaron was convicted of arranging the murder. Allred's brother, Owen, then took over the organization.

Ammann, Jakob: Jakob Ammann (c.February 12, 1644-?), initiator of the Amish split from the Mennonites, was born in Switzerland. Little is known of the details of his personal life. He first gained public attention in the 1690s as the minister of a Mennonite congregation in Emmenthal, Switzerland, where he had introduced some unusually strict practices. Whereas Menno Simons (1496?-1561), founder of the Mennonites, had advocated a strict use of "shunning," that is, avoidance of those who had been excommunicated or who were otherwise under the "ban," or period of chastisement, the practice had been liberalized since his time. Ammann insisted on strict observance, meaning that one could not even eat or sleep with a spouse under the ban.

Further, Ammann reintroduced foot-washing as a regular part of worship, insisted upon uniformity of dress, made lying an excommunicable offense, and taught that only those of the Mennonite/Brethren tradition would be saved and go to heaven. In 1693 he began visiting other Mennonite congregations, seeking agreement with his various positions. Mennonites generally sought to move by consensus, but Ammann's tendency to excommunicate all those who disagreed with him made that difficult.

Within a year the Mennonites in Switzerland and in the Alsace region of today's France were split over his leadership, with perhaps a third following Ammann. In 1694 he moved to Alsace, the region of his greatest support. He expressed concern about the split in the fellowship and admitted that his own harsh manner had contributed to the situation. Attempts were made to reunite the Mennonites, but ultimately there was no change in the issues and the split remained.

Ammann faded from public view and passed away sometime between 1708, when he was listed on a census, and 1730, when his daughter joined the Reformed Church and stated that he was dead. Today there remain numerous Amish groups, particularly in the United States, and they are notable for the attempt to retain such things as the dress and transportation modes of the seventeenth century.

Anandamurti, Shrii Shrii: Shrii Shrii Anandamurti (b. 1923), founder of the Ananda Marga Yoga Society, was born Prabhat Rainjan Sarkar in Jamalpur, India. He was the son of a railway accounts clerk, and when his father died prematurely, he had to leave school to work for the railroad. In 1955 he announced that he had achieved enlightenment. He left the railroad position and founded Ananda Marga (literally, "bliss path"), a yogic philosophy. He took the name Shrii Shrii Anandamurti, which roughly means, "one upon seeing him falls into bliss," and took the vows of a renounced life.

In 1958, under his birth name, he also founded Renaissance Universal, a system of social action based upon his Progressive Utilization Theory (Prout), and aimed at organizing the lower classes in opposition to both communism and the ruling government. He marketed Ananda Marga and Renaissance Universal as the spiritual and social answers to the human condition, and particularly to the ills of Indian society. Ananda Marga/ Prout candidates ran for public office in 1967 and 1969 and there were numerous clashes between the government and group supporters. Ananda Marga by that time had gained enormous popularity, with over 400 schools and a membership past one million.

In 1969 the government forbade any government employee to have membership in Ananda Marga (an order eventually overturned by the courts) and in 1971 Anandamurti was arrested on the charge of conspiring to murder former members. The charge was generally understood to have been politically motivated, with no basis in fact. In 1975 Indira Gandhi proclaimed Emergency Rule and banned many organizations, including Ananda Marga. Anandamurti was tried and found guilty under rigged conditions (e.g., he was unable to call any witnesses on his behalf). With the lifting of Emergency Rule, however, he was retried in 1978, found innocent, and released. Since then he has continued to lead the organizations, now international in scope.

Anderson, Victor H.: Victor Anderson (b. 1917), cofounder with his wife, Cora, of the tradition of Faery Wicca, was born in New Mexico, but the family soon moved to Oregon. He later reported that at age nine he was initiated into witchcraft by witches, originally from the southern United States, who called themselves faeries. Their celebrations included music, dancing, magic, and communion with nature.

In 1950 he married Cora, who had Alabama roots in folk magic, and they settled near San Francisco. He first gained prominence in 1960 with the publication of *Thorns of the Blood Rose*, a collection of pagan poems.

Over several years he worked with his wife and one of his first initiates, Thomas DeLong (Gwydion Pendderwen), to put together the materials, including some from the Alexandrian Wicca Tradition, that became the Faery Wicca Tradition. Although Anderson has remained a low-profile figure, a number of his students have become quite well-known in Neo-Pagan circles, including Alison Harlow, Valerie Voigt, Aidan A. Kelly, Michael Thorn, and Starhawk.

Andrae, Johann Valentin: Johann Andrae (August 7, 1586-January 27, 1654), probable founder of the Rosicrucian story, was born in Germany. His father, a Lutheran pastor and abbot, died in 1601 and his mother moved the family to Tübingen, where Andrae entered the university. After graduation he became a Lutheran pastor in Stüttgart, but resigned in 1607 from poor health.

From 1607 to 1614 he lived in Tübingen with his mother, who had become court apothecary to Frederick I, the Duke of Württemberg. Andrae enjoyed the rich social life brought by such surroundings and was introduced to mysticism and the occult by Christoph Besold. In 1614, with his health improved, he married and became the deacon at Vaihingen. That year he published a pamphlet, *Fama Fraternitatis*, under the pseudonym of Christian Rosencreutz (C.R.), and the following year published an anonymous pamphlet, *Confessio*. These told the story of Christian Rosencreutz, who traveled to the Mediterranean in the 1400s, where he learned all occult wisdom and connected with a secret fraternity dating back to ancient Egypt. Rosencreutz, according to these booklets, died in 1484, having initiated others into the secret Rosicrucian Order. Another book, *The Hermetic Romance or the Chemical Wedding; written in High Dutch by Christian Rosencreutz*, appeared in 1616.

As these documents circulated they brought forth a number of reactions from the public. On the one hand, many thought it was a hoax and dismissed it. On the other hand, many thought the books revealed an actually existing occult order and sought to join it. In 1619 Andrae published *The Tower of Babel*, in which he confessed to writing the anonymous or C.R. books and that the Rosicrucian Fraternity was a fiction. He apparently created its symbolism from his family's coat of arms. By 1619, however, Rosicrucianism was indeed a reality.

Although the concept soon moved beyond his control, commentators have suggested that he likely created the Rosicrucian story to stimulate thinking about certain social issues. In any case, he went on to become an overseer at Kalw, then Court Prelate at Stüttgart, and finally, in 1650, an abbot in Bavaria. In all, he wrote more than one hundred books, though only the few on Rosicrucianism gained him fame.

Andrews, Lynn V.: Lynn Andrews (b. 1945), popular New Age author and teacher, has revealed few details of her early life. She has stated that in 1978 she began looking for spirit guides in the course of her travels as a collector of Indian art. She eventually met Agnes Whistling Elk and Ruby Plenty Chiefs, who served as her guides.

Over the course of a half-dozen best-selling books, Andrews has informed the public of her subsequent experiences within mystical Native American shamanism. These experiences often were incredible adventures reminiscent of the stories told by Carlos Casteneda, whose earlier work was reportedly inspirational for Andrews. She has claimed initiation into the Sisterhood of the Shields, an ages-old secret organization of Native American women that decided the time was right to let in a white woman and publicly reveal their rituals and teachings.

Andrews has communicated her ideas and experiences, not only through her books, but through seminars and workshops. What she shares is a blend of various Native American and New Age elements. Although a popular and successful figure, she has been criticized by scholars, Native Americans, and even some New Agers for presenting as fact what must be from her own imagination. These critics point to the presence of ghost-writers, made-up characters, and erroneous descriptions of traditional cultures to make their case.

Aquino, Michael A.: Michael Aquino (b. October 16, 1946), founder of the Temple of Set, was born in San Francisco, California. After earning a B.A. (1968) in political science from the University of California, Santa Barbara, he joined the Army as an officer working in the area of psychological warfare. Just before a two-year tour of duty in Vietnam he joined the Church of Satan, founded by Anton LaVey. In 1971 he returned to the United States and was assigned a post in Kentucky. He continued his involvement in the Church of Satan, organizing a local "grotto" and receiving ordination as a Satanic priest.

In 1972, troubled by several conflicts with LaVey's leadership, Aquino left the church and began working on a new interpretation and approach. In 1975 he founded the Temple of Set by ritually invoking the Prince of Darkness, who reportedly gave Aquino a document to follow, *The Book of Coming Forth By Night.* Aquino teaches that what Christianity has called

Satan is a corruption of the Egyptian figure of Set. Set is not deemed to be an evil deity, but one who works to expand human potential. Members can work on their evolution in solitary fashion, through a correspondence course, or can join local groups, called pylons.

Aquino has continued his Army career, receiving his M.A. (1976) and Ph.D. (1980) degrees from the University of California, Santa Barbara. He married Lilith Sinclair, who had previously led a large Church of Satan group in Spottswood, New Jersey. Because of the connection with the figure of Satan, Aquino and the Temple of Set have been subject to various ungrounded allegations and criticism. The accusation that he was involved in child molestation at the San Francisco Presidio, for example, was refuted by a Presidio investigation.

Herbert W. Armstrong
Courtesy: The Worldwide Church of God

Armstrong, Herbert W.: Herbert W. Armstrong was the founder of the Worldwide Church of God. Originally influenced by his wife's observance of the Sabbath, Armstrong became interested in the Bible, and in 1931 he was ordained in the Oregon Conference of the Church of God. He became a preacher and, in 1934, he started a radio ministry called "The World Tomorrow," and began publishing the periodical *The Plain Truth*. Disagreements about the observance of feast days and about the interpretation of the Old Testament caused a fracture within the Church of God. Armstrong followed the minority faction and was listed among the seventy elders of a new conference called the Church of God (Seventh Day) in Salem, Virginia, in 1933. The Salem group had chosen to observe the feast days, but in the following years disregarded the practice, which led Armstrong to withdraw and continue his ministry as Radio Church of God.

Armstrong's ministry expanded considerably after World War II; in 1947 he moved to Pasadena, California, where he opened Ambassador College. In 1953 he brought his work to Europe and, in the 1960s, his son, Garner Ted Armstrong, began a television ministry. The church acquired its present name in 1968, and continued its expansion through the 1970s, during which the circulation of *The Plain Truth* quadrupled. Joseph W.

Tkach, Sr. succeeded Armstrong at his death in 1986.

Shortly before his death in 1986, Herbert Armstrong confided in Tkach that he felt some of what he had taught—particularly about healing—was deficit, and asked that the Church's teaching on this point be re-examined in light of the Scriptures. This request set in motion a series of dramatic changes that led it to abandon its unique doctrines, which for most of its institutional life taught a form of Christianity at variance with mainstream Evangelical Christianity. The upheaval was so thorough-going that by the spring of 1997 the Worldwide Church of God had been admitted into the National Association of Evanglicals.

Arnold, Eberhard: Eberhard Arnold (July 26, 1883-November 22, 1935), founder of what today is known as the Hutterian Brethren of New York, was born in Konigsberg, Germany. His father was a professor of church history at the University of Breslau and his parents raised him in a strongly Christian atmosphere. At age 16 he had a significant religious experience that heightened the teaching he had received from his parents about seeing the world through the eyes of the poor. He began to work among the poor in association with such groups as the Salvation Army. He continued his schooling and received his doctorate in 1907.

In 1909 he married Emmy von Hollander and spent much of his time as a traveling speaker. This took a toll on his health, however, and in 1913 he moved to the Tyrolean Alps for recuperation. He took advantage of the opportunity to write and study the history of the radical Reformation. In 1915 he moved to Berlin to be literary director of Furche-Verlag. In 1919 he led an important Student Christian Movement meeting in Marburg, where he was energized to create a living community to follow the radical ethical demands of Jesus' Sermon on the Mount (Matthew 5-7). He founded such a community the following year and was very successful until the German financial crisis of 1922 led to its disintegration.

In 1926 Arnold began another community at a farm near Rhon, which became known as the Bruderhof. They held all things in common and ran their own school for the children. In 1930 he united that group with the Hutterian Brethren in the United States. In the early 1930s the Bruderhof experienced rising pressure from the Nazis, who did not like their pacifism or their communalism. Out of safety concerns, the children were moved to Lichtenstein, where another community was begun. Arnold raised funds for it through a successful lecture tour in Europe in 1935, completed shortly before his death following leg surgery. In 1936 the group, now with a collective leadership, was expelled from Germany and finally ended up in the

United States (New York) in 1954, where Arnold's son, Heini (d. 1982) became presiding elder.

Arthen, Andras Corban: Andras Arthen (b. November 20, 1949), cofounder of the EarthSpirit Community, was born in Spain. In 1972 he received a B.A. in English and education from Curry College and did post-graduate work in education at Harvard University. In 1969, while still an undergraduate, he entered the world of Neo-Paganism through initiation into a Scottish family of witches.

Gradually developing his knowledge of witchcraft and settling in Massachusetts, in 1975 he founded the Glainn Sidhr Order, which highlights shamanism within the craft. This gained such positive response that he was later able to organize the covens based upon it into the Athanor Fellowship and begin a related magazine, *Crossroads*. In 1979 he organized the first Rites of Spring Pagan Celebration, which has in the years since become the largest annual pagan gathering of its kind in the United States.

In late 1980, with his new wife, Deirdre Pulgram Arthen, he founded the EarthSpirit Community in the Boston area as a broadbased, accessible, pagan organization. It was the first legally incorporated pagan church in Massachusetts, and has become one of the largest such groups in the United States. Arthen has become well-known as a spokesperson for Neo-Paganism, having served as the National Public Information Officer for the national association of Wiccan groups, the Covenant of the Goddess. He has also worked with law enforcement groups on issues of occult-related crimes.

Arthen, Deirdre Pulgram: Deirdre Arthen (b. November 5, 1956), cofounder of the EarthSpirit Community, was born in Atlanta, Georgia. She received a B.A. in history and drama in 1978 from Tufts University in Medford, Massachusetts. In June 1980 she was initiated as a witch in the Glainn Sidhr Order, founded by Andras Corban Arthen, whom she married. In late 1980 she and Andras Arthen founded the EarthSpirit Community as a broadbased, accessible, pagan organization in the Boston area. It has become one of the largest such groups in the country, with several thousand participants.

Arthen publishes the group's journal, *Fireheart*, as well as a monthly newsletter. She has taken responsibility for development of the Rites of Spring Celebration, begun by her husband in 1979, and it has become a nationally-known, pan-pagan event. She has also developed other corresponding pan-pagan seasonal events, Suntide Celebration, Twilight

Covening, and Hearthfire Gathering, and runs the training group of the Glainn Sidhr Order.

From her participation in the pagan community, Arthen became interested in the power of rituals for personal healing. In 1986 she received an M.A. in counseling psychology from Wellesley College and has combined traditional and holistic methods as a spiritual counselor. She has become a popular workshop leader and lecturer on behalf of the Neo-Pagan movement.

Shoko Asahara
Courtesy: AUM Shinrikyo

Asahara, Shoko: Shoko Asahara founded AUM Shinrikyo in Tokyo in 1987. Asahara made international headlines in the wake of a poison gas attack that occurred on March 20, 1995 in the crowded Tokyo subway system. Twelve people died and many others were injured. Within a few days of the attack, AUM Shinrikyo was fingered as the most likely suspect. The leadership was eventually arrested and the organization disbanded.

A form of Tantric Buddhism, AUM Shinrikyo's teachings emphasized yoga practices and spiritual experiences. Master Asahara, whose original name was Chizuo Matsumoto (b. 1955), had traveled to India seeking enlightenment. Before returning to Japan, he sought out the Dalai Lama and received what he believed was a commission to revive true Buddhism in the land of his birth. By the time of the subway incident, Asahara had acquired a large communal facility near Mt. Fuji and a following of approximately 10,000 members in Japan (with an estimated 30,000 followers in Russia).

In addition to the usual teachings that go hand in hand with mainline Buddhism, Master Asahara was also fascinated with seeing into the future. His preoccupation with divination may have grown out of the weakness of his physical senses, as he was born blind in one eye, with only partial use of the other. Before undertaking yoga and meditation practices, Asahara pursued the study of such divinatory practices as astrology. Like many other Japanese spiritualists, he was fascinated by Western biblical prophecies as well as by the prophecies of Nostradamus. Perhaps influenced by the apocalyptic flavor of these predictions, Asahara himself began preaching an apocalyptic message to his followers. In particular, he prophesied a confrontation between Japan and the United States before the end of the century that would in all likelihood decimate his home country.

Asahara was, in fact, so certain about an impending conflict between Japan and the U.S. that he actually began preparing to wage war. Unable to match the conventional military might of the United States, AUM scientists investigated unconventional weapons, from biological agents to poison gas. The Tokyo gas attack was motivated by increased police scrutiny of the AUM Shinrikyo, with the idea of distracting police attention away from the movement.

In the end, it was Asahara's own pronouncements that led the police to the door of AUM Shinrikyo. In particular, Master Asahara had predicted that gas attacks by terrorists would occur in the not-too-distant future. This made him an obvious target of suspicion. Hence the subway attack, far from diverting attention away from AUM Shinrikyo, actually had the opposite effect.

Atkinson, William Walker: William Atkinson (December 5, 1862-November 22, 1932), popularizer of both New Thought and Hinduism, was born in Baltimore, Maryland. Not much is known about his early life. In 1894 he passed the Pennsylvania bar exam and began practicing law. After several years of stressful work, however, he had a nervous breakdown and began searching for spiritual comfort.

Eventually he found New Thought and became so committed to it that he moved to Chicago in order to be in a major arena of New Thought activity. In 1899 he married Margaret Foster Black and the following year became editor of *Suggestion*, a New Thought periodical. In 1901 he joined forces with New Thought publisher Sydney Flowers and edited his *New Thought* magazine until 1905. He also established the Psychic Club and the Atkinson School of Mental Science in rooms adjacent to the enterprises Flower was running. He began writing New Thought books and became a leading figure in New Thought circles.

Atkinson reestablished himself as a lawyer, passing the Illinois bar in 1903. He also expanded his religious interests into Hinduism and in 1903 began publishing books on Hindu topics under the name of Swami Ramacharaka. These books proved to be even more popular than his New Thought books and he became the first major popularizer of Hinduism in America. He was extremely prolific, writing over 30 books on New Thought-related topics and about as many as 20 on Hindu-related topics. From 1916 to 1919 he edited the journal *Advanced Thought*.

Sri Aurobindo
Courtesy: American Religion Collection

Aurobindo, Sri: Sri Aurobindo (August 15, 1872-December 5, 1950), a major channel for Hindu teachings to reach the West, was born Arvinda Ackroyd Ghose, in Calcutta, India. He received a western education, including schooling at Cambridge University. He returned to India in 1893 as a professor at Baroda University. In 1906 he became principal of Bengal National College in Calcutta and co-founded *Bande Mataram*, official organ of the Bengal National Party.

By 1908 he was head of the Bengal National Party and a key leader in the movement for national independence. He also began to immerse himself in the Indian traditions and literature, particularly of yoga. In 1908 he was arrested on the charge of sedition and held for one year, though he was never convicted. While in prison he was able to concentrate on his reading and yogic practice, reporting remarkable progress in his mental discipline.

In 1910 he settled in French-controlled Pondicherry and founded an ashram. In 1914 he met Mira Richard (1878-1973), a French woman who had met the god Krishna in a dream, only to find that Aurobindo matched the figure in the dream. She stayed to become his main associate and came to be called the Mother. During these early years his teaching and writing focused on what he called integral yoga, which sought to unite the spiritual and the material, rather than disengage from the material. He pictured yoga as the means of engaging the evolutionary growth toward the divine life.

On November 24, 1926 he proclaimed the "Day of Siddhi," meaning that the god Krishna had descended into the physical. After this time he communicated with people only indirectly through his writings and the Mother. He developed numerous followers in the West and after his death the Mother continued supervision of the international centers.

B

Baal Shem Tov, Israel: Israel Baal Shem Tov (Elul 18, 1698-Sivan 6, 1760), the founder of Hassidic Judaism, was born Israel Eliezer in Akop in the Carpathian Mountains of southern Poland. Much of his personal biography, especially his early life, is difficult to ascertain through the layers of stories that have arisen about him. He was orphaned at age five and was raised by friends and neighbors in Akop.

At about the age of ten he went to live with Reb Meir, a tar maker by occupation, but otherwise known as a *tzaddik*, or mystic teacher, and member of the Nistarim, a secret mystic order led by Rabbi Adam Baal Shem. Israel became a full member of the Nistarim in 1712. In 1716 he obtained the position of assistant religious teacher to the children in the town of Brody. In 1719 he became the *shamash* (like a church sexton) in his hometown of Akop and shortly thereafter married. By that point he was the leader of the Nistarim.

About this time the son of Rabbi Adam Baal Shem came to town and conferred upon Israel his deceased father's manuscripts on the kabbalah, the occult interpretation of the Bible originating in medieval Judaism. This son stayed to study the manuscripts with Israel, but soon passed away. Israel's wife also died, and after a period on his own he married Leah Rachel, daughter of a rabbi, and moved to Brody. In 1724 he had a vision of the biblical prophet Ahiya (or Ahijah) of Shilo (see 1 Kings 14:2-6 or 2 Chronicles 9:29; 10:15). For the next ten years he lived alone in the mountains, communicating with that prophet and mastering occult knowledge.

In 1736, now known as the Baal Shem Tov, or one who wields mystic power, he moved to Mezshbozsh and began to teach what became known as Hassidism. He emphasized a sense of piety for even the most mundane parts of everyday life, and prayer as seeking oneness with God. He urged followers to express through dance and song the joy of seeking and finding God. He became famous throughout Europe as a teacher and worker of miracles and a large percentage of pre-World War II Jews in Europe were Hassidim.

Meher Baba
Courtesy: American Religion Collection

Baba, Meher: Meher Baba (February 25, 1894-January 31, 1969), influential independent spiritual teacher, was born Merwan Sheriar Irani in Poona, India. He was raised as a Zoroastrian, but while attending Decca College met Hazrat Babajan, a Muslim mystic and teacher. He became her student and gained self-realization. As he then traveled around the country, other spiritual leaders identified him as an avatar, an incarnation of God.

In 1922 he founded his first ashram near Bombay and the title "Meher Baba," or "compassionate father," became the popular name for him. In 1924 the headquarters was moved near Ahmednager and expanded into a whole community called Meherabad, including a poorhouse, hospital, and free school. In 1925, following an ancient tradition, he became silent, and remained so the rest of his life. He communicated and dictated his books at first through the use of an alphabet board and then through sign language. One of the explanations of this silence is that he did not intend to found a new religion, but rather to encourage people to live according to the high ideals already spoken by various teachers. Thus, more speech by him would be superfluous. In fact, the words of those various teachers might have been his anyway, as he claimed to be another incarnation of the same being that had been known as Jesus, Krishna, Buddha, etcetera.

Meher Baba made several trips to the United States, beginning in 1931, where he gained many followers, but did not organize them into one group. The result is that a number of centers and organizations (like Sufism Reoriented) have arisen that promote his ideas as part or all of what they do. Baba's religious tenets were very basic, centering on love of God and humanity. He suggested both very practical, service activities to actualize love of humanity, and mystical goals of union to actualize the love of God.

Baha'u'llah: Baha'u'llah (November 12, 1817-May 29, 1892), founder of the Baha'i Faith, was born Mirza Husayn-Ali in Persia (today's Iran). He received no formal education, as that was a privilege reserved only for families of religious figures. His father, Mirza Buzurg, was an influential government figure, so the family did lead a comfortable existence; Baha'u'llah was able to afford to marry three wives as a young man.

In 1844, when Baha'u'llah was about 27, Siyyid Ali Muhammad proclaimed himself the Bab, or Gate, through which news would come of this promised Mahdi, the Hidden One, successor to Muhammad, founder of Islam, whose coming would set the world right. Baha'u'llah was caught up in the movement and became one of the Bab's chief assistants. The movement endured much persecution, especially in the turmoil following the Bab's execution by authorities in 1850. Baha'u'llah was imprisoned in 1852, and during his many months of incarceration came to believe that he himself was the holy figure of whom the Bab spoke.

In 1853 Baha'u'llah and other followers were exiled to Baghdad. He maintained his leadership, but kept his new-found identity to himself. In 1863 he moved to Constantinople (today's Istanbul) and for the first time revealed his identity to an inner circle. A few months later, still under persecution, he moved to Adrianople (today's Edirne, in Turkey) and widely advertised his identity, sending letters to prominent people around the world. He took the name Baha'u'llah, meaning Glory of God. He claimed that, as the culmination of all the great religious leaders of the past, he could bring ultimate wisdom to bear on all the religious and social ways to combat injustice and fulfill humanity.

From 1868 to the end of his life, Baha'u'llah was either in a prison barracks or under house arrest in what is today Acre, in Israel. There he wrote a great deal, still mostly untranslated into English. His most important work was the Kitab-i-Aqdas (Most Holy Book) of laws. After his death his devoted son, Abdul-Baha, led the movement.

Bailey, Alice LaTrobe Bateman: Alice Bailey (June 16, 1880-December 15, 1949), founder of the Arcane School, was born in Manchester, England. She was raised in the Church of England and served it as a Sunday School teacher, but was aware of a mystical side to her nature. This expressed itself one day when she was fifteen years old as she had a vision of a man wearing a turban visiting her home to tell her she was destined for important work. She believed this to be a vision of Christ.

As an adult, Bailey worked for the Young Men's Christian Association (Y.M.C.A.) in many places around the world. She met Walter Evans in

India. They married in 1907 and moved to Ohio, where he studied to be an Episcopal priest. They later moved to California, but the marriage did not last. They were separated in 1915 and divorced by 1919.

In 1915 Bailey encountered Theosophy through a group in Pacific Groves, California. There she saw a picture on the wall of a man she identified to be the same man of her teenage vision. The Theosophists said he was Koot Hoomi, a spiritual master who helped direct Helena Blavatsky, founder of the Theosophical Society. Soon Bailey was editor of the group's periodical, *The Messenger*, and romantically involved with Foster Bailey, the society's national secretary.

In 1919 another spiritual entity, Djwhal Khul (spelled by Theosophists Djual Khool and sometimes called D. K. or the Tibetan), reportedly contacted her and proposed channeling a number of wisdom books through her. After the publication of the first of nineteen books, *Initiation: Human and Solar*, internal conflict caused Bailey and Foster Bailey to leave the Theosophical Society. They married in 1921 and by 1923 founded the Arcane School, along with a magazine, *The Beacon*, and the Lucis Trust for their publications. She taught that the powers of the spiritual hierarchy could be accessed at certain times and places, particularly in full-moon meditation ceremonies.

Her efforts to help bring in a new world era have included founding the Triangles in 1937, groups of three around the world who unite daily in meditation. That year she also published "The Great Invocation," a short prayer seeking the realization of God's plan for earth. Foster Bailey (d. 1977) continued the work after her death.

Arthur Balfour
Courtesy: American Religion Collection

Balfour, Arthur J.: Arthur J. Balfour (1848-1930), also known as the first Earl of Balfour, was very interested in psychical research and the question of survival, like his brother Gerald W. Balfour and his sister, the wife of Henry Sidgwick. Born at Whittinghame, East Lothian, Scotland, he studied law and philosophy at Eton, and Trinity College, Cambridge University. After being a member of the British Parliament from 1874 to 1885, he became Prime Minister in 1902, First Lord of the Admiralty in 1915, and Foreign Secretary in 1916. In 1894 he became president of the Society for Psychical Research, occupying a position which had previously been held by his brother.

He held many seances with Mrs. Willett who, in one series of communications received by automatic writing and referred to as the Palm Sunday Case, mentioned Mary Lyttelton, who died shortly before her engagement to Arthur Balfour was to have been announced. The Palm Sunday Case was considered one of the most striking evidences of survival after death utilizing the method of cross-correspondences. Balfour never married and died fifty-five years after the death of his beloved Mary, whose ghostly presence in Balfour's house was occasionally perceived by Mr. Willett.

Ballard, Edna Anne Wheeler: Edna Ballard (June 25, 1886-February 10, 1971), cofounder of I AM Religious Activity, was born in Burlington, Iowa. In 1912 she became a concert harpist. She married Guy Ballard in 1916 and one of their common interests was the occult. They soon moved to Chicago, where she edited *The American Occultist* and worked in the Philosopher's Nook bookstore.

In 1930, while hiking on Mt. Shasta in California, Guy Ballard reported an encounter with Saint Germain, an 18th century occultist who was now an "Ascended Master." The Ballards subsequently founded the I AM Religious Activity and the Saint Germain Foundation to spread the message of the Ascended Masters, which focused on getting people to attune themselves to the God within. When her husband died in 1939 she became sole leader of the nationwide organization.

For the next 18 years she struggled with a court battle that severely hurt the group. The Ballards were accused of mail fraud, gaining money for promoting beliefs they knew to be false. The case went all the way to the Supreme Court, which ruled on April 24, 1944 that people do not have to prove the truth of religious claims, even if they seem unbelievable to others. Despite this victory, the group did not regain use of the mail until 1954 and did not regain religious tax-exempt status until 1957. Still, the 1950s marked the beginning of recovery. In 1951 a conference site near Mt. Shasta was purchased and later a radio program, still on the air today, was begun.

Ballard, Guy Warren: Guy Ballard (July 28, 1878-December 29, 1939), cofounder of the I AM Religious Activity, was born in Newton, Kansas. After attending business college he supervised his uncle's lead and silver mine in Tucson, Arizona. In 1916 he married Edna Wheeler, a concert harpist who, like him, was interested in the occult.

They soon moved to Chicago, where his wife found a position editing *The American Occultist*. He was often out of town on business and in 1930 was able to hike around Mt. Shasta in California, a place he knew from Theosophical writings to be a spiritual power point. On the mountain he reportedly met the Comte de Saint Germain, an 18th century occultist who was now an "Ascended Master" looking for someone to help usher in a new spiritual age.

Saint Germain chose Ballard and his wife for that task, and they accordingly established the "I AM" Religious Activity and the Saint Germain Foundation to spread the teachings of Saint Germain and the other Ascended Masters. According to Ballard, "I AM" is the God power within each person, and the goal is to activate that power and act in harmony with it. One means toward that is the repetition of affirmations, or "decrees."

Often under the pseudonym of Godfre Ray King, Ballard published a number of books, beginning with *Unveiled Mysteries* in 1934. He also led numerous classes and traveled as lecturer. By the time of his death in late 1939 the organization had affiliated groups stretching across the country. He did not live to see the prolonged court battle over the accusation of fraud, which ended with the Supreme Court decision in their favor in 1944.

Ballou, Adin Augustus: Adin Ballou (April 23, 1803-August 5, 1890), founder of the Hopedale Community, was born in Cumberland, Rhode Island. His father ran a farm and a sawmill, but Ballou's persistent ill health turned him away from farm work toward other pursuits. A religious experience at age eighteen led him into the ministry. In September 1821 he was ordained a minister in the Christian Connection, to which his parents belonged.

He was a popular preacher and spent some time as a traveling evangelist. He had relatives who were Universalists, and in studying it for the purposes of condemning it, he was instead converted. He left the Christian Connection and on December 10, 1823 was ordained as a Universalist minister. Until 1827 he served a church in Milford, Connecticut, then he moved to the Prince Street Church in New York City.

In less than a year he returned to Milford, where he engaged in the troublesome issue of whether, at death, people were immediately reconciled with God, or if they had to undergo a time of reflection and instruction first. Most Universalists took the former position, but Ballou took the latter. He was forced to leave the Milford church and was immediately offered a church in Menden, Connecticut. He and like-minded Universalists founded the Massachusetts Association of Independent Restorationists and he founded and edited its journal, *The Independent Messenger*.

Ballou became a prominent voice in reform issues. He strongly believed in working to create God's kingdom on earth, and thus sought to end slavery, gain equal rights for women, end war, and stop the liquor trade. He became convinced that founding a community to embody "practical Christianity" would trigger a mass movement. In 1841 he bought a farm near Milford, Connecticut, founded a stock company, began a newspaper, *The Practical Christian*, and in 1842 about thirty people moved there to begin Hopedale Community.

For over a decade it flourished, gaining over 100 residents, but ended suddenly in 1856 when two brothers, who had bought up three-fourths of the stock, decided to liquidate the company. Ballou became minister of the reorganized community church, which affiliated with the Unitarians, and remained there until his retirement in 1880.

Beissel, Johann Conrad: Johann Conrad Beissel (1690?-1768) was an early Seventh-Day Baptist leader and founder of the Ephrata Cloister. The son of a drunken baker, he was finally apprenticed to a musically inclined baker after both his parents died.

When he was twenty-five years old, Beissel joined the Pietists, an independent German movement emphasizing personal spirituality as opposed to the formality of the state church. Soon after Beissel moved to Heidelberg, he was arrested and banished for attending the Collegia Pietistica, and sought refuge at Schwarzenau, like other Pietists. After joining the Community of True Inspiration, he became affiliated with Alexander Mack and the Church of the Brethren. However, after a short stay, he began wandering around Germany, and eventually headed to Pennsylvania in search for the community known as the "Society of Woman in the Wilderness" which, by this time, had long been disbanded. Beissel found the leader of the American Church of the Brethren Peter Becker, to whom he apprenticed himself in order to learn the weaver's trade.

In 1721 he and three other followers journeyed into the wilderness and established a communal life near Conestoga. In 1724 they were contacted by a group of male Brethren who had split from the Germantown congregation. Among them was Peter Becker, who baptized Beissel and who was voted leader of a congregation established at Conestoga. However, when he began to advocate what many called a Mosaic legalism, emphasizing the virtues of celibacy and Sabbatarianism, he ran into conflict with the congregation, and in 1728 a schism occurred, with the formation of a Sabbath-keeping congregation at Conestoga. But after four years he disappeared into the wilderness again, settling near Cocalico Creek, where he founded what was to become the Ephrata Community, with some of his followers.

After Alexander Mack's death in 1735, more people, such as the leaders Peter Miller and Conrad Weiser, moved from the Church of the Brethren to Beissel's community, where the followers were organized into three groups: householders, solitary brethren, and spiritual virgins. The Kedar, a large community house, was erected, the community businesses were developed by Israel Eckerlin, a distinctive habit was worn, and new names were given. Beissel, who became "Friedsam Gottrecht," began a publishing enterprise that by the mid-1740s became a major competitor of Benjamin Franklin's printing monopoly. Eckerlin was expelled after a power struggle with Beissel who, after his death, was followed by Miller. The work of the community was eventually absorbed by the Seventh-Day Baptists.

Bell, Eudorus N.: Eudorus N. Bell (June 27, 1866-June 15, 1923), a founder of the Assemblies of God, was born in Lake Butler, Florida, with twin brother Endorus. His father died two years later and the family struggled financially. Still, Bell managed to graduate in 1903 from the University of Chicago and become a Southern Baptist pastor in Texas.

In 1907 Bell received the "gifts of the Spirit," left the Baptist ministry, and moved to a Pentecostal congregation in Malvern, Arkansas. He became editor of a magazine serving a number of like-minded Pentecostal groups, *Word and Witness*, and in 1909 married Katie Kimbrough. In 1913 he called for a gathering of Pentecostals to discuss doctrinal standards and areas for mutual cooperation. In 1914 he chaired that national meeting of Pentecostals, marking the beginning of the Assemblies of God, and subsequently he was offered a teaching position at the Gospel School in Findlay, Ohio. In 1915 he was converted to an anti-trinitarian, "Jesus Only," belief and was expelled from his teaching position. The following year he returned to Trinitarianism and helped draft a faith statement on that issue passed by the Assemblies of God in 1916.

In his remaining years Bell was an honored leader of the church, returning in 1918 as editor of the church's magazine, renamed the *Evangel*, serving as General Secretary in 1919-20 and as chairman from 1920 to his death in 1923. The Assemblies of God, now with over two million members, has become one of the largest denominations in the United States.

Elbert Benjamine (C.C. Zain)
Courtesy: Church of Light

Benjamine, Elbert: Elbert Benjamine (December 12, 1882-November 18, 1951), founder of the Church of Light, was born in Iowa. He became interested in the occult as a teenager and at age 18 joined the Hermetic Brotherhood of Luxor and its more esoteric, inner group, the Brotherhood of Light. He began studying astrology with a leader of that group, Minnie Higgins, while working a number of odd jobs to support himself.

In 1907 Higgins died and Benjamine moved to headquarters in Denver to become the group's lead astrologer. The following year, at the request of the other two main leaders, he agreed to write a series of lessons on the occult sciences to use for membership outreach. After several years of further study, he began writing in 1914, but that year the organization dissolved. He moved to Los Angeles and began teaching privately, using drafts of courses he had written under the name of C. C. Zain. In 1918 he opened his classes to the public and among his students was Elizabeth Dorris, whom he married in 1919.

In 1932, having finally completed all 21 projected lessons on occult sciences, Benjamine incorporated the Church of Light. It was seen as successor to the earlier group, which claimed to be part of a tradition dating back to 2400 B.C. in Egypt. After 1932 he began publishing books under his own name on various aspects of astrology, and became one of the best-known astrologers in the United States. The Church of Light has continued its work since his death.

Berg, David Brandt: David Brandt Berg (1919-1994) was the founder of the non-traditional Christian missionary movement known as The Family (formerly the Children of God). Virginia Brandt Berg, David's mother, had a considerable influence on him. She was raised in a Christian home, but eventually became a virtual atheist. However, an accident which left her bedridden for nearly five years led her to a conversion experience. After she was miraculously raised from her death-bed, she spent the rest of her life with her husband in active Christian service as a pastor and evangelist.

In 1944, Berg met and married Jane Miller, an active member of the Alliance church in Sherman Oaks, California. In late 1948 he began min-

Father David
Courtesy: The Family

istering at a small Christian and Missionary Alliance church in rural Arizona, built a new church for his congregation, and opened it to the Native and Mexican-American population of the community. The white church board members were disappointed, and in early 1951 he was forced to resign his pastorate.

For the next 15 years, Berg taught secondary school, held a number of other secular jobs, attended several secular and Christian colleges, opened and ran a small center for missionaries, and traveled the U.S. booking an evangelical program on radio and television. He also applied for a mission to Southeast Asia. He eventually became more convinced of the ineffectiveness of organized, traditional "Churchianity" and its emphasis on ceremonialism and lavish buildings, as well as its general lack of interest in evangelical outreach. These convictions were later adopted by the Children of God and later The Family.

In 1962, while facing a serious illness, he desperately asked God if there was a particular message that he was supposed to preach. The book of Jeremiah was indicated as the message for modern America. After this episode, however, David sensed that he had not yet found God's full calling for his life.

In the mid-1960s, Berg began traveling with his four children in evangelistic outreach, and in early 1968 he and his family journeyed to Huntington Beach, California, a beach town that had become a gathering place for thousands of hippies. Here he found his life's calling, and the movement now known as the Family was founded. He began ministering to the youth in a small Christian coffee house, the Light Club, which, within a few months, was full every night. Hundreds of followers had become Christans and stopped taking drugs.

Berg's new ministry to the hippies marked his total rupture with mainstream Christian denominations. At Huntington Beach, he became convinced that the time had come for a complete break, and sensed that his newly saved hippie congregation wanted the raw truth of the Gospel, rather than the version that had permeated mainstream Christianity. In a talk given in September 1968, at the Light Club, he explained that Jesus was a true revolutionary.

During this period, Berg met his second wife, Maria, who in January

1969 was working as a secretary in Tucson, Arizona, when a few members of his "Teens of Christ" visited from California. She returned to Huntington Beach with them. She remained Berg's constant companion for 25 years, from the spring of 1969 until his passing in 1994.

In 1970, the "Teens of Christ," who were likened by a newspaper reporter to "Moses and the Children of God," settled at an abandoned ranch in Texas that had formerly been Fred Jordan's Texas Soul Clinic. There Berg wanted to implement his vision for a true New Testament community. After nearly a year in Texas, David and Maria left for Europe, looking for new regions to evangelize, including Israel where, however, there were actually very few similarities between his brand of Christian communalism and the cooperative lifestyle of the Israeli kibbutzim.

During these travels abroad, Berg had a new calling from God, one of providing written counsel, teaching and guidance to his followers. For the balance of his life he remained behind the scenes, constantly teaching and advising, while the Children of God and later The Family were rapidly expanding throughout the world. His writings focused upon the fundamental teachings of the Bible, as well as the mission of his new movement. At the heart of his teaching was the conviction that the love of God, as manifested in the Bible and the person of Jesus, was the solution to every human need, and that the Christian's primary responsibility is to dedicate time, energy and resources to sharing the Gospel with others.

Among Berg's most controversial beliefs was his adherence to the principle that he called the Law of Love, that he applied most shockingly to matters of sex. He claimed that sex was not inherently evil in the eyes of God, and that loving heterosexual relations between consenting adults were permissible, as long as no one was hurt or offended. In 1976, he also proposed to his followers that in certain circumstances, it would be acceptable for a Christian to have sexual relations with someone in an effort to give them a tangible manifestation of God's love, thereby helping them to come to a saving knowledge of Jesus Christ. This doctrine, which became known as "Flirty Fishing," was practiced by some Family members until 1987, when it was officially discontinued.

Berghes, Prince Rudolphe François Edouard De Landas: Prince Rudolphe François Edouard De Landas Berghes (November 1, 1873-November 17, 1920), co-founder of the North American Old Roman Catholic Church, was born in Naples, Italy, to Austrian nobility. After attending the Universities of Cambridge and Paris he received a Ph.D. from the University of Brussels. He served for a time with the British Army and was in the Sudan around 1911. Back in England he was introduced to Arnold Harris Matthew of the Old Roman Catholic Church, and that changed the direction of his life.

De Landas Berghes was quickly caught up in Matthew's plans to spread Old Catholicism throughout Britain. He was ordained by Matthew in November 1912 and was consecrated by him in June 1913. His plans to become a missionary bishop in Scotland were cut off by the tensions leading to World War I. When England announced a state of war with Austria, de Landas Berghes, as a prominent Austrian, avoided imprisonment only by virtue of his relationships with nobility all over Europe. England decided instead to deport him to the United States, where he arrived on November 7, 1914. He became the second person, after Joseph René Vilatte, to bring Old Catholic orders to America directly from Europe.

He eventually decided to found a new branch of Matthew's work, and in October 1916 consecrated William H. F. Brothers and Carmel Henry Carfora as charter bishops of the enterprise. Brothers, however, soon withdrew and it was only with de Landas Berghes and Carfora that the North American Old Roman Catholic Diocese was formally launched in 1917. Finding or creating real congregations with real people proved difficult, though, and de Landas Berghes became too frustrated, returning to the Roman Catholic fold on December 22, 1919.

In 1920, as his part of the agreement with the church, he became a novice with the Order of St. Augustine and was appointed to teach French at Villanova University near Philadelphia. Their part of the agreement was to recognize his (retired) episcopal status, but this did not come to pass and he began to rethink the whole situation. He told Carfora he wanted to return to what was now called the North American Old Roman Catholic Church, but died before further action was taken. His legacy remains as a major American source of Old Catholic orders.

Bernard, Pierre Arnold: Pierre Bernard (1875-September 27, 1955), founder of the Tantrik Order in America, was born Peter Coons in Leon, Iowa. After working odd jobs in various states, he met Mortimer K. Hargis in 1905, and with him founded the Bacchante Academy in San Francisco. The academy provided classes in hypnotism and sexual relationships, but was destroyed with the earthquake in April 1906.

In 1909 in New York City he founded the Tantrik Order in America, combining hatha yoga with his version of Tantric Hinduism, wherein sexual energies are used as a means to enlightenment. He took the title Oom the Omnipotent, but was powerless to stop two women in the group from complaining to the police that he was keeping them against their will and conducting orgies. He was arrested but the charges were dropped and he continued his business, which later expanded into the New York Sanskrit College and a physiological institute. At that time he took the name Dr. Pierre Arnold Bernard.

About 1918 he married Blanche DeVries, a woman of wealth, although she performed as an oriental belly dancer. She completely changed his life, introducing him to high society, including her cousin Mary Baker Eddy, founder of the Church of Christ, Scientist. In 1924 he moved to a 78-acre estate in Nyack, New York, where he built a significant library in occult and oriental materials and created a center to welcome gurus and other guests. He engaged in a number of charitable activities befitting his now impeccable status in the community. For the rest of his life he contributed in a quite reputable way to the American acquaintance with Hinduism.

Annie Besant
Courtesy: American Religion Collection

Besant, Annie Wood: Annie Besant (October 1, 1847-September 21, 1933), a leader of the Theosophical Society, was born into a devoutly Christian family in London, England. Her father died when she was five. In 1866 she married Frank Besant, a minister, with whom she had two children. Her changing religious views, among other things, led to an eventual divorce.

Besant became a colleague of atheist Charles Bradlaugh in 1874, wrote for his magazine, *National Reformer*, and lectured on women's rights. In 1876 she and Bradlaugh founded the Freethought Publishing Company; at one point they published birth control information, which led to their brief arrest on obscenity charges. Over time, Besant and Bradlaugh went their separate ways and Besant joined a number of socialist-oriented groups.

In 1888 she discovered the Theosophical Society and its founder, Helena Blavatsky, and was quickly converted. Besant was soon co-editor of *Lucifer* magazine and a key leader of the organization. After Blavatsky's death in 1891 she became leader of the Esoteric Section for Europe and India, while William Q. Judge headed the American Esoteric Section and Col. Henry S. Olcott remained at the headquarters in India as international president. Besant solidified her position with the publication in 1892 of two books, *Seven Principles of Man* and *Karma*, and her well-received representation of Theosophy at the 1893 World's Parliament of Religions in Chicago.

In 1895 Judge led most of the American followers into the independent Theosophical Society, and those that remained loyal to the Indian headquarters became known as the Theosophical Society in America. Besant gradually rebuilt the American following and upon Olcott's death in 1907 became international president. In 1909 she declared that a new world avatar was to appear and soon was convinced that Jiddu Krishnamurti, under the tutelage of Charles Leadbeater in India, was that person. He was formally announced in 1912, but personally renounced that role in 1929. She continued to lead the embattled society until her death in 1933.

Yogi Bhajan
Courtesy: Sikh Dharma

Bhajan, Yogi: Founder of the Sikh Dharma and of the 3HO organization (Health, Happy, Holy Organization), Harbhajan Singh Khalsa Yogi was born in Kot Harkan, Tehsil Wazirabad, India (now Pakistan) on August 29, 1929. The adopted name "Khalsa" replaces his family name, which was traditionally associated with one's subcaste—a social arrangement opposed by orthodox Sikhism. The center of Sikh religious authority in Amritsar conferred on him the title Siri Singh Sahib.

After receiving his B.A. from Punjab University in 1954, Bhajan married the lecturer and counselor Inderjit Kaur, with whom he had three children. From 1954 to 1969, he worked as a customs official and Interpol officer. In 1969 he moved to Los Angeles, where he founded the 3HO Foundation, a teaching and outreach organization combining traditional Sikhism and yoga. Young Americans and Canadians who by 1975 had adopted the Sikh lifestyle through 3HO numbered in the thousands and lived in ashrams and teaching centers throughout the country.

Bhajan's teachings represent a synthesis of Sikhism and a type of Kundalini yoga. Because Sikhs believe in being completely self-supporting, 3HO members run several kinds of businesses, and generally lead prosperous lifestyles. He has been co-president of the World Parliament of Religions, co-chairperson of the World Fellowship of Religions, director of the Unity of Man Conference, a member of the Interreligious Council of Southern California, as well as of the board of directors of the American Council of Executives in Religion.

H.P. Blavatsky
Courtesy: American Religion Collection

Blavatsky, Helena Petrovna: H.P. Blavatsky (July 30, 1831-May 8, 1891), co-founder of the Theosophical Society, was one of the modern occult's most influential leaders. She grew up in Russia and in 1848 married General Nikifor Blavatsky, but after a few months left him and moved to Constantinople. The details of much of her life are obscure. She claimed to have spent the next 25 years exploring the occult and meeting key religious figures. In Egypt she founded a spiritualist society that disintegrated after fraudulent activities were exposed.

By the early 1870s she had arrived in the United States, still active in spiritualism, holding seances and giving lectures. In 1875 she founded the Theosophical Society with Col. Henry S. Olcott and William Q. Judge. This was more occult than standard spiritualism, emphasizing ancient wisdom, reincarnation, and karma. In her 1877 book, *Isis Unveiled*, she repudiated spiritualism as focused on mere matter and began to focus on the Far East and wisdom gained from a hierarchy of spiritual masters. In 1879 she and Olcott left the United States to establish a new headquarters in Adyar, India.

Much of the rest of her career was spent in a struggle over the issue of the existence of the masters. In 1884 an associate claimed that written messages from the masters that "appeared" in a cabinet in her home, were fraudulent. The Society for Psychical Research sent an investigator, who discovered secret passages and confirmed the fraudulent activity. The announcement severely hurt the organization and Blavatsky moved to London, where she continued her writing and development of the local lodge. Thanks to Olcott's devoted organizational work and the development of Annie Besant's leadership, the Theosophical Society was experiencing a significant resurgence by the time of Blavatsky's death in 1891.

Bonewits, Philip Emmons Isaac: Isaac Bonewits (b. October 1, 1949), founder of Ar nDraiocht Fein, was born in Royal Oak, Michigan. After deciding against becoming a Roman Catholic priest, he enrolled in the University of California, Berkeley, interdisciplinary studies program. For a time he roomed with Robert Larson, previously a student at Carleton College in Minnesota, where in 1963 the Reformed Druids of North America was formed. The group began as a joking critique of compulsory chapel attendance, but became more substantial. Larson and Bonewits formed a local "grove," and in 1969 Bonewits was ordained a Druid priest. In 1970 he graduated with a degree in magic, thus garnering some media attention.

In 1973 he became editor of *Gnostica*, a Pagan periodical based in Minneapolis, and was married. He began a new Druid group, the Schismatic Druids of North America, and in 1976 published *The Druid Chronicles (Evolved)*, containing the history, rituals, and customs of the various Reformed Druid groups. That year he got a divorce and moved back to Berkeley. In 1978 he began *The Druid Chronicles* (later renamed *Pentalpha Journal*), but experienced little success and about 1979 withdrew from the Reformed Druids.

Still seeking a stable niche, he had a second marriage from 1979 to 1982. In 1983 he married Sally Eaton and joined the New Orthodox Order of the Golden Dawn as a third degree priest. He moved to New York City, where he met Shenain Bell, with whom he began Ar nDraiocht Fein (Our Own Druid Faith), conceived as a Neo-Pagan form of Druidism, not narrowly Celtic-based, but pan-Indo-European in heritage. The group began in 1984 with the first issue of *The Druids' Progress*. Later he obtained another divorce and in 1988 married Deborah Lipp, a Gardnerian priestess.

Booth, William: William Booth (April 10, 1829-August 20, 1912), founder of the Salvation Army, was born in Nottingham, England. His family's difficult financial straits forced him to leave school and apprentice to a pawnbroker at age 13. His father passed away a few years later. By the time Booth began work as a pawnbroker on his own in London in 1849, he had also found religion. After a time in the Methodist Church he joined a splinter group, the Reformers.

In 1852 he became a full-time preacher for the Reformers, shifting in 1854 to the New Connection, another group with Methodist roots. He was assigned to the staff of a London church and was extraordinarily successful as an evangelist specialist, converting 3,000 people in 1855. That year he married Catherine Mumford. In 1858 he moved to pastor the Gateshead Church, a moribund congregation that he soon revived. After three years he left the New Connection in a dispute over his desire to focus exclusively on evangelism. In 1865 he and his wife jointly began preaching in the slums of London, with great success. They founded the East London Christian Mission, which sprouted many branches, and the periodical, *East London Evangelist*.

Over the next several years the idea of a "salvation army" took shape. The name of the magazine was changed to the *Salvationist*, Booth took the title of "general" and workers gained military-type uniforms. In 1888 he added the other major component of the developing organization, that of social service. Working daily in the slums, he was acutely aware of the physical needs of the people he preached to and decided that basis relief services needed to be a part of the gospel presentation. His most famous book, *In Darkest England, and the Way Out* (1890), described the nature of urban poverty and presented his ideas for eliminating the problem.

After his wife died in 1890, Booth traveled a great deal, overseeing the spread of the movement into 58 countries. He was honored by the president of the United States, the king of England, and the city of London. Oxford University presented him with an honorary doctorate.

Bradley, Marion Zimmer: Marion Zimmer was born June 3, 1930, in Albany, NY, in a Lutheran family. She spent three years at New York State Teachers College in Albany, but did not graduate. In 1949 she married Robert A. Bradley, a railroad employee, and had a son, Paul. They moved through a series of small towns, and in the early 1950s she was a member of the Rosicrucians. Marion taught herself to write by writing short stories for the pulp fiction magazines, and then paperback novels, the first, *Seven from the Stars*, being published in 1955.

In 1959 Bradley left her husband, and moved to Abilene, where she finished college at Hardin Simmons University, majoring in education, psychology, and Spanish, and earning a teaching certificate. However, the romance novels she wrote to finance her education sold so well that she never had to go into teaching. In 1963 she moved to Berkeley, California, and did graduate work in psychology at the university of California, Berkeley, from 1965 to 1967.

In 1964 she married Walter Breen, and became a member of an occult organization that Breen had conceived of in Texas, the Aquarian Order of the Restoration, whose purpose was to restore worship of the Goddess. The Order had about 18 members at its peak, and dissolved in 1982, feeling that its purpose had been accomplished. In the meantime, in the late 1970s, Bradley became involved with the Neopagan Witches in Berkeley.

She joined a women's group that included Starhawk, and then, with Diana Paxson, Anodea Judith, and others, helped found the Dark Moon Circle, working in it for about five years; it later evolved into the Fellowship of the Spiral Path. This period in her life coincided with the writing of *The Mists of Avalon*, her best-known novel, and one of the most-popular books ever written about the foundation myths of Neopagan Witchcraft.

Since the mid-1980s Bradley has very much gone her own way, turning out a series of novels, some connected with *Mists*, most not. She has refused to stay "active" in the Neopagan community because of her profound disagreements with many stances currently considered to be "politically correct" by most Neopagan Witches.

Branham, William Marrion: William Marrion Branham (April 6, 1909- December 24, 1965), founder of the Branham Tabernacle and Related Assemblies, was born in Burkesville, Kentucky, the son of a part-time logger and alcoholic. From early in his life, despite his troubled home life, Branham knew he was destined for something great. At age seven he heard a voice that told him the future held a special work for him. Later he joined the Pentecostal Church and experienced a call to the ministry, though that ministry was not at first to be Pentecostal.

In 1933 he began an independent Baptist tent ministry and established the Branham Tabernacle. In 1934 he married Hope Brumbech. His ministry ran into a series of problems. It was not immediately self-supporting and he was forced to take a day job as well. His hoped-for association with Baptists did not bear fruit, as he spoke of his unBaptist-like continued visions and heavenly visitations. In 1937 his wife and child were killed in the Ohio River flood and he moved into a long period in which he sought guidance for his future work.

In 1946 he had a vision of an angel promising him healing power and foreknowledge. He began to heal with great success and started *The Voice of Healing* magazine in 1948, later followed by the Spoken Word Publications. His now clearly Pentecostal ministry attracted a number of other healers, such as Morris Cerullo and Asa Allen, who associated with him. In 1955 his organization was hurt by a well-publicized struggle with the IRS, but he remained a powerhouse in the field until the early 1960s, when he began to reduce his healing emphasis and focus more on controversial doctrines like "Jesus Only" anti-trinitarianism and the approaching destruction of the United States in the end times. When he died in a car accident in Amarillo, Texas, his organization was much reduced in size, but his influence as a healer remained strong.

Bresee, Phineas Franklin: Phineas Franklin Bresee (December 31, 1838-November 13, 1915), founder of the Church of the Nazarene, was born on a farm in Franklin Township, New York. He experienced conversion at age 17 and joined the Methodist Episcopal Church. In 1856 the family moved to Iowa and, with an exhorter's license, preached often. He added the middle name of Franklin after his birthplace, and in 1858 became a full-time Methodist minister. He developed a mail correspondence with Maria Hibbard and married her in 1860 without having seen her in person. In 1866 he experienced sanctification, what the holiness movement sees as a second part to conversion, enabling one to be made perfect in love.

In 1883 Bresee accepted the pastorate of the First Methodist Church in Los Angeles, California, and over the next ten years served in other important positions, including that of Los Angeles District Superintendent. He also gradually increased his commitment to the holiness movement, not a commitment shared by most of his Methodist colleagues. In 1894 he requested a special appointment to the Penial Mission, an ecumenical holiness center in Los Angeles, and that request was denied. He then dropped his long career in Methodism to go to Penial, but in less than a year needed to look elsewhere.

In October 1895 Bresee and some followers founded the Church of the Nazarene and almost immediately experienced great success. By 1905 he was superintendent of a number of churches spread across the country. In October 1907 the church merged with the Association of Pentecostal Churches and in October 1908 merged with the Holiness Church of Christ. This last merger is considered the official beginning of the Church of the Nazarene. Bresee continued to lead the church from the Los Angeles church until his death.

Britten, Emma Hardinge: Emma Britten (1823-October 2, 1899), a major occult leader of the nineteenth century, was born in London, England. Her father, a sea captain, died when she was still a child. Her musical abilities were such that as early as age eleven she was giving vocal and piano concerts. Her mother helped cultivate this talent and also supported her interest in the occult. As a youngster, Britten learned the arts of mediumship and clairvoyancy through membership in a secret occult society. Her birth surname was Floyd, but she took the Hardinge name after a member of her occult group claimed to have married her while she was in a trance. She never recognized the relationship, but took the name to irritate the claimant.

In 1855 she moved to New York City to perform at the Broadway

Theater and other venues, and found a long-term position as musical director of the Dodsworth House. During this time she also became one of the most popular trance speakers in a culture infatuated with Spiritualism. During the early 1860s her favorite project was the development of a "Self-Sustaining Institution for Homeless and Outcast Women," a project that gained little support.

She returned to England from 1865 to 1869, where she wrote *Modern American Spiritualism* (1870), then returned to New York to help with its publication. At this time she met and in 1870 married William Britten. That year they began an occult periodical, *The Western Star*, in Boston, but a fire destroyed the work and they moved back to New York City. There she met Madame Blavatsky and was present at the founding meetings of the Theosophical Society in 1875.

Her growing attachment to Theosophy did not sit well with her Spiritualist colleagues, who thought of themselves more as scientists than occultists. As far as is known, she never formally joined the Theosophical Society, and during her remaining years of writing and lecturing she was independent in her views and associations. Her *Ghostland* (1876) and *Art Magic* (1876) showed theosophic beliefs and the latter also remains important to the Church of Light for its articulation of the teachings of the Brotherhood of Light.

Brooks, Nona Lovell: Nona Brooks (March 22, 1861-March 14, 1945), a leader of the Church of Divine Science, was born in Louisville, Kentucky to an upper-class Presbyterian family. She graduated from the Charleston Female Academy about 1878 and after her father's death in 1880 moved to Pueblo, Colorado, to join other family members. Invalidism seemed to run in her family, particularly affecting her mother and a sister, Alethea, and in the early 1880s Nona Brooks was stricken as well. She was diagnosed with ulcers of the throat and by 1887 was dangerously thin.

A friend, Kate Bingham, who had been trained in New Thought by Emma Curtis Hopkins, finally convinced Brooks and sister Alethea to attend her New Thought classes, and soon Brooks was healed. The Presbyterian church expelled them upon hearing of their new way of thinking. Brooks decided to become a teacher, attending Pueblo Normal School and Wellesley College in Massachusetts to gain her credentials. She taught for two years in Pueblo before moving to the Denver school system. About 1890 Brooks and sisters Alethea and Fannie (James) connected with Malinda Cramer's Divine Science in San Francisco and under her direction built a Divine Science teaching and healing practice in Denver. In 1895 Brooks left the school system to devote herself full-time to Divine Science.

In October 1898 she went to San Francisco to take Cramer's theological courses and was ordained by Cramer on December 1, 1898. She returned to Denver and presided over the new Divine Science Church services. In March 1901 she performed the first wedding ceremony ever done by a woman minister in Colorado. In 1902 she began the periodical *Fulfillment*, which is still running today as *Aspire to Better Living*.

When Cramer was killed by the April 1906 San Francisco earthquake, the center of Divine Science shifted to Denver. Fannie James led the college and Nona Brooks led the church. After Fannie died in 1914 the burden of both fell on Brooks. During the 1920s she traveled widely and opened branch churches across the country. In 1934 and 1935 she retired from the church and college, respectively, and settled in Chicago. In 1938 she returned to head the college and retired again in 1943, but remained active as a teacher.

Brothers, William Henry Francis: William Brothers (April 7, 1887-July 21, 1979), leader of the Old Catholic Church in America, was born into a Roman Catholic family near Nottingham, England. "Brothers" was his mother's maiden name; he added it to his name as an adult. The family moved to Waukegan, Illinois in the 1890s, where his father built a pioneering lace-making factory.

In 1908 Brothers joined the American Congregation of the Order of St. Benedict, an independent group founded by Dom Augustine de Angelis Harding and friendly with the Old Catholic Church in America, led by Jan Francis Tichy. In 1909 the congregation moved about 150 miles north to Fond du Lac, Wisconsin, where it was courted by Protestant Episcopal Church Bishop Charles Chapman Grafton. He gave them a building they named St. Dunstan's Abbey, but the group did not finally affiliate with the Episcopal Church. On October 3, 1911 the group gave the abbey to the Old Catholic Church in America and Tichy ordained Brothers a priest that day. Priests in that church were not celibate and Brothers is known to have married at some point.

In 1914 Tichy, debilitated by a stroke, named Brothers head of the Old Catholic Church in America. Brothers received episcopal consecration on October 3, 1916 by Rudolphe de Landas Berghes et de Rache and merged with his Old Roman Catholic Church. Within a year, however, Brothers left de Landas Berghes and reformed the Old Catholic Church in America. He established a congregation in Chicago and began adding ethnic-based leaders and congregations in the East and Midwest. In 1924 he established new headquarters in New York City. By 1936 the church had 24 parishes and almost 5,500 members.

In the 1950s the church slowly broke apart and on March 21, 1962, Brothers merged the church into the Russian Orthodox Church, accepting reordination as mitred archpriest. In 1967 he left that church and joined the Holy Ukrainian Autocephalic Orthodox Church in Exile. Still not satisfied, he left that body in 1969 and reestablished the Old Catholic Church in America, consecrating Joseph Anthony MacCormack as his successor. Brothers, through his participation in numerous consecrations, is known for being a primary source of independent American episcopal orders.

Broughton, Luke Dennis: Luke Broughton (April 20, 1828-1898), famous nineteenth century astrologer, was born in Leeds, Yorkshire, England. Like his father and grandfather, he grew up to be a physician who was also an astrologer. In 1854, two years after his marriage, he moved to the United States. He supported himself as a weaver while attending the Eclectic Medical College in Philadelphia. In 1860 he began issuing *Broughton's Monthly Planet Reader and Astrological Journal*, which ran until 1869.

In 1863 Broughton opened a medical office, utilizing herbs and astrology in addition to the standard medical tools. During the 18th and 19th centuries, with the Age of Enlightenment, astrology went into a period of decline, almost disappearing in many parts of the United States and Europe. Desiring to gain a broader audience for astrology, Broughton began giving public lectures in 1866, which proved popular. Soon he was also the country's main source for astrological literature.

Broughton was a key figure in the revival of astrology in the West and fared well in debates with debunkers like astronomer Richard Proctor. Broughton himself was quick to denounce any would-be astrologers he felt to be unqualified. Astrology became a common topic of conversation for many people, and a number of early 20th century professional astrologers owed their commitments to his influence. Several of his books became classics that still have importance.

Brown, Henry Harrison: Harrison Henry Brown (June 26, 1840-May 8, 1918), early New Thought leader and founder of the "Now" Folk, was born in Uxbridge, Massachusetts. He attended Nichols Academy in Dudley, Massachusetts and in 1857 began a teaching career. During the Civil War he served part of the time as a lieutenant for a black regiment, the 29th Connecticut Volunteers. After the war he returned to teaching and married

Fannie M. Hancox in 1873 (whom he later divorced).

In 1880 Brown left teaching for life as a traveling lecturer on topics ranging from social reform to Spiritualism. In 1887 he graduated from the Unitarian Divinity School in Meadville, Pennsylvania and served parishes at Petersham, Massachusetts (1887-88) and Salem, Oregon (1890-92). By 1893 he had converted to New Thought and left the church to again travel as lecturer, this time on New Thought topics.

About 1900 he arrived in San Francisco and organized the "Now" Folk, a group dedicated to the exploration of metaphysical healing and the harnessing of the cosmic energy. Brown began a periodical, *Now*, and became a prolific author, publishing at least 16 books from 1900 until his death in 1918. In addition to the standard New Thought topics such as the attraction of wealth, his classes and books also covered hypnotism, telepathy, clairvoyance, and other occult phenomena. He was rather unusual among New Thought leaders in desiring to express his convictions about the unity of life through the establishment of a cooperative community. Beginning at a residence, in 1906 it expanded into some acreage at nearby Glenwood. Although the community did not survive his death, the periodical, courses, and other works were continued for a number of years by a disciple, Sam E. Foulds.

Buchman, Frank Nathan Daniel: Frank Buckman (June 4, 1878-August 7, 1961), founder of Moral Re-Armament, was born in Pennsburg, Pennsylvania. Raised a Lutheran, he graduated from Lutheran Theological Seminary in 1902 and became a pastor in Overbrook, Pennsylvania. For six years he was very successful, building a hostel for poor, young men, but in 1908 a quarrel with the trustees forced him to leave. Angry and depressed, he went to England and eventually found renewal in Keswick Chapel.

Back in the United States he became Y.M.C.A. secretary at Pennsylvania State College, and then in 1916 extension lecturer at Hartford Theological Seminary. Both positions, especially the latter, allowed a flexible schedule for meeting and speaking with people internationally. The substance of his talks was the lesson he learned at Keswick Chapel, namely, that estrangement from God comes from moral compromise, and that new life comes from confession, honesty, and love.

In 1918, on a trip to China, he organized what would become his trademark, a "house party," in which the participants are encouraged to confess sins openly in an atmosphere of trust, seek God's guidance, and commit to a life of high moral standards. Such intimate and powerful gatherings gained popular momentum and in 1921 the First Century Christian Fellowship was founded on its principles. Occasionally, as at Princeton University in the late 1920s, the group was accused of actually promoting low moral standards through presumably lurid sharing sessions, but such charges were consistently refuted.

In the 1930s the group was popularly known as the Oxford Group because of its popularity at Cambridge and Oxford Universities. In 1938 Buchman changed the Oxford Group to Moral Re-Armament (MRA), believing that as the world was arming for war, he needed to offer an alternative. Some detractors claimed he was sympathetic to Nazism, a claim since shown to have no foundation, although he did show naiveté about Hitler's goals. After the war, especially through a new, unofficial headquarters in Caux, Switzerland, the MRA played a prominent role in bringing together former combatants. Buchman continued to lead the MRA until his death, and it remains a strong organization with offices in 28 countries.

Buckland, Raymond: Raymond Buckland (b. August 31, 1934), founder of the Seax-Wica Tradition, was born in London, England. He was raised in the Church of England, but as a teenager became fascinated with the occult. He went to King's College in London, served in the Royal Air Force for two years, and married Rosemary Buckland, who shared his occult interests.

About 1961 they settled in New York and soon thereafter they read Gerald Gardner's *Witchcraft Today* (1954), which struck such a responsive chord that they began corresponding with Gardner at his home on the Isle of Man. In 1963 they visited him and were initiated into the first two degrees of witchcraft during their three-week stay. Rosemary Buckland took the craft name of Lady Rowan and he took the name Robat. Upon return to New York, the Bucklands began a Gardnerian coven, the first in the country, and in 1966 founded the Museum of Witchcraft and Magic, based on Gardner's museum on the Isle of Man.

Thanks to the museum and their eagerness to promote witchcraft, the Bucklands became widely known and soon there were Gardnerian covens spread across the country. He wrote a number of books on witchcraft to help fill the gap in the literature, especially as Gardner's books were out of print. In 1973 the situation changed, however, as the Bucklands divorced and she subsequently exited from any affiliation with Gardnerian covens. Leadership of Gardnerian Wicca was turned over to Judy and Tom Kneitel (Lady Theos and Phoenix).

Raymond Buckland moved to New Hampshire and married Joan Helen

Tayler, who helped him develop a new wiccan approach called Seax-Wica. The book of rituals for this group, called *The Tree*, was published in 1974, and within a decade covens had been established in many states and internationally. There is a training seminary in Charlottesville, Virginia, although the Bucklands now live in Southern California.

Budapest, Zsuzsanna E.: Z. Budapest (b. January 30, 1940), a leader of Dianic Wicca, was born Zsuzsanna Mokcsay in Budapest, Hungary. At age 16, with the turmoil in Hungary after the revolt against Soviet control in 1956, she left the country. After a brief time in Austria she obtained a scholarship at the University of Chicago and moved to the United States.

After a failed marriage that produced two children, Budapest moved to Venice, California, in 1970 and opened a bookstore. She became involved in witchcraft and the women's movement, and in 1971 helped found the Susan B. Anthony Coven, which has since become a major branch of feminist or Dianic Wicca. Since 1979 Budapest and the Susan B. Anthony Coven headquarters have been located in Oakland, California.

Dianic Wicca places central emphasis on Goddess worship and posits a prehistoric time of matriarchal peace, disrupted by the rise of patriarchies and male deities. Budapest's first book, *The Feminist Book of Lights and Shadows* (1976), immediately became an authoritative text for Dianic Wicca groups. She currently runs workshops, trains priestesses, and conducts a cable television show, "13th Heaven," in the Oakland-San Francisco area. She is considered by many a founder of the women's spirituality movement and taught Starhawk, another well-known feminist Wiccan.

Burgoyne, Thomas H.: Thomas Burgoyne (April 14, 1855-March 1894), a founder of the Hermetic Brotherhood of Luxor, was born in Scotland. Even as a child he was reportedly able to see the spiritual entities some have called the Brotherhood of Light, though he did not learn about the brotherhood until he met occultist M. Theon as an adult.

In 1880 Burgoyne moved to the United States and joined forces with a retired British Army captain named Norman Astley, a member of the Brotherhood of Light in New York City with his wife, Genevieve Stebbins. Burgoyne quickly became a prominent member of the East Coast occult community, writing articles on the tarot for *The Platonist* in 1887 and 1888. Burgoyne then moved with the Astleys to their estate in Carmel, California, and wrote a series of occult lessons that were published as *The Light of Egypt*, vol. 1, in 1889.

The Brotherhood of Light claimed to be part of a tradition that dated back to a group of adepts in Egypt in 2400 B.C., and Burgoyne's lessons provided the opportunity to found the Hermetic Brotherhood of Luxor as the exoteric, or public outreach arm of the Brotherhood of Light. Burgoyne was its leader until his premature death in 1894. Some of his working manuscripts were organized and published after his death, including *Celestial Dynamics* (1896) and *The Light of Egypt*, vol. 2 (1900).

It is sometimes difficult to ascertain the facts of the often obscure lives of occult leaders. Researcher Arthur Edward Waite has claimed that Burgoyne was actually Thomas Henry Dalton, a convicted fraud, who left England with his partner, Peter Davidson (AKA M. Theon; Norman Astley). Whatever its origins, the Hermetic Brotherhood is continued today as the Church of Light.

C

Cabot, Laurie: Lauri Cabot (b. March 3, 1933), founder of the Witches' League for Public Awareness, was born in Wewoka, Oklahoma. She reportedly was initiated at age 16 into Druid-Celtic witchcraft by three priestesses. She continued her private studies of witchcraft through junior college, Massachusetts College of Art, and the Rhode Island School of Design.

As an adult she developed connections between witchcraft and occult sciences like magic. In 1971, for the Wellesley Adult Education program, she gave her first classes on "Witchcraft as a Science," and for most of the 1970s taught the course at the Cambridge Center for Adult Education and at Salem State College. She founded the Temple of Isis in Salem and did both private consultations and work with public agencies, including a number of police departments.

In April 1977 she was given the Paul Revere Patriots Award for her work with special needs children. Governor Dukakis took the occasion to informally designate her "The Official Witch of Salem." This sparked a heightened media interest in her that made her a major spokesperson for the Neo-Pagan community. She founded the Witches' League for Public Awareness to activate the Neo-Pagan network for defense against anti-Pagan programs and actions. Finally, in the late 1980s she found time to put some of her knowledge of witchcraft down on paper as *Power of the Witch: The Earth, the Moon, and the Magical Path to Enlightenment* (1989).

Caddy, Peter: Peter Caddy (b. 1917), cofounder of the Findhorn Community and pioneer New Age leader, was born in England. His father regularly visited Spiritualist mediums and so introduced Caddy to alternative spiritualities at a young age. At age 17 Caddy began a career in the hotel and catering business. In World War II he joined the Royal Air Force and was sent to Burma, where he had the opportunity to continue his study of various metaphysical and occult paths. He became a student of Ram Sareek Singh.

After the war he remained in the Royal Air Force and married Sheena Govan, a spiritual mentor. In 1953, while stationed in Iraq, he had an affair with Eileen Combe, and soon they both obtained divorces and married each other. He left the service and in 1956 found a hotel management position in Scotland. In 1962 he was fired from that position and they settled in Findhorn Caravan Park, near Inverness, along with a friend, Dorothy McLean, a former student of Govan.

Eileen began to receive spiritual guidance concerning their new life there, particularly how to live in harmony with their environment. Gardening was difficult in the shallow, sandy soil, but after learning to communicate with plant and other nature spirits, their garden grew huge vegetables. Visitors began coming to witness the garden and hear about the Caddys' spiritual way of life. Gradually the Findhorn Community was formed and Caddy began connecting with like-minded people and groups internationally. Numerous books about Findhorn were written, and it became a major force in the emerging New Age movement.

Caddy moved to the United States in the late 1970s and obtained a divorce in 1982. He moved to Mt. Shasta with his new wife, Paula, and founded The Gathering of the Ways community after the Findhorn model.

Cady, Harriette Emily: Harriette Cady (September 12, 1848-January 3, 1941), famous New Thought author, was born on a farm in Freeville, New York. She was the niece of the well-known feminist Elizabeth Cady Stanton. She graduated from the Homeopathic Medical College in New York City, making her among the first women physicians of any kind in New York.

She began to believe in non-medical healing through the preaching of Albert B. Simpson, founder of the Christian and Missionary Alliance, but after reading the New Thought books of Warren Felt Evans came to accept the New Thought interpretation of metaphysical healing. In November 1887 she attended a class by visiting New Thought teacher Emma Curtis Hopkins and found the healing power for herself. She wrote a booklet, *Finding the Christ in Ourselves* and a copy made its way into the hands of Charles and Myrtle Fillmore, founders of Unity School of Christianity. They invited her to contribute to *Unity Magazine*, which she did, beginning with the January 1892 issue.

This began a long and rewarding association with Unity. Her articles gained such a positive reader response that the Fillmores asked her to write a lesson series on faith basics. Her twelve articles began with the October 1894 issue and their tremendous impact led the Fillmores to reprint them as a booklet, *Lessons in Truth* (1895). Still today it is a required text for all beginning Unity students and is one of the best-selling New Thought books of all time. It has been translated into eleven languages and Braille. Despite the close association with the Fillmores, she never visited Unity Village in Missouri, and they never met personally until the Fillmores went to New York City about 1927. In her final years she was afflicted by near blindness and became almost a recluse.

Joseph Campbell
Courtesy: Joseph Campbell Archives and Library
Photo by Kathlee Thormod Carr

Campbell, Joseph: Joseph Campbell is a scholar and writer who, shortly before his death in the early eighties, became something of a popular culture phenomenon. Campbell was at the forefront of the group of thinkers through whose work "myth" was reevaluated by the mass consciousness of Western society, so that the term now means more than just "false story." Mythology, in the sense of "sacred story," is now viewed as something worthwhile, and even necessary for human beings. Campbell's now-classic early work on Hero myths, *The Hero With a Thousand Faces*, was consciously appropriated by creative writers, and even by movie producers such as George Lukas, producer of the popular *Star Wars* series. Partially because of his influence on popular culture, Campbell appeared on TV in a series of interviews with Bill Moyers, which is how his work was brought to the attention of the general public.

Campbell worked within the larger tradition of Jungian psychology, a school of thought that examines mythology for the light it throws on psychological processes. Jung understood myths as manifestations of the collective unconscious, the part of the mind that acts as a storehouse of myths and symbols to which all human beings have access, and which is viewed as the ultimate source of every society's mythology. Campbell did not develop a new view of mythology, but, rather, is responsible for popularizing the Jungian view.

Carey, Ken: Ken Carey's *Starseed Transmissions, channeled during an 11-day period in the winter of 1978-79* was based on an experience that occurred one September afternoon when, bedridden with a cold, he felt a presence. He was living in the countryside, where he had moved with his family after leaving his post office job. There he farmed for seven years, apprenticed to an Amish carpenter, and read the Bible.

In the book *The Starseed Transmissions* Carey describes the content of a series of messages—metaconceptual information—from "spatial intelligences," regarded as angels or extraterrestrials or as "informational cells" belonging to some kind of Galactic organism. The purpose of the channeled material contained in The Starseed Transmissions is typical of much of contemporary channeled literature, which aims to assist human evolution by lifting "the spell of matter" and giving birth to a new "Planetary Being." Humankind is viewed as ready for a momentous transformation that can occur with the help of advanced intelligences.

The book of channeled material, whose author is listed as Raphael, although the source seems to be Jesus Christ, is considered a masterpiece by many in the New Age movement. It also echoes *A Course of Miracles* and works channeled from Bartholomew and Emmanuel, especially in its analysis of the human psyche. Other works have been channeled by Ken Carey, such as *Notes to My Children: A Symplified Metaphysics* (1984), as well as *Vision*, and *Terra Christa* (1985), in which the channeled information is presented so as to appeal to a Christian audience.

In his *Return of the Bird Tribes* (1988) he describes a number of encounters that occurred in the winter of 1986-87 with a circle of angels actively involved in the founding of the Iroquois League in North America, regarded by some as the basis of the U.S. Constitution. Since then, Carey has written a number of magazine articles and has participated in certain conferences, such as the Whole Life Expo.

Carfora, Carmel Henry: Carmel Henry Carfora (August 27, 1878-January 11, 1958), co-founder of the North American Old Roman Catholic Church, was born in Naples, Italy. He was ordained a Roman Catholic priest on August 15, 1901 and was sent to the United States as a missionary to Italian immigrants through the Order of Friars Minor. In a dispute with his superiors, he left the order in 1908 and established his own missions, establishing a pastorate in Youngstown, Ohio in 1910. His theological orientation was pre-Vatican I, except for allowing a married priesthood.

In 1912 Carfora was consecrated a bishop by Paolo Miraglia Gulotti, founder of the Italian National Episcopal Church, but did not join that body. On June 14 of that year he incorporated his work as the National Catholic Diocese in North America. That work struggled, however, and on October 4, 1916, he was consecrated by Prince Rudolphe de Landas Berghes, creating with him in 1917 the North American Old Roman Catholic Diocese. In 1919 de Landas Berghes returned to the Roman Catholic Church and Carfora changed the name of the group to the North American Old Roman Catholic Church.

In the following years, from his headquarters in Chicago, Carfora was successful in pulling together numerous congregations, most of them non-English-speaking immigrants, dissatisfied with Roman Catholic or Anglican structures. After World War II he tried to unite with the Ukrainian Orthodox Church. Although the merger did not go through, 32 of his parishes left him for that church. Carfora dealt with this kind of loss many times in his career.

He consecrated at least 40 people over the years and thus was known far beyond his particular jurisdiction as a key source of Old Catholic orders. In the last years of his life his health deteriorated due to asthma and heart trouble. He was succeeded by Hubert Augustus Rogers, a product of his West Indian congregations.

Caro, Roger: Roger Caro (b. January 30, 1911), is patriarch of the Église Universelle de la Nouvelle Alliance (Universal Church of the New Alliance), based in France. He was ordained priest on June 5, 1972, by Armand Ghislain Toussaint of the Rosicrucian Apostolic Church, and was consecrated on November 6, 1973, by Joseph Paul Fernand Dupuis of the Catholic Charismatic Church of Canada. He has had numerous other consecrations, including from Georges Bellemare of the Universal Church of the New Alliance on June 27, 1977.

As current head of the Universal Church of the New Alliance, Caro supervises one of the larger and more influential of the European independent bishop groups. In 1983 he claimed more than 15 bishops, 28 clergy, and 40 seminarians in France and other French-speaking countries. His group has a distinctly gnostic or mystic orientation. He often goes by the religious names of Pierre Phoebus or Stephanos and serves as the Commander of the Patriarchal Order of the Holy Cross of Jerusalem, headed by Maximos V Hakim, Patriarch of the Melkite-Greek Catholic Church.

Carus, Paul: Paul Carus (July 18, 1852-February 11, 1919), philosopher and a significant factor in the introduction of Buddhism to the United

Paul Carus
Courtesy: American Religion Collection

States, was born in Ilsenburg, Germany. His father was the First Superintendent of the Protestant state church of Prussia and although Carus followed this interest in religion, he did not follow his father into the ministry. He received a Ph.D. in 1876 from the University of Tübingen and accepted a teaching position at a military academy in Dresden. His liberal religious views soon forced him to leave, however, and after a brief stay in England he moved to the United States in 1884.

In 1887 Carus became editor of *Open Court*, a Chicago-based journal of ideas. His regular contributions developed his philosophy that supernatural concepts like immortal souls or God have no ontological reality, but rather are traditional ways of discussing life experiences. He found that Buddhism shared his practical, common-sense approach and committed much of his adult life to understanding it, though he never claimed to be a Buddhist himself. In 1888 he married Mary Hegler, daughter of Edward G. Hegler, the industrialist founder of *Open Court*. In 1890 Carus expanded his duties to include founding and editing the *Monist*, a magazine dedicated to exploring his philosophically-monistic world view.

In 1893 Carus met Anagarika Dharmapala and Soyen Shaku, Buddhist delegates to the World Parliament of Religions at the Chicago World's Fair. He was so impressed with them that he agreed to sponsor their future activities in America and in the process he became the first major American spokesperson for Buddhism. He sponsored the American branch of Dharmapala's Maha Bodhi Society and conducted Dharmapala's 1896 national tour. When Zen master D. T. Suzuki arrived in the United States in 1897 he stayed with Carus until 1909 and they worked together translating a number of Buddhist texts. Carus himself published dozens of books, the most successful of which was the widely acclaimed *Gospel of Buddhism* (1894). Some of his poems were later set to music and became hymns used today by the Buddhist Churches of America.

Castanda, Carlos: Carlos Castanda is a popular writer trained as an anthropologist who wrote a series of books recounting his training as a "sorcerer" under Don Juan, a Yaqui Indian shaman. Castanda presents himself as a skeptical social scientist who gradually enters into the Don Juan's world, eventually taking on the goals and values of his Yaqui mentor through a series of best-selling books. In the first few volumes of the series, Don Juan attempts to shatter Carlos's convential world view through controlled experiences with psychedelic substances. Initially published during the peak of the sixties drug culture, *The Teachings of Don Juan: A Yaqui Way of Knowledge* became an overnight sensation because of the support it seemed to offer for the drug culture's contention that psychedelics opened the mind to new realities. In later volumes, however, the importance of drugs are diminished, relativized as rather crude tools necessary for piercing Carlos's stubborn grip on ordinary reality.

Critics have dismissed Castanada's work as pure fiction, exploiting a gullible public's desire for ancient wisdom, myth, and magic in a guise palatable to modern temperaments. Native American critics in particular have harshly attacked Castanada for exploiting the New Age's interest in romanticized and sensationalized American Indian religious practices. However, whether fictional or not, Castanda's books have created an appealing world in which an entire generation of readers have imaginatively participated.

Beyond psychedelics, Don Juan instructed Carlos in other techniques for "stopping the world" (interrupting the plausibility structure of ordinary reality). One of these approaches is what would nowadays call lucid dreaming, the becoming aware that one is dreaming during a dream and exercising control over one's dream experience. More advanced techniques involve what the Western occult tradition would call astral projection—separating one's consciousness from the body and gazing back at one's physical form.

Edgar Cayce
Courtesy: A.R.E.

Cayce, Edgar: Edgar Cayce (March 18, 1977 - January 3, 1945), was an early twentieth-century "psychic" best known for his pronouncements on health and reincarnation. He was born near Hopkinsville, Kentucky, the son of Leslie B. Cayce, a businessman and tobacco farmer, and Carrie Elizabeth Cayce. Cayce was raised in the Christian Church (Disciples of Christ), and eventually taught Sunday school. He dropped out of school to became a photographer's apprentice, and made his living as a photographer. Married to Gertrude Evans in 1903, he fathered two sons.

Cayce developed a case of severe laryngitis in 1900. During this crisis, an acquaintance hypnotized Cayce (according to some accounts, the trance was self-induced). During the trance, Cayce diagnosed his own health problem and prescribed a cure. Soon after this experience, he began to perform the same trance prescriptions for others, and his reputation gradually grew.

In 1909, Cayce met a homeopathic physician, Dr. Wesley Ketchum, who requested that Cayce give him a reading. Ketchum's illness was cured, and he publicized his story and the story of other cures widely. Some of Ketchum's remarks about Cayce were quoted in an article that appeared in the *New York Times* in September 1910. After this exposure, Cayce, now widely known as the "Sleeping Prophet," was sought after by thousands of ailing people. His prescriptions varied from psychic treatments to home remedies to advising the patient to see a particular medical doctor. In time, he performed distance reading, prescribing cures to people who wrote letters requesting medical assistance.

A turning point in his readings began in 1923 when Cayce met Arthur Lammers, a wealthy printer and student of theosophy and Eastern religions. Cayce traveled to Dayton, Ohio, to conduct a series of private readings. One of Lammers' central articles of faith was belief in reincarnation, and Cayce mentioned Lammers' past lives in one of the private readings. Cayce subsequently began to explore the past lives of his other clients, including past lives in such exotic lands as Atlantis. He soon added past-life readings to his health readings. Not long after his sessions with Lammers, he closed his photography studio and moved to Ohio.

After Lammers suffered some financial reverses, Morton Blumenthal, a New York stockbroker, offered to finance a center and hospital on the East Coast. Cayce then moved to Virginia Beach, where he resided for the balance of his life. The Hospital opened in 1928 and Atlantic University in 1930. In 1931, however, Blumenthal's business failed, a casualty of the Great Depression. Without Blumenthal, both the hospital and the university had to be shut down.

In spite of these setbacks, Cayce's readings were still his principal asset. Following the closings, the Cayce family and some supporters set up the Association for Research and Enlightenment (A.R.E.) as a vehicle for Cayce's work. Also, the Edgar Cayce Foundation was established to preserve the Cayce papers. Cayce gave readings for the rest of his life, until shortly before his death.

Clutterbuck, Dorothy: Gerald Gardner had claimed that he had been initiated into the Craft (witchcraft) in 1939 by "Old Dorothy" Clutterbuck (this usage of "Old" being an English usage conveying affectionate respect), but little was known about her until 1980, when Doreen Valiente, annoyed by Jeffrey Burton Russell's assertion that Dorothy Clutterbuck had probably never existed, decided to try to track her down, and succeeded in doing so, finding the key documents in various British government offices, as she reported in an Appendix to the Farrars' *A Witch's Bible*.

It turns out that Dorothy was born on January 19, 1880, in Bengal, to Captain (later Major) Thomas St. Quintin Clutterbuck and Ellen Anne (Morgan) Clutterbuck. Dorothy returned to England, and married a man named Fordham, and became quite affluent. Living in a mansion in the New Forest area, she was a leading member of the Fellowship of Crotona and its Rosicrucian Theater Group. Ronald Hutton has found an elderly gentleman who, as a boy in the 1930s, was a member of the Order of Woodland Chivalry (one of the less-paramilitary alternatives to the Boy Scouts), which used a ritual, based on what was at the time thought to be Native American religious practices, that included casting a circle, calling to the four directions, invoking the Great Spirits of Nature, drumming, dancing, and eating a small feast. This gentleman remembers the night, he told Hutton, when Dorothy Clutterbuck's Rosicrucian Theatre Group came to their circle as guests—and this solves the problem of where the basic Gardnerian ritual format came from.

Clutterbuck apparently kept the coven going during much of World War II, and was also active, as was Gardner, in defense work on the home front. After the war she apparently was not too active in the coven, but still managed to keep Gardner on a fairly short leash. It was only after her death in 1961 that Gardner began proclaiming the Gardnerian foundation myth: that the New Forest Coven had survived from times past.

Valiente feels that her establishing the Clutterbuck did exist proves that the coven had survived from the past—but it does not; it merely proves that the coven existed about 1939, just when Gardner and some others say that it did. The most likely possibility is that Clutterbuck and the others in the occult circles of London, Brighton, etcetera, had begun the coven—perhaps building on experiments by a Pentangle Club at Cambridge in the mid-1930s—a year or two earlier as an attempt to recreate the Pagan religion described by Margaret Murray. The best evidence for this is the fact that, according to a pamphlet that Gardner published about his museum on the Isle of Man, Dorothy Clutterbuck owned the sword that ended up in Gardner's museum, that was used by Gardner and "Dafo" to initiate Doreen Valiente in 1953, and that was also used every year by the Ancient

Order of Druids for its ceremonies at Stonehenge, because its hilt happened to fit exactly into the hole in the Hele Stone. That is, it is no accident that the Ross Nichols whom Gardner thanks in the preface to *Witchcraft Today* was a member of the Ancient Order of Druids, and became its Chosen Chief in the same year that Gardner died.

Andrew Cohen
Courtesy: Moksha Foundation

Cohen, Andrew: Andrew Cohen has been a teacher of Enlightenment since the mid-1980s. Cohen was born in New York City in 1955, where he spent his childhood and early adolescence, traveling abroad to complete his education before returning again in his early twenties. Unable to forget a spontaneous spiritual experience that occurred when he was sixteen, Cohen eventually decided to abandon all other aspirations and at the age of twenty-two became a serious spiritual seeker. After pursuing many different spiritual teachers and paths, his seeking finally led him to India, where in 1986 he met a little-known teacher named H.W.L. Poonja. This meeting was the catalyst for a spiritual awakening that completely transformed his life. Cohen's natural gift for communicating the understanding of awakening drew people to him almost immediately, and his teaching was born.

Since that time Cohen has continued to travel and teach extensively throughout the world, giving public talks and leading intensive retreats. Evolving over the course of his career, Cohen's teaching is now characterized by his distinction between Personal Enlightenment and what he calls, Impersonal Enlightenment. In this, he seeks to convey his discovery that spiritual liberation's true significance is its potential to radically transform not only the individual personally, but the entire way that human beings, as a race, live together. Inspired by Cohen's message, communities of students dedicated to living his teachings have opened public centers throughout the world. Cohen devotes much time and energy to these communities, bringing people together in a common vision of unity, and a shared commitment to living spiritual life not for personal gain, but for the purpose of demonstrating the profound significance that embracing an enlightened life, a life free from fear, ignorance and selfishness, can have for the race as a whole.

Cohen's continual questioning of certain popular paradigms in the modern spiritual world has made him an unusually controversial figure. In particular, he contends that the depth of awakening of a spiritual master can be clearly discerned by their behavior. This view, coupled with the uncompromising nature of his own life and teaching, has created significant tension in the spiritual world at large and has elicited, at times, strong opposition.

Cohen's active investigation into the nature of spiritual understanding and the spiritual pursuit has also led him to initiate meetings with teachers, scholars and leaders in many different fields in order to explore and elucidate the fundamental truths at the heart of human life. This passion for ongoing spiritual inquiry has also found expression in the magazine *What Is Enlightenment?*, a popular and highly respected biannual publication founded by Cohen. *What Is Enlightenment?* brings together pioneering thinkers and teachers from a broad spectrum of paths and disciplines, providing a dynamic forum for investigating the most important spiritual questions of our time. Cohen is also the author of a number of books including *An Unconditional Relationship to Life, Autobiography of an Awakening, My Master Is My Self, Freedom Has No History* and *Enlightenment Is a Secret.* In 1997 he established an international retreat center in western Massachusetts where he currently resides.

Collin, Michel: Michel Collin (September 13, 1905-June 24, 1974), founder of the Église Catholique Renoveé (Renovated Catholic Church), was ordained a Roman Catholic priest on July 9, 1932 in Lille, France. On April 28, 1935 he had a vision of receiving an episcopal consecration. On October 7, 1950 he had another vision in which Christ gave him full apostolic authority, placing him on a par with the pope. The following year the Roman Catholic Church removed him from his priestly office.

Collin then went into a time of reflection until December 25, 1958, when he publicly proclaimed himself Pope Clement XV and founded the Renovated Catholic Church. He made his headquarters at a farmhouse in Clemery, Lorraine, France and called it Le Petit Vatican de Marie Coredemptrice. He arranged for a more earthly consecration on October 23, 1966 from Jean Damgé of the Sainte Église Catholique Gallicane Autocephale. During his papal reign, Collins achieved an international following. After his death the group split into several competing factions.

Cooper, Irving Steiger: Irving Steiger Cooper (March 16, 1882-January 17, 1935), the first regionary bishop of the Liberal Catholic Church in the United States, was born in Santa Barbara, California. After graduating from one of the University of California campuses, he was introduced to Theosophy. Within a few years he was a leading figure in Theosophy and in 1911 traveled to the international headquarters in Adyar, India.

He remained in India for some years as secretary to Charles Webster Leadbeater and began writing his first books on Theosophy. In 1914 Leadbeater moved to Australia and Cooper followed in 1917. Cooper helped Leadbeater and Bishop James Ingall Wedgwood (formerly of the Old Roman Catholic Church) put together the beginnings of the Liberal Catholic Church, a mixture of the Old Catholic and Theosophic traditions. Cooper was ordained a Liberal Catholic priest in 1918 and the following year was sent to the United States as its first regionary bishop.

He set up his headquarters in Hollywood, California and built St. Alban's Cathedral. In 1926 he toured the world with Annie Besant and Theosophy's new World Teacher, Jiddu Krishnamurti. In 1927 he married Susan L. Warfield and the following year presided over the church's first Provincial Convocation. In the years before his death he suffered from poor health, but managed to complete his most important book, *Ceremonies of the Liberal Catholic Rite* (1934), a revision of the church's liturgy that became standard.

Costa, Carlos Duarte: Carlos Duarte Costa (July 21, 1888-March 26, 1961), founder of the Igreja Católica Apostólica Brasileira (Brazilian Catholic Apostolic Church), was born in Rio de Janeiro, Brazil. Little is known about his early life. He was ordained a Roman Catholic priest on April 1, 1911 and with an exemplary record of service rose steadily in prominence. He was consecrated a bishop on December 8, 1924 by Sebastiao Leme da Silveira, the Roman Catholic bishop of Rio de Janeiro.

Costa was assigned as Bishop of Botucatu in Brazil until his early retirement in 1937. After 26 years of service he was still only 49 years old. Perhaps he retired at such a young age because he was already having ideological difficulties with the hierarchy. During World War II he became involved in an anti-papal campaign that accused the Roman Catholic Church of secretly helping the Italian fascists. For these activities the Vatican excommunicated Costa in June 1945 and the following month, on July 6, he founded the Brazilian Catholic Apostolic Church.

The changes from traditional Catholic practice Costa introduced in his church include a vernacular Portuguese liturgy, abolishment of the sacrament of penance, and permission for clergy to marry. Since Costa's death the church has been led by Luís Fernando Castillo-Méndez.

Cramer, Malinda Elliott: Malinda Cramer (February 12, 1844-August 2, 1906), founder of the Divine Science Federation International, was born into a Quaker family in Greensboro, Indiana. As a young woman she became afflicted with the invalidism so common among women of the time and moved to San Francisco in an attempt to find better health. There she married Charles Lake Cramer in 1872. He was also a Quaker and ran a photography studio.

In 1885 she had a religious healing experience, possibly as a result of receiving ministry from New Thought lecturer Miranda Rice. She began teaching New Thought classes in 1887, perhaps after attending Emma Curtis Hopkins' class of April 1887. In May 1888 she incorporated her work as the Home College of Spiritual Science and began the periodical *Harmony* in August 1888. The magazine gained a wide readership in New Thought circles. She began to establish branch centers in the San Francisco Bay Area and one in Denver in 1890. By that time she had renamed her work Divine Science.

In May 1892 Cramer founded the International Divine Science Association and held its first convention that December in San Francisco. It was ecumenical in nature, not limited to Divine Science adherents, and became the first New Thought ecumenical convention to last beyond two meetings—there were five altogether, ending in 1899. Cramer was the first person after Emma Curtis Hopkins to ordain New Thought clergy. She ordained Nona Brooks for the growing Denver work in December 1898. Cramer's career was cut short by the April 1906 earthquake in San Francisco; she died a few months later from injuries sustained at that time, and the Divine Science headquarters shifted to Denver, Colorado.

Crawford, Florence Louise: Louise Crawford (September 1, 1872-June 20, 1936), founder of the Apostolic Faith Church (Mission), was born in Coos County, Oregon. She grew up imbued with the freethought/atheist persuasion of her parents, but remained curious about Christianity. She experienced conversion at a party sometime after her marriage to Frank M. Crawford when she heard a voice say, "Daughter, give me thine heart." Believing this to be a directive from heaven, she joined the Methodist Church and was soon one of its most active workers in social reform and as president of the California Woman's Christian Temperance Union.

In 1906 she heard about the new Pentecostal experience at the Azusa Street church in Los Angeles. She visited there several times and experienced sanctification on one occasion and speaking in tongues on another occasion. She was also healed of several maladies, including spinal meningitis. She left the Methodist Church and became a traveling home missionary for the Azusa Street church, led by William J. Seymour. In December 1906, while in Oregon preaching, she was invited by a Portland church to become their permanent pastor. She accepted, left Seymour's church, and at first named her independent ministry Apostolic Faith, later renamed Apostolic Faith Church (Mission).

As head of her own church, Crawford's personal beliefs came more to the fore. She refused to take offerings at regular meetings, preached a strict moral code, and added footwashing to baptism and the Lord's Supper as a third ordinance. A son, Raymond Robert, was ordained and became her assistant. In 1908 she began *The Apostolic Faith* magazine and the church steadily grew. In 1913 she began evangelizing the sailors at Portland harbor with some success. By the time she died over twenty years later the church had a solid base in the Pacific Northwest and had an international presence in Norway, Sweden, Canada, and several other countries.

Creme, Benjamin: Benjamin Creme (b. 1922), founder of Share International Foundation (known in the United States as the Tara Center), was born in Glasgow, Scotland. He began painting as a teenager and after a brief time in the Glasgow School of Art became a professional artist.

He was very interested in the occult and read many theosophical works, particularly those of Alice Bailey, founder of the Arcane School. In her last major work, *The Reappearance of the Christ* (1948), she reactivated the long-standing theosophist hope of a new world teacher by stating that such a one would appear by the year 2000. Creme was greatly influenced by that book, and by the Aetherius Society, a group that believes in communication with extraterrestrials.

In 1959 Creme began receiving messages from the spiritual masters believed by theosophists to be directing the destiny of earth. He was told that Lord Maitreya, a bodhisattva who has also appeared as Jesus Christ, would arrive on earth in approximately twenty years. In 1975 he received the message that he needed to prepare humanity for this reappearance of Christ. He stepped up his writing and speaking activities toward that end. In 1977 he began channeling messages from Maitreya indicating that the earth could perish if the people did not begin to manifest divine love more adequately, particularly by justly sharing the earth's resources, including education and health care, with the poor.

Creme founded Share International to coordinate the work and indicate the key concept of sharing. On April 25, 1982 he took out large ads in many major newspapers announcing that "The Christ Is Now Here!" and would be known to all within two months. When Christ failed to appear, Creme lost much of his following, which had tended to be in New Age circles. He has continued to promote Maitreya's coming, and in 1988 circulated pictures of his brief appearance in Kenya.

Sir William Crookes
Courtesy: American Religion Collection

Crookes, Sir William: Sir William Crookes (1832-1919), one of the greatest physicists of the 19th century, and one of the first prominent investigators of spiritualist mediums. Born June 17, 1832 in London, England, he was the son of a prosperous tailor. Following graduation from the Royal college of Chemistry, he became Superintendent of the Meteorological Department at Radcliffe Observatory, Oxford, in 1854, where he devised an automated method for recording instrument data. The next year he joined the faculty of Chester Training College as a professor of chemistry. Because Chester would not provide him with a research laboratory, he resigned in 1856. Most of his life's research was carried out at a home laboratory.

In the same year in which he resigned from Chester, Crookes married Ellen Humphrey, with whom he had eight children. Crookes initially supported his family by writing and editing articles for photography journals. Eventually, in 1859, he initiated his own periodical, *Chemical News*. Later, he also assisted with the founding and editing of the *Quarterly Journal of Science*. In 1861 Crookes discovered the element thallium and accurately measured its atomic weight. Two years later, he was elected a Fellow of the Royal Society of London for Improving Natural Knowledge.

Crookes found the phenomena associated with Spiritualism fascinating. He systematically studied mediumship from 1869 to 1875, and attended seances with such well-known mediums as D. D. Home, Frank Herne and Charles Williams. He chose to devote most of his time to the former, perhaps because Home always held seances in good light, as well as because he welcomed scientific research into his abilities.

Crookes went beyond simple observation to investigate Home's phenomena in controlled, scientific environments. Often he had Home perform one of his remarkable feats of psychokinesis (moving physical objects without touching them) while he and other scientists of repute watched and took notes. Rather than claiming that disembodied spirits were reponsible for the observed phenomena, he postulated that they were the result of some sort of psychic force projected by the medium.

Crookes is also remembered for his study of Florence Cook. In 1872 Cook requested an investigation after an attendee at one of her seances had grabbed the full-form materialization of her spirit guide, Katie King, and claimed that it was Cook herself. Crookes studied her mediumship closely, and for some four months she lived with him and his family. Skeptics have suggested that Crookes was having an affair—or was at least infatuated—with Cook, which would explain why a scientist of Crookes's stature could be easily tricked. This "theory" is, however, pure speculation, based on little more than circumstantial evidence.

Crookes lent his support to the Society for Psychical Research (SPR) after its formation in 1882—even serving as president in 1886—but he never became really active in it. In 1875, the Royal Society awarded Crookes its Royal Medal. In the next year he devised the radiometer, an instrument that measured the impact of radiation on objects in a vacuum, and a special tube called the Crookes' tube. This line of research led more or less directly to his discovery of cathode rays, which soon led to discoveries (by other scientists) of x-rays and the electron.

From 1887 to 1889, Crookes served as president of the Chemical Society. From 1890 to 1894, he also served as president of the Society of Electrical Engineers. In 1897, he was knighted. In 1898 he became president of the British Association for the Advancement of Science. In 1903, Crookes invented an instrument used in the study of subatomic particles, the spinthariscope. In 1910, he was awarded the Order of Merit, one of England's highest non-military honors. From 1913 to 1915 he served as president of the Royal Society.

Crowley, Aleister Edward: Aleister Crowley (October 12, 1875-December 1, 1947), the most famous and influential ritual magician of the twentieth century, was born Edward Alexander Crowley in Leamington, Warwickshire, England. His father was a preacher for the Exclusive Plymouth Brethren, and he soon rebelled against his strict, fundamentalist upbringing. He was a student at Trinity College in Cambridge from 1894 to 1897, but dropped out before completing a degree. His interests in the occult and sexual activ-

Aleister Crowley
Courtesy: American Religion Collection

ity crowded out his studies.

In 1898 he was initiated into the Hermetic Order of the Golden Dawn (O.G.D.), an occult group focused on ritual magic (magick). In 1903 he married Rose Edith Kelly. He seemed destined for leadership in the O.G.D., but was denied higher grades of initiation because of his homosexual activities. Samuel (MacGregor) Mathers, one of the founders of the O.G.D., gave Crowley the higher grades anyway, thus causing a split in the organization. By 1904 Crowley decided to exit the O.G.D. and was seeking another avenue of expression. Visiting in Cairo, Egypt, in April 1904, he reportedly received a communication lasting several days from a spirit entity named Aiwass. The result was *The Book of the Law*, an outline of his Egyptian brand of magick, which he called Thelema, from the Greek word for Will. Crowley taught that "'Do what thou wilt' shall be the whole of the Law," which is to say that training the will to achieve the fulfillment of one's destiny is crucial for magical activity.

In 1907 he founded his own order, Argenteum Astrum (Silver Star), and two years later began the semiannual periodical, *Equinox*, the collected issues of which later became an important source of magical material. Also in 1909 he obtained a divorce. In 1912 he met Theodore Reuss, head of the Ordo Templi Orientis (O.T.O.), an occult group that taught sex magick at its higher levels. Crowley joined the O.T.O. and soon was made the head of its British branch. He added rituals for homosexual magick.

Crowley went to the United States in 1914 and met with the few O.T.O. adherents there at that time. At some point he discovered and was inspired by the sex magick theories of P. B. Randolph, founder of the Fraternitas Rosae Crucis in America, and over the following years altered the O.T.O. sex magick rituals to accommodate his new findings. In 1919 he moved to Italy, where he continued his training and reached "ipsissimus," the highest possible magical level. In 1922 he succeeded Theodore Reuss as outer head of the O.T.O.

In 1923 Mussolini, as part of a move against occultists, forced Crowley to leave Italy, and he went first to Tunis, then France (from which he was expelled about 1930), then to England, where he remained for the rest of his life. In 1929 he married Maria Theresa Ferrari de Miramar. Despite

Crowley's dedicated leadership, the O.T.O. did not grow, but steadily diminished. Perhaps it was because Crowley's energies were diverted by an addiction to heroin, or perhaps the times were not conducive to occultists generally. At the time of his death, there was only one remaining center of the O.T.O., and the group almost disappeared entirely until its surprising resurgence in the 1970s. Crowley's impact has continued to be tremendous among almost all the magical groups.

Cummins, George David: David Cummins (December 11, 1822-June 26, 1876), founder of the Reformed Episcopal Church, was born in Smyrna, Delaware. In 1836, at age 14, he entered Dickinson College to study law, but a conversion experience three years later caused him to leave the school and enter the Methodist ministry. After serving several pastorates (and ordination in 1842) he left to join the Protestant Episcopal Church, for which he was ordained priest on July 6, 1845. After a year at Christ Church in Baltimore, he spent six years at Christ Episcopal Church in Norfolk, Virginia. There, on June 24, 1847, he married Alexandrine Balch. Later pastorates included St. James in Richmond, Trinity Church in Washington, D.C., St. Peter's Church in Baltimore, and Trinity Church in Chicago.

On November 15, 1866 he was consecrated bishop and became Assistant Bishop of Kentucky. Still carrying the evangelical style of his Methodist ministry and downplaying the importance of liturgy, he was thus identified with the "low church" elements of the denomination. This was not a major problem until he agreed to participate in the 1873 meeting of the Evangelical Alliance of the World in New York City, at which he spoke and partook of communion. The latter action was believed by many to be contrary to church policy and he was severely criticized. Believing that the "high church" elements were thwarting the church's mission, he resigned on November 10, 1873.

On December 2, 1873 he founded the Reformed Episcopal Church. He maintained the office of bishop, but eliminated the House of Bishops as a separate order of ministry. He taught that the "real presence" of Christ in communion happened within the believer, not in the bread and wine. Although he led the church for only three years before his death, he lived to see it create seven jurisdictions in the United States and Canada.

Cunningham, Sara: Sara Cunningham, a former Episcopalian, found the Craft (Wicca) movement in the late 1960s, and by 1970 was running the Albion Training Group in Pasadena, California. In 1970 she was one of the founding members of the Church of the Eternal Source, but separated from them in 1971 after a dispute over eclecticism, which she favored, versus as pure a reconstruction as possible of Egyptian religion, which Harold Moss and the others favored. She founded the Temple of Tiphareth, which combined ceremonial magic, Egyptian religion, and Wicca, and also ran Stonehenge, an occult supply house in Pasaena. Hans Holzer found the store, and wrote about her in his books at that time. She may have been one of Starhawk's first teachers. In 1973, she moved to Wolf Creek, Oregon, and founded Lady Sara's Coven. About a year later, *Womanspirit* began in that community, and ran for the next decade. There was an offshoot of her Oregon coven in Salt Lake City in the late 1980s. Her books include *AUM: The Sacred Word* and *The Hermetic Art* (both published by the First Temple of Tiphareth in Glendale, Oregon, in 1975); *Candle Magic* (Hollywood, CA: Phoenix House, 1974); and *Questions and Answers on Wicca Craft* (Wolf Creek, OR: Stonehenge Farm, 1974).

Cunningham, Scott: Scott Cunningham was born in Royal Oak, Michigan, on June 27, 1956. He was a prolific author of books on the occult and the modern Craft movement. He died March 28, 1993, at the age of 36, in San Diego, California, of AIDS. Scott met a Witch for the first time in 1971, at age 15, and was initiated soon after he became an adult. He practiced the Craft as his religion for his entire adult life, and was universally respected as a tireless researcher and meticulously professional writer.

His writings were being published by the time he was 18. His first Llewellyn book was published in 1982, and he proceeded to turn out several dozen more on such topics as herbalism, incenses, crystals, aromatherapy, and food magic, as well as such basic texts as *The Truth About Witchcraft Today, Earth Power, Wicca: A Guide for the Solitary Practitioner*, and *Earth, Air, Fire, and Water*.

He was hospitalized in 1990 with fungal meningitis, his first AIDS-related illness, and was the focus for a national healing and fund-raising campaign. He kept the illness secret from all but his closest friends for awhile, afraid that the ostracism possible with AIDS might interfere with sales of his books and hence with his ability to pay the mounting medical bills. However, he did give permission for the truth to be told in the fall of 1992 (according to the eulogy on p. 7 of *Green Egg* No. 101). His optimistic attitude about life, his work, and the reincarnation promised to initiates never wavered, according to those who knew him well.

Cutler, Alpheus: Alpheus Cutler (February 29, 1784-August 10, 1864), founder of the Church of Jesus Christ (Cutlerite), a branch of the Church of Jesus Christ of Latter-day Saints, was born in Plainfield, New Hampshire. Trained as a stone mason and architect, he married Lois Lantrop in 1808 and soon thereafter moved to Upper Lisle, New York. He was a captain in the War of 1812 and the following decade moved to Chautauqua County, New York.

In 1832 he housed a group of Mormons traveling through town. They healed his daughter of a serious illness and converted the family. He was baptized on January 20, 1833 and moved to Kirkland, Ohio, to help build the temple. Later, he was licensed to preach and did some evangelizing in Iowa. In 1839 he moved his family to Missouri and became operator of a grist mill near the new Mormon settlement at Far West. He was the main architect of the temple there, but construction had barely begun when attacks on the community drove them to Nauvoo, Illinois.

In Nauvoo he joined the High Council and worked on plans for the temple. In 1843 he was named by founder Joseph Smith, Jr. to the Quorum of Seven, those capable of leading the Mormons should the need arise. After Smith's death in 1844, Cutler was part of the westward move in 1846 to Council Bluffs, Iowa, though he had problems with Brigham Young's leadership. He then went on a multi-year mission to the Indians (Lamanites) and thus did not join in the further westward move to Utah. He returned to Iowa in 1852 and joined a small group of Mormons at Manti, Iowa. In 1853, after a vision, he decided to use his authority from the Quorum of Seven to reorganize the church, doing so on September 19, 1853. The church reached a high of 183 members. After Cutler's death the group, under Chauncey Whiting, moved to Minnesota, and in 1928 some settled in Independence, Missouri, where they remain today.

D

Darby, John Nelson: John Darby (November 18, 1800 - April 29, 1883), the originator of dispensationalism and the major founder of what has become the Plymouth Brethren group of churches, was born in Westminster, Ireland. He graduated from college at age 19 and seemed headed for a brilliant law career. Instead, following a conversion experience, he trained for the Anglican priesthood and was ordained a priest in 1826.

In 1827, while convalescing from a fall, Darby became concerned about the dangers of the close relationship between church and state. He resigned from his rural curacy (though remained an Anglican priest for many years) and began meeting with others of like mind. In his first pamphlet, "The Nature and Unity of the Church of Christ" (1828), he attacked denominationalism and state churches as artificial. Church unity, he taught, can only come through spiritual unity.

In 1832 Darby, along with B. W. Newton and George V. Wigram, founded a congregation at the preaching chapel at Plymouth, England. Soon Darby began traveling on behalf of the Plymouth Brethren, spending significant time particularly in Switzerland and the United States. He established local assemblies, each independent, with no separate order of clergy, and with no formal creed. He also taught his new kind of theology, called dispensationalism, which divides history into seven periods, each characterized by a different method used by God to relate to humans. This helped harmonize some apparent contradictions in the Bible and supported an apocalyptic worldview, as the current dispensation is the next-to-last one. He taught a relatively new end-time schema, called premillennialism, in which the saved are secretly taken by Christ (raptured) prior to the seven years of tribulation, at the end of which Christ visibly comes to bind Satan and initiate the millennium of peace, followed by the Day of Judgment.

In the late 1840s the Plymouth Brethren divided into Open and Exclusive branches, over the issue of whether to commune with other Christians or only with other Brethren. Darby was a staunch exclusivist. At his death he left behind a huge volume of writings, plus a theological movement that would lead to the Scofield Reference Bible, the Companion Bible, and Fundamentalism.

Baba Hari Dass
Courtesy: Sri Rama Foundation

Dass, Baba Hari: Baba Hari Dass was a yogi all his life, and practiced continual silence (*mauni sadhu*) for over 45 years. He became well-known as a teacher of Baba Ram Dass, via Baba Ram Dass's book, *Be Here Now*. Students persuaded him to come to the United States in 1971. Since then, he has taught a traditional form of yoga known as Ashtanga Yoga (or Raja Yoga), and has given regular classes on the *Bhagavad Gita* and the *Yoga Sutras* of Patanjali.

Following the example of Baba Hari Dass, Sri Rama Foundation was created to establish an orphanage, school, and health clinic for needy children in India. This goal has been met, and Shri Ram Ashram in Haridwar, India, now provides a home for 30 children and schooling for 200 additional students from surrounding villages. Sri Rama Foundation also publishes the philosophical teachings of Baba Hari Dass, as well as musical recordings of India's sacred music performed by Western artists.

In addition to the orphanage in India, Baba Hari Dass has been the inspiration for several large projects. These include the Mt. Madonna Center in Watsonville, California, one of the largest retreat centers on the West Coast, the Mt. Madonna School, a PK - 12 private school, the Pacific Cultural Center, a satsang center in Santa Cruz, California, the Salt Spring Centre, a retreat facility in British Columbia, and the Ashtanga Yoga Fellowship in Toronto, Ontario.

Ram Dass, Baba: Baba Ram Dass (b. April 6, 1931), founder of the Hanuman Foundation, was born Richard Alpert in Boston, Massachusetts. After receiving his Ph.D. from Stanford University in 1957 he became professor of psychology at Harvard University. Another faculty member in his department was Timothy Leary, and together they began experiments with hallucinogens, particularly LSD. Eventually the university decided that the experiments were inappropriate and expelled both Leary and Alpert in 1963.

Alpert became a major spokesperson for the counter-culture of the 1960s and 70s, though he came to discourage the use of drugs in the quest for spiritual experience. He became a disciple of Neem Karoli Baba, a Hindu teacher in India, who in 1967 gave Alpert the religious name of Ram Dass ("God's servant"). Also during his time in India he studied under Maharaji ("great king," not to be confused with the Maharaji of Elan Vital), from whom he learned raja yoga and worshipful devotion to Hanuman, the monkey-faced deity of popular piety in India.

Upon Ram Dass's return to the United States he took up residence in New Hampshire and kept busy as a speaker and writer. In 1971 he published what is perhaps still his most famous book, *Be Here Now*, a plea for people to focus on present experiences rather than dwelling in the past or future. The Hanuman Foundation was incorporated in 1974 as a means of preserving and disseminating the teachings of Ram Dass and his teacher, Neem Karoli Baba. The Neem Karoli Baba Hanuman Temple is located in Taos, New Mexico.

In the mid-1970s Ram Dass began an association with spiritual teachers Hilda Charlton and Joya Santayana (Jaya Sati Bhavagati Ma), though he broke away from Santayana two years later. Through the 1980s and 1990s he has remained a prolific writer and is a sought-after New Age workshop leader.

Andrew Jackson Davis
Courtesy: American Religion Collection

Davis, Andrew Jackson: Andrew Jackson Davis (August 11, 1826-January 13, 1910), the most widely-read philosopher of Spiritualism and the movement's dominating intellectual figure, was born in Blooming Grove, New York. He apprenticed to a cobbler in 1841 in Poughkeepsie, New York and in 1843 a local tailor dabbling in mesmerism found him an exceptional subject. For some years he traveled as the "Poughkeepsie Seer," exhibiting his clairvoyant abilities while in a trance (a trance he later discovered could be self-induced).

His career was expanded in 1844 when he claimed to have begun spirit contact with such deceased luminaries as the ancient Greek physician Galen and the eighteenth century visionary Emanuel Swedenborg. He claimed to receive through them valuable medical and philosophical information. He established healing clinics in New York and from 1847 to 1849 ran a periodical, *The Univercoelum*. In 1848 he married a woman named Della. His trance lectures so impressed Professor George Bush of New York University, a Swedenborgian himself, that he endorsed Davis in his book, *Mesmer and Swedenborg* (1847).

Davis's many writings laid out his ideas in great detail. He modified Swedenborg's belief in the six spheres surrounding earth into six spiritual spheres that humans can evolve through toward God. This undergirded Spiritualism because those spirits still closest to the earth presumably lent themselves most easily to spiritualist contact. His philosophy also was compatible with the American belief in progress, as spirits could progress eternally, even after death. His books became best-sellers. *The Harmonial Philosophy* (1852), for instance, went through twenty-four editions in thirty years.

His most controversial ideas dealt with persons finding their soul-mates, not usually their spouses. He became paired with a married woman, Mary Love, and the relationship cost Davis a great deal of support. She eventually obtained a divorced and married Davis on May 15, 1855. In 1857, in an attempt to set the record straight about his life and beliefs, he published an autobiography, *The Magic Staff*. In 1886 he combined his clairvoyant healing with a regular medical degree from the United States Medical College, and continued an active public life until shortly before his death.

Romana Cardona Delfin
Courtesy: Eclesia Catolica Christiana

Delfin Roman Cardona: Delfin Roman Cardona was born in Puerto Rico in 1918. Raised a Roman Catholic, he was introduced to Spiritualism as a teenager. He soon discovered that he had clairvoyant and healing abilities. In 1956 he founded the Spiritualist Cristiana Church after moving to New York City, but changed the name in 1969 to the Eclesia Catolica Cristiana to differentiate its more traditional Christian orientation from that of other Spiritualist churches.

Cardona modeled the Eclesia

Catolica Cristiana on the structure of the Roman Catholic Church, and was elected and installed as its pope by the Church's College of Priests. Cardona believed that the Roman Catholic Church was not as catholic (universal) as it could be, and he therefore developed what he called a universalist catholicism or the Delfinist Doctrine. Theologically, he draws primarily upon traditional Christianity and the teachings of Allan Kardec, the French writer and medium who brought Spiritualism into Brazil. The Kardec brand of Spiritualism was distinctive at the time for its emphasis on belief in reincarnation and karma.

After hundreds of testimonies and witnesses attesting to the many miracles that Delfin has performed, the faithful voted by sealed envelope to proclaim him a Living Saint on October 28, 1978, and he became known as Saint Delfin the First. To date, healings of paralysis, blindness, deafness, cancer, aids and other terminal illnesses have been attributed to the Saint. For many years, he has also anointed and taught his disciples to perform healing.

After Delfin had completed a twenty-five-year process of martyrdom and purification, during which he was pronounced Pure and Divine Avatar, and the spirit of a Solar Angle, who is the Promised Comforter, he was proclaimed Second Savior and New Messiah of this planet on September 31, 1997, by the Spirit of Christ. The College of Priests and the faithful at Eclesia Catolica Cristiana recognize him as a Second Savior, whose messianic mission is to restore the teachings of Christ, to clarify His parables, and to define God and creation through enlightened reason and logic.

DeLong, Thomas (Gwydion Pendderwen): Thomas DeLong was born in Berkeley, California, on May 21, 1946. He was 13 when he met Victor Anderson, with whom he cofounded the Faery Tradition of Witchcraft. He studied with Anderson until he was in his early twenties, learning about the Craft, Celtic folklore and other systems, such as Huna and Haitian and West African Voudoun. He was particularly influenced by Robert Graves's theories of Goddess as muse and poet as sacred king. Pendderwen and Anderson developed and wrote much of the liturgical material of the Faery Tradition, incorporating Gardnerian materials as they became available in the late 1960s and early 1970s.

He attended California State University at Hayward, where he majored in theater and earned a bachelor of arts degree. He disliked modern theater, preferring dromenon, drama in its original form as religious or mystical ritual. He learned Welsh, which led to a long correspondence with a friend in Wales, who interested him in Celtic nationalism. He was active in historically oriented groups, including the Society for Creative Anachronism (SCA), serving as Court Bard for the society's Kingdom of the West.

With Alison Harlow, an initiate of the Faery Tradition and a fellow member of the SCA, Pendderwen founded Nemeton in 1970 in Oakland. Nemeton, which means "sacred grove" in Welsh, originally served as a neo-Pagan networking organization; it was intended to be the West Coast equivalent of the Pagan Way, which at first was primarily active in the East and Midwest. In 1972 Pendderwen's first recording, Songs of the Old Religion — songs for each sabbat, the seasons and love songs to the Goddess — brought him fame within the Pagan community. He was married briefly, then divorced. In 1974 Nemeton published three issues of *Nemeton* magazine, then folded. Regional secretariats of the Nemeton organization spread across the United States, playing a key role in early Wiccan and Pagan networking and growth there. Because of his personal connections with the founders of the Pagan Way movement, he was able to help coordinate a series of Pagan Ecumenical Council meetings. This led to his being one of the architects and founders of the Covenant of the Goddess.

On a vacation to the British Isles, Pendderwen reached a turning point in his life. He met his Welsh correspondent, Deri ap Arthur, and others active in the Wiccan movement, including Alexander Sanders and Stewart Farrar. At the Eistedffodd in Wales he was profoundly moved by being honored on stage as foreigner of Welsh descent. On his return home he quit his Federal job, and began homesteading on his land, Annwfn, in Mendocino County. He lived in a circular, two-story cabin that he built himself — with no electricity or running water. He worked on his writing, and started to hold tree plantings every winter on his own and nearby land. The outgrowth was Forever Forests, formed in 1977 to sponsor annual tree plantings and encourage ecological consciousness as a magical process in harmony with Mother Earth. In 1978 he merged Nemeton with the Church of All Worlds, and it became the Church's publishing arm.

He emerged from seclusion in 1980 to appear in concert and ritual at the first Pagan Spirit Gathering. In 1981 Gwydion's Forever Forests sponsored an immense Midsummer Pagan Festival at the Big Trees Meadow campground of the East Bay Regional Park System in Contra Costa County, California (i.e., the Oakland hills); there were 150 people in the New, Reformed, Orthodox Order of the Golden Dawn circle. However, it turned out to be a one-time event. He was arrested for civil disobedience, along with members of Reclaiming, at a demonstration at Lawrence Livermore Laboratory in California in 1982.

Pendderwen tried to establish an extended family on Annwfn, but personal differences with friends and a constant shortage of money impeded him. Those who knew him well report that he was witty, eloquent, and highly respected, but also given to outbursts of temper that made some of his personal relationships difficult. On November 9, 1982, returning home after an evening out visiting friends, his truck went off the winding dirt road at Annwfn and over the side of a steep hill. He was thrown out, and the truck rolled over him, crushing him to death.

Pendderwen's published works, all through Nemeton, include: *Wheel of the Year* (1979), a songbook of music and poems; *The Rites of Summer* (1980), two musical fantasies performed at the 1979 Summer Solstice gathering at Coeden Brith, a 200-acre piece of wilderness owned by Nemeton and adjacent to Annwfn; and *The Faerie Shaman* (1981), songs of trees, country life, British Isles history, and Pendderwen's love for Wales. However, much of his poetry, rituals and liturgical material remains unpublished. His cabin is maintained as a temple by the Church of All Worlds, which inherited Annwfn as a sanctuary; and his birthday is observed as a memorial day by some CAW members.

Gayatri Devi
Courtesy: Vedanta Center

Devi, Gayatri: Srimata Gayatri Devi (1906-1985) was born and reared in India. A mystic by temperament, she was close to the poet, Rabindranath Tagore and an early follower of Mahatma Gandhi. Inspired by the teachings of Vivekananda, she came to the United States when she was nineteen and took her place as the first Indian woman and youngest sister in the monastic community. Believing in the full equality of women and recognizing the depth of her illumination, Swami Paramananda ordained Sister Devamata to teach Vedanta. During his lifetime, women monastics carried major responsibility in every area of the work.

Until his death in 1940, all of the centers founded by Swami Paramananda were part of the Ramakrishna Math (monastery) and Mission whose headquarters were at Belur, Calcutta, India. At his death, his centers were excommunicated from Ramakrishna Math and Mission because he designated Srimata Gayatri Devi as his spiritual successor.

After his death, she took her place as the leader of the community, spiritual guide, editor of the publications and teacher to thousands here and abroad. She continued to minister to Vedanta groups in Switzerland and Germany. She lived a consecrated life for 69 years and served as the spiritual leader for 55 years until her death in 1995.

Anagarika Dharmapala
Courtesy: American Religion Collection

Dharmapala, Anagarika: Anagarika Dharmapala (September 17, 1864–April 29, 1933), founder of the Maha Bodhi Society and one of the first Buddhist teachers in the United States, was born David Hewivitarne in the British colony of Ceylon (today's Sri Lanka). His parents sent him to British schools, and though he thus was thoroughly immersed in Christian beliefs, he remained Buddhist. In 1883 he left St. Thomas's Collegiate School after witnessing a Christian-led attack on a Buddhist procession.

That year he joined the Theosophical Society, a western-based organization that nevertheless seemed to have a strong appreciation for Buddhism. He visited Helena P. Blavatsky, the group's founder, at her headquarters in India, who encouraged him to study Pali, the language of the ancient Buddhist scriptures. In 1884 Blavatsky's colleague, Colonel Henry S. Olcott, persuaded the British government to make several policy changes, including designating Buddha's birthday (Wesak) a holiday. With such strong credentials, Olcott and Dharmapala worked together a number of years to strengthen Buddhism in the colonies. At that time he took the name Anagarika Dharamapala, meaning "homeless protector of the Dharma."

In 1891 he visited the Bodh Gaya, where the Buddha attained enlightenment, and was shocked at the site's poor condition. He founded the Maha Bodhi Society to care for the site and in 1892 founded the *Maha Bodhi Journal*. In 1893 he was one of the several Buddhist representatives at the World Parliament of Religions in Chicago. There he met Paul Carus and persuaded him to head an American branch of the Maha Bodhi Society. He also conducted the first Buddhist initiation of a Westerner in the West—Theosophist and Swiss citizen C. T. Strauss.

In the following years Dharmapala was a frequent international traveler. In his 1896-97 tour of the United States he led the first American celebration of Wesak. In his 1925-26 tour of England he founded another branch of the Maha Bodhi Society and in 1927 led England's first Wesak festival. On January 13, 1933 he was ordained a monk by a Sinhalese group at Sarnath, India. This was the first Buddhist ordination done on Indian soil in over seven centuries.

Dingle, Edwin John: Edwin Dingle (April 6, 1881-January 27, 1972), founder of the Institute of Mentalphysics, was born in Devonshire, England, and grew up in Cornwall. His father, a journalist, died when Dingle was still young, and he and his brother went to live with grandparents. Dingle also became a journalist and in 1900 went to Singapore as a correspondent for the Far East. At that time he began studying meditation and yoga.

On February 22, 1909 he left Singapore for a combination pilgrimage and newspaper assignment to write about the geography of central China. Surviving malaria and political unrest, he arrived at a Tibetan monastery, where he spent nine months studying with its masters. They reportedly taught him how to remember his past lives, how to breath so as to absorb energy (or prana) from the air, and so on.

Upon return to England, Dingle did not initially make much public mention of his religious experiences. He published *Across China on Foot* (1911) and *China's Revolution, 1911-1912*. In 1913 he returned to China, not to meditate, but to found the Far East Geographical Establishment and publish the "New Map of China" (1914), *Dingle's New Atlas and Commercial Gazeteer of China*. He also began a weekly magazine, *China and the Far East Finance and Commerce*. These efforts earned him a handsome living and membership in the Royal Geographical Society.

In 1921, at the age of 40, he retired to Oakland, California, but not until 1927, on a visit to New York, did he begin lecturing on his mystic experiences. He gained a following that formally incorporated in 1934 as the Institute of Mentalphysics. His first headquarters was the International Church of the Holy Trinity in Los Angeles ("Trinity" referring to Body, Mind, and Spirit), and he took the religious name of Ding Le Mei. In 1941 a 385-acre retreat facility in Joshua Tree, California, was purchased, and remains the center of the international organization.

Divine, Father Major Jealous: Father Divine (1877?-September 10, 1965), founder of the Peace Mission Movement, may have been born George Baker in Savannah, Georgia, in 1877, but there is little reliable information about his early life. His followers suggest an alternative chronology with the claim that he married his first wife, Penninah (d. circa 1941) on June 6, 1882.

Father Devine
Courtesy: American Religion Collection

In any case, he first became a public figure in 1919 by beginning a ministry in Brooklyn, New York. He soon moved his small group of followers to a home in Sayville, Long Island, where he developed a reputation for being able to find employment, provide free meals, and give purpose to followers. He claimed he was the Second Coming of Christ and preached the virtues of sobriety, hard work, honesty, and celibacy. Previously known as Major Jealous Divine, in 1930 he took the name of Father Divine. About that time his church gained the name of the Peace Mission Movement.

The busloads of visitors to his church led to his arrest in November 1931 as a "public nuisance." After a lengthy trial the judge gave him the maximum sentence of one year in jail and $500 fine, but three days later, on June 7, 1932, the judge died of a heart attack. Divine commented, "I hated to do it." The sentence was soon reversed, and his claim to divine powers was reinforced for hundreds of followers. In 1933 he moved his headquarters to Harlem, and he was soon among the most influential African Americans in New York City. The church acquired numerous businesses, which Divine used, not only to continue to provide his followers with basic needs, but to pressure politicians to enact legislation to help the poor, especially the blacks.

Divine promised his followers heaven on earth, and modeled that by living in lavish estates and driving a Rolls Royce. The generous banquet table was the center of the church's gatherings and was intended to follow the pattern of the daily communions of early Christians. On April 29, 1946, he married a young, white, Canadian woman named Edna Rose Ritching and designated her his successor.

Dow, Lorenzo: Lorenzo Dow (October 15, 1777-February 2, 1834), the forerunner of Primitive Methodism, was born in Coventry, Connecticut. During childhood he reported numerous prophetic visions, including one at age fourteen that called him to become a preacher. At age seventeen he was converted by the Methodists, but when he tried to preach, his parents did not approve.

About two years later, in 1796, Dow began to travel with an itinerant preacher, and received a license to preach from the local Methodist conference. He was appointed to a circuit in Canada, but left without notice in 1799 to preach in Ireland. This move turned out badly, as he met with little response and almost died of smallpox. He returned to the United States in 1801 and was allowed to renew his relationship as a preacher with the Methodist Church. However, after a few months he again left the conference to travel as an independent evangelist. A large part of his support came from a talent for land speculation.

In 1804, along with marrying Peggy Holcombe on September 3, he began issuing a periodical called *Journal*, in which he expressed his views on excessive administrative control in the church and other issues. That year he also published an autobiography. In 1806 he again visited Ireland, this time going to England as well, and had much more success. In particular, he spoke with interested parties of the benefits of camp meetings. As a result, Hugh Bourne led a camp meeting in Mow Cop, England, at the end of May 1807. It and following camp meetings had great success, but Bourne's Wesleyan Methodist Connection was dismayed by disorder and excesses of the meetings. Bourne and a colleague, William Clowes, were dismissed, camp meetings were forbidden, and those converted at them were not allowed to become members. The result was the founding of the Primitive Methodists.

Dow, meanwhile, was dismissed from the Methodist Church in America, but continued his itinerant preaching. In 1816 he bought land in Wisconsin, where he intended to found an ideal community, the City of Peace, but land deed problems prevented its realization. His wife died in January 1820 and he married Lucy Dolbeare on April 1, 1820. He was aware of the growth of the Primitive Methodists in England; they did not establish themselves in America until shortly before his death.

Dowie, John Alexander: John Dowie (May 25, 1847-March 9, 1907), founder of the Christian Catholic Church, was born in Edinburgh, Scotland. He had very little formal schooling because of chronic dyspepsia, but read the Bible seriously as part of a very pious family. When he was a teenager the family moved to Australia and his illness gradually disappeared.

As an adult he became a minister in the Australian Congregational Church, but was dissatisfied until, during the plague of 1876, he discovered he had healing power. That year he married his cousin, Jeanne Dowie, and established an independent congregation in Sydney. In 1882 he founded the International Divine Healing Association. His condemnation of liquor and tobacco won him praise from many quarters, but his equal condemnation of prescription drugs, newspapers, theaters, and most other congregations was more controversial, and he endured numerous threats against his life.

In 1888 Dowie left his church position to travel and preach, touring the United States for several years. In 1891 he settled in Chicago and in 1893 built a church near the entrance of the World's Fair. He formally incorporated his work in 1896 as the Christian Catholic Church. In 1901, chafing at the continuing obstacles presented by those opposed to his preaching, and being unable to rid the city of physicians and drugstores, he led the congregation in buying 6,600 acres on Lake Michigan, and as many as were able moved there to build Zion.

Zion was proposed by Dowie as a holy city built from scratch to prevent sinful practices from gaining a foothold. He saw himself as Elijah the Restorer (Malachi 4), the fulfillment of biblical plans to renew humanity. Zion was soon thriving with many businesses, and Dowie himself as healer was still an attraction for many visitors. After a few years, however, the city's fortunes went downhill, and Dowie, partially paralyzed by a stroke, did not provide the necessary leadership. In 1906, when Dowie went to Mexico City to establish another Zion, the citizens replaced him with a new leader, Wilbur Glenn Volivia. Dowie died less than a year later. His legacies, the town of Zion and the church, both still exist, though the town has come to look much like any other.

Sir Arthur Conan Doyle
Courtesy: American Religion Collection

Doyle, Sir Arthur Conan: Creator of the famous detective Sherlock Holmes, Sir Arthur Conan Doyle (1858-1930) profoundly believed in spiritualism and in the power of mediums. After participating in table-turning seances at the home of the mathematician General Drayson, he started being interested in paranormal phenomena and became a member of the Society for Psychical Research. Doyle embraced the faith of Spiritualism after 30 years of study, and started lecturing with his second wife, who also began automatic writing after the loss of her brother during World War I. He lectured in Great Britain, Northern Europe, South Africa, America and New Zealand, and he published *The New Revelation* (1918) and *The Vital Message* (1919).

He supported spirit photography and the search of proof of fairies, which had interested him all his life. He was particularly excited by a letter received from a Spiritualist friend who maintained that the existence of fairies could be proven through photographs taken in Yorkshire by two young girls, Elsie Wright and her cousin Frances Griffiths. The Theosophist Edward L. Gardner, who was asked to investigate, pronounced the photographs genuine, although they looked faked.

The Coming of Fairies, published in 1922, contained a full account of the two girls' case and documented other fairy evidence. But upon his return from a trip to Australia, he found out that the photographs were pronounced false, and that he was victim of a hoax, admitted later by the two girls.

In the same year he argued with his friend Harry Houdini over a seance, during which the only sitters in addition to Houdini were Doyle and his wife, who was supposed to put the magician in touch with his deceased mother, through her automatic writing. They later had other quarrels, such as that about the question of Mina Stinson Crandon's mediumship, which was examined by a committee of the Scientific American without the presence of Houdini, although he was a member of it.

Dresser, Horatio Willis: Horatio Dresser (January 15, 1866-March 30, 1954), New Thought historian and lecturer, was born in Yarmouth, Maine. His parents, Julius and Annetta Dresser, were students of Phineas P. Quimby, a founding figure of New Thought. Quimby died a few months after Horatio Dresser's birth and the family moved to Denver, Colorado and then to Oakland, California, as Julius Dresser found positions editing newspapers. Horatio Dresser left school at age thirteen to help support the family.

In 1882, possibly because of the success of Mary Baker Eddy, another Quimby student, the family moved to Boston and Julius and Annetta Dresser began a healing practice. Julius Dresser engaged in a very public controversy with Eddy over the extent to which Quimby was the unacknowledged source of her Christian Science teachings. Meanwhile, Horatio Dresser became sufficiently self-educated so as to enter Harvard University in 1891. He was forced to drop out in 1893 after the death of his father and began what was to be his major career pattern of lecturing and writing on New Thought topics.

The year 1895 was significant for Dresser—he published his first two books, *The Immanent God* and *The Power of Silence,* and was a major organizer of the Metaphysical Club of Boston. He founded two journals, the *Journal of Practical Metaphysics* (1896-98) and *The Higher Law* (1899-1902) and wrote for several other periodicals. In 1898 he married Alice Mae Reed. In 1903 he returned to Harvard and received his Ph.D. in Philosophy in 1907, giving him the most significant academic credentials of any contemporary New Thought advocate. Except for a brief period teaching at Ursinius College in Philadelphia (1911-13), he spent the rest of his life lecturing and writing on behalf of New Thought.

Perhaps his most significant contributions to New Thought were as historian, particularly through the *History of the New Thought Movement* (1919) and his edition of *The Quimby Manuscripts* (1921), in which he carried on his father's argument for recognition of Quimby's importance. In 1919 he was ordained as a minister of the General Convention of the New Jerusalem, a Swedenborgian church, and from time to time served local parishes. Toward the end of his life he worked in a Boston clinic that explored both religious and medical approaches to illness.

Drummond, Henry: Henry Drummond (December 5, 1786-February 20, 1860), a founder of the Catholic Apostolic Church, was born in Hampshire, England. At age eight his banker father died and left him a fortune. He attended Harrow and Oxford, but did not complete a degree. He married Henrietta Hay about 1808 and went into banking. He was elected to the House of Commons in 1824, but ill health caused him to withdraw.

In 1826 Drummond held the first of many annual conferences on prophetic issues at his huge Albury estate. These Albury conferences, usually composed of about thirty men, became famous, and influenced John Nelson Darby and many others. Drummond's notes on the meetings were put together in the three-volume *Dialogues in Prophecy* in 1833. The consensus of opinion from the beginning of the meetings was that the Second Coming of Christ was imminent and that signs of the end times, such as the Jews returning to their homeland and the advent of charismatic spiritual gifts, would shortly appear.

In 1830, gifts of healing, speaking in tongues, and prophesy appeared in John Campbell's congregation in Scotland, then spread to Edward Irving's congregation in London. By 1832 Drummond had the experience and, like the others, separated from the established church. In December 1832, through the exercise of prophetic gifts in an Albury prayer meeting, that group approved Drummond as its minister. In 1833 he became one of twelve Apostles for the various groups bonding together to become the Catholic Apostolic Church. In 1836 he announced that each Apostle would be responsible for one of twelve areas of the world. He was assigned Scotland and Switzerland.

Drummond spent the rest of his life helping the church financially and organizationally. He edited the *Testimonies*, the church's major statements to the world, wrote several other works, and was re-elected to the House of Commons in 1847. After the death of the last Apostle in 1901 the church declined and is now virtually defunct, except for a branch, the New Apostolic Church, begun in Germany.

Durham, William H.: William Durham (1873-July 7, 1912), developer of the "Finished Work of Calvary" theology within Pentecostalism, was born in rural Kentucky. At age 25, in 1898, he had a conversion experience within the Baptist tradition, but two years later experienced sanctification and joined the Holiness movement. Soon he was ordained and began pastoring a small Holiness church on North Avenue in Chicago.

In 1907 he visited William Seymour's Azusa Street church in LA and there received the Pentecostal baptism of the Holy Spirit. Back in Chicago his ministry expanded greatly and the following year he began issuing *Pentecostal Testimony*. In his theological reflections he decided that, contrary to what was taught among both Holiness and Pentecostal churches, sanctification (the perfecting of one's sinful nature) was not a "second work" of grace available to some as a post-conversion experience. It was rather part of the salvific work already accomplished by Jesus on the cross and thus available to everyone through faith.

This was the first major theological innovation in Pentecostalism and there was much resistance to it at first. Durham tried preaching it in Los Angeles in 1911 with mixed results. William Seymour condemned the idea, but enough people were persuaded that Durham was able to start his own church in Los Angeles. In February 1912 he returned to his work in Chicago, but complications from a cold soon took his life at the young age of 39. His "Finished Work" message eventually gained a wide acceptance among Pentecostals.

Dylks, Joseph C.: Joseph Dylks (early 1800s), a mysterious and charismatic leader, appeared one day in August 1828 in the small town of Salesville in Guernsey County, Ohio. Over the next several weeks he lectured on the Bible at a number of worship meetings and stayed with several families. He began to confide to individuals that he was the messiah, come to establish the new Jerusalem. He claimed he was immortal and those who followed him would also become immortal.

One by one he converted many leading citizens, including Michael

Brill, the town's founder, and Robert McCormick a United Brethren preacher and the town's schoolteacher. After three weeks he accompanied McCormick on a tour of the surrounding area, called Leatherwood. Upon return to Salesville, McCormick testified that he had seen Dylks fight and defeat Satan and heal the son of a minister in a nearby town. Dylks then made his first public statement of his identity and mission, and announced the conversions already made. Much of the rest of the town was then converted and the single community church building was claimed for Dylks's "little flock."

This did not come without opposition. Within a few days a mob attacked Dylks and carried him to court, but the judge did not find him guilty of any crime and released him. The mob then chased him into the woods. On October 28, 1828, after the town had settled down, he returned and told his followers that his work would continue in Philadelphia. With McCormick and two other "apostles," he traveled to that city, at its border sending McCormick and one of the other apostles on ahead with plans to meet later. The McCormick pairing never saw Dylks again, and returned sadly to Salesville.

A portion of the "little flock" continued to meet for years in hopes of Dylks's return. After seven years, the apostle who had remained with Dylks at Philadelpia returned just long enough to claim that he had seen Dylks ascend into heaven and that Dylks would shortly return. That apostle was never seen again. Dylks might never have gained wider attention except for a novel that appeared in 1870, *The Leatherwood God*.

E

Eddy, Mary Baker Glover: Mary Baker Eddy (July 16, 1821-December 3, 1910), founder of the Church of Christ, Scientist, was born into a pious Congregational family in Bow, New Hampshire. Her early life was filled with hardship. Her first husband, George W. Glover, died in 1844, one year after the marriage. Struggling to raise their one child, she faced continuing health problems, the death of a serious suitor and then, in 1849, the death of her mother. In 1853 she married Daniel Patterson, but the relationship was not a close one and she eventually divorced him in 1875.

Ever interested in trying new cures for her ailments, she visited Phineas P. Quimby, a mental healer, in 1862 at his office in Portland, Maine. She was so pleased with the results that she stayed as a devoted student, along with a handful of others, including Warren Felt Evans and Julius and Annetta Dresser. Unfortunately, her ailments revisited her occasionally and when he died she was distraught that she could no longer turn to him. On February 1, 1866, two weeks after his death, she fell on some ice and thought she could not recover. However, she reported that lying in bed three days later reading the Bible, the truth of God's healing power was revealed to her and she was permanently cured.

Soon she experienced success in healing others and began gathering students, teaching what she came to call Christian Science. In 1875 she published the first edition of her major textbook, *Science and Health*. She married Asa Gilbert Eddy in 1877 and in 1879 founded the Church of Christ, Scientist. The "Mother Church" was established in Boston and soon many branch churches were founded.

In 1883 she sued Edward J. Arens for plagiarism of her material, and he counter-sued with the support of Julius Dresser that her material was itself a plagiarism of Quimby's teaching. The suit was settled in her favor, but the issue remained because the Quimby family would not release Quimby's manuscripts for the purposes of the trial. Scholars today have tended to agree that, although she shared some basic ideas with Quimby, her general approach, particularly her emphasis on its Christian character, was quite her own.

Eddy ran the church in such a way that allowed no deviation from her ultimate authority. She did not ordain clergy, but instead used lay readers of her material at Sunday services. Her success is undeniable; she created an international organization that is still the largest of the "metaphysical" groups, many of the founders of which were her students.

Effendi, Shoghi: Shoghi Effendi Rabboni (March 1, 1897-November 4, 1957), the last great individual leader of the Baha'i Faith, was born in Akka, Palestine (today Acre, in Israel). The Baha'i Faith began with the announcement of Mirza Ali Muhammad (The Bab), that the promised mahdi, who would set the world right, was soon to come. Baha'u'llah, Shoghi Effendi's great-grandfather, announced that he was that figure. When he died in 1892 the Baha'i Faith was led by his son, Abdul-Baha (Abbas Effendi), who organized the teachings and spread the movement internationally. Shoghi Effendi, Abdul-Baha's grandson, was groomed his whole life to take over the movement, and was college educated in England and Israel. In 1921, at the age of 24, Abdul-Baha died and Effendi stepped into the leadership role.

Effendi very capably took a fledgling international group and transformed it into a large, stable, world religion, for which work he became known as the Guardian. He further clarified the belief elements and insisted that Baha'i Faith followers could not also belong to other religions. A major task he undertook was the translation into English of some of Baha'u'llah's writings. Effendi's own works, though not included in Baha'i scripture, are considered authoritative for the faithful. He arranged that future leadership of the Baha'i Faith would not be individual, but corporate, a move perhaps encouraged by the fact that he had no children of his own. After his death in London in 1957, leadership was transferred to an interim committee until an elected group, the Universal House of Justice, took over in 1963.

Eielsen, Elling: Elling Eielsen (September 19, 1804-January 10, 1883), founder of the first Norwegian-American Lutheran synod, was born in Voss, Norway. He was confirmed in 1820, but several years later experienced renewed religious devotion. He found himself patterning his life after personal friend Hans Nielsen Hauge (1771-1824), a famous lay evangelist who spoke of the need for repentence and a true morality.

Eielsen became an itinerant lay evangelist, speaking throughout the Scandinavian countries. He was arrested in 1837, as Hauge had been arrested, for violating the law against itinerant preaching. Eielsen decided to move to America, where there were no such restrictions. On September 22, 1839 he preached his first sermon in the United States, to Norwegian immigrants in Chicago. He then concentrated his efforts among Norwegian settlements in Illinois and Wisconsin. He was ordained in October 1843 by Francis Alex Hoffman of the Ministerium of Northern Illinois, and thus became the first ordained Norwegian Lutheran in the country.

In April 1846 in Jefferson Prairie, Wisconsin, Eielsen founded the Evangelical Lutheran Synod in America, wrote its constitution, and was elected its president. The constitution supported lay preaching and leadership, and insisted on proof of conversion before admittance to membership. In 1848 two other pioneer Norwegian clergy, Anderson and Andrewson, organized a split from the synod. In 1856 Rasmussen led another split over the issue of requiring conversion before membership. Although Eielsen lost half of his following in this episode, his continuing evangelistic efforts made up for it.

In 1875 yet another split occurred over the conversion issue and the majority of Eielsen's following left to form Hauge's Norwegian Evangelical Lutheran Synod in America. Once again, Eielsen regrouped his loyalists around the original constitution and carried on. The Evangelical Lutheran Church in America (Eielsen Synod) continues today, though with less than fifty members.

Evans, Warren Felt: Warren Felt Evans (December 23, 1817-September 4, 1889), early New Thought popularizer, was born on a farm in Rockingham, Vermont. After two years of college he left to become a Methodist minister. He married Charlotte Tinker in 1840 and served a number of pastorates in the Northeast, but gradually his beliefs began to move away from standard Methodist fare. He read a number of books by Swedish visionary Emanuel Swedenborg and moved toward belief in the "law of correspondence" between the material world and the spiritual world, with the latter in control and the former having only a shadow form of reality.

This new concept was reinforced for him when he visited Phineas P. Quimby, a mental healer in Portland, Maine, for relief from chronic ill health. Upon being healed by Quimby, Evans learned what he could from him and then, with his blessing, opened his own healing ministry in Claremont, New Hampshire. He also left the Methodist ministry and joined the (Swedenborgian) Church of the New Jerusalem. In 1867 he moved his practice to Boston, then in 1869 moved again to Salisbury, where he and his wife received patients until his death in 1889.

Evans participated in no New Thought organization and took no students, as far as is known. What he did do was write, and his first book, *The Mental Cure, Illustrating the Influence of the Mind on the Body, Both in Health and Disease, and the Psychological Method of Treatment* (1869), was the first New Thought book in the United States. He wrote about ten books altogether, including two on Swedenborgianism. His books on New Thought, which became very popular, were key in introducing the American public to "metaphysical" ideas.

F

Farrakhan, Louis: Louis Farrakhan (b. May 11, 1933), founder of the Nation of Islam, was born in New York City as Louis Eugene Walcott and grew up as an Episcopalian. He attended Winston Salem Teachers College in North Carolina for two years before deciding to devote himself to a musical career. He married Betsy Walcott and settled into the nightclub circuit and the parenting of nine children.

In 1953 he was first introduced to black Muslims and in 1955 he heard Elijah Muhammad, leader of the Nation of Islam, speak for the first time. He soon joined the group, becoming a member of the New York Temple and its branch of the Fruit of Islam (FOI), the group's fraternal and security society. Following black Muslim practice, he dropped his last name as a name of slave heritage and became known as Louis X. Eventually Muhammad gave him the name Farrakhan, the meaning of which is unclear, but seems related to the word "khan" in Arabic, or "ruler."

Farrakhan rose to become an important figure in the Nation of Islam as a temple minister and through the marriage of two of his daughters to relatives of Muhammad. After Muhammad died in 1975, Farrakhan gained a national ambassadorial position in Chicago, but he became increasingly disenchanted by the changes in the organization as it moved into more mainstream Islamic practice, changing its name to the American Muslim Mission and opening membership to whites.

In 1978 Farrakhan left the American Muslim Mission and founded another Nation of Islam in Chicago, returning to Elijah Muhammad's old organization in both name and practice. Over the next several years he built a number of mosques and a following of at least five thousand. In 1984 he was a strong supporter of Jesse Jackson's bid for the presidency, and thus gained national media attention. Some of Farrakhan's public remarks, however, were seen as anti-Semitic, and relations with Jackson were strained. Since then he has worked to build relations with Muslim nations around the world and to create community self-help programs in the United States. He has also tried to build relations with black members of Congress, but various controversial issues, particularly that of apparent anti-Semitism in his organization, have remained as stumbling blocks.

Farrar, Janet & Stewart: Janet Farrar was born Janet Owen on June 24, 1950, in Clapton, London, England. Her mother Ivy died when Janet was five. After graduation from the Royal Wanstead High School for Girls in Sawbridgeworth, Hertfordshire, she went to work as a model and receptionist. In 1970 she was initiated into Alex and Maxine Sanders' London coven, where she met Stewart Farrar.

Stewart was born June 28, 1916, in Highland Park, Essex. He was raised as a Christian Scientist, but became an agnostic in College. In 1937 he graduated from University College, London, where he studied journalism. In 1939 he volunteered for the Army, and served until 1946, when he was discharged with the rank of Major. In 1947 he began a long career in journalism: 1947-50, working for Reuters; 1953-54, reporter for the Communist Party's *Daily Worker*; 1956-62, scriptwriter for Associated-British Pathe and for A.B.C. (now Thames) television, and freelancing for the BBC; 1969-74, feature writer for *Reveille*. This last post connected him with the Craft: sent to do a story on Alex Sanders in 1969, he ended up being initiated into the London coven (where he met Janet) on February 21, 1970, and subsequently writing a book, *What Witches Do* (1971), on its practices.

The social life of London occultism affected Farrar's life: his wife Isabel left him to marry the writer Francis King, and Stewart fell in love with Janet. On December 22, 1970, Janet and Stewart left the Sanders' coven to found their own, which they continued building up until 1976. They were handfasted in 1974, then legally married in 1975. In 1976, they turned the coven over to Susan and David Buckingham, and moved to Ireland, which does not tax the income of professional writers. Here they founded a new coven, which has hived off others, and began co-authoring a steady stream of books that have been influential worldwide in defining the current self-concept of the Craft as a religion. They have been particularly influential in correcting the grandiosities within the Alexandrian Tradition caused by Sanders' particular personality.

Fetting, Otto: Otto Fetting (November 20, 1871-January 30, 1933), founder of the Church of Christ (Fettingite), was born in St. Clair, Michigan. He grew up in the Reorganized Church of Jesus Christ of Latter Day Saints and was ordained a priest in 1899. In 1925 he broke off that career and switched to a schismatic group, the Church of Christ (Temple Lot), that owned the site Joseph Smith, Jr., founder of Mormonism, had originally designated for the building of the temple.

Fetting immediately became a leader and in 1926 was ordained one of the group's 12 apostles. In February 1927 Fetting began receiving messages from a spirit identified as John the Baptist. In accordance with these messages the Church of Christ (Temple Lot) broke ground for the building of the temple, finding Joseph Smith's original foundation markers in the process. The message of July 18, 1929, however, was not easily accepted by the church membership. It was interpreted to mean that the entire congregation had to be rebaptized. This message was rejected and those who had gone ahead with a new baptism, including Fetting, were ejected from the church.

Taking about 1,400 followers (one-third of the group) with him, Fetting founded the Church of Christ (Fettingite), which he led for the rest of his life. He continued to receive angelic messages, some thirty in all. Since his death, despite several controversies, the group has continued a solid existence.

Fillmore, Charles Sherlock: Charles Fillmore (August 22, 1854-July 5, 1948), co-founder of the Unity School of Christianity, was born in St. Cloud, Minnesota. His father was often absent as a traveling Indian trader and his mother was a seamstress. He had little formal schooling and was reared as an Episcopalian, though as a youth he was attracted to Spiritualism and other occult paths. At about the age of 20 he moved to Denison, Texas to take a position as a railroad freight agent and there he met Myrtle Page at the meetings of the local Literary Club. They married on March 29, 1881, by which time he had established a real estate, assay, and insurance office in the boom town of Pueblo, Colorado.

In 1884 they moved to Kansas City, Missouri, where Myrtle Fillmore's long-standing bout with tuberculosis took a turn for the worse. Seeking any possible cure, they attended a New Thought lecture in 1886. Charles was not impressed, but Myrtle was quickly convinced by the affirmation she had learned: "I am a child of God and therefore do not inherit sickness." Her gradual self-healing and ability to heal others finally convinced Charles, and in April 1889 he left real estate to found the magazine *Modern Thought*.

This is generally considered the founding event for what became known by 1914 as the Unity School of Christianity.

For a time the Fillmores closely associated with New Thought teacher Emma Curtis Hopkins, attending her seminary in 1890 and receiving ordination from her in 1891. In 1890 Myrtle Fillmore began what came to be known as Silent Unity, people agreeing to sit, either alone or with others, and meditate in unity at a given time, as directed in the magazine. From this point their following, nurtured also through Sunday worship services, grew rapidly. In 1903 their work was incorporated as the Unity School of Practical Christianity.

Charles Fillmore oversaw the beginning of another magazine, *Weekly Unity*, in 1909, the creation of Unity Inn in Kansas City in the 1920s, and the founding in 1924 of yet another magazine, Unity Daily Word, which became one of the biggest-selling devotional magazines in the country. His wife died in 1931 and in 1933 he married Cora G. Dedrick. By the time of his death, Unity was by far the largest New Thought organization in the world.

Fillmore, Myrtle: Myrtle Fillmore (August 6, 1845-October 6, 1931), co-founder of Unity School of Christianity, the largest New Thought organization in the world, was born into a pious Methodist family in Pagetown, Ohio. Her birth name was Mary Caroline Page, but she was called "Myrtle" from childhood. In 1867 she took the one-year "Literary Course for Ladies" at Oberlin College, was licensed as a teacher, and moved to a school in Clinton, Missouri. In the 1870s her health deteriorated and she moved to Denison, Texas, known as a resort for consumptive (tuberculosis) patients.

In Denison she met Charles Fillmore and married him on March 29, 1881, by which time he had established a real estate office in Pueblo, Colorado. In 1884 they moved to Kansas City, Missouri, and her health took a turn for the worse. Desperate for a cure, in 1886 they attended a New Thought lecture and she was converted, especially by the affirmation: "I am a child of God and therefore do not inherit sickness." During the course of the next two years she slowly completed her cure and convinced her husband of its truth.

In 1889 Charles Fillmore left real estate to begin the magazine *Modern Thought*. In April 1890, through the pages of that periodical, Myrtle Fillmore called for the formation of the Society of Silent Help, later renamed Silent Unity. Persons, either alone or in groups, would agree to meet and pray at a certain time each week. By 1906 some 15,000 memberships had been issued for Silent Unity. Their work also grew by Sunday worship meetings.

The Fillmores were ordained in Chicago in 1891 by New Thought teacher Emma Curtis Hopkins, having attended her seminary course. In 1891 Charles came up with Unity as the common name for their work, and in 1903 they incorporated as the Unity School of Practical Christianity (renamed in 1914 the Unity School of Christianity).

Her particular interests in Unity were Silent Unity—the heart of the organization's growth—and work with families and children. In 1893 she began the magazine *Wee Wisdom* which, before its demise in 1991, was the nation's longest-running children's magazine.

Fitch, Ed: American Wiccan, high priest, and a key founder of the Pagan Way. 1970. He was born in Roxboro, North Carolina, to a family with Russian roots; they moved frequently as he grew up because his father worked in the construction trade. Fitch spent four years at the Virginia Military Institute. After graduation, he entered the Air Force and was sent to Japan, where he ran a courier station, carrying secret documents from a spy organization that evesdropped on Soviet activities in Siberia. After three years, Fitch returned to civilian life in the United States, working as a technical writer and electronics engineer in Washington, D.C. It was now the 1960s, and modern Witchcraft and Neopaganism were spreading around the country. Fitch was initiated into the Gardnerian tradition of Witchcraft by Raymond and Rosemary Buckland, and eventually rose to the rank of high priest. He was also trained in trance channeling by Spiritualist mediums from the Church Of All Worlds.

The Air Force called him back to duty during the Vietnam war and stationed him in Thailand, which provided him with an opportunity to learn about Eastern religions and mysticism. In Thailand, Fitch wrote two books that were never formally published but that later circulated in the Pagan community and became "underground classics": *The Grimoire of the Shadows,* a book of magical training techniques, and *The Outer Court Book of Shadows,* which reconstructs the magical and seasonal rituals of ancient Crete, Greece and Druidic Europe. Twenty years later, material from these books was still surfacing in new traditions and rituals, sometimes being labeled as an "ancient Celtic tradition from Ireland and Scotland."

After Thailand, Fitch was reassigned to North Dakota to work on the redesign of Minuteman rockets. During this time he became part of an informal group that created the Pagan Way. Fitch composed introductory and background materials and public rituals, and worked with Donna Cole and Herman Enderle to found the first Pagan Way grove, in Chicago. The Air Force sent Fitch next to southern California. He left the military as a captain and obtained a master's degree in systems management from the captain and obtained a master's degree in systems management from the University of Southern California. He went to work for a major aerospace firm as a research and development engineer.

When Joe Wilson, an Air Force Sergeant, was transferred to England in 1970, Fitch took over editing the *Waxing Moon*, which Wilson had founded in 1964; Fitch later renamed it the *Crystal Well* when Joe began a new *Waxing Moon* in England. His articles in it were later collected as *Magical Rites* from the *Crystal Well* (1984). In the growing Pagan movement, Fitch helped to organize and chair two Pagan Ecumenical Councils, and was a signatory to the charter that established the Covenant Of The Goddess as a church for Witches in 1975. In the 1980s Fitch remained active as a Gardnerian high priest and became involved in Odinism, a form of Norse Paganism that stresses conservative, family-oriented values. Fitch lives in the outskirts of Los Angeles with his wife and two sons.

Flower, Joseph James Roswell: Joseph Flower (June 17, 1888-July 23, 1970), a founding leader of the Assemblies of God, was born in Belleville, Ontario, Canada, and as a child was raised a Methodist. When he was a teenager the family moved to Indianapolis and joined the Christian and Missionary Alliance Church there. In 1907 his parents became part of the new Pentecostal movement and the following year he also received the "baptism of the Spirit" (speaking in tongues).

Flower began doing missionary work in Indiana and founded a periodical, *The Pentecost* (later renamed *Grace and Glory*). He married Alice Marie Reynolds in 1911 and about 1912 he was ordained by D. Wesley Myland's World's Faith Missionary Association. He created a new periodical for that group, *The Christian Evangel*. Flower was a major figure at the first national meeting of Pentecostals in 1914, out of which was born the Assemblies of God. In 1915 he moved to St. Louis, Missouri, where his magazine was joined with Eudorus Bell's *Word and Witness* to become *Pentecostal Evangel*.

He was secretary of the General Council from 1914 to 1917, head of the publishing house in Springfield, Missouri, from 1917 to 1919, and secretary for foreign missions from 1919 to 1925. At that point his career was derailed by his backing of an unpopular constitutional proposal, and he moved to a local church pastorate in Scranton, Pennsylvania. By 1931, however, he was back as assistant general secretary, moving up in 1935 to general secretary and then treasurer. He retired in 1959.

Ford, Arthur Augustus: Arthur Ford (January 8, 1897-January 2, 1971), the most famous Spiritualist medium of the twentieth century, was born in Titusville, Florida. He was raised as a Baptist, but was ejected from the church when he was sixteen for unacceptable views. He then joined the Christian Church (Disciples of Christ) and decided to train for the ministry.

During World War I service, Ford began having spontaneous psychic experiences, such as hearing names spoken of people who would soon die in battle. In 1920 he became pastor of the Christian Church in Barbourville, Kentucky, and he took every opportunity to learn more about psychic phenomena. He married Sallie Stewart in 1922. About that time he discovered he could put himself into a trance and thereby met Fletcher, his spirit-guide for the rest of his career.

These new-found abilities enabled him to leave the ministry and found the First Spiritualist Church of New York City. His belief in reincarnation, rather unusual among Spiritualists, led to difficulties with the National Spiritualist Association, and in 1936 he formed the rival International General Assembly of Spiritualists. In 1937 he moved to Hollywood where he established himself as a popular lecturer. Also that year, having obtained a divorce from his first wife in 1927, he married Valerie McKeown.

For most of the rest of his career, Ford was an independent medium and speaker, except for a brief leadership of the Church of Metaphysical Science in Miami, Florida, after World War II. In 1956 he helped create the Spiritual Frontiers Fellowship, a nondenominational group through which many mainstream church members were enabled to explore paranormal abilities. Over the years he devoted much time to this organization.

In 1965 he gained much media attention after giving a positive reading for Sun Myung Moon, founder of the Unification Church. Two years later he was again in the spotlight conducting a seance for Episcopal Bishop James Pike on Canadian television. Pike was convinced he had made contact with his dead son and was significantly affected by the event. After Ford's death it was discovered he had faked that seance, and perhaps others as well, though followers insisted this was no proof he did not have genuine powers.

Ford, Arnold Josiah: Arnold Josiah Ford (1890?-1935?), colleague of Marcus Garvey and an early leader in the movement to build black Judaism in America, was born in Barbados, West Indies. His father was an evangelical preacher, but he revolted against this upbringing. He became a music teacher in the British Navy and moved to the United States in 1912.

In New York City Ford became bandmaster of the New Amsterdam Musical Association, a position he held for eight years. He made contact in that city with some proponents of black Judaism, and this changed forever his religious outlook. He studied the Hebrew language and Jewish traditions, becoming convinced that Judaism was the true, indigenous African religion. In 1917 he met Marcus Garvey, a fellow West Indian, who was creating the Universal Negro Improvement Association (UNIA) and promoting "back to Africa" ideas. This appealed to Ford's theology, believing that God would lead blacks in America back to their homeland in Ethiopia. Ford joined the UNIA as its bandmaster and choirmaster. He co-wrote (with Ben Burrell) the National Anthem of the UNIA, "Ethiopia, Land of Our Fathers," and wrote much of the UNIA's official hymnbook, *The Universal Ethiopian Hymnal.*

Ford tried to convince Garvey to convert to Judaism and to promote it as the UNIA's official religion, but with no success. Perhaps this was the cause of a rift with Garvey about 1923. Whether Ford actually left the UNIA or participated on a lower-profile level is unclear. What is clear is that in 1924 his energies were shifted in a new direction, founding the Beth B'nai Abraham Congregation. About that time knowledge was spreading about the discovery of a group of Ethiopian Jews called Falashas and this seemed to Ford to be confirmation of his beliefs about black Judaism.

Ford determined to go to Ethiopia to learn about the Falashas firsthand. He turned over his foundering congregation to Wentworth A. Matthew of the Commandment Keepers Congregation of the Living God, and arrived in Ethiopia with his family soon after the coronation of Haile Selassie in November 1930. The remainder of his days were spent in the vicinity of Addis Ababa, apparently once again making a living with his music. The extent or nature of his religious work there is unknown, and he is said to have died soon after the invasion of Ethiopia by Italy in 1935.

Fortune, Dion: Violet Mary Firth was born in 1891 to a family of Christian Scientists. In her twenties she was a law analyst at a medical-psychological clinic in London, and began to study psychology to work on her own development. In 1919 she was initiated into the Alpha et Omega Lodge of the Stella Matutina, the HOGD offshoot presided over by Mathers' widow, Moina Bergson Mathers. Taking the name Dion Fortune (adapted from her "magical motto," Deo Non Fortuna, taken when she joined the Lodge), Violet studied under J. W. Brodie-Innes. In 1922 she organized the Community of the Inner Light as an "outer court" for the AEO. She and Mrs. Mathers clashed more and more as Violet matured as

Dion Fortune
Courtesy: American Religion Collection

a leader; when Mrs. Mathers expelled her in 1927, Firth, now using the name Dion Fortune, took the (now) Fraternity of the Inner Light with her. It is still active in London as the Society of Inner Light, and is the ancestor of many other important magical organizations now functioning in England.

Fortune worked as a psychiatrist, specializing in helping people recover from and counter "psychic attacks," the topic of her best-known book, *Psychic Self-Defense*. She wrote prolifically during the 1920s and 1930s, and her novels are still a source of inspiration to modern Witches. She died in 1946.

The Fraternity of the Inner Light was divided into at least two autonomous inner sections, one of which was avowedly "pagan"—that is, non-Christian. The acting heads of the pagan section from the mid-1930s into the 1940s were Charles R. F. Seymour (1880-1943) and Christine Hartley, who have been ably brought to public notice by Alan Richardson's recent [ital] Dancers to the Gods. Seymour had written an essay, "The Old Religion—A Study in the Symbolism of the Moon Mysteries," in 1937. In another essay, "The Ancient Nature Worship," also written in 1937, Seymour says, "The witch-hunting of the fourteenth to eighteenth centuries was an effort to stamp out an old religion surviving from pre-Christian days. Its sin was that it celebrated with joy and laughter the great nature festivals." In his diary on June 21 (summer solstice), 1938, he wrote, "I got the idea of linking the old symbolism of indigenous women's mysteries with the pagan mysteries of England right down to the present day and through the witchcraft period." That is, he had obviously been reading Margaret Murray.

Christine Hartley, who worked as Seymour's High Priestess, recorded in her diary on June 28, 1938, "Started when I walked over the threshold of the house and felt witchcraft all around me. Went upstairs extremely desirous of being a witch. When we had settled down I kept getting little pictures of Ishtar worship through the ages, the most constant being one of silhouetted witches in pointed hats and ragged skirts dancing round a fire. Then…I was aware of the goddess standing before us mistily veiled."

Seymour and Hartley were certainly in the occult circle surrounding the people who began the New Forest coven in 1939, and their own ideas were obviously pointing in that direction as well. Hartley had told an interviewer before her death that she had belonged to a coven in the 1940s. It is therefore curious that the party line of the Society of Inner Light has long been that the Society has absolutely no connection with Witchcraft. It is true that the SIL is not itself a Witchcraft organization, but its connections with the Craft movement are plainly evident.

Fox, Emmet: Emmet Fox (July 30, 1886-August 13, 1951), New Thought leader and minister of perhaps the largest church in the United States in the 1940s, was born in Ireland. He was raised a Roman Catholic and attended the Stamford Hill Jesuit College in London, though without completing a degree. On his own he studied engineering and eventually found employment as an electrical engineer.

By that time he had left Catholicism and spent his spare time studying New Thought, particularly the works of Thomas Troward. Fox attended the meeting of the International New Thought Alliance in London in 1914. In 1928 he began lecturing on New Thought topics and found enough success to be able to give up his engineering career. In 1931 he visited New York on a lecture tour and was asked to be the new minister of the Church of the Healing Christ, founded in 1906 by William John Murray. The church, once a powerhouse with a regular Sunday attendance in the ballroom of the Waldorf-Astoria Hotel of over 1,000, had suffered through the death of Murray in 1924, the brief pastorate of Albert C. Grier for a few months in early 1925, and a succession of temporary leaders since then.

Fox accepted the pulpit and immediately began midweek meetings across the city as well as Sunday services in the Biltmore Hotel. He was ordained for the task by Nona Brooks of Divine Science, the denomination with which the church was affiliated. His significant oratorical abilities, plus his popular message that humans can experience unity with God and thus the peace, harmony, and power that comes with that realization, led to huge audiences. He had to move to the Astor Hotel, then to the Hippodrome, to accommodate everyone. Finally, by 1940, his weekly Sunday services filled Carnegie Hall to capacity and on Wednesday nights similar crowds filled the Manhattan Opera House.

Fox did not write a large number of books, but the ones he did were best-sellers. *The Sermon on the Mount* (1934) by 1940 was in its nineteenth edition and became something of an American religious classic. It and others of his works popularized New Thought in the sense that most readers did not realize the books were authored by a New Thought minister.

The Fox Sisters: Margarett, Leah, Kate
Courtesy: American Religion Collection

The Fox Sisters: Fox, Leah (or Anne) (c.1814-November 1, 1890), Catherine (or Kate) (c.1836-July 2, 1892), and Margaret (c.1835-March 8, 1893), often collectively referred to as the Fox sisters, gained an enduring place in history as the first mediums of the modern Spiritualist movement. In 1847 a Methodist farmer, John D. Fox, his wife, and their six children moved into an old house in Hydesville, New York. The house was rumored to be haunted, and in March of 1848 the two youngest children, Kate and Margaret, found they could communicate by making rapping sounds with a spirit they called Mr. Splitfoot (i.e., the devil).

They soon became a local sensation and two committees could find no logical accounting for the phenomenon. The sisters found that their mediumship was not confined to the house or to that one entity, and on November 14, 1849, they first appeared in public with admission charged. In 1850 they went to New York, where they made a believer out of famous newspaperman Horace Greeley. An older sister, Leah (or Anne) became something of a manager, and they began tours of the country.

Although mediumship had been known and practiced prior to this time, the Fox sisters ignited a Spiritualist movement that became practically a national pastime. The personal lives of the sisters saw much tragedy, however. Margaret became the romantic partner of Arctic explorer Elisha Kent Kane and did not tour for a time. When he died in 1857 she had fought successfully for his modest legacy. Leah, divorced in the 1830s, married again but became a widow in 1853. She married again in 1858, to Daniel Underhill, and semi-retired.

Kate continued demonstrating and lecturing on her own, but was plagued by alcoholism. She married Henry Jencken in 1872, but was widowed in 1881, and deteriorated to the point where her children were removed from her care in 1888. At that point Margaret came to her defense by claiming that the alcoholism was due to the stress of hiding their career-long hoax. The spiritualist community and the nation at large was shocked by this revelation. Although Margaret tried to retract the confession the next year, there was no longer an audience, and Kate and Margaret lived out the rest of their lives in obscurity and poverty.

Fox, Matthew Timothy: Matthew Fox (b. December 21, 1940), controversial Roman Catholic theologian, was born Timothy James Fox in Madison, Wisconsin. He was paralyzed with polio at age 12, but after six months in the hospital regained the use of his legs. He knew at that time he would become a priest. After high school he entered the Dominican College of St. Rose of Lima at River Forest, Illinois. In 1960 he joined the Dominican order and in 1964 received his B.A. He received his M.A. from the Aquinas Institute of Philosophy and Theology in Dubuque, Iowa, in 1967 and was ordained a priest, taking the religious name of Matthew.

At that point, on the advice of Thomas Merton, he went to Paris to study the ancient Catholic mystics. During the social upheavals in Paris in 1968 he was politicized. He received his S.T.D. in 1970 from the Institut Catholique de Paris and then taught theology for a couple of years back at the Aquinas Institute in Iowa. From there he taught first at Barat College in Lake Forest, Illinois, then at Mundelein College in Chicago, both women's schools. The Barat experience especially introduced him to a feminist perspective.

Fox's scholarly work during this time and ever since has been both derided and praised as popular in nature and cutting edge in content. Although some have identified his teachings as New Age, he insists he is firmly within the Catholic tradition. In 1977 he founded the Institute for Culture and Creation Spirituality as a means of furthering his belief in creation as a blessing and a spirituality that is informed by the mystic tradition. In 1983 he moved the institute to Holy Names College in Oakland, California, and invited Native American shamans and the Neo-Pagan priestess Starhawk to teach.

In 1984 Cardinal Joseph Ratzinger asked the Dominican Order to investigate Fox's teachings. After a year, the committee said they could find no heresy in his books. Still, Fox's references to God as "She," his de-emphasis of "original sin" in favor of "original blessing," criticism of priestly celibacy, advocacy of women priests, etc., led to further problems with the hierarchy. In 1988-89 he accepted a year of public silence from Cardinal

Ratzinger. In 1992 he was asked to return to his Dominican home province in Chicago. Refusing to do so, he was dismissed from the Dominican Order in March 1993. He is still a priest, but is not allowed to publicly administer the sacraments.

Fox, Selena: Selena Fox (b. October 20, 1949), founder of Circle Sanctuary and one of the most well-known Wiccan priestesses, was born in Arlington, Virginia. Not much has been written about her early life. She received a B.S. in psychology in 1971 from the College of William and Mary and did further studies in clinical and social psychology at Rutgers University, the University of Wisconsin, and the Mendota Mental Health Institute.

Along the way she studied a variety of religious paths, from Druidism to Native American shamanism, and participated in a large number of workshops, meditations, and ritual experiences. In 1974 she founded the Church of Circle Wicca as informal gatherings in Madison, Wisconsin. In June 1975 she and her partner, Jim Alan, moved the setting to a farm near Sun Prairie, Wisconsin. Alan wrote well-received music for the group and published a songbook in 1977. Through this music and their international networking among pagan groups they became major figures in the field.

The church was incorporated in 1978, one of the first Wiccan churches in the United States to be officially recognized by the government. In 1980 Fox began the *Circle Network News*, which has become the most popular Neo-Pagan periodical in the country. After local pressures forced several moves, 200 acres were purchased near Barneveld, Wisconsin as a permanent headquarters, and the name was changed to Circle Sanctuary.

Fox teaches an eclectic blend of spiritual approaches she terms Wiccan Shamanism or Nature Spirituality. She formed the Pagan Spirit Alliance to help connect Neo-Pagans around the world, regardless of particular orientation. In 1984 she severed her relationship with Alan and in 1986 married Dennis Carpenter. In 1988, after a two-year legal battle, the church won local zoning rights to function as a church. In the process, Fox founded Pagan Strength Web to help defend pagan religious rights.

Frost, Gavin: Gavin Frost (b. November 20, 1930), co-founder of the Church and School of Wicca, was born in Staffordshire, England. After receiving a doctorate in physics and math from London University he entered the aerospace industry, which took him to Southern California. He was already interested in the occult, having begun with a study of Stonehenge in England.

Gavin Frost
Courtesy: Church and School of Wicca

About 1962 he met Yvonne Wilson, who shared his occult interests, and they moved to St. Louis. There they were initiated into Wicca and in 1965 founded the Church and School of Wicca. Its correspondence course soon attracted hundreds of students, some of whom eventually developed branch covens across the United States. The church was incorporated in 1968, vying with the Church of All Worlds as the first incorporated Wiccan church in America, and in 1972 it received tax-exempt status from the Internal Revenue Service.

The Frosts have authored several books on witchcraft, but some of their views have separated them somewhat from the mainstream of the Neo-Pagan community. In particular, while most Neo-Pagans emphasize Goddess worship, the Frosts recognize an impersonal deity that ultimately cannot be defined.

Yvonne Frost
Courtesy: Church and School of Wicca

Frost, Yvonne: Yvonne Frost (b. 1931), co-founder of the Church and School of Wicca, was born Yvonne Wilson in Los Angeles, California. She was raised in a conservative Baptist family, but as a young adult began to search for an alternative religious identity. She married in 1950, right out of high school, but obtained a divorce in 1960. She enrolled in the community college of Fullerton, California, and also began to explore spiritualism and the occult.

After graduating from the community college in 1962 she met Gavin Frost, who shared her religious interests. They moved to St. Louis, where they were initiated into a Celtic form of Wicca. In 1965 they founded the Church and School of Wicca. Their widely advertised correspondence course continues to draw several thousand students, though only a fraction complete the school, which is geared to serious study. In 1968 the church was incorporated, vying with the Church of All Worlds as the first incorporated church of the Neo-Pagan movement in the United States. The Frosts married in 1970.

The Frosts have published several books on witchcraft, but their views have not always been accepted within the larger Neo-Pagan community. In particular, they do not focus on Goddess worship, but affirm an impersonal God who cannot finally be defined. This has set the Frosts somewhat apart from the majority of Neo-Pagans, though relationships and dialogue continue.

G

Ga, Macario V.: Macario V. Ga is the leader of one of the two groups using the name Iglesia Filipina Independiente (Philippine Independent Catholic Church). Information about his birthdate and early life is unavailable. He was one of the clergy of the Philippine Independent Catholic Church when it gained communion and episcopal succession in 1947 from the Protestant Episcopal Church (now just the Episcopal Church) in the United States. He was consecrated on September 17, 1950 by Norman S. Binstead of that church and beginning about 1970 became primate of the Philippine Independent Catholic Church. Ga was a popular leader and was consistently re-elected to successive four-year terms as primate.

In 1980 a new constitution for the church was proposed that Ga and some others interpreted as biased against Catholic elements in the church. Ga and some other bishops declared the new constitution null, but the committee working on it accepted it on May 8, 1981, along with a new primate. The church was split just about in half over this issue as Ga led his followers out of communion with the Episcopal Church. Issues of politics and nationalism were also involved in the split, with most of Ga's supporters loyal to the then-ruler of the Philippines, Ferdinand Marcos, a member of the church. (Marcos fled the country in February 1986 and died on September 28, 1989). The result of the church split was parallel churches with virtually the same name, an issue that will likely require court resolution.

Gardner, Gerald Brousseau: Gerald Gardner (June 13, 1884-February 12, 1964), founder of the contemporary Wicca movement, was born into a Scottish family in Blundellsands, England. Childhood asthma prevented a normal schooling, and he gained most of his education through his own reading. He worked on a plantation in Ceylon (today's Sri Lanka) from 1900 to 1923, when he became a civil servant.

Over the following years, Gardner became an amateur anthropologist, as his various government jobs took him and sometimes his wife, Donna (whom he married in 1927), into numerous Asian countries. In 1936 he published *Kris and Other Malay Weapons*, which became the standard work on that topic. He was particularly interested in magical and religious practices, and sought out local leaders in those areas. For a time he joined a Masonic lodge in Ceylon.

Just prior to World War II he retired and returned to England, where he joined the Corona Fellowship of Rosicrucians. Through those connections he was supposedly introduced to Dorothy Clutterbuck, the priestess of a group of practicing witches. She agreed to initiate him into practices handed down through many generations, though the practice of witchcraft was unlawful and she swore him to secrecy, at least during her lifetime. He did manage to talk about wiccan practices indirectly through his 1949 novel, *High Magic's Aid*, published under the pseudonym of Scire. He also opened a witchcraft museum near his home on the Isle of Man.

In 1951 the final law against witchcraft was struck down, and in 1954 Gardner published his landmark book, *Witchcraft Today*, describing the craft and lamenting its apparent imminent demise. The book, however, attracted the attention of a number of people who came to him and his high priestess, Lady Olwen (Monique Wilson), for initiation. Gardnerian Wicca thus made its way into the United States through initiates Raymond and Rosemary Buckland in 1963 and initiate Alexander Sanders several years later.

After Gardner's death on an ocean voyage his papers and effects were sold to *Ripley's Believe It or Not*. These have clearly shown that Gardner did not learn witchcraft from a living tradition as he had claimed during his life, but in fact created all the rituals and beliefs himself. He created the witch's ritual knife, the *athame*, from his knowledge of the *kris*, the Malaysian ceremonial weapon. He created the major holy days, or *sabbats*, from the eight ancient pagan agricultural festivals, and then added the *esbats*, or biweekly meetings. He created the practice of nude (or "skyclad") worship from his experience sunbathing after recovering from a leg injury. Other sources included the medieval book, *Greater Key of Solomon*, Masonic books, Aleister Crowley books, and elements of Asian cultures. Whatever the sources, Gardnerian Wicca is the source of the practices of most Wiccan groups, and has become its own living tradition.

Garvey, Marcus Mosiah: Marcus Garvey (August 17, 1887-June 10, 1940), founder of the Universal Negro Improvement Association and major religious figure for many African Americans in the early twentieth century, was born in St. Ann's Bay, Jamaica. He was raised Roman Catholic and went to work for a printing firm. In 1908 he went into journalism and founded the National Club and the *Watchman* paper to persuade the white and mulatto officials to support labor reforms. After seeing no progress, he moved on to other jobs in Costa Rica and Panama.

From 1912 to 1914 he lived in England and wrote for Duse Mohammed Ali's *African Times and Orient Review*. He then returned to Jamaica and, inspired by Booker T. Washington's work, founded the Universal Negro Improvement Association (UNIA) on August 1, 1914. His first project was a Jamaican trades school. In the search for funding, he decided to accept a standing invitation from Booker T. Washington and visit him. Garvey arrived in New York in March 1916, only to find that Washington had recently died.

Undaunted by this development, Garvey began to travel from city to city, speaking in black churches and elsewhere about the UNIA and his plans for racial unity and self-help. In January 1918 he began publishing *Negro World*, a weekly newspaper, and within a year developed a large, international subscription list. This gave him the money to buy Liberty Hall in Harlem, New York City, as headquarters for the UNIA. The combination of the paper and his powerful skills as an orator enabled the organization of hundreds of UNIA chapters across the country.

Over the next several years he sold stock to develop the Black Star Line of steamers and a number of other black-run enterprises. His first marriage, to his secretary, Amy Ashwood, lasted from December 1919 to June 15, 1922, and in July 1922 he married his new secretary, Amy Jacques. A major triumph was the UNIA international convention in August 1920, which brought thousands of delegates from around the world to New York. This showed that Garvey was the leader of the largest mass movement of blacks the United States had ever seen. The convention called for the liberation of Africa and named Garvey the provisional president of the yet-to-be Republic of Africa.

The appeal of Garvey was multidimensional, including the desire for self-improvement and freedom, the excitement of following such a charismatic leader, and the romance of having a black-run shipping line connect with Africa. He was also an original and forceful theologian who saw religion as a crucial part of his vision. He asserted that God, Christ, and the Madonna were all black and believed that participation in white churches was counterproductive. The UNIA, through George Alexander McGuire, developed *The Universal Negro Catechism* and *The Universal Negro Ritual* to express the spiritual component of its vision. Garvey believed that the spiritual and physical redemption of American blacks could only come by separating completely from the white population and rebuilding a homeland in Africa. He himself never visited Africa.

Garvey's program was opposed by many African Americans, for whom any "Back-to-Africa" program was illusory and a retreat. Leaders like W. E. B. DuBois were suspicious of his finances and pointed to his meeting with Ku Klux Klan leaders in 1922, when Garvey agreed that the United States is rightly a "white man's country" and that labor reforms are useless. In 1921 the shipping line suffered major losses and virtually went out of business, though stock continued to be sold. Garvey was arrested for stock fraud and ultimately spent about three years in jail before being deported to Jamaica in late 1927.

In the following years he tried unsuccessfully to rebuild the UNIA. He moved to London in 1935, where he published a periodical, *Black Man* and offered correspondence courses in the School of African Philosophy. He died of a stroke in 1940 and left behind an important legacy of achievement.

Gestefeld, Ursula Newell: Urusla Gestefeld (April 22, 1845-October 22, 1921), founder of the Church of the New Thought, was born in Augusta, Maine. She married Theodore Gestefeld, a newspaper editor, in the 1860s, and bore four children. She was almost forty years old and living in Chicago when she encountered the teachings of Mary Baker Eddy, founder of Christian Science. Gestefeld had coped with a life-long sickliness, but she reportedly cured herself in three months by applying the principles of Eddy's *Science and Health with Key to the Scriptures.* In May 1884 she enrolled in a class Eddy held during a tour through Chicago and quickly became a leader in Christian Science circles.

In 1887 Gestefeld gave Eddy further evidence of her promise as leader by the publication of a 16-page booklet, *What Is Mental Medicine?* However, her 1888 full-length book, *Ursula N. Gestefeld's Statement of Christian Science,* displeased Eddy. The book gave Eddy full credit, but only briefly, and did not mention *Science and Health,* which Gestefeld thought was a confusing book. Eddy expelled her from the church, and Gestefeld reacted by writing *Jesuitism in Christian Science* (1888). She became an independent healer and studied under Emma Curtis Hopkins for a time.

About May 1891, perhaps occasioned by her husband's death, she moved from Chicago to Philadelphia, then to New York City from 1892 to 1895, then back to Chicago. In 1896 she founded a magazine, *The Exodus* and in 1897 founded the Exodus Club, which became a church as well, with Sunday services. In November 1902 the church name was changed to the Church of the New Thought and the club was separated from it as the College of the Science of Being.

Branch congregations of the Church of the New Thought were founded at least in Detroit and Minneapolis and probably elsewhere, each with women pastors. She founded the Gestefeld Publishing Company to circulate her several books, and was active in the International Metaphysical League. Her church did not long survive her death, but other aspects of her work remained influential.

Goddard, Dwight: Dwight Goddard (July 5, 1861-July 5, 1939), founder of Fellowship Following Buddha and one of the first non-Asian Buddhists in the United States, was born in Worcester, Massachusetts. About 1881 he graduated from Worcester Polytechnic Institute and began a career as a mechanical engineer. This ultimately did not prove fulfilling, however, and in 1891 he entered Hartford Theological Seminary. Upon graduation in 1894 he went to China as a Baptist missionary and there married his first wife, a medical missionary.

Over the following years Goddard became frustrated with the lack of progress in the church's mission and decided that more success would come if the church were more informed by the prevailing religion of Buddhism. In 1924 he proposed the formation of the Christian and Buddhist Fellowship. When this fell through he moved to Japan to study with Roshi Taiko Tamazaki at the Shokoku monastery. In 1927 he published his first book, *Was Jesus Influenced by Buddhism?*

Not long after writing that book Goddard decided that he was no longer interested in joining together Christianity and Buddhism, and in fact had left Christianity behind in favor of (Zen) Buddhism. He divorced his first wife, was briefly married to another, then finally settled near Union Village in Vermont. There he built a temple and began the magazine *Zen*. In 1934 he founded the Fellowship Following Buddha to spread Buddhism among non-Asian Americans. He published a number of books, the most important of which was *A Buddhist Bible* (1938), containing many first-time English translations of key Buddhist scriptures. Although his organization did not long survive his death, his writings helped produce an indigenous Buddhist following in the United States.

Goldsmith, Joel Sol: Joel Goldsmith (March 10, 1892-June 17, 1964), founder of the Infinite Way, was born in New York City. His parents were Jews by heritage but not by practice, and Goldsmith's religious training was basically limited to the bar mitzvah.

Goldsmith became interested in Christian Science when his girlfriend, a Christian Scientist, successfully cured his father of a life-threatening illness in 1915. Goldsmith thereupon became a student of Mary Baker Eddy's teachings, a study that was interrupted by World War I and his tour of duty with the Marines. After the war, Goldsmith went into his father's import business, but the business went so poorly that he was forced to leave and take a job as a salesman. Then his own health deteriorated and he was diagnosed with tuberculosis. Given only a few months to live by the doctors, he requested treatment by a Christian Science practitioner and was healed.

In 1928 he was once again treated by a practitioner, this time for a cold, and was unexpectedly cured also of all interest in tobacco, alcohol, and gambling. He additionally discovered that he was now able to effect cures for other people. At that point he formally joined the Church of Christ, Scientist, and began a new career as a practitioner. This new business was very successful and he eventually had offices in Boston across the street from the Mother Church.

In 1943 his wife died and he moved to Santa Monica, California, where he remarried in 1945. Partly because of bureaucratic pressures from the church, the following year he left Christian Science and semi-retired. He continued his personal spiritual explorations, however, and achieved what he termed a mystical initiation into a new level of understanding. He wrote a book based on this experience, *The Infinite Way* (1947), and began touring as a lecturer to explain his ideas. In the early 1950s he moved to Honolulu, Hawaii, was divorced in 1956 and married a student, Emma Lindsey, in 1957.

His basic message was that all people have the opportunity to connect with God through meditation, and when this is done we can use this experience of transcendence and the divine power to live a fulfilled life, not wanting for health or any other need. He did not found a new organization, but his students gathered loosely around newsletters, books, and tapes, and continue to do so through the work of surviving family members in Arizona.

Gómez, Clemente Dominguez: Clemente Dominguez Gómez (b. April 23, 1946), founder of the Holy Palmarian Church, began seeing visions of the Virgin Mary in 1968. As a result of these experiences he predicted a split in the Roman Catholic Church after the death of Pope Paul VI and a communist revolution in Spain after the death of General Franco. In 1970 the archbishop of Seville, Spain, denounced the visions as invalid, but groups in various parts of the world interested in Marian apparitions had already spread them to a wide audience.

Gómez and his followers formed the Carmelite Order of the Holy Face and sought out a traditionalist bishop who would support their work. They found such a person in Pierre Martin Ngo-Dinh-Thuc, former Archbishop of Hue, Vietnam, who was retired and living in Italy. Ngo-Dinh-Thuc ordained Gómez on January 1, 1975 and consecrated him on January 11, 1976. That September all persons involved were excommunicated by the Vatican, but that did not prevent Gómez from founding the Holy Palmarian Church.

After the death of Pope Paul VI, Gómez claimed a mystical consecration to the papacy in August 1978 and took the name Pope Gregory XVII. In the years since then he has reportedly consecrated dozens of people, though it is difficult to ascertain the real extent and strength of his following.

Govinda, Anagarika: Anagarika Govinda (May 17, 1898-January 14, 1985), founder of Arya Maitreya Mandala, was born Ernst Lothar Hoffmann in Waldheim, Germany. An exceptionally gifted individual, he grew up speaking three languages and studied at the Universities of Freiburg, Naples, and Cagliari. As a youth he was attracted to Buddhism and his first book, *The Fundamental Ideas of Buddhism and Their Relation to the Concept of God*, was published when he was only eighteen years old. He quickly gained stature as a major European spokesperson for Buddhism.

In the 1920s he moved to Ceylon (today's Sri Lanka) to study with Mahathera Nyanatiloka, Brahmacari Govinda, and became a lama (priest) in 1928. He supported himself as a university lecturer in archeology and was also an artist of some note. In 1931 he traveled to India to study under Tomo Geshe Rinpoche and in 1933 he founded the Arya Maitreya Mandala. He intended it as an order that would seek ways of awakening the "Buddha-nature" within people in the context of contemporary issues and concerns, particularly in the West. Although he himself was not an independence leader, his friendship with Jawaharlal Nehru and others caused him numerous difficulties with the British government in the 1940s. When India achieved independence in 1947 Govinda became an Indian citizen and married Li Gotami.

Over the next thirty years Govinda and his wife traveled extensively around the world. He wrote a number of books, perhaps the most famous being *The Way of the White Clouds: A Buddhist Pilgrim in Tibet* (1966). An American branch of Arya Maitreya Mandala was established in San Francisco in 1967 and Govinda made his first visit to the United States the following year. After 1976 he traveled mostly in North America and made his home in Mill Valley, California.

Grant, Frederick William: Frederick Grant (July 25, 1834-July 25, 1902), the leader of an important branch of the Plymouth Brethren, was born in London, England. At age 21 he moved to Canada, where he was ordained by the Church of England in Canada, despite not having attended a seminary. After a few years, however, he was converted to the Plymouth Brethren (an independent fundamentalist movement founded by John Nelson Darby), and moved to Plainfield, New Jersey, where he led a home congregation, lectured, and wrote books.

Grant was among the more strict, or exclusive Brethren, who did not fellowship with non-Brethren groups. This did not mean he had no disagreements with John Nelson Darby (d.1883). Contrary to Darby, he believed that even persons who lived prior to the birth of Jesus achieved salvation, and that Christians may be justified and not know it. Arguments for these positions were presented in his 1883 book, *Life and the Spirit* (later renamed *Life in Christ and Sealing with the Spirit*), which provoked much heated discussion. In 1885 the Montreal assembly of Plymouth Brethren excommunicated him.

Grant and his supporters then formed what became known as Plymouth Brethren (Exclusive: Grant Brethren), a separate branch of the Exclusive Brethren. The Loizeaux Brothers, owners of the major North American Brethren publishing company, became his supporters and over the years published his many books. A theme Grant became known for in his theological works was finding hidden patterns in the Bible. Finding what he believed to be a five-fold arrangement within the Psalms, he went on to outline similar numerical structures he found throughout the Bible, culminating in a multi-volume work, *The Numerical Bible* (1892-1903).

Beginning even during Grant's lifetime and coming to a head particularly in the late 1920s, many Grant assemblies moved toward an open position and are now, including the publishing house, an integral part of the Open Brethren or Christian Brethren. Those Grant assemblies that remained exclusive merged with other exclusive bodies.

Gross, Darwin: Darwin Gross (b. January 3, 1918), founder of Ancient Teachings of the Masters (ATOM), was born the third of five children in Denhoff, North Dakota. His paternal grandfather was a minister in the Mennonite Brethren Church and Gross as a youth rejected his strict upbringing in that religious tradition. The family moved to Portland, Oregon about 1930. He eventually served a term in the military, attended Portland State College briefly, and worked variously as a musician and an electronics engineer.

Over the years Gross explored numerous spiritual paths, particularly in eastern traditions. One night in 1966, while driving home from his electronics job, his car was bathed in a bright light and a voice began speaking to him. He began receiving regular instruction from the voice. In 1969 he joined ECKANKAR when he identified the voice as belonging to Paul Twitchell, the head of that group. After Twitchell's death in 1971 Gross succeeded him as leader of ECKANKAR, being formally designated the 972nd Living ECK Master. This surprised many of those who had been in the organization longer than Gross and a number of them left.

On October 27, 1972, Gross married Twitchell's widow, Gail Atkinson Twitchell and for a time the organization moved solidly behind his leadership. He wrote several books for the general public and circulated some "in-house" material as well. After his divorce from Gail on December 31, 1977, the organization began to deteriorate from internal conflicts. In October 1981 Gross named Harold Klemp as his successor, but remained as president of the corporation. In 1983 all ties between Gross and ECKANKAR were severed in a bitter dispute and he founded Sounds of Soul to maintain what he considered the true ECK teachings through his own books and music. In 1989 he phased out the Sounds of Soul name in favor of the Ancient Teachings of the Masters (ATOM), indicating his belief that the human soul is an atom.

Gurdjieff, Georgei Ivanovitch: Georgei Ivanovitch Gurdjieff (1866?-October 29, 1949), an important Sufi-influenced spiritual teacher who inspired the creation of numerous religious groups, was born in Armenia. His exact date of birth is a subject of some controversy, and may have been as late as November 1877. Many other elements of his early life are unknown as well. As a young man he reportedly spent much time with the dean of a Russian Orthodox Cathedral, asking many questions about science and miracles. In 1896 he decided to satisfy his curiosity by travel.

For a number of years he wandered and studied, from Asia to Africa, supporting himself through various trades. He later claimed to have joined

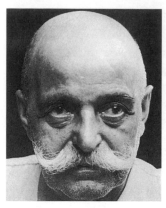

Georgei Ivanovitch Gurdjieff
Courtesy: American Religion Collection

the Seekers of the Truth, a legendary group that sought esoteric wisdom. The greatest influence on him came from Turkish Sufism, and his work is generally categorized under the broad heading of Islam. Between 1912 and 1917 he taught and organized groups in Russia and out of those would come Pyotr Demianovitch Ouspensky, his most famous pupil. Gurdjieff married the Countess Ostrowsky in 1914.

As the Russian Revolution neared (1917), Gurdjieff and his inner circle moved to Paris, and in nearby Fountainebleau he founded the Institute for the Harmonious Development of Man in 1922. The institute attracted a number of well-known artists and intellectuals interested in Gurdjieff's message that humans are "asleep" on many different levels, and must find ways to "wake up" before they can take charge of their lives. A controversial method he found for achieving this was placing the person under severe psychological stress, enabling the breakdown of normal thinking patterns and the creation of a new kind of awareness. Another technique he developed was a series of dance-type movements, also designed to create a new awareness.

Gurdjieff's system of spiritual mastery is represented by the Enneagram, a nine-pointed symbol in a circle. His approach has been called the Fourth Way, a spiritual method distinguished from the methods of the fakir, yogi, or monk by immersion in ordinary life.

In 1924 he made his first visit to the United States, where Ouspensky's well-known book, *Tertium Organum* (1920) had already helped create an interested audience. The only book by Gurdjieff published during his lifetime was *The Herald of Coming Good*. Gurdjieff closed the institute in 1933 and spent his remaining years teaching and writing. After his death, his long-time secretary and student, Jeanne de Salzmann, created the Gurdjieff Foundation (1950) in Paris, and similar organizations have since arisen in major cities around the world. Only posthumously, with the publication of more of his writings and the activities of his followers, has Gurdjieff become well-known beyond a relatively small circle.

H

Harlow, Alison: Alison Harlow (b. August 29, 1934), co-founder of both the Covenant of the Goddess and Nemeton, was born in New York City. She received an M.A. in 1962 from Columbia University in mathematics and began a career in the computer industry. She grew up in an agnostic household, but in 1966 had a religious experience that connected her with Goddess worship.

In 1970 she began to study in the San Francisco area with Victor H. Anderson, an early Neo-Pagan leader of the Faerie Tradition. In 1972 she joined with Thomas DeLong (Gwydion Pendderwen) in creating the *Nemeton Journal* and the Nemeton Fellowship, which has primarily functioned as a publishing association. In 1972 Nemeton published *Songs for the Old Religion*, indicating Harlow's interest in developing a collection of quality music for use by Neo-Pagan groups.

In 1975 she founded the Wings of Vanthi, a coven that combines the Faerie Tradition with Gardnerian witchcraft. The group reveres Vanthi, a winged Goddess connected with the Dark (New) Moon. In 1975 she teamed with Gwydion Pendderwen and Aidan A. Kelly to create an ecumenical organization that would facilitate communication and cooperation among all the various Neo-Pagan groups, and thus the Covenant of the Goddess was founded. The Covenant of the Goddess has since been a major force in the Neo-Pagan community and has served an important public relations role with those outside the community.

Harper, Merydydd: In 1979, Jean Michele M., in Ramsey, NJ, the inventor of Wombat Wicca and author of "The Wombat Laws," had become coordinator of the Mensa Witchcraft, Occult, and Paganism Special Interest

Group, and founded its newsletter, *Robin Hood's Barn*. Members of the group at that time included Pete Davis (founder of the Aquarian Tabernacle Church in Seattle), David Gray (Founder of the Neo-Animist Church), Steve McNally (founder of the Asatru Free Assembly), and Valerie Voigt. When her full name was accidentally published, Jean changed it; she is actually a rather well-known writer of fantasy and science fiction.

In 1981, wildly enthusiastic letters from a science-fiction fan named Jani H. in Dayton, Ohio, began appearing in the national Craft journals: Jani had discovered the Craft. During the next two years, she was initiated by and worked with Jean Michele. In 1983, having moved to the San Francisco Bay area, Jani H. changed her name to Meredydd Harper, and founded the Moonsilver Outer Grove of the Circle of Our Lady of the Well in Berkeley, California.

Meredydd now declared her goal of founding the first official Gardnerian coven in northern California, and proceeded to do so. In this new Gardnerian coven were trained Brendan (Joe M.), Lady Marian of Beannacht Danaan, and Lady Bride (Joann H.). The California Lineage published a manifesto in *The Hidden Path* in 1988 proclaiming its independence from the Protean Lineage. Meredydd thus continues to function as the reigning Queen of an autonomous Tradition.

Harris, Thomas Lake: Thomas Harris (May 15, 1823-March 23, 1906), founder of the Brotherhood of the New Life and Spiritualist innovator, was born in Buckinghamshire, England, but moved with the family to New York five years later. His mother died soon afterward, and when a stepmother entered the household in 1832, Harris ran away from home. Despite his young age, he managed to survive and did not return home. Revolting against his strict Calvinist upbringing, he became a Universalist minister in the New York area and married Mary Van Arnum in 1845.

Soon after the marriage he was converted to Swedenborgianism and in 1947 became pastor of the Swedenborgian First Independent Church Society of New York. In 1851 he learned trance mediumship from J. D. Scott, and even ran Scott's community in Fayette County, Virginia, for a year. He then moved to pastor the Swedenborgian church on Washington Square in New York City and became a popular trance lecturer. His first wife having died in 1850, he married Emily Isabella Waters in 1855.

In 1861 Harris founded the Brotherhood of the New Life near Wassaic, New York, moving in 1863 to Amenia, New York. In 1867 a wealthy British convert, Laurence Oliphant, joined the group and enabled a move to a better site in Brocton, New York. In 1875 the group founded the Fountain

Grove community in Santa Rosa, California, reportedly to better connect with the little spirits, fairies, who prefer warmer weather. By 1881 the Brocton site was completely closed.

Harris gained some notoriety for his brand of Spiritualism, which required the finding of a spiritual counterpart, always of the opposite sex and usually not one's spouse, to function as one's new life partner. This new relationship was not to be sexual in nature, however, as Harris counseled celibacy for all followers. In 1891, six years after the death of his second wife, he married Jane Lee Waring. The couple soon moved back to New York and the California community never recovered from this blow. By 1900 it was down to a handful of members and finally disappeared in 1934.

Judith Harrow
Courtesy: Judith Harrow

Harrow, Judith: Judy Harrow grew up in the Bronx. Although a New York City kid, she was active with the Girl Scouts and spent many summers away at camp, developing a deep love of the Northeastern woodlands. She graduated from the Bronx High School of Science in 1962 and received her B.A. from the Western College for Women in 1966.

Judy attended her first Pagan Way ritual at Samhain, 1976. In this religion, based on the seasons and cycles of Mother Earth, she found a home. She joined a pre-initiatory study group and received her First Degree Initiation in the Gardnerian Tradition of Witchcraft in September of 1977, then was elevated to Second Degree early in 1978, in the Coven of Iargalon.

Iargalon was the first coven in New York to affiliate with Covenant of the Goddess. Judy received a CoG ministerial credential in 1979. The New York City Clerk's office refused to enter holders of CoG credentials in their registry of clergy empowered to perform legally binding marriage ceremonies. After a long battle, and with much assistance from the New York Civil Liberties Union, in January, 1985, Judy became the first Witch to sign the registry book. Many more have since followed.

Judy, and her first working partner, Fred Kuhn, formed the Inwood Study Group at Midsummer of 1980. After she received her Third Degree that November, the study group evolved into Proteus Coven. This coven is

Gardnerian in heritage, with a liberal theological orientation and a strong emphasis on nature spirituality and personal creativity in ritual (and elsewhere).

Judy received her M.S. in Counseling (with honors) from City College of New York in 1979, so her training in Witchcraft and in Counseling took place during the same period of her life. Since the insights and skills gained during counseling training and practice have been useful to her as a coven leader, she feels called to share these with others who lead covens and similar small, close-knit worship groups.

In response, Judy founded the Pagan Pastoral Counseling Network in 1982, and served as first editor of the Network's publication. She co-created a workshop series on Basic Counseling Skills for Coven Leaders, which has successfully run many times, most often as a weekend intensive. She founded the New York Area Coven Leaders' Peer Support Group, and served as Program Coordinator for eight regional Pagan gatherings. Her book, *Wicca Covens*, published in 1999, integrates secular research on group dynamics with the experiential comments of over 30 coven leaders from the United States, Canada and Britain.

Proteus Coven affiliated with Covenant of the Goddess in August, 1981. Judy was convening First Officer of CoG's Northeast Local Council in 1983, National First Officer of CoG in 1984, and co-Chair of CoG's Grand Council in 1985. She has held various other positions on the CoG National and Local Council Boards of Directors, most recently National Public Information Officer from 1993-1995.

For two years, Judy produced "Reconnections," a weekly feature on the activities of religious progressives of all faiths, for WBAI radio in New York. She has contributed essays to the "Witchcraft Today" anthology series and to the volume *Magical Religion and Modern Witchcraft* published by SUNY Press. She has also written for *AHP Perspective*, (the Newsletter of the Association for Humanistic Psychology), *Counseling and Values* (the journal of the Association for Spiritual, Ethical and Religious Values in Counseling), *Gnosis* and such small Pagan publications as *Six Roads, Hidden Path, Harvest* and the CoG *Newsletter*. Some of Judy's writing is also available on the World Wide Web.

Judy is a member of the Association for Humanistic Psychology and of the American Counseling Association. Within ACA, she belongs to two special interest subgroups: The Association for Spiritual, Ethical and Religious Values in Counseling and the Association for Specialists in Group Work. She is also a member of the Interfaith Council of Greater New York, and served that group as Program Coordinator for 1996-1997.

Haywood, Garfield Thomas: Garfield Haywood (July 15, 1880–April 12, 1931), first presiding bishop of the Pentecostal Assemblies of the World, was born in Greencastle, IN. He finished two years of high school before being hired as a cartoonist for the black-run weekly papers *Freedman* and *Recorder*. He was deeply committed to church life, serving as church school superintendent for both a Methodist and a Baptist church. He married Ida Howard in 1902.

In 1908 he was converted to Pentecostalism and joined the Apostolic Faith Assembly in Indianapolis. In 1909 he became pastor of the tiny congregation and the following year, using a printing press he set up in his home, began issuing the *Voice in the Wilderness*. He authored many hymns and published a hymnal, *The Bridegroom Cometh*. Under his leadership the congregation steadily grew, affiliating with the Pentecostal Assemblies of the World (PAW) in 1912. In 1918 he was elected secretary-treasurer of the PAW and the editor of the new magazine *Christian Outlook*. He was known as a progressive, well-read thinker.

By 1924 Haywood was pastoring one of the largest Pentecostal churches in the world, Christ Temple, in a new, 1200-seat sanctuary. That year the previously integrated PAW fell victim to racial tensions and most of the white members left. In the reorganization that followed, the office of bishop was created and Haywood, now the clearly dominant figure in the church, was elected to fill that office. He held that position, as well as the pastorate of Christ Temple, for the rest of his life, with great success.

Heindel, Max: Max Heindel (July 23, 1865–January 6, 1919), founder of the Rosicrucian Fellowship, was born into an aristocratic family in Germany. At age 16 he went to study engineering in Glasgow, Scotland, and eventually became chief engineer on one of the Cunard oceanliners. In 1895 he moved to New York City as a consulting engineer and married. In 1903 he moved to Los Angeles and encountered the occult through the Theosophical Society in America, led by Katherine Tingley. He joined that group and quickly rose through the ranks, serving as an occasional traveling lecturer on astrology. His wife passed away in 1905.

In 1907 he made a visit to Germany, where he was reportedly visited by a spiritual entity that led him to the Temple of the Rosy Cross near the Bohemian border. There he stayed for a month, while receiving the information he put into *The Rosicrucian Cosmo-Conception* (1909). He returned to the United States and founded the Rosicrucian Fellowship in Columbus, Ohio, in 1908. His teachings were a mixture of Rosicrucian tradition with Theosophy, Rudolph Steiner (whom he may have met in Germany), and particular emphases on Christian symbols, vegetarianism, and astrology.

By 1910 Heindel had established other centers along the West Coast. That August he married Augusta Foss (d. 1938). In 1911 he established new headquarters at Mt. Ecclesia near Oceanside, California, where he built a sanctuary, offices, cafeteria, and other structures to accommodate students and visitors. He wrote a number of books and produced a monthly magazine, *Rays from the Rosy Cross*. The organization has continued since his death, and its annual *Ephemeris* and *Table of Houses* are widely used among astrologers.

Hensley, George Went: George Hensley (d. July 25, 1955), founder of the Church of God with Signs Following, introduced the practice of snake handling into Pentecostalism. Little is known of his early life, and he was probably in his thirties when he was converted and joined a Holiness church in 1908. Soon thereafter he began preaching. His career was changed forever when some hecklers let loose some poisonous snakes in front of him while he was preaching. Instead of stopping the service, Hensley picked them up and used it as an illustration of Mark 16:17-18 and the signs of true believers.

His fame soon spread, and he was asked to introduce the practice to the Church of God (Cleveland, TN). About 1914 he started a congregation in Grasshopper Valley, Tennessee, and many years went by with no incident. When a member was bitten and almost died, however, the congregation dwindled and he relocated to Pine Mountain, Kentucky, and the East Pineville Church of God. He was forced to take a lower profile after the 1928 pronouncement of the Church of God against snake handling, but he did not stop, and often traveled to encourage the practice in independent churches.

In the early 1940s he became pastor of a church in Brightsville, Tennessee, and in 1948 moved to an ideal position, that of assistant pastor of the South Chattanooga Church of God, where he was given plenty of time for his evangelistic tours. Despite his claims to have been bitten hundreds of times to no ill effect, he died in Florida the day after being bitten by a rattlesnake during a worship service.

Herr, John: John Herr (September 18, 1782-May 3, 1850), founder of the Reformed Mennonite Church, was born in Lancaster, Pennsylvania. His father, Francis Herr, left the Mennonite Church in 1800, believing that the church had become lax and forgetful of founder Menno Simons' teachings.

He began to hold informal meetings in his house, gathering like-minded people.

After Francis Herr died in 1810, John Herr took over the leadership. Not previously very religious, John Herr became convicted of his sin and rose to the occasion. On May 30, 1812, he was baptized by a member of the group and ordained as the group's minister and bishop. That November they dedicated the first meeting house for what was becoming the Reformed Mennonite Church. They immediately began issuing pamphlets charging the Mennonite Church with being worldly and corrupt.

Herr wrote a number of books outlining his beliefs, which did not differ in doctrine from the Mennonite Church, but in practice. He advocated foot washing, the holy kiss, strict use of disciplinary excommunication and shunning, and no fellowship (communion) with those of other churches. Under Herr's leadership the church grew to about 2,000 members, but since his death it has steadily declined.

Hicks, Elias: Elias Hicks (March 19, 1748-February 27, 1830), founder of a Society of Friends (Quaker) group, Friends General Conference, was born in Hempstead Township, New York. He had little formal schooling as a child and learned mostly on his own. His mother died when he was eleven and he spent most of his teen years living with his older brother's family. Between 1765 and 1771 he was apprenticed to a carpenter. On January 2, 1771 he married Jemima Seaman, daughter of a prosperous Long Island farmer, whose farm Hicks then ran for the rest of his life.

A few years after his marriage he experienced deep spiritual turmoil that culminated in a new dedication to his Quaker heritage. In 1775 he began speaking for the first time in the local congregation, and became active in the struggle against slavery and participation in the American Revolution. In 1778 he became a minister, and his oratorical abilities made him a popular speaker at Quaker meetings all over the new United States.

Theologically, he was known for opposing Deistic tendencies among Quakers. Instead of rationalism, he emphasized mystical elements and the importance of listening to the Inner Light. He became very controversial after the turn of the century when he turned his attention to the growth of evangelical sentiments among Quakers. A strong individualist, he resisted any move to create a uniform "Discipline" for Quakers, or formulate a creed, or develop planned worship services. He insisted that even the authority of the Bible must be tested by inward experience.

In 1827, after years of tension, the pro-Hicks faction split from the Philadelphia Yearly Meeting, and similar splits followed in other meetings.

At the time of his death, there were about seven Hicksite meetings. Not until 1900 did a General Conference emerge to aid in their common efforts.

Holdeman, John: John Holdeman (January 31, 1832-March 10, 1900), founder of the Church of God in Christ, Mennonite, was born in New Pittsburg, Ohio. He grew up as a Mennonite but was not very religious. In 1852 he married Elizabeth Ritter, who was already pregnant, and the ensuing scandal caused him to reflect on what he considered his profligate youth. In 1853 he had an experience of cleansing and a call to the ministry.

For the next six years Holdeman did little else but study the Bible, Mennonite history, and languages. In 1859 he began to take his message on the road, the message being that the Mennonites were too lax in their commitments and too worldly. His revivalistic style of evangelism was a first for the Mennonites and his primary success came in the immigrant communities, particularly among the Russian Mennonites in McPherson County, Kansas and in Manitoba, Canada. He organized his followers into the Church of God in Christ, Mennonite.

In 1882, after the death of his mother, he sold the family farm and moved to Jasper County, Missouri. There, among numerous followers, he established a headquarters and continued his lecturing and writing. The last three years of his life were in McPherson County, Kansas, the site of his first major evangelistic success.

Holmes, Ernest Shurtleff: Ernest Holmes (January 21, 1887-April 7, 1960), founder of the United Church of Religious Science, one of the most successful New Thought groups, was born in Lincoln, Maine. He left home at age fifteen and worked a number of jobs around Boston, Massachusetts. Although his formal education was limited, he had a gift for public speaking and was an avid reader.

In 1908 he decided to act on his public speaking abilities by earning a 2-year certificate from the Leland Powers School of Expression. While there he was introduced to Christian Science and founder Mary Baker Eddy's book, *Science and Health with Key to the Scriptures*. From this point he became intensely interested in Christian Science and the related New Thought groups and authors, particularly Thomas Troward, a British judge in the Punjab.

In 1912 he moved to Venice, California, where his brother, Fenwicke Holmes, was a Congregationalist minister, and took a job with the city. He continued his New Thought study with a correspondence course from Christian Larson and eventually converted his brother. In 1917 they founded the Metaphysical Institute in Los Angeles, opened a Metaphysical Sanitarium in Long Beach, and began the magazine *Uplift*. They became popular lecturers and authors and were partners until 1924. In that year Holmes was the last pupil of New Thought pioneer Emma Curtis Hopkins in New York City, from whom he gained a mystical dimension. Holmes was among the first New Thought writers to include from the developing field of psychology the difference between waking consciousness (what Holmes called objective mind) and the subconscious (subjective mind).

In 1927 Holmes married Hazel Durkee Foster and began what would be his permanent organization, the Institute of Religious Science and School of Philosophy, and a new periodical, *The Science of Mind*. He developed a large Sunday congregation, an audience enhanced beginning in 1949 by a radio show, "This Thing Called Life." In 1953 he changed the name of the organization to the Church of Religious Science and designated the numerous branch groups across the country as churches. Opposition to this move led to Religious Science International and other splinter groups.

Hopkins, Emma Curtis: Emma Curtis Hopkins (September 2, 1849-April 8, 1925), a major early figure in the New Thought movement, was born in Killingly, Connecticut. She married George Irving Hopkins, a high school English teacher, on July 29, 1874. For a time they lived in Nantucket, Massachusetts, moving to Manchester, New Hampshire, about 1881. In October 1883 she heard a talk by Mary Baker Eddy, founder of Christian Science, and soon was healed by an Eddy disciple, Mary Berry. Hopkins was converted and enrolled in Eddy's course in December 1883. Hopkins separated from her husband about this time, though a formal divorce was not obtained until November 1900. Hopkins thereafter apparently led a life of celibacy.

She quickly became a favorite of Eddy's, who appointed her editor of the *Journal of Christian Science* beginning in September 1884. Hopkins was dismissed from that post and expelled from Christian Science in October 1885, for reasons not entirely clear, and then served for some months as editor of A. J. Swarts' *Mind Cure Journal* while he was out of town. In the summer of 1886 she teamed with another former Eddy student, Mary Plunkett, to create the Emma Curtis Hopkins College of Christian Science in downtown Chicago. Soon a student group, the Hopkins Metaphysical Association, was formed, and began to establish branch groups. By the end of 1887 there were 21 Hopkins Metaphysical Associations across the country, connected by *Truth: A Magazine of Christian Science*. This was the first New Thought national organization.

In January 1888 Plunkett moved to New York to establish a related group, the International Christian Science Association, but in mid-1889 a scandal involving Plunkett caused Hopkins to sever that relationship. Hopkins continued her teaching work, which she had recast to emphasize its religious nature. In the summer of 1888 she changed the school's name to the Hopkins Theological Seminary, and in December 1888 the Hopkins Metaphysical Associations became the Christian Science Associations.

The first class from her seminary graduated on January 10, 1889 and Hopkins ordained them (most of them women) as clergy. Hopkins thus became the first woman in modern times to act in the role of a Christian bishop and ordain others. She realized that this was not just a religious, but a feminist action, and believed that God's feminine side was in the process of showing more of itself, leading naturally to women on earth taking on new leadership roles.

By the end of 1893 Hopkins claimed that 350 students had been through the basic course and 111 students had completed the theological course. She not only taught at the Chicago school but traveled across the country holding classes. From 1890 to 1898 she wrote commentaries on the International Sunday School Lessons for the *Chicago Inter-Ocean* newspaper. These efforts earned her the title of "Teacher of teachers" in New Thought. Her students included the founders of Divine Science, Unity School of Christianity, Homes of Truth, and Religious Science.

On November 12, 1894, tired of the efforts of being a school administrator, Hopkins closed the successful seminary and moved to an apartment in New York City. There she remained in semi-retirement, maintaining only a small number of private students and patients, including socialite Mabel Dodge Luhan and writer Maurice Sterne. About 1919 she began writing her last and most famous book, twelve studies in *High Mysticism*.

Houteff, Victor T.: Victor T. Houteff was a reforming Adventist and the founder of a small splinter group called the Davidians. The original name of the group was Shepherd's Rod. The Branch Davidians are by far the most well-known group directly influenced by Houteff. Houteff was born in Raikovo, Bulgaria on March 2, 1885. He immigrated to the U.S. in 1907, worked in a restaurant in Milwaukee and operated a small hotel in Rockford, Illinois. In 1918 he attended a Seventh-day Adventist tent meeting and was converted to Adventist teaching. Houteff moved to Los Angeles and actively served as the assistant superintendent of his church's Sabbath

School. Houteff had limited formal education, but he did not passively accept Adventist doctrine. Instead, he studied Adventist literature, and in 1929 he began to set forth ideas of his own in a series of tracts later published as the *Shepherd's Rod.*

Houteff believed that only the Seventh-day Adventists possessed the correct interpretation of scripture regarding the future, Sabbath observance and dietary regulations. He poured his energies into both understanding the signs of the second advent of Christ and preparing followers for the event. He relied on earlier Adventist teaching, particularly the writings of Ellen G. White. He believed, however, that he had additional insights which had never been revealed to the church before. His core idea was that the General Conference of the Seventh-day Adventists had grown worldly, formal and institutional. Christ could never return to this compromised church. It was therefore essential to call the General Conference to reform. When 144,000 faithful Adventists had responded to his reform message, the new era would begin.

The General Conference rejected Houteff's teaching, arguing that he misrepresented the views of White and the Adventist heritage. Houteff responded by moving to central Texas (near Waco) in 1935, where he organized some sixty followers to print his teachings and communicate his ideas to the parent body. Houteff led the community for twenty years—until his death in 1955.

—William L. Pitts

L. Ron Hubbard
Courtesy: Church of Scientology

Hubbard, L. Ron: Lafayette Ronald Hubbard (Mar. 13, 1911 - Jan. 24, 1986), writer and founder of Dianetics and Scientology, was born in Tilden, Nebraska, the son of Ledora May Waterbury and Harry Ross Hubbard, an officer in the U.S. Navy.

Hubbard spent much of his youth with his maternal grandfather in Montana due to his father's service in the Navy. In 1923-24, Hubbard lived in Washington, D.C., and, again, after 1929, graduating from high school there in 1930. Between 1927 and 1928 Hubbard traveled throughout the Far East. In 1930 he entered George Washington University, but left before graduating. Hubbard spent some of the early 1930s as an aviator and aviation correspondent. His major vocation by 1934, however, was as a prolific and increasingly successful fiction writer. His stories of the 1930s and 1940s were predominantly action and adventure, and included westerns and science fiction.

Hubbard married three times—in 1933 to Margaret Louise Grubb; in 1946 to Sara Northrup; and in 1952 to Mary Sue Whipp. There were six children. During World War II he was a Navy lieutenant, serving in both the Pacific and Atlantic, and spent time in 1943 and 1945 as a patient in a naval hospital for ulcers and injuries to eyes and hip. In 1950 he published his most famous book, *Dianetics: The Modern Science of Mental Health*. This work, on a new form of therapy Hubbard labeled dianetics, became an instant bestseller, generating numerous articles, discussion groups and conversations.

Due to *Dianetics'* popularity the Hubbard Dianetics Research Foundation was established in May 1950 in Elizabeth, New Jersey, with offices in Los Angeles, Chicago, Honolulu, and Washington, D.C. *Dianetics* was opposed by the medical, psychological and psychiatric professions, which all published articles discouraging its use. Despite these attempts, by late September 1950, over 750 Dianetics groups were established with over 250,000 individuals applying the techniques described in *Dianetics*.

In the fall of 1951 Hubbard felt he had isolated "life energy" or "life source"—the individual himself, which he termed "thetan" (the human "soul"). Hubbard concluded that the thetan was able to leave the body and exist independently of the flesh. In March 1952, he moved to Phoenix where he announced the establishment of the Hubbard Association of Scientologists International (HASI). In 1954, Scientologists and Dianetics practitioners in Los Angeles formed the Church of Scientology.

Scientology expanded rapidly in the United States and abroad, with hundreds of churches and centers appearing after 1954, and millions of people passing through Scientology classes and counseling by the 1980s. Between 1951 and 1954, Hubbard wrote some twenty Scientology books and gave more than 1,100 lectures.

In 1959, Hubbard moved to England, where he started the Hubbard College of Saint Hill, in Sussex. There he lectured and supervised the education of "auditors"—people trained to deliver and apply Dianetics and Scientology processes and procedures. He also developed his ideas on the "operating thetan" (OT)—Hubbard's concept of the state of spiritual freedom, and the ultimate goal of Scientology processing.

In 1966 Hubbard resigned all adminstrative positions in the Church, and the next year set to sea with a handful of veteran Scientologists, called the Sea Organization, with the goal of researching and developing procedures for achieving the state of "OT." In 1975, he settled in Dunedin, Florida, and a year later moved to a Southern California desert ranch in La Quinta. In 1982, Hubbard retired to a private life in San Luis Obispo County, devoting the majority of his time before his death four years later to writing and completing research on the state of "OT."

Hunt, Ernest: Ernest Hunt (August 16, 1878-February 7, 1967), founder of the Western Buddhist Order of the Honpa Hongwanji, was born in Hertfordshire, England. He spent some years traveling the world as a seaman, then attended Eastbourne College with the aim of becoming an Anglican priest. The day before his ordination, however, he decided to convert to the Buddhism he had encountered on his travels.

In 1915 he and his wife, Dorothy, moved to the Hawaiian islands to work with the plantation-based Buddhist community, eventually opening Sunday schools for English-speaking Buddhist children. In 1924 Bishop Yemyo Imamura of the Honpa Hongwanji Buddhists ordained both Hunt and his wife and Hunt took the religious name of Shinkaku, or "true light-bearer." In 1926 Hunt became head of the Honpa Hong-wanji English Department, an office created by Imamura in 1918 to coordinate the work with English-speaking Buddhists. In addition, Hunt did much work among non-Buddhists, and in 1928 those new initiates founded the Western Buddhist Order as a nonsectarian branch of the Honpa Hongwanji Mission (which is otherwise of the Pure Land or Shin Buddhist tradition) intended to spread Buddhism to non-Buddhist Westerners.

Bishop Imamura was key to the support of these path-breaking ventures and in 1929 he founded the Hawaiian branch of the ecumenical International Buddhist Institute, making Hunt vice-president and editor of its new journal, *Navayana*. That year Hunt published *An Outline of Buddhism*, leading the Burmese Theravada Buddhists to ordain both Hunt and his wife and grant the honorary degree Doctor of the Dharma. Hunt organized many social aid programs, including prison and hospital visitations.

Bishop Imamura died in 1932 and his successor was not ecumenically- or Western-minded. The Institute and the English Department were dismantled and Hunt was forced to move to a Soto Zen temple, where he was ordained a priest in 1953. In 1963 he became the only Caucasian priest in the West to achieve the Soto rank of Osho.

Hurley, George Willie: George Hurley (February 17, 1884-June 23, 1943), founder of Universal Hagar's Spiritual Church, one of several predominantly African-American spiritualist churches, was born in Reynolds, Georgia. He became first a Baptist minister, then a Methodist minister, and married Cassie Bell Martin. They moved to Detroit in 1919, where he became a minister of the Triumph Church and Kingdom of God in Christ, a holiness church. Over the next several years he became that group's Presiding Prince of Michigan.

About 1922 he was converted to Spiritualism and became a minister in the International Spiritual Church. After receiving a vision he interpreted as a command to found a new church, he established Universal Hagar's Spiritual Church on September 23, 1923, in Detroit. The following year he began the School of Mediumship and Psychology, which eventually became an inner auxiliary of each congregation. Complementary to this was the Knights of the All-Seeing Eye, a secret lodge open to men and women members of the church.

Hurley incorporated concepts from Catholicism, astrology, Ethiopianism, and other sources for the group's belief system. He taught that the original Hebrews were black people and that white skin was the sign of Cain's curse. At some point he began teaching that just as Jesus was the God of the Piscean Age, he was the God of the Aquarian Age, which began after World War I and would usher in universal peace and harmony. Toward this end he was a strong critic of racism and the practice of segregation. At the time of his death there were between thirty and forty congregations spread over eight states, approximately the same as the status of the church today.

Hutter, Jacob: Jacob Hutter (?-1536) was born and raised in the hamlet of Moos (South Tyrol, Italy), where he became leader of the Brethren. His followers were being persecuted when he decided to move to Moravia. In Austerlitz he found and joined the group led by Jacob Wiedemann, and then returned to the Tyrol in order to organize his own movement. A faction emerged among the Austerlitz group that protested Wiedemann's authoritarian leadership, and in winter of 1530, 350 members established themselves at Auspitz.

Hutter was eventually asked to arbitrate and work out an agreement between the two groups, that he reorganized under the leadership of a third group located at Rossitz. When in 1533 Hutter arrived in Auspitz, the group at first did not accept his leadership. Hutter, who believed that the group's misfortunes were due to insufficient detachment from worldly goods, accused the wife of one of the leaders of hoarding money. After it was discovered that this was true, Hutter was elected chief elder, or *Vorsteher*, and began reorganizing the group and strenghtening it both communally and economically.

However, in 1535, after King Ferdinand of Austria demanded the expulsion of the Brethren from Moravia, the group scattered and Hutter returned to Tyrol, where he wrote a remonstrance citing the peaceful nature of the Brethren. Ferdinand placed a price on the head of Hutter, who was arrested with his wife on November 29, 1535. He was eventually burned alive and his wife executed two years later.

Hutter's followers, who were forced to migrate several times to locations in Europe and Russia, finally migrated to North America in the 1870s and spread colonies across the prairies in Canada, as well as in Montana, North, and South Dakota, becoming the most successful communal group in modern history.

I

Irving, Edward: Edward Irving (August 4, 1792-December 7, 1834), a founder of the Catholic Apostolic Church, was born in Annan, Scotland. At age thirteen he entered Edinburgh University, graduated in 1809, and entered Divinity Hall to work towards ministry in the Church of Scotland. Supporting himself by teaching, he finally finished his training in 1815, but did not find a parish position until 1819, when he became assistant at St. John's Parish in Glasgow. This soon led to his own parish, the Caledonian Chapel at Hatton Garden in London.

His congregation grew steadily and on October 13, 1823 he married Isabella Martin. At that time he was running a campaign to expand the chapel into the National Scots Church for London, and the new structure was finished in May 1827. Meanwhile he associated with Henry Drummond and his famous Albury Conferences on issues of prophecy, which met annually beginning in 1826. Early on the conferences reached a consensus that the end-times, with the signs of the Spirit and the second coming of Christ, were near. The expected signs of the Spirit—prophecy, speaking in tongues, and healing—appeared in a Scotland congregation in 1830 and then in Irving's congregation in 1831.

That year the Church of Scotland condemned Irving's controversial Christological views as published in his *Orthodox and Catholic Doctrine of Christ's Human Nature* (1830), but the church's trustees had stood behind him. Now the presence of tongue-speaking in worship was too much for them. They asked for a trial before the London presbytery, which in 1832 declared Irving unfit and took away his pulpit. He responded by forming another congregation, the first in what became the Catholic Apostolic Church. He led that congregation until September 1834, when he felt a call to preach in Scotland. There, within a few months, he fell ill and died.

Henry Drummond, one of the designated twelve Apostles, emerged as the main leader of the church, which declined after the death of the last Apostle in 1901.

Itkin, Mikhaël Francis Augustine: Augustine Itkin (February 7, 1936-August 1, 1989) was the founder of the Community of the Love of Christ (Evangelical Catholic) and one of the first openly homosexual religious leaders in the United States. He was ordained in 1952, at the age of sixteen, by Rev. Claude Williams, head of the People's Institute of Applied Religion/The Way.

In 1955 Itkin became licensed with the Eucharistic Catholic Church in Atlanta, Georgia, the first exclusively homosexual congregation in the country (founded in 1946). The founder of that church, George Augustine Hyde, gained episcopal orders in 1957 from John C. C. Sherwood of the American Holy Orthodox Catholic Eastern Church. Hyde then reordained Itkin on May 6, 1957, but Itkin left him two years later, claiming that Hyde was moving "back into the closet."

Itkin was consecrated on November 12, 1960 by Christoper C. J. Stanley of the United Old Catholic Patriarchate of the World and at that point had the credentials to lead his own organization, which went through a number of name changes, beginning with Primitive Catholic Church (Evangelical Catholic). After a few years he received permission to reformulate Ulric Vernon Herford's Evangelical Catholic Communion in the United States. In 1963 this new organization was supplemented with an internal religious order called Brotherhood of the Love of Christ (later the Community of the Love of Christ).

During the 1960s Itkin developed a theological emphasis on pacifism, freedom from oppression (especially oppression of homosexuals), and civil rights. In 1968 he was one of the first Old Catholic bishops to ordain a woman and the action caused a schism among his followers. Those against the move retained the Evangelical Catholic Communion name, and Itkin led the rest into a new group, the Community of the Love of Christ (Evangelical Catholic).

In the early 1970s he moved to Los Angeles and briefly renounced his episcopal orders while taking on a Mennonite theology. In 1974, however, he resumed his past activities, including participation in a number of multiple consecrations (a common Old Catholic practice). He moved to San Francisco and further established himself as a gay religious activist, though with a limited church following. He died from complications of the AIDs virus and was succeeded by Marcia Alice Mari Herndon.

J

James, William: William James (1842-1910) was a well-known American psychologist and philosopher, perhaps best remembered as an advocate of the philosophy of pragmatism. Spiritualism was a popular movement during his lifetime, and he made significant contributions to what we would today call psychical research. He was fascinated by the phenomenon of mediumship, and studied many mediums.

He was born into a wealthy, New York family. His father was the equally famous Henry James, who was an adherent of the ideas of Emanuel Swedenborg. James graduated from Harvard University with a medical degree at the age of 27, and within a few years was teaching physiology, psychology and philosophy at his *alma mater*. An interesting blend of scientist and spiritual seeker, James was interested in religious experiences and mystical states. He is justly celebrated for his *Varieties of Religious Experience,* a book that is still a standard reference for scholars in that field.

James was also interested in paranormal phenomena, an interest that manifested as early as 1869. While in London in 1882, he encountered—and even participated in the research of—the new Society for Psychical Research (SPR). His appreciation of the British society was such that, in 1885, James helped found the American Society for Psychical Research. Psychical research was also carried on at the Lawrence Scientific School which he founded at Harvard. He was deeply committed to the goal of subjecting so-called psychic phenomena to scientific methods.

James was particularly interested in the Boston medium Leonara Piper. James gave a famous lecture called the "white crow" lecture in 1890 in which he asserted that "to upset the conclusion that all crows are black, there is no need to seek demonstration that no crows are black; it is sufficient to produce one white crow; a single one is sufficient." He further asserted that Ms. Piper was just such an exception.

James was also deeply interested in the question of the survival of the soul after death. While never asserting that survival had been proven beyond a shadow of a doubt, he cited spiritualist phenomena as strongly supporting such a view. This point was well argued in several essays. He passed away at his summer home in Chocura, New Hampshire on August 26, 1910. Current mediums and channels often claim contact with James, and relay his supposed teachings from the other side.

Jansson, Eric: Eric Jansson (December 19, 1808-May 13, 1850), founder of the Bishop Hill religious community in Illinois, was born in Bishop-skulla, Sweden, and had access to very little formal education. In 1830, when he was twenty-two, he suffered a severe attack of rheumatism, which led to a religious experience. He realized his status as a sinner and saw the Lutheran Church as at best unhelpful in teaching the power of Jesus. He came to believe that the believer, who was justified and sanctified at the moment of salvation, could go on to lead a perfectly sinless life through the power of Jesus, who could also heal all afflictions.

Jansson was healed and began to share his new ideas. He gathered a few followers and married Maria Kristina Larsdotter in 1835, but by 1841 general hostility forced him to move northward to Halsingland. There he had more success, gaining a loyal assistant in Jonas Olsson. In 1844 he moved permanently to Stenbo. Later that year he sponsored two book burnings directed at Lutheran clergy and was arrested briefly. In 1845 he was arrested again, but followers helped him escape to Norway.

In 1846 Jansson led about 1200 on a migration to the United States, where they began the Bishop Hill (after Bishopskulla, Jansson's home town) community near what today is Galva, Illinois. For some years they attempted to hold all goods in common and also experimented with enforced celibacy, but both courses were eventually abandoned. The community did very well until 1849, when a cholera epidemic killed about one-quarter of the residents, including Jansson's wife. This shook the community's faith in faith healing.

Jansson married Anna Sophia Gabrielson on September 16, 1849, and tried to restore a sense of normalcy, but a new difficulty arose. John Root decided to leave the community but his wife refused to go with him. Neither would the community release goods he wished to take with him. At one point he kidnapped his wife and the community took her back. Finally, in May 1850, Root killed Jansson. The group stayed together under Jonas Olsson until 1857, and then quickly dissipated.

Jaya Sati Bhagavati Ma
Courtesy: Richard Rosenkrantz

Jaya Sati Bhagavati Ma: Ma, born Joyce Green, was formerly a housewife in Brooklyn, New York. Her life began to change radically, however, in December 1972 when she had a vision of someone she, though Jewish, recognized as Jesus Christ. He would reappear three more times. She turned for guidance to residents of a nearby Jesuit seminary who offered her both sympathy and understanding. Then in the spring of 1973 she had a second set of apparitions, this time of a person who called himself Nityananda. He appeared to her almost daily for a year and taught her.

At the time Nityananda appeared, she had no knowledge that such a person had actually lived in India, had begun a movement then headed by Swami Muktananda, and had a disciple named Swami Rudrananda who initially brought his teachings to America. Nityananda, as he appeared to her, taught her about what he termed *chidakash*, the state in which love and awareness are one. He gave her a new name, *Jaya* (Sanskrit for "victory" or "glory") and mentioned a woman named Hilda. Green, who began to call herself Joya Santanya, soon found Swami Rudrananda and a short time later was led to Hilda Charlton, an independent spiritual teacher in Manhattan who encouraged her to become a teacher.

Through the mid 1970s, Joya Santanya's teachings activity led to the founding of some thirteen small communities where people lived cooperatively and gathered for daily satsang for meditation. In July 1976 she moved to Florida where land was purchased and Kashi Ashram was established. Over the next few years she traveled around the country visiting the several houses and expanded her teaching work to the West Coast. In 1978 she fell ill and many thought she might die. The majority of the people living in the cooperative houses moved to Florida to be near her. Fortunately, she recovered, and the people decided to stay and expanded the ashram to around 80 residents. During the next decade it would double in size.

John-Roger: John-Roger Hinkins, generally called John-Roger, was born in 1934 at Rains, Utah. In 1958 he earned the bachelor degree in Psychology at the University of Utah, and in 1960 and 1961 he obtained the Secondary Teaching and the Secondary Life Teaching Credentials at the Uni-

John-Roger
Courtesy: Church of the Movement of Spiritual Awareness

versity of Utah and at the University of California at Los Angeles. In Los Angeles, he pursued post-graduate work at the University of California, at the University of Southern California, and at the California State University.

In 1963 he experienced a nine-day coma, while undergoing surgery for a kidney stone, after which he claimed that a new personality had superseded his old personality. In 1971 he founded in Los Angeles the Church of the Movement of Spiritual Inner Awareness (MSIA), a nondenominational church focusing on soul transcendence.

For over thirty years, John-Roger has traveled around the world teaching and lecturing about the wisdom of the spiritual heart. Among the organizations that he has founded and with which he works closely are: the Institute for Individual and World Peace, of which he is president; the University of Santa Monica, of which he is Chancellor; and the Peace Theological Seminary and College of Philosophy, of which he is president.

He published a number of works, such as the best-sellers *You Can't Afford the Luxury of a Negative Thought* (1988), *Life 101* (1990), *Do It! Let's Get Off Our Buts* (1991), *Wealth 101: Wealth is Much More Than Money* (1992), and *We Give to Love* (1993). Among other works are: *Forgiveness – The Key to the Kingdom, The Tao of Spirit, Journey of a Soul, The Path to Mastership, The Power Within You, Inner Worlds of Meditation, Wealth & Higher Consciousness, God is Your Partner, Walking With the Lord, Dream Voyages* and *Spiritual Warrior.*

Jones, Charles Price: Charles Jones (December 9, 1865-January 19, 1949), founder of the Church of Christ (Holiness) U.S.A., was born in Texas Valley, Georgia. As a young man he moved to Arkansas and joined the Locust Grove Baptist Church in Crittendon County. In 1887 he received a license to preach and pastored several churches briefly. He graduated from Arkansas Baptist College in 1891 and accepted the pastorate of Bethlehem Baptist Church in Searcy, Arkansas, moving the following year to Tabernacle Baptist Church in Selma, Alabama.

In Alabama Jones discovered the holiness movement, which was based on a post-conversion experience of grace, enabling one to become perfect in love. He had this experience in 1894 and when he moved the following year to Mt. Helm Baptist Church in Jackson, Mississippi, began preaching holiness. He associated with Charles Harrison Mason, another African American Holiness Baptist and founder of the Church of God in Christ. Both encountered much opposition among Baptists to the holiness teaching. In 1902 Jones was finally forced to leave his church and in response he founded the Christ Temple Church, associating it with the Church of God in Christ.

In 1907 Mason was converted to Pentecostalism and his denomination split over the issue. In 1909 Jones founded a new, non-Pentecostal denomination, the Church of Christ (Holiness) U.S.A., which he headed for the rest of his career. In 1917 he founded the Christ Temple Church in Los Angeles, which thereafter served as his headquarters. In 1918, two years after the death of his first wife, he married Pearl R. Reed. He authored several books and hundreds of hymns.

Jones, James (Jim) Warren: Jim Jones (May 13, 1931-November 18, 1978), founder of the People's Temple, was born in Lynn, Indiana. His father was an alcoholic road construction worker. He married Marceline Baldwin in 1949 and attended college briefly, but left it to become minister of the Somerset Methodist Church in Indianapolis.

Before receiving final elder's orders he left the Methodist Church and founded an independent congregation called Community Unity. There he put into place his vision of a Pentecostal-style worship and a social service activism across racial boundaries. By the late 1950s the congregation was renamed the People's Temple and began to emulate many of the features of Father Divine's Peace Mission. Jones saw Father Divine (d. 1965) as a role model and although Jones was white most of his followers were black. In 1960 the People's Temple affiliated with the Christian Church (Disciples of Christ) and the following year Jones received a B.S. from Butler University in Indianapolis.

In 1964, after returning from a two-year travel sabbatical to diffuse community controversy about the congregation's activities, he was ordained as a Christian Church (Disciples of Christ) minister. Believing that Indianapolis was a dangerous area for a future nuclear war, he moved the congregation to Ukiah, California. The success of his ministry there made him wealthy and influential, and he added a congregation in Los Angeles. His social work earned him community awards and praise in church journals.

There were areas of concern, however. He began claiming he could raise people from the dead. It was rumored he held dictatorial control over the personal lives of followers and abused some children. In 1977, facing media exposure, he moved to a colony in Guyana, South America, he had founded in 1973, and it soon swelled to more than 900 inhabitants as "Jonestown." The group still faced court charges, and Jones began to speak of the possibility of group suicide. In November 1978 Congressman Leo Ryan and others visited Jonestown to investigate. Ryan and most of his group were shot to death and almost all the residents of Jonestown also died via poison or gunshot. The name "Jonestown" has since served for many to stand for and sum up the dangers of religious "cults," though some, like Michael Meiers, have suggested the C.I.A. had a role in the incident.

Marc Edmund Jones
Courtesy: The Sabian Assembly

Jones, Marc Edmund: Born in St. Louis Missouri, Marc Edmund Jones (1888-1980) was a famous occultist and astrologer. He studied at the Theological Seminary of the United Presbyterian Church, and in 1948 he earned the Ph.D. in education at Columbia University. During his long life, he worked as astrologer, editorial consultant, Protestant minister, as well as motion-picture scenarist.

After becoming involved in astrology (1913), he established the Sabian Assembly (1923), and some 20 years later he became president of the American Foundation for Metaphysical Arts and Sciences in New York City. He was also an early member of the American Federation of Astrology, as well as of the Astrologers' Guild of America, of which he was vice-president from 1941 to 1942. He died in Stanwood, Washington.

Known as one of the most famous astrologers in America, he utilized horoscope patterns to his approach to delineation, which like the approach to degree interpretaions, became very popular among astrologers. Both these methods were popularized by Dane Rudhyar. Among his most famous works are *Guide to Horoscope Interpretation* (1941), *How to Learn Astrology* (1941), and the *Sabian Symbols* (1953).

Jordan, Clarence: Clarence Jordon (July 29, 1912-October 29, 1969), founder of the Koinonia Community, was born in Talbotton, Georgia. He graduated from Georgia State College of Agriculture in 1933, then received his Th.M. (1936) and Ph.D. (1939) from Southern Baptist Theological Seminary. He worked his way through school by pastoring part-time and a short teaching assignment at Simmons University, a black-oriented Baptist school in Louisville, Kentucky.

By the time he finished his schooling, Jordan was convinced that racism was a major problem in the Southern Baptist Convention as well as the country as a whole. He became director of the Sunshine Center in the black section of Louisville, then later was named superintendent of missions for the Long Run Baptist Association. During this time he was an active member of the Fellowship of Reconciliation, a pacifist group, and a study group called *Koinonia*, named for the New Testament word for close Christian community.

In 1941 he and a missionary, Martin English, decided to put together a practical plan for living out what had become deeply held convictions about the communal sharing of property, racial equality, and non-violence. In the following year Koinonia Farm was founded on 400 acres near Americus, Georgia as a communal, Christian, multi-racial community, self-supporting through the sale of agricultural products. In 1948 the farm members campaigned against the post-war draft and local relations became so strained that the Rehobeth Baptist Church expelled Jordan and some others in 1950.

In 1956 Jordan and the farm gained larger public attention when he tried to help integrate a college, resulting in acts of violence and harassment by such groups as the White Citizens Council. These experiences led Jordan to create the Cotton Patch approach to the New Testament, which placed biblical stories in the contemporary South. In 1968 the farm was reorganized as Koinonia Partners, focused on educating visitors and raising capital funds for the poor.

Jouret, Luc: Luc Jouret (1947-1994), founder of the Solar Temple, was born in Kikwit, Belgian Congo (present-day Zaire), from Belgian parents on October 18th, 1947. Fear of violence against Belgian citizens at the time of decolonization persuaded his parents to settle back in their home country, where Luc enrolled in the Department of Medicine of the Free University of Brussels. In the 1970s the Belgian police opened a file on Jouret as a a member of a small Communist group, the Walloon Communist Youth. In 1974 he graduated as a medical doctor. In 1976 he enlisted as a paratrooper and took part in the Kolwezi raid, which allowed Belgian troops to bring back home a group of fellow-citizens threatened in Zaire. The prevailing ideas among paratroopers were diametrically opposed to Luc Jouret's

Communism but, according to a former college mate, Marc Brunson, now a veterinarian, the young doctor asserted that, at the time, joining the paratroopers "seemed the best way to infiltrate the Army with Communist ideas." After the military experience, his interests focused on alternative forms of medicine. He studied homeopathy and later became a registered homeopathic practitioner in France (in many French-speaking countries homeopathy is in fact regulated by law). In 1977 he had visited the Philippines (later he reported also visits to "China, Peru and India") in order to study the techniques of local spiritualist healers. According to Jean-François Mayer, a Swiss scholar of non-traditional religions, Jouret claimed—in a long interview he had with him in December 1987—that the experience in India was crucial for turning to homeopathy, although he had been in contact with European homeopatic practitioners before. For a short while he supposedly became a follower of guru Krishna Macharia. In the early 1980s he started a homeopathic practice in Annemasse, France, receiving clients also from nearby Switzerland. His success as a homeopathic doctor was remarkable. People came to him from as far as the other side of the Ocean and, after a few years, Jouret had several practices in France, Switzerland and Canada.

In the 1980s, besides continuing with his homeopathic practice, Luc Jouret became also a lecturer on naturopathy and ecological topics, active in the wider circuit of the French-speaking New Age movement. About 1981, he established the Amenta Club, an organization managing his conferences. He spoke in New Age bookstores (in France, Switzerland, Belgium and Canada) and in eclectic esoteric groups such as the Golden Way Foundation of Geneva (previously called La Pyramide, which had as its leader Joseph Di Mambro, 1924-1994, who later became the co-founder—and largely the real leader—of the Solar Temple, while the Golden Way became for all purposes the parent organization of the Atlanta, Amenta and later Archédia clubs and groups). In 1987, Jouret was able to be received as a paid "motivational speaker" by two district offices of Hydro-Québec, the public hydroelectric utility of the Province of Québec. Besides getting paid 5,400 Canadian dollars for his conferences in the period 1987-89, he also recruited executives and managers who later followed him to the end. On October 4th and 5th, 1994, fifty-three people died—some suicides; most murders—in Switzerland and in Canada in adherence with the apocalyptic ideas propagated by Jouret and the Solar Temple.

—Massimo Introvigne

Judith, Anodea: Anodea Judith, formerly named A. Judith Mull (and sister of the actor Martin Mull), is director of Lifeways, a school for the study of consciousness and healing arts, located in northern California, which she founded in 1983. She pursued undergraduate work in psychology at Clark University, Worcester, MA, 1971-73, then studied Fine Arts at the California College of Arts and Crafts, Oakland, CA, 1973-74. From 1975 to 1986 she studied Bioenergetics with various teachers in the San Francisco area. In 1977 she resumed her studies in psychology at John F. Kennedy University, Orinda, CA; and in 1978-79 studied at the Berkeley Psychic Institute.

Her path to Neopaganism led through the circle of people around Marion Zimmer Bradley in Oakland, CA, and she initially worked in the Dark Moon Circle that has since evolved into the Fellowship of the Spiral Path. Anodea was ordained a Priestess in the Church of All Worlds in 1985, and served as CAW's President 1985-91. In 1988 she received the M.A. in Clinical Psychology from the Rosebridge Graduate School of Integrative Therapy. From 1991-93 she studied Somatic Experiencing with Peter Levine. She notes that in the course of her training, she has studied acupressure, yoga, bioenergetics, psychic healing and reading, gestalt therapy, radical psychiatry, ritual magic, and shamanism.

Currently living in Sebastopol, California, she helps oversee CAW's subsidiary organizations, which include Forever Forests (which she helped to found in 1977), Nemeton, the Ecosophical Research Association, and the Holy Order of Mother Earth (HOME). She is an ordained minister and Elder of the Covenant of the Goddess, and has served as one of its officers. She can be reached via Church of All Worlds, 2140 Shattuck #2093, Berkeley, CA 94704.

She is the author of several books, including *Wheels of Life: A User's Guide to the Chakra System* (Llewellyn, 1986), widely regarded as one of the best books ever written on the Chakras; and, with Selene Vega, *The Sevenfold Journey* (Crossing Press, 1992). She has published many articles in *Green Egg* and *Circle Network News*, and her writings have also appeared in the *San Francisco Chronicle*, the *Oakland Tribune*, and anthologies edited by Marion Zimmer Bradley and by Chas Clifton. She co-authored two articles with her husband, geologist Richard Ely, in Frank Joseph's anthology on *Sacred Sites*. She appears regularly at Neopagan festivals across the continent, and on various broadcast media.

— Aidan A. Kelly

William Q. Judge
Courtesy: American Religion Collection

Judge, William Quan: William Q. Judge (April 13, 1851-March 21, 1896), co-founder of the Theosophical Society and founder of the Theosophical Society in America, was born to a Methodist family in Dublin, Ireland that moved to the United States in 1864. His poor health in childhood followed him into adulthood. In 1872 he became a naturalized citizen and a lawyer, specializing in commercial law. Two years later he married Ella M. Smith.

In 1874 he became a follower of Madame Blavatsky and in 1875 helped her and Col. Henry Olcott found the Theosophical Society. When Blavatsky and Olcott moved to India in 1878 to establish a new headquarters, Judge was the main person left in the United States, but was ill-equipped to lead, what with frequent illnesses, trips abroad, and limited occult knowledge. He made the best of it and improved his knowledge and confidence with a visit to India in 1884. When the American section was officially organized in 1886 he was elected general secretary. In 1888 he became a leader of the new Esoteric Section, a group for serious Theosophist students.

By this time he felt able to contribute to Theosophy through writing. He began two new journals, *The Path* (1886) and *The Theosophical Forum* (1889), and wrote several books, including the well-known *Ocean of Theosophy* (1893). When Blavatsky died in 1891, Judge became leader of the American Esoteric Section and Besant took the European and Indian Esoteric Sections, while Olcott remained in India as international president. All did not go smoothly, however, but major arguments were postponed until after the orchestration of a successful Theosophy presence at the 1893 World's Parliament of Religions at the Chicago World's Fair.

Just as Blavatsky had regularly received written messages, supposedly from the spiritual masters, so did Judge. Just as Blavatsky was accused of writing the notes herself, so was Judge. He managed to clear his name within the organization, but the newspapers got hold of the story and played it up at his expense. He believed that Besant was to blame for the whole affair and in April 1895 declared the American Theosophists independent. He took 75 of the 89 branches with him, thus forming what came to be called the Theosophical Society of America. After his premature death the following year he was succeeded by Katherine Tingley.

C.G. Jung
Courtesy: American Religion Collection

Jung, Carl Gustav: Carl Jung, the famous Swiss Psychologist (1875-1961), was born at Kesswil, Thurgau, Switzerland. He is considered to be the originator of analytical psychology. His ideas have had considerable influence on contemporary popular culture through the medium of such thinkers as Joseph Campbell, and through certain movements such as the men's movement, which has been considerably influenced by the Jungian tradition.

He studied medicine at the University of Basel, Switzerland, and took his M.D. in 1902 at the University of Zurich. Between 1907 and 1913 he became a disciple of Freud, but their collaboration did not last. They both studied dreams, but Jung advanced an approach that did not depend heavily on sexual problems, in contrast with Freud who insisted upon the sexual roots of neurosis. Jung was more interested in the archetypal symbols that appeared in dreams, rather than focusing purely on what dreams revealed about personal wishes and repressed fears.

Also Jung, whose thought was deeply influenced by his own Christian background and commitment to religious humanism, believed that religion represented a fundamental element of the psychotherapeutic process as well as of life, whereas Freud insisted upon an entirely biological understanding of psychoanalysis. The paper on *Symbols of the Libido,* which appeared in 1913, marked Jung's break with Freudian theory, and the psychology that emerged afterwards focused on the division between conscious and unconscious, and on the vision of the personal unconscious as a branch on the tree of the collective unconscious. According to Jung, one could bring unconscious contents into consciousness through a process of individuation, or the journey of the soul, which he called *Heilsweg.* Jung's analytical psychology emphasized the importance in this spiritual journey of archetypal symbols, which had a universal application in human life, as well as individual symbols, appearing in waking or dreaming life.

After the break with Freud, Jung went through a period of inner disorder and seeking, during which he carried out a journey of exploration into his own unconscious mind. He published only a few works during that period, such as his *Psychology of the Unconscious,* and *VII Sermones ad Mortuos,* written in three evenings in a semi-automatic way and published anonymously. In the same period, Jung's household seemed to be bothered by ghostly entities. In his interpretation of the spiritual journey of the human being, he also drew upon Eastern philosophies and various occult ideas, such as alchemy. The supernatural was an object of preoccupation for Jung, and it played a considerable part in his life. He had visions during his childhood as well as later life, and had an experience with the spirit medium Miss S.W. that encouraged his reading into the philosophical aspects of occultism. Some of his reminiscences are recorded in *Memories, Dreams, Reflections*, an autobiographical memoir which, like *The Soul and Death*, deals with death and afterlife.

Among Jung's other most significant works are *The Theory of Psychoanalysis* (1916), *Psychological Types* (1923), *Modern Man in Search of a Soul* (1933), *Psychology and Religion* (1938), *Psychology and Alchemy* (1953), *The Interpretation of Nature and the Psyche* (1955), and *Archetypes and the Collective Unconscious* (1959).

K

Roshi Philip Kapleau (left) with spiritual director of the Rochester Zen Center, Bodhin Kjolhede
Courtesy: Rochester Zen Center

Kapleau, Philip: Philip Kapleau (b. 1909), is founder of the Zen Center of Rochester and one of the most popular Buddhist authors in the United States. Kapleau first encountered Buddhism as a court reporter in Japan for the war crimes trials in 1946. Once back in the United States he attended D. T. Suzuki's Zen philosophy lectures at Columbia University and was prompted to move to Japan in 1953 for a traditional Zen meditation training.

His first six months he trained with Soen Nakagawa Roshi at the Ryutakuji Monastery, then spent three years with Harada Roshi at the Soto Zen Monastery of Hosshin-ji. In November 1956 he began studying with Yasutani Roshi and remained with him for ten years. He experienced *kensho* (a significant state of realization) in the summer of 1958 and eventually was ordained a Zen monk and authorized to teach Zen. In 1965 he published *The Three Pillars of Zen*, one of the first detailed looks at the meditative process behind the Zen philosophy, and it became a best-seller.

Chester Carlson, founder of the Xerox Corporation and a supporter of Buddhism, read the book, helped get it into many libraries, and invited Kapleau to visit his home in Rochester, New York. In 1966 Kapleau made that visit and stayed to found the Zen Center of Rochester. Over the next twenty years half a dozen affiliate centers were begun in various places around the world. A periodical, *Zen Bow*, was founded in 1968. Kapleau maintained an active schedule of speaking and writing. In 1987 he turned over the administration of the center to a new abbot, Bodhin Kjolhede.

Kardec, Allan: The French doctor Hippolyte Leon Denizard Rivail (1804–1869) was the founder of Spiritism, also called Kerdecism, which differs from Anglo-American Spiritualism primarily because of its emphasis on reincarnationist beliefs. His pseudonym, Allan Kardec, is attributed to information he received about past lives during which his name was Allan and Kardec. This information was received through Celina Japhet, a professional somnambulist with whom he used to participate in seances.

Many scripts, produced while in trance, called for compulsory reincarnation, and *The Book of the Spirits,* published in 1856, explained these concepts. Its 1857 revision became the guidebook of spiritist philosophy, and, with Kardec's other works, *The Book of Mediums* (1864), *The Gospels According to Spiritism* (1864), *Heaven and Hell* (1865), *Genesis* (1867), *Experimental Spiritism and Spiritualist Philosophy,* and *The Four Gospels* (1881), have had a particular influence in Brazil.

According to Kardec, reincarnation through many lives is necessary to achieve spiritual progress. Also, the interference of past incarnations may be the cause of such problems as epilepsy, schizophrenia, and multiple personality disorders, so that understanding past lives may heal these disorders. This, it should be noted, is the basic premise of past-lives therapy, which Kardec anticipated by a century. Kardec encouraged the practice of healing/therapy through the acceptance of spirit communications. He also criticized contemporaneous psychical research through the monthly magazine *La Revue Spirite,* and the Society of Psychologic Studies, of which he was president.

Kawate, Bunjiro (Konko Daijin): Bunjiro Kawate (September 29, 1814–October 10, 1883), founder of Konko Kyo, a form of Shinto worship, was born Genshichi Kandori in the Bitchu Province of Japan. As the second son, he was subject to the common practice of adopting out to a family with no son for inheritance. At age eleven, he was adopted by the Kawate family in Otani and renamed Bunjiro Kawate.

His adoptive father died in 1831, leaving Kawate to run the farm and conduct the necessary community duties of the family. Kawate was very successful in these new responsibilities, adding greatly to the family assets. On December 13, 1836 he married Tose Furukawa. About that time, a visit to a Buddhist temple on Shikoki Island stirred him from his religious complacency and he became very devout in his Shinto observances.

In the 1850s some misfortunes led him to believe he may have offended Koijin, a presumably malevolent Shinto deity. A revelation came to him, however, that Koijin was actually benevolent. In 1858 he was attracted to another deity, Kane no Kami, and later received a revelation that that deity and Koijin were one and the same. In 1859, obeying further revelations, Kawate retired from his regular duties and became a full-time disciple of Tenchi-Kane no Kami, the Principal Parent of the Universe. He developed the practice of toritsugi (mediation), in which Kawate, much like a Catholic priest in confession, hears the burdens of the people and intercedes with the deity on their behalf. On May 1, 1860 he began keeping a toritsugi record book, and many consider Konko Kyo to date from that point.

Followers constructed a temple in 1861, in 1864 he was officially permitted to conduct religious services, and in 1867 was made a Shinto priest by the government. Shortly thereafter a new revelation gave him the name (Ikigami) Konko Daijin, meaning Living God of Golden Light. He emphasized sincere piety and taught that God needs people to carry out his plans. He therefore encouraged social concern activities, such as building hospitals. The basically monotheistic sect was temporarily suppressed in 1872-73, but in 1882 was named one of the thirteen approved forms of Shinto in Japan.

Keil, William: Willian Keil (March 6, 1812-December 30, 1877), founder of the Aurora and Bethel communes, was born in Prussia and grew up in Germany with little formal schooling. In 1838 he migrated to New York City, where he opened a successful tailoring shop. Dissatisfied with Lutheranism, he tried Methodism for a while, but then tired of that.

Not able to find a religious home to his liking, he determined to make one. In 1843 he sold his business and moved to an area of German immigration in western Pennsylvania, where he began gathering a community interested in following his message of love and unselfishness. Unfounded rumors, however, suggested that Keil wanted people to worship him and many therefore turned against him. More than once he faced mob violence.

In 1844 he and some loyal followers moved to a 5300-acre parcel in Shelby County, Missouri, where he could both get a fresh start and put into action his developing beliefs in the communal sharing of goods. There the Bethel community was formed, based only on the belief in God's love, shared property, and in Keil as leader. Even the shared property was not strictly adhered to, as some property owners were permitted to join. Despite such a loose bonding structure, it was very successful, and by 1855 reached 1000 inhabitants.

In about 1856 a new community, called Aurora after one of Keil's children, was added in the Willamette Valley of Oregon. Keil helped establish it, and lived in the meantime (1855 to 1857) in Portland working as a magnetic healer. The Aurora community was also very successful, reaching about 1000 inhabitants during the 1860s. Neither community, however, survived long after his death. Bethel disintegrated in 1880 and Aurora in 1881. Even so, they were two of the most successful communes of the nineteenth century.

Kelly, Aidan A.: Aidan Anthony Kelly was born October 22, 1940, to Marie Cecile Kelly, in Colon, Panama, where his father, Lieutenant John Patrick Kelly, was on his first assignment, in the U.S. Canal Zone, after graduating from West Point in 1939. After traveling around the world, the Kellys settled in Mill Valley, California, where Aidan graduated from Tamalpais High School. He was raised as a Roman Catholic, but became an agnostic in his teen years, under the influence of Bertrand Russell and Alan Rein.

Aidan studied at the University of California, Berkeley, and at San Francisco State University, from where he received a B.A. (1964) and an M.A. (1968) in Creative Writing. He worked as an editor for Stanford University Press 1964-66, and on the staff of W. H. Freeman and Company in San Francisco 1968-73. In 1967 he and other friends founded the New, Reformed, Orthodox Order of the Golden Dawn, for which Kelly created an original Book of Shadows during the next seven years.

In 1971 he married Alta Picchi, and on January 12, 1973, they became parents of a daughter, Maeve Adair Kelly. At the end of 1973 he resigned from his staff position, and became a freelancer, in order to begin a Ph.D. program at the Graduate Theological Union in Berkeley. In 1975 he helped found the Covenant of the Goddess [x-ref], serving as one of its Directors 1975-77. In 1977, to deal with some personal problems, he began working a Twelve-Step Program, and in 1978 became a practicing Roman Catholic again. He received the Ph.D. in Theology from the GTU in 1980. From 1979 to 1988 he taught at various San Francisco Bay Area schools, mainly at the University of San Francisco.

In 1988 he was divorced from Alta, became an active member of the Craft again, and with his third wife, Julie, received training and initiation in the Protean Gardnerian Lineage in New York. In 1989 they relocated to southern California, at first to Santa Barbara, where he and Julie had a son, Aidan Edward O'Ryan-Kelly, on March 21, 1990; and then to Los Angeles, where he worked on staff for Jeremy Tarcher. Recently he has been working as a freelance editor, as well as on founding his own publishing company. In 1991 he founded the Aradianic Faerie Heresy [x-ref]. In 1992 he and Julie joined the Church of All Worlds, and in 1993 became resident members of the Star City Nest. After relocating to Santa Rosa, they separated in June 1994, and Kelly returned to the Los Angeles area, where he has been working as a writer and teacher.

Kelpius, Johannes: Johannes Kelpius (1673-c.February 1708), founder of the Society of Woman in the Wilderness, was born in Halwegen, Transylvania. He was orphaned in childhood, but was able to make the most of his gifted intelligence. He received a Ph.D. in theology from the University of Altdorf in 1689, when he was only sixteen.

He associated with scientist Johann Jacob Zimmerman, who introduced him to mystical pietists who combined science, theology, and the occult arts. These groups had gained some disfavor for lack of enthusiasm for the state church. Zimmerman decided to move to America, where they could freely set up a commune and prepare for Christ's imminent return. Zimmerman died just before the group set sail, and Kelpius became the new leader.

They arrived in Pennsylvania on June 23, 1694, and purchased land on Wissahickon Creek in Germantown. The group became popularly known as the Woman in the Wilderness (cf. Revelation 12:14-17) and was the first occult organization in the area of the United States. Members observed celibacy and practiced astronomy, astrology, magic, and the Bible. They provided many friendly services to the people of the area, including horoscopes, amulets, and medical assistance, and so were welcomed. Kelpius organized an education program for the area children. He negotiated a settlement of some differences among the Seventh-Day Baptists and helped dedicate the Swedish Lutheran Church at Wicacoa.

Always of frail health, he contracted tuberculosis, but continued to believe he would live to see the return of Christ. He died at the young age of thirty-five and the community soon dissipated. Its mystical ideas permeated other groups and it was influential in the founding of Irenia, or the True Church of Philadelphia or Brotherly Love about 1697 at nearby Plymouth, led by Henry Bernhard Köster.

Kent, Grady R.: Grady Kent (April 26, 1909-March 31, 1964), founder of the Church of God (Jerusalem Acres), was born in Rosebud, Georgia. Like many in that rural environment, Kent had formal education only through the third grade. At age 21 he was converted to a Holiness group, but soon became Pentecostal and joined the Church of God (Cleveland, Tennessee). He hoped the church would let him serve as minister without attending their seminary, and for a time traveled and presented himself as a Church of God preacher, until church officials found out and expelled him.

He finally found ordination in 1932 in the Church of God of Prophecy and served as an evangelist in several states. In 1938 he settled as pastor of a congregation in Georgia. There he had trouble with the Ku Klux Klan and one night almost lost his life at their hands, a story he told in his book, *Sixty Lashes at Midnight* (1963). He later moved to a Church of God of Prophecy congregation in Cleveland, Tennessee, and at the same time led the Church of God Marker Association, which sought ways of commemorating significant events in the Church of God history. He initiated the Field of the Woods site in North Carolina to honor Ambrose J. Tomlinson, founder of the Church of God of Prophecy and hero to Kent.

In 1957 Kent left the Church of God of Prophecy, upset with changes made by Tomlinson's successors, and founded with 300 supporters the Church of God (Jerusalem Acres) in Cleveland, Tennessee. He felt the end times were near and banned Christmas, Halloween, and Easter as pagan festivals. The birth of Christ was celebrated in October. He coined the term "New Testament Judaism" in 1962 to refer to the church's incorporation of Hebraic symbols and practices.

Ketcham, Robert Thomas: Robert Ketcham (July 22, 1889–August 21, 1978), a founder of the General Association of Regular Baptist Churches, was born in Nelson, Pennsylvania. He left home at age sixteen and never finished high school. At age 20 he experienced a call to ministry and in 1912 became the pastor of the First Baptist Church in Roulette, Pennsylvania. He married Clara Ketcham, who died in 1920. He was ordained in 1915 and went on to serve other churches in Pennsylvania.

Ketcham identified solidly as a fundamentalist, resisting any modernist or liberal moves to alter traditional ideas concerning such things as the virgin birth of Jesus or biblical inerrancy. In 1919 he saw liberal tendencies in a program of the Northern Baptist Convention (now the American Baptist Churches in the U.S.A.) called the New World Movement and wrote a pamphlet that made him well-known in fundamentalist circles, *A Statement of the First Baptist Church, Butler, Pennsylvania, with Reference to the New World Movement and the $100,000,000 Drive*. In 1922 he married Mary Smart.

About that time he began serving churches in Ohio and in 1923 attempted to unify fundamentalist individuals with the Bible Baptist Union. In 1932 the Bible Baptist Union was replaced by the General Association of Regular Baptist Churches. Although he was not present at its first meeting, he was a guiding force, becoming its leader in 1934 and remaining so until 1960. He pastored the prestigious Walnut Street Baptist Church in Waterloo, Iowa, from 1939 to 1946 and worked full-time for the association, editing *The Baptist Bulletin* from 1938 to 1955. He had a heart attack in 1960 and his long struggle with an eye affliction called keratocoma steadily worsened. From 1960 until his retirement in 1966 he was the association's national consultant.

Hazrat Inayat Khan
Courtesy: Sufi Order International

Khan, Hazrat Inayat: Hazrat Inayat Khan (July 5, 1882-February 2, 1927), founder of the Sufi Order, was born in India. At age twelve he left home to pursue a musical career. After some time he became a court musician for the Nizam of Hyderabad, and joined the Chishti (Sufi) Order, one of the larger Indian Sufi groups. Eventually Khan received the mantle of succession from Murshid Khwaja Abu Hashim Madani and he embarked on a pilgrimage of India. While in Calcutta he founded a music school, but did not settle there, as he decided that his mission was to introduce Sufism to the West in the hope of bringing greater unity to the world.

Khan left for New York City on September 13, 1910, and became a lecturer in music and Sufism at Columbia University. When time permitted, he lectured across the country. At a lecture in Berkeley, California, he gained his first convert, Mrs. Ada Martin, whom he gave the initiate name of Rabia, and soon there were numerous followers in various cities. In Nyack, New York, he met Ora Ray Baker, the cousin of Church of Christ, Scientist founder Mary Baker Eddy. Because of her family's objections, they had to pursue the relationship abroad, and they were married in England on March 20, 1913.

Khan decided to stay for a time in England, founding the Sufi Order in London in 1916, and eventually a quarterly magazine, *Sufism*. This was the first Sufi organization in Europe and the first in the United States as well. After World War I he moved the headquarters to France and visited the United States with lecture tours in 1923 and 1925. In 1926 he built the Universal Temple in Suresnes, France, to signify his belief that all religions are basically one.

His unexpected death the following year on a visit to India raised problems of succession. Most in the United States followed Rabia Martin, who had become a murshid. Most in Europe followed Khan's surviving family members, who did not accept Martin's leadership. They waited for his son, Pir Vilayat Inayat Khan, then eleven years old, to complete his training and take control of the organization. In the 1960s he reintroduced the Sufi Order in the West to America, as the Martin branch had gone in a different direction and reorganized as Sufism Reoriented.

Pir Vilayat Inayat Khan
Phot by: Valerie and Prasad

Khan, Pir Vilayat Inayat: Pir Vilayat Inayat Khan is the head of the Sufi Order International. ("Pir" is a title designating the living leader of a Sufi School.) The Sufi Order International was founded in 1910 by Vilayat Inayat Khan's father, Hazrat Inayat Khan, who believed that his "Sufi Message" of the modern era could unite East and West through its teachings of universal brotherhood, attunement to cosmic principles of unity, and the awakening of humanity to the divinity within.

Vilayat, Hazrat's oldest son, attended the Sorbonne, and studied musical composition with Nadia Boulanger. After World War II, having served minesweeper duty with the Royal Navy, Pir Vilayat began his quest for the techniques of spiritual attainment. After long pilgrimages and retreats with the great dervishes and rishis of Indian and the Holy Land, he was confirmed as Pir by a council of Chisti Pirs. Taking up his father's mantle, his lectures and seminars in the U.S. and Europe inspired a resurgence of interest in the teachings of Inayat Khan. The Sufi Order grew rapidly during the 1960s and 1970s.

During the 1970s, the Sufi Order purchased a Shaker village in New Lebanon, New York. This site, renamed the Abode of the Message, continues to be a spiritual hub of Sufi Order activities, and is home to Omega

Publications which publishes and distributes much of the writings of Inayat Khan and Pir Vilayat. The esoteric school of the Order utilizes the traditional teacher/disciple (murshid/mureed) structure of traditional Sufism.

The North American Secretariat of the Order, located in Seattle, Washington, publishes *Heart & Wings*, a quarterly newsletter, recent updates on the teachings of Pir Vilayat, and provides support to centers throughout North America. Pir Vilayat resides in Suresnes, a suburb of Paris. Pir Vilayat is the author of *The Message in our Time*, *Toward the One*, *The Call of the Dervish*, *Introducing Spirituality into Therapy and Counselling*, and *That Which Transpires Behind That Which Appears*.

George King
Courtesy: Aetherius Society

King, George: George King (1919-1997) was the founder of the Aetherius Society, probably the most well-known flying-saucer religion. Born in Wellington, Shropshire, England, King developed a deep interest in the occult and, it is said, became a master of yoga. In May 1954, he received a command from interplanetary sources to become "the Voice of Interplanetary Parliament." Subsequently, he continually received trance messages and/or telepathic communications from various beings, mainly from different planets in the solar system.

The Aetherius Society was founded in London in 1955. King visited the United States in 1959, where he established a center in Los Angeles to serve as the North American headquarters for the work of the Society. His eminence Dr. George King, as the members of the Society usually addressed him, was lavished with innumerable titles, academic degrees, and honors. He also authored many books.

The Society publishes Dr. King's books and taped lectures, a newsletter, *The Cosmic Voice*, which has been in print since 1956, and a quarterly *Journal of Spiritual and Natural Healing* which, a few years ago, was replaced with *The Aetherius Society Newsletter*. This newsletter covers many topics, including information from the Society's headquarters and various branches, activities of members, and columns on the Cosmic Teachings.

King, Joseph Hillery: Joseph Hillery King (August 11, 1869-April 23, 1946), leader of the Pentecostal Holiness Church, was born into a large, poverty-stricken family in rural South Carolina. At age sixteen he experienced conversion and then sanctification, joining the Methodist Church as a Holiness advocate (believing in sanctification as a second act of grace, eliminating one's inherent sinful nature).

In the late 1880s King became interested in the ministry, and after a period of military service and then marriage to Willie Irene King in 1890, began to pursue that career. His wife was opposed to that kind of life, however, and the marriage soon ended. Beginning in 1892 he served a number of pastorates and attended the School of Theology at U.S. Grant University in Chattanooga, Tennessee. Upon graduation in 1897 he left Methodism for the Fire-Baptized Holiness Association. By 1900, after two years evangelizing in Canada, King was in Iowa as assistant to the leader, Benjamin Irwin. About that time a scandal caused Irwin to leave the church and King was elected general superintendent and editor of the church's periodical, *Live Coals of Fire.*

In 1907 King accepted Pentecostalism and eventually persuaded the entire church to accept it as a new way of experiencing "fire-baptism." In 1911 he began a two-year world mission tour, though still managed to negotiate a merger with the Pentecostal Holiness Church that year, which name the new group took. King was named assistant general superintendent and head of the mission board. From 1917 to his death he was general superintendent of the Pentecostal Holiness Church. In 1920 he married a second time, to Blanche Leon Moore. Under his leadership the church, distinctive among Pentecostals for its insistence on the need for a prior experience of sanctification, became a significant religious force.

Klemp, Sri Harold: Sri Harold Klemp is the current spiritual leader of Eckankar, the Religion of the Light and Sound of God, that was founded by Paul Twitchell in 1965.

Klemp grew up on a Wisconsin farm. During his youth, he attended a two-room country schoolhouse. He attended high school at a religious boarding school in Milwaukee, Wisconsin. Following college training as a preministerial student in Milwaukee and Ft. Wayne, Indiana, he enlisted in the U.S. Air Force. There he trained as a language specialist at the University of Indiana and as a radio intercept operator at Goodfellow AFB, Texas. Then followed a two-year stint in Japan when he first encountered Eckankar.

In October 1981, he became the spiritual leader of Eckankar. In this role, his full title is Sri Harold Klemp, the Mahanta, the Living ECK Mas-

Sri Harold Klemp
The Mahanta, the Living ECK Master
Courtesy: Sri Harold Klemp

ter. As the Living ECK Master, Klemp is responsible for the continued evolution of Eckankar's teachings. His stated mission to help people find their way back to God in this lifetime. He has written many books, discourses, and articles about the spiritual life.

Among the over 30 books Klemp has written to date are *The Wind of Change, Soul Travelers of the Far Country, Child in the Wilderness,* and *The Living Word,* books 1 and 2. Also included are *The Book of ECK Parables,* volumes 1-4; *The Spiritual Exercises of ECK, Ask the Master,* books 1 and 2; *The Dream Master; We Come as Eagles; The Drumbeat of Time;* and *The Slow Burning Love of God.* He has also written many series of twelve-month discourse lessons for those who take up the teachings of Eckankar. Among these are *The Easy Way Discourses, The ECK Dream 1 Discourses, The ECK Dream 2 Discourses, The Master 3 Discourses,* and *Letters of Light & Sound 1 and 2.*

Each year Klemp speaks at Eckankar international seminars. He has visited many parts of North America, Europe, the South Pacific, Africa, Australia, and New Zealand, meeting with spiritual seekers and giving inspirational talks around the world. There are more than 60 videocassettes and 116 audiocassettes of his public talks available.

Knapp, Martin Wells: Martin Knapp (March 27, 1853-December 7, 1901), founder of the International Holiness Union and Prayer League, was born in Clarendon, Michigan. He was raised a Methodist, but did not give it much attention until he met Lucy Glenn at Albion College. Under her guidance he experienced conversion and soon felt the call to preach. They married in 1877 and he began serving Methodist Episcopal churches in Michigan.

In the early 1880s Knapp discovered the holiness movement, which taught a post-conversion experience of sanctification that cleansed one of sin in preparation for a life of love. After his own experience of sanctification, he oriented his ministry toward holiness. In 1887 he took a leave from congregation ministry to try evangelism and running a periodical, *The Revivalist.* However, his wife's ill health (she died in 1890) and other problems prevented much success.

In 1892 he moved to Cincinnati, married Minnie C. Ferle, and started the periodical again. In 1894 he started Beulah Heights School on property near Flat Rock, Kentucky, and held annual camp meetings there. In 1897 he began a congregation in Cincinnati, still under the authority of the Methodist Episcopal Church. He was a primary agent (with Seth Cook Rees) in creating the International Holiness Union and Prayer League that year, intended as a holiness support group. Under increasing pressure from the Methodist Episcopal Church, no longer favorably inclined toward the holiness movement, he took an early retirement in 1899.

In 1900 Knapp founded God's Bible School and placed it on a secure footing before his death from typhoid fever in 1901. The school and other aspects of his work lived on in the International Holiness Union and Prayer League, which became its own denomination and ultimately became a constituent part of the Wesleyan Church.

J.Z. Knight
Courtesy: J.Z. Knight

Knight, J. Z.: J. Z. Knight (b. March 16, 1946), well-known New Age channel, was born in Dexter, New Mexico. Her birth name was Judith Darlene Hampton and her parents, farm laborers, raised her as a fundamentalist Baptist. At the Artesia High School in Artesia, New Mexico, she was a popular figure, and even was elected rodeo queen. She married Otis Henley, with whom she had two sons.

After she divorced Henley she married Jeremy Burnett, a dentist, and, in 1977, while experimenting with the presumed powers of pyramids to do such things as help preserve foods, she had her first vision of Ramtha, who indicated he was there to guide her to enlightenment. Uncertain about the experience, she contacted spiritualist Lorraine Graham, who helped her understand that Ramtha was a spiritual entity she was spontaneously channeling. After some more sessions with Ramtha she decided to share him with the public, and had her first public channeling on December 17, 1978. Soon she was traveling and holding workshops across the United States.

Ramtha is described as a 35,000 year old warrior from the now submerged continent of Lemuria in the Pacific Ocean. He had avoided death by discovering how to alter his body into light vibrations. Traveling to India, he later became the source of the stories of the avatar Rama. His teachings are those common to the New Age movement, emphasizing the divine nature within each person and the power of beliefs to create reality.

Knight's channeling of Ramtha became extraordinarily popular and her life was completely changed. She appeared on numerous talk shows and gained the endorsement of such Hollywood stars as Shirley MacLaine. She received some criticism for the high cost of her workshops. She also received criticism from the anti-cult movement after a group of devoted followers began living near her home in Yelm, Washington.

Knoch, Adolph Ernst: Ernst Knoch (December 12, 1874-March 28, 1965), founder of the *Unsearchable Riches* periodical and author of the Concordant Version of the Bible, was born in St. Louis, Missouri and moved to Los Angeles at age ten. As an adult he entered a career as a printer, married Olive Elizabeth Hyde, and affiliated with the Plymouth (Open) Brethren.

A serious student of the Bible, Knoch began to come to some conclusions at variance with the Brethren, and was excommunicated from them about 1900. In 1906 he published in *Things To Come*, a British journal run by dispensationalist scholar Ethelbert W. Bullinger, an article on spirit baptism as superseding water baptism. This began an association with Bullinger and another reader of that journal, Vladimir Galesnoff (d. 1921). In October 1909 Knoch and Galesnoff began publishing *Unsearchable Riches*, a magazine covering Knoch's theology and his progress in writing the Concordant Version of the Bible. The goal of the Concordant Version was to create a literal translation of the Bible, limited only by decent grammatical structure, wherein each original word would be assigned a standard English word.

Knoch published the Concordant Version of Revelation in 1919 and finished the New Testament in 1926, the year his wife died. During a long trip to Germany and the Holy Land to prepare for Old Testament work, he met and married (1932) Countess Sigrid von Kanitz. He stayed in Germany to work on a German Concordant Version and returned to the United States in 1939. He finally finished the Old Testament Concordant Version, but most of it was published posthumously.

While scholars did not embrace the Concordant Version, it became influential in many circles, particularly those related to *Unsearchable Riches*, which is still published today. Theologically, he helped spread the popularity of dispensational thinking, which divides God's methods of dealing with humans into about seven periods. Knoch differed from many in teaching universal salvation and Saturday as the sabbath.

Koresh, David: David Koresh, leader of the Branch Davidians, was born Vernon Howell. An illegitimate child, he dropped out of high school in 1974 before completing the 10th grade. His passions as a teenager were playing guitar and studying the Bible. In the years that followed, he held a succession of short-term, menial jobs, devoting most of his attention to playing the guitar and restoring cars.

In 1979, Vernon Howell began participating in study sessions at a Seventh-Day Adventist Church in Tyler, Texas, that his mother attended. Howell learned of the Branch Davidians from an SDA friend and began working as a handyman at Mt. Carmel in 1981. He became a favorite of the Davidian leader, 67-year-old Lois Roden. Rumors began circulating that the two were lovers. The relationship elevated Howell's status with the group and gained for Lois Roden an ally in her struggle with her son, George Roden, for control of the Branch Davidians.

Lois Roden attempted to resolve the power struggle by naming Howell as her successor and inviting Branch Davidian adherents to come to Mt. Carmel to listen to his teachings and prophecies. Howell was able to attract young adults to the group due to his own youthful demeanor and his musical and automotive interests. This was something that the Rodens had been unable to do. Converts point to Howell's biblical knowledge more than any other single factor in explaining their own attraction to the Branch Davidians.

Vernon Howell enunciated his controversial "New Light" doctrine in 1989. He asserted that as a messiah, he became the perfect mate of all the female adherents. Part of his mission was to create a new lineage of God's children from his own seed. These children would ultimately rule the world. In 1990 Vernon Howell legally adopted the name David Koresh. "Koresh" is Hebrew for Cyrus, the Persian king who defeated the Babylonians 500 years before the birth of Jesus.

Acting on rumors that the Davidians were illegally modifying firearms, a force of 76 agents of the ATF raided the Branch Davidian commmunity on February 28, 1993. The raid turned into a shoot-out between federal agents and Branch Davidians. The resulting standoff turned into a 51-day siege that ended on April 19 when federal agents launched a new attack on the Davidian complex. During the second assault, a fire ignited in the buildings and over 80 members died, including David Koresh.

Krishnamurti, Jiddu: Jiddu Krishna-murti (May 11, 1895-February 17, 1986), born of middle-class Brahmin parents, was acclaimed at age fourteen by the Theosophists as the coming World Teacher. He was made head

J. Krishnamurti
© *Karsh, Ottawa*

of Annie Besant's newly formed worldwide religious organization, the Order of the Star in the East, in 1911. But, in 1929, after many years of questioning, he dissolved the Order, repudiated its claims and returned all assents given to him for its purpose.

Krishnamurti claimed allegiance to no caste, nationality or religion, and considered himself bound by no tradition. He traveled the world and spoke spontaneously to large audiences until his passing at age ninety. He asserted that human beings have to free themselves of all fear, conditioning, authority and dogma through self-knowledge, and that this will bring about order and psychological transformation. The conflict-ridden violent world cannot be transformed into a life of goodness, love and compassion by any political, social or economic strategies. It can be changed only through the transformation in individuals brought about through their own observation without any guru or organized religion. The rejection of all spiritual and psychological authority, including his own, was a fundamental theme of his teaching.

In establishing the many schools he founded in India, England, and the U.S., Krishnamurti envisioned that education should emphasize the integral cultivation of the mind and the heart, not mere academic intelligence. For decades he engaged in dialogues with teachers and students to emphasize the understanding that it is only unconditioned mind that truly learns.

The Krishnamurti Foundation of America was established as a charitable trust in 1969. The main purposes of the foundation are the administration of the Oak Grove School; the maintenance of the Krishnamurti Archives and Library; the production, publication and distribution of Krishnamurti books, videocassettes, films and audio recordings; the sponsorship of workshops, retreats, annual gatherings and of videotape showings for interested groups throughout the country, including on cable television.

Kuhlman, Kathryn: Kathryn Kuhlman (May 7, 1907-February 20, 1976), faith healer and founder of the Kathryn Kuhlman Foundation, was born in Concordia, Missouri. She grew up attending both Methodist and Baptist churches and experienced conversion at age fourteen. After two years of high school she dropped out and headed west, preaching primarily to Baptists.

About 1930 she made her way to Denver, Colorado, and her preaching was so impressive that she was offered the pastorate of the Denver Revival Tabernacle. To enable this, she was ordained by the Evangelical Church Alliance. In 1938 she married fellow evangelist Burroughs Waltrip, but they divorced several years later. Unable at that point to remain in that congregation, Kuhlman moved to pastor a small church in Franklin, Pennsylvania. Within several months a woman was reportedly healed of a tumor and a man of blindness. Kuhlman promptly shifted the focus of her ministry to this new phenomenon and her following grew quickly.

In 1947 she began holding her weekly services in Carnegie Auditorium in Pittsburgh, and soon added regular services in Youngstown, Ohio and Los Angeles, California. A radio program added to her audience, and she traveled widely as a popular speaker. Her first book, *I Believe in Miracles* (1962), was a best-seller and provided a platform for a weekly television show that began soon thereafter and continued until her death. She also created the Kathryn Kuhlman Foundation, which supported overseas radio stations, foreign missions, and various other ministries.

Kuhlman's magnetic style and remarkable abilities made her one of the most famous healers of her day. Her services were marked by spontaneous healings, as reported by those who were invited on stage to testify to their healing. She died from a long bout with heart disease.

Kushi, Michio: Michio Kushi (b. 1926), teacher of macrobiotics and founder of the East West Foundation, was born in Wakayama Province, Japan. His father was a university professor who saw to it that his son received a higher education as well, at Tokyo University. He was too young to enter the military during World War II and was able to continue his studies.

After the war, Kushi joined the World Federalist Movement, a group striving for world peace. About the same time he encountered George Ohsawa, founder of the macrobiotic philosophy, which combines a certain kind of vegetarian diet with an ancient Asian world view based on balancing the universal forces of yin and yang. In 1949, with the help of the World Federalist Movement, Kushi traveled to the United States. He became a student at Columbia University and worked with Herman and Cornelia Aihara to build a macrobiotics following through the Ohsawa Foundation. He married Tomoko Yokohama, today known as Aveline Kushi.

In 1965 a woman following a strict form of the diet died and the organization fell upon troubled times. Then in 1966 Ohsawa died and Kushi decided to go independent. He founded the Order of the Universe Publications and in 1967 began a periodical, *The Order of the Universe*. In 1968 he opened a macrobiotic restaurant and founded another periodical of more general interest, *East West Journal*. In 1972 he created the East West Foundation to oversee all of his work and in 1977 he began the Kushi Institute in Beckett, Massachusetts, primarily geared toward training macrobiotic leaders.

By the 1980s there were about a dozen affiliated centers across the United States and more abroad. In 1986 he returned to his World Federalist Movement interests by beginning the One Peaceful World campaign, aimed a promoting a peaceful lifestyle at the local community and individual levels.

L

Lake, John Graham: John Lake (March 18, 1870-September 16, 1935), independent Pentecostal healer, was born into a large Methodist family in Ontario, Canada. In 1890 he moved to Chicago and in 1891 became a Methodist Episcopal minister, though he did not take a church position and started a newspaper and insurance business instead. In 1898 he married Jenny Stevens and soon became a convert of John Alexander Dowie, whom he credited with healing his wife, brother, and sister of various ailments. He moved to Zion, Illinois, where Dowie built his spiritual community, and worked as the building manager while still maintaining his insurance work.

In 1904 the Zion commune was beginning to fall apart and Lake moved back to Chicago, where his business expanded successfully. He served as a lay healing evangelist on the side and in 1907 was converted to Pentecostalism. This gave him new energy for religious work and the following year he gave up his business and moved to Africa as a missionary. He became pastor of the Apostolic Tabernacle in Johannesburg in 1910 and returned to the United States after his wife's death in 1912. He married Florence Switzer in 1913 and founded the Apostolic Church in Spokane, Washington, in 1914. Over the next twenty years he established branch churches in Portland and San Diego and was instrumental in launching the career of Gordon Lindsey.

Larson, Christian Daa: Christian Larson (1874-?) was an influential New Thought author and editor. Little is known of his early life. In January 1901 he founded the New Thought Temple in Cincinnati, Ohio. It began offering Sunday morning services in November 1902. In 1907 he resigned to write full-time and was succeeded by George Milton Hammel, a former

Methodist minister. The church reached its greatest height under the leadership of Leila Simon from 1912 to 1918, when its regular attendance of 1,100 to 1,500 made it the largest New Thought Sunday audience in America.

Despite such a significant church-building beginning, it was his writing that gave Larson his lasting claim to fame. In September 1901, soon after he founded the New Thought Temple, he produced the first issue of *Eternal Progress*, a New Thought magazine that quickly became very popular. The magazine stated that it would be devoted to "those principles, laws, and scientific facts that are directly conducive to the development of genius, superiority, and worth." In 1909 the magazine's name changed to *Progress Magazine* and continued its run until February 1916, with a brief reappearance in 1920 and 1921.

He wrote over thirty books, placing him among the more prolific of the New Thought authors. He followed a common business/success orientation, with such titles as *Mastery of Fate* (1907) and *Thinking for Results* (1911). Larson's popularity and influence were shown by his being elected an honorary president of the 1916 New Thought Congress in Chicago. In addition to his periodical and book writing, he offered correspondence courses for the more serious of his widespread followers. Ernest Holmes, founder of Religious Science, was one of his correspondence students about 1913. In 1929 Larson was named associate editor of the Religious Science organ, *Science of Mind*, and remained in that position for a number of years.

LaVey, Anton: Anton LaVey (b. April 11, 1930), founder of the Church of Satan, was born Howard Anton Szander LaVey in Chicago, Illinois. His father was a traveling salesman and the family moved to San Francisco while LaVey was still an infant. As a teenager he studied various avenues of the occult, as well as hypnotism and music. He dropped out of high school to join the Clyde Beatty Circus and worked as a calliope player and big cat trainer, later learning stage magic as well.

He married in 1950 and about that time took a job as a police photographer, but in 1955 returned to organ playing. He obtained a divorce in 1960 in order to marry Diane Hegarty. Drawing on his circus and occult backgrounds, he began to conduct "midnight magic seminars" at his house. This proved popular enough for him to found the Church of Satan on April 30, 1966. His showmanship encouraged significant media coverage of such events as the first Satanic wedding and the first Satanic funeral, worship with a nude woman lying on the altar, and his small role as the Devil in the movie "Rosemary's Baby."

While anti-cult groups have made much of the Church of Satan, it is not the dangerous group it has sometimes been made out to be. The church is not interested in such things as blood sacrifice and does not condone the breaking of laws established for the common good. LaVey in fact denies the actual existence of Satan, instead suggesting that Satan is a mythical figure representing sensual indulgence, unrestricted wisdom, and basic animal vitality. After the group suffered from organizational splintering in the mid-1970s, it reorganized with a much lower public profile. LaVey passed away in 1997.

C. W. Leadbeater in 1931
Courtesy: American Religion Collection

Leadbeater, Charles Webster: C.W. Leadbeater (February 16, 1854-March 1, 1934), a leader in the Theosophical Society and a bishop of the Liberal Catholic Church, was born in Stockport, Cheshire, England. His father, a railroad employee, died when Leadbeater was still young, and the family was thus unable to afford a college education. His uncle, W. W. Capes, a reader in ancient history at Queen's College in Oxford, arranged for him to have the training necessary to be an Anglican priest.

Leadbeater was ordained on December 21, 1879 and appointed to Cape's Church at Bramshott, Hampshire. Pursuing an interest in psychic phenomena, he discovered the Theosophical Society and its leader, Helena P. Blavatsky. He joined in late 1883 and soon received letters from Koot Hoomi, one of Theosophy's spiritual masters, advising him to join Blavatsky at the headquarters in India. This he did, arriving in early 1885, and was rewarded with the positions of recording secretary and editor of *The Theosophist* magazine. After Blavatsky's death in 1891 he became good friends with her successor, Annie Besant, and often toured with her.

In 1906 he was charged with sexual improprieties in relation to a group of boys in his care at the headquarters and was forced to resign his positions. He remained a part of the society only because of Besant's friendship. A couple of years later he became convinced that another boy who had come to live at the headquarters, Jiddu Krishnamurti, was the promised world teacher. By 1909 he had also convinced Besant, who brought him back to an official position in order to work with Krishnamurti. Krishnamurti's father objected to these new proceedings and sued to regain custody, renewing sexual molestation charges against Leadbeater. The society won in court, but Leadbeater was forced to leave.

In 1914 he moved to Sydney, Australia, where he met James I. Wedgwood, a founder of the Liberal Catholic Church, which combined Catholicism and Theosophy. Wedgwood consecrated him Regionary Bishop for Australia on July 22, 1916, and in the following years Leadbeater wrote key theological works for the church. From 1923 until his death he was presiding bishop of the church.

LeBaron, Ervil Morrell: Ervil LeBaron (February 22, 1925-August 16, 1981), founder of the Church of the Lamb of God, was born in Colonia Juarez, Chihuahua, Mexico. The LeBaron family was excommunicated from the Church of Jesus Christ of Latter-day Saints in 1944 for a number of reasons, including continued advocacy of polygamy. The family then aligned itself with other polygamy leaders, Joseph Musser, Rulon Allred and Margarito Bautista. Bautista baptized Ervil and his brother Joel in 1951.

In 1955 Joel had a revelation that he was the "One Mighty and Strong" the Mormon founder Joseph Smith, Jr. had prophesied would come at a time of need to set things straight (*Doctrines and Covenants* 85). Joel founded the Church of the First Born of the Fulness of Time and appointed Ervil president of the Mexican missions. In 1961 Ervil became patriarch, second in power only to Joel.

Over time, Ervil became more and more controversial within the church, advocating civil enforcement of church attendance and exercising autocratic authority over church members. Joel removed him from the patriarch office in 1969 and, after Ervil threatened violence, excommunicated him in 1971. Ervil publicly suggested that such treatment deserved death, and on August 20, 1972, his followers killed Joel. Ervil was sentenced to twelve years for this, but served only one year before a higher court reversed the ruling. In 1975 an associate of Joel's, Dean Vest, was killed and Ervil was again convicted, serving eight months in prison.

About this time Ervil founded his own organization, the Church of the Lamb of God, but still seemed obsessed with his rivals. He ordered the death of Rulon Allred in 1977, was captured by the authorities in 1979, and sentenced to life in prison. He died of a heart attack about two years later in Utah State Prison. His church is now apparently defunct.

LeBaron, Joel Franklin: Joel LeBaron (July 9, 1923-August 20, 1972), founder of the Church of the First Born of the Fulness of Times, was born in Laverkin, Utah. His family followed Mormon belief, but also believed in polygamy, which the Church of Jesus Christ of Latter-day Saints had formally disavowed in 1890. Shortly after Joel's birth the family moved to Colonia Juarez, Mexico, to facilitate following a polygamous lifestyle.

In 1944 the LeBaron family was excommunicated from the Church of Jesus Christ of Latter-day Saints and connected with other Mormon polygamists such as Rulon Clark Allred and Margarito Bautista, both of the United Order Effort (later the Apostolic United Brethren). Bautista baptized Joel and his brother Ervil in 1951, and the same year Joel married Magdalena Soto. In 1955 Joel had a vision of his identity as the "One Mighty and Strong" prophesied (*Doctrines and Covenants* 85) by Joseph Smith, Jr., founder of Mormonism, who would come to set the church on the proper path. He thereupon founded the Church of the First Born in the Fulness of Times and appointed his brother Ervil as head of the Mexican mission.

One of Joel's doctrinal emphases was that Christ would return only in response to the obedience of a community of people. To this end he thought that the Ten Commandments should be the basis of civil order, and even forged an interfaith organization, the Alliance for Pastors and Christian Teachers (now called the Christian Judaic Evangelical Brotherhood) of others who felt the same way. His brother Ervil, since 1961 in the position of patriarch in the church, became increasingly autocratic and unstable, and in 1969 Joel removed him from the patriarch office. In 1971, after threats of violence from Ervil, Joel excommunicated him. The following year Ervil's followers killed Joel. Ervil was convicted, served some time in jail, and was released only to oversee more killings. Ervil eventually died in jail in 1981. Joel's church was taken over by another brother, Verlan LeBaron.

Lee, Ann: Ann Lee (February 29, 1736-September 8, 1784), founder of the group commonly called Shakers, was born Ann Lee in Manchester, England. As a teenager she went to work in a textile mill. In 1758 she joined an ecstatic "Shaking Quakers" group that included dancing, speaking in tongues, and belief in the imminent return of Christ. On January 5, 1762, she married Abraham Stanley, a blacksmith trained by her father, who arranged the marriage. The relationship was poor and tragic; all four children died, three of them at birth. Lee interpreted it all as a judgment upon her sins.

In 1770 she reported a vision of Jesus, who told her that human sin was based on sexual activity. She began to preach and attracted some followers. She was arrested several times and in 1774 sailed for America with her husband, brother, and six disciples. Her husband tired of the celibate lifestyle and soon left. In 1776 they settled on land near Niskeyuna, New York. Lee maintained a low profile during the Revolutionary War, but her pacifism led to another brief arrest. Later, she traveled widely, preaching equality of the sexes, abolition of slavery, pacifism, confession of sin, and a celibate communalism.

By the time of her death, eleven communities had been founded. The name formally was the United Society of Believers in Christ's Second Appearance, but was commonly called the Shakers. Members believed that Mother Ann Lee was, in fact, the second coming of Christ, in the form of Holy Mother Wisdom. The term "Shakers" came from the ecstatic form of worship, which was not individual frenzy, but stylized dance and motion. The communities included men and women, but no romantic involvements were allowed. Numeric growth came from conversion of outsiders and from rearing orphans, who often chose to stay upon reaching maturity. Just before the Civil War there were 19 communities with as many as 6,000 Shakers. The handful that remain today have an agreement not to admit new members, but to let it die out naturally, having fulfilled its function.

Lee, Gloria: Gloria Lee (March 22, 1926-December 2, 1962) was founder of the Cosmon Research Foundation, one of the first UFO contactee groups. She was born in Los Angeles, California and for a time was a child star in Hollywood. As an adult she became an airline stewardess at Los Angeles International Airport. She married William Byrd in 1952 and shifted her career to that of ground hostess. In November of that year George Adamski became the first person to prominently advertise contact with extraterrestrials, and in September 1953 Lee experienced alien-directed automatic writing at the airport.

Lee joined a number of psychic and occult groups in an effort to find out more about her experience, and continued to receive messages, sometimes telepathically from J. W., identified as a resident of Jupiter. In 1959 she founded the Cosmon Research Foundation and published *Why We Are Here!*, a book containing her conclusions about the meaning of her contact. She was basically theosophical in orientation, except that the "Ascended Masters" had become a hierarchy of space leaders.

In 1960 Lee visited Mark-Age, a new contactee group in Florida, and became closely involved with them. In September 1962, after being given plans for a spaceship by J. W., Lee went to Washington, D. C. to discuss the plans with government officials. Following J. W.'s instructions, she began a fruit juice fast and waited in a hotel for officials to visit. None did, and she died of her fast on December 2. On December 12, Mark-Age psychic

Yolanda claimed to have contacted her. The following month, Verity, a New Zealand psychic, also claimed contact, and spoke of her continuing life among the space beings.

Lefebvre, Marcel: Marcel Lefebvre (November 29, 1905-March 25, 1991), founder of the Society of St. Pius X, was born in Switzerland. He was ordained a Roman Catholic priest in 1929 and spent many years in Africa as a missionary. After World War II he elected to stay in Africa, becoming vicar-apostolic of Dakar in 1947 and apostolic delegate for French-speaking Africa in 1948. In 1955 he became Archbishop of Dakar and in that capacity served on the Central Preparatory Commission of Vatican II.

In 1962 Lefebvre was appointed Bishop of Tulle, France, and observed with interest the workings of Vatican II (1962-65). When it rejected the work of his commission and instituted many liberalizing changes, Lefebvre was disheartened and decided to retire in 1968 (from his current post as Superior General of the Holy Ghost Fathers). So many traditionalist seminary students sought him out in retirement that, with the approval of local bishops, he finally agreed to open a traditionalist seminary, the Fraternite Sacerdotale de Saint Pius X, first at the University of Fribourg, then moving to Econe, Canton of Valais, Switzerland.

The seminary became very popular and Lefebvre achieved renown as a champion of Catholic traditionalism, but by 1975 the hierarchy felt that such a seminary was undermining the authority of Vatican II and thus approval of the seminary was withdrawn. Although he closed the seminary he persisted in teaching students and in June 1976 performed unauthorized ordinations for 13 of them. Pope Paul VI suspended his priestly credentials on July 22 and for a number of years Lefebvre and the Vatican jousted with no clear culmination. He was finally excommunicated by Pope Paul II on June 30, 1988 and consecrated four bishops to continue his work, known in the United States as the Society of St. Pius X. It has become the largest of the traditionalist Catholic groups, with about 300 priests and as many as 100,000 adherents around the world, 15,000 of them in the United States. Franz Schmidberger succeeded Lefebvre upon his death in Martigny, Switzerland.

Lenz, Frederick (Rama): Rama (b. February 9, 1950), sometimes called Zen Master Rama, founder of the Rama Seminars, was born Frederick Lenz in San Diego, California. At age two the family moved to Stamford, Connecticut, where his father eventually became mayor. He received a B.A. from the University of Connecticut, then a Ph.D. in 1979 from the State

University of New York. While working on his graduate degrees he was a lecturer in English at the New School for Social Research.

Meanwhile, beginning at age 18, he studied yoga under Sri Chinmoy, who gave him the name Atmananda. As Atmananda he taught yoga classes in New York. In 1979, after finishing his degree, he moved to San Diego, California, and opened a Chinmoy meditation center. The following year he closed the center, moved to Los Angeles, and founded Lakshmi, after the Hindu goddess. He quickly gained a large following after students reported that during meditation sessions he could levitate, disappear, or exude beams of light.

At first teaching under his own name, he began to emphasize his previous incarnations as a Zen master. He taught what he called Tantric Zen. In 1983 he announced his new name of Rama, to indicate his status as the ninth incarnation of Hindu god Vishnu. He has suggested that such a rare incarnation was due to the fact that the present dark age was ending and Vishnu is needed to make the transition. By 1985 he had about 800 full-time disciples in four centers--San Diego, Los Angeles, San Francisco, and Boston. To accommodate the new growth he dismantled Lakshmi and re-incorporated as Rama Seminars. He later disbanded Rama Seminars. He authored several spiritual novels, including *Surfing the Himalayas*. Rama died unexpectedly in a drowning accident near his home in 1998.

Lewis, Harvey Spencer: Harvey Lewis (November 25, 1883-August 2, 1939), founder of the Ancient and Mystical Order of the Rosae Crucis (AMORC), was born in Frenchtown, New Jersey and grew up in New York City. Although his family was Methodist, as a young man he became interested in the occult. In 1904, as he was starting a journalism career, he founded the Rosicrucian-oriented New York Institute for Psychical Research. Over the following several years he associated with various British occult groups.

In 1909 he traveled to Toulouse, France, where he was initiated by members of the International Rosicrucian Council and given authority to begin an order in the United States. By 1915 the new group was strong enough to begin issuing a periodical, *The American Rosae Crucis*, and branch groups were established. At the 1917 convention a correspondence course was approved, which enabled the organization to gain many more adherents than it otherwise could have.

On June 17, 1918, Lewis was arrested for selling fraudulent bonds and collecting money under false pretenses. The charges were dropped, but Lewis felt it prudent to move his headquarters to San Francisco. There he met

Aleister Crowley, head of the Ordo Templi Orientis (OTO), and maintained friendly relations with that group, though he did not agree with its practice of sex magick. In 1925 the headquarters was moved again to Tampa, Florida, then moved a final time in 1927 to San Jose, California.

In common with the general Rosicrucian tradition, Lewis taught the mastery of mental imaging to recreate one's reality. His many books helped popularize AMORC, which became the largest Rosicrucian organization in the world. One famous book, Lemuria, the Lost Continent of the Pacific (1931), was written under the pseudonym W. S. Cerve.

Lewis, Samuel Leonard: Samuel L. Lewis (October 18, 1896-January 15, 1971), influential Sufi leader in the United States, was born in San Francisco to Jewish parents. In 1915, at the San Francisco World's Fair, he discovered Theosophy and studied that for several years. In 1919 he joined a newly organized group led by Rabia Martin, a disciple of Hazrat Inayat Khan, founder of the Sufi Order. When Khan visited the United States in 1923, he initiated Lewis formally as a Sufi. In 1925 Khan gave Lewis the title, "Protector of the Message," and after Khan's death in 1927, Lewis worked closely with Martin, Khan's successor, in the development of the California work.

Lewis, during this same time, continued his exploration of other religious paths. He met Zen master Nyogen Senzaki in 1920, studied under him, and helped him establish centers in San Francisco (1928) and Los Angeles (1929). He sat with Shigetsu Sasaki Roshi in 1930, who recognized him as a worthy Zen teacher. In the 1930s Lewis studied yoga under Ramana Maharshi. From 1942 to 1945 Lewis served in the U.S. Army Intelligence. After Martin's death in 1947, her successor, Ivy Oneita Duce, accepted Meher Baba as the new avatar (incarnation of god) and changed the group's orientation accordingly. Lewis did not share this enthusiasm and left the group in 1949.

Lewis continued his own spiritual journey, achieving initiation by Hindu Swami Ram Dass of Kanhangad, India (1953), into Shingon Buddhism in Japan (1956), into the Naqshbandi order of Sufis in Pakistan (1956), into the Rifai and Shadhili Sufi orders in Egypt (1960-62), and into the Khalandar and Khidri-Chishti-Kadri Sufi orders of Pakistan (1960-62). He was ordained a murshid by the Chishti, Kadri, and Sabri orders.

He returned to San Francisco in 1962 and in 1966 founded a Sufi center, the Mentorgarten, in San Francisco. In 1967 he was ordained a Zen master by Kyung-Bo Seo. By this time Hazrat Inayat Khan's son, Vilayat Inayat Khan, had arrived in the United States to reestablish the Sufi Order, and in 1968 Lewis integrated his work into the new Sufi Order.

Lewis is perhaps most remembered for his use of spiritual dances, derived from the dervish dances of the Middle East. The dances and walks, often combined with patterned breathing and the repetition of mantras, were designed to lead one into a mystical state and connection with Allah. In 1977 some of his followers left the Sufi Order to found the Sufi Islamia Ruhaniat Society.

Lindsey, Gordon J.: Gordon Lindsey (June 18, 1906-April 1, 1973), founder of Christ for the Nations and the Full Gospel Fellowship of Ministers and Churches, was born in Zion, Illinois, the site of John Alexander Dowie's religious commune. That experiment fell apart soon after Lindsey's birth and his family eventually moved to the Pisgah Grande commune in southern California. That disintegrated as well and the family shifted to Portland, Oregon.

At age 14 Lindsey visited John D. Lake's Apostolic Church in Portland and heard Pentecostal founder Charles Fox Parham preach. Within days Lindsey had the Pentecostal experience of speaking in tongues and from that point decided to enter the ministry. In 1924 he moved to San Diego, where John Lake had another church, and through that connection received a large tent for evangelistic work. The next twenty years were spent as a traveling preacher and as pastor of churches in California, Washington, and Montana. He married Freda Schimpf in 1937.

In 1944 he became pastor of an Assemblies of God church in Ashland, Oregon. In 1947 he left Freda in charge of the congregation to become a manager of William Marrion Branham's healing ministry. In this capacity he founded the *Voice of Healing* magazine and in 1949 the Voice of Healing Fellowship. In 1952 Lindsey moved out on his own, creating a new headquarters for the *Voice of Healing* in Dallas. He published a steady stream of his own books and pamphlets and gathered an increasing number of likeminded clergy. In 1962 the Voice of Healing Fellowship was transformed into the Full Gospel Fellowship of Ministers and Churches. While that maintained its separate existence, in the late 1960s Lindsey changed his other Voice of Healing work into Christ for the Nations.

Lloyd, Frederick Ebenezer John: Frederick Ebenezer John Lloyd (June 5, 1859-September 11, 1933), the second leader of the American Catholic Church (after Joseph René Vilatte), was born in Milford Haven, South Wales, and grew up in England. He graduated from Dorchester Missionary College and was ordained a deacon in the Church of England in preparation for missionary work in Canada. After the required three years he decided to remain and was ordained a priest by the bishop of Quebec.

Lloyd was stationed at Levis, Quebec, until 1894, when he transferred to the Episcopal Church in the United States. He pastored St. Matthew's Episcopal Church in Bloomington, Illinois; Trinity Episcopal Church in Hamilton, Ohio; St. Mark's Episcopal Church in Cleveland, Ohio (1898-1903); and St. Peter's Episcopal Church in Uniontown, Pennsylvania. He gained a well-known name by editing the denomination's *American Church Directory* (also called *Lloyd's Clerical Directory*) for a number of years and by founding (1903) the Society of St. Philip the Apostle to train missionary priests.

In 1905 he was elected bishop coadjutor for Oregon, but objections raised by an Oregon group (the nature of which are unknown) caused him to withdraw. This incident apparently began a long period of religious searching. In 1907 he left the denomination to join the Roman Catholic Church. As he was married, there was no possibility of becoming a Roman Catholic priest, and lay status was unacceptable. So he returned after a few years and pastored Grace Episcopal Church in Oak Park, Illinois (1911-14). In 1914 he left the denomination again and the following year joined the American Catholic Church, led by Joseph René Vilatte. Vilatte consecrated him a bishop on December 29, 1915. In 1917 he married a second time, to Philena Peabody, widow of millionaire Hiram P. Peabody.

In 1920 he succeeded Vilatte as head of the American Catholic Church and over the next dozen years brought in several ex-Episcopal priests to serve as bishops. The number of faithful congregants, however, did not grow correspondingly, and the church remained small. In 1932 he turned the church over to Daniel C. Hinton.

M

Machen, John Gresham: J. Gresham Machen (July 28, 1881-January 1, 1937), prominent theologian, teacher, and founder of the Orthodox Presbyterian Church, was born in Baltimore, Maryland. He graduated from Johns Hopkins University at the age of 20, then earned a B.D. and M.A. at Princeton Theological Seminary. During a year of post-graduate studies in Germany, Machen was shaken by the new waves of biblical and religious criticism there, but managed to find ways of resolving his doubts and retained his staunchly conservative form of Presbyterianism.

Machen became a professor at Princeton Theological Seminary and over the years provided the most lucid, scholarly presentation of traditional, evangelical Protestantism over against the liberal theological perspectives. His seminal book, *Christianity and Liberalism* (1923), argued that liberal Christianity, with its reinterpretations in the light of biblical criticism and modern culture, was no longer Christianity at all, but an entirely different religion.

His position did not win the day at Princeton, however, and in 1929 the school reorganized, leaving traditionalists in the distinct minority. This, plus the publication in 1932 of *Re-Thinking Missions*, which seemed to some to emphasize social and physical needs at the expense of saving souls, led to several conservative responses. First, Westminster Theological Seminary in Philadelphia was formed as a traditionalist stronghold, then Machen and others created the Independent Board of Presbyterian Foreign Missions. Finally, after Machen's presbytery tried and convicted him of schismatic actions, he and his supporters left to found, in 1936, the Orthodox Presbyterian Church. Machen passed away shortly afterwards, but the denomination has remained in place.

Mack, Alexander, Sr.: Alexander Mack (July 1679-February 19, 1735), founder of the Church of the Brethren, was born in the Palatinate in Germany. His father, a successful miller and one-time mayor, was a prominent person in the town of Schriesheim and a member of the Reformed Church. In 1702 Mack and his brother inherited their father's mill.

Over the next several years, Mack became involved with pietists, those who rejected the formalism of the state church in favor of an emphasis on more personal religious experience. Local authorities began harassing pietist activities, and in 1706 Mack sold his half of the mill to his brother and moved to a more liberal atmosphere at Schwarzenau in Wittgenstein. In 1708 he and a small group of other pietists began focusing on the necessity of believers' (adult) baptism and rebaptized each other by a three-fold immersion. This was the beginning of what after 1908 was known as the Church of the Brethren. Until then the formal title was German Baptist Brethren, though they were commonly called "Dunkers" or "Tunkers" because of their distinctive baptism.

As the church grew, Mack was the first recognized minister. He taught that only the baptized could be admitted to the Lord's Supper (Holy Communion), which was taken in conjunction with a full meal, called a love feast, which included foot washing and other observances. He also taught pacifism. In 1720, as Wittgenstein showed signs of becoming inhospitable, Mack and many followers moved first to the Netherlands, and then in 1729 to America, where they settled in Pennsylvania and joined other Brethren who had migrated there earlier. For the rest of his career he led the Germantown church.

MacLaine, Shirley: Shirley MacLaine (b. April 24, 1934), famous actor and New Age spokesperson, was born Shirley MacLean Beatty in Richmond, Virginia. By high school she was dancing professionally and looking forward to a career in the entertainment field. She moved to New York after high school and married Steve Parker in 1954. That year she gained the lead in the Broadway musical *The Pajama Game*, and went on to become a major Hollywood star.

During the 1960s she became a political activist on behalf of the Democratic Party, stopping the Vietnam War, and other liberal causes. In the mid-1970s her marriage ended and she began to explore new spiritual interests. A number of significant sessions with Swedish medium Sture Johanssen and San Francisco medium Kevin Ryerson convinced her of the truth of channeling (as it has come to be called) and she ventured into a number of psychic adventures within the New Age movement, as outlined in both *Out on a Limb* (1983) and *Dancing in the Light* (1985). In the early 1980s she associated for a time with J. Z. Knight, channeler of Ramtha.

After the film version of *Out on a Limb* aired on television in 1987, MacLaine began holding Higher Life seminars, in which she shared the results of her spiritual learnings and raised money for the establishment of New Age centers, the first one being Ariel Village in Crestone, Colorado. In 1989 she published a book on meditation, *Going With: A Guide for Inner Transformation*.

Maharaji: Maharaji (b. December 10, 1957), leader of Elan Vital, was born Prem Pal Singh Rawat in Hardwar, India. His father, Shri Hans Maharaj Ji, was a spiritual teacher of surat shabda yoga (the yoga of the sound current), using four distinctive techniques or kriyas. Shri Hans founded the Divine Light Mission in 1960 and at his death in 1966 was succeeded as leader by his youngest son, Prem Pal Singh Rawat (Maharaji), then only eight years old.

Maharaji had already been recognized as spiritually precocious, meditating at the age of two and lecturing at the age of six. In 1971 he made his first visit to the United States, combining the work of a spiritual master with such childhood interests as visiting Disneyland. He (known at that time as Guru Maharaj Ji) instructed his followers (at that time called premies) in the four yoga techniques and gave other kinds of spiritual discourses. He was accepted by followers as an embodiment of God.

In November 1973 the Divine Light Mission suffered the first of several setbacks. It failed to fill the Houston Astrodome for its widely publicized Millennium 73 program, thus placing it in financial difficulties. The publicity made it a new target for anti-cult groups. The following month Maharaji turned 16 and took over the administration of the organization from his mother and older brother. In May 1974 he married his 24-year-old secretary, Marolyn Johnson, stating that she was the incarnation of the Hindu goddess Durga. His mother decided that this showed he was unprepared to run the organization, and moved to make his older brother the new leader. The court settlement gave his mother and brother control of the group in India and he gained control of the group outside India.

In the 1980s Maharaji made many changes. He shortened his name, began wearing western clothes, and disbanded the Divine Light Mission with its ashrams. He has chosen instead to relate to followers directly through personal appearances, writings, and a new organization, Elan Vital, based at his residence in Malibu, California.

Malcolm X: Malcolm X (May 19, 1925-February 21, 1965), the most prominent figure of the "black Muslim" movement, was born in Omaha, Nebraska. His father, a Baptist preacher who was often in danger for speaking
up against the poor treatment of blacks, died suspiciously when Malcolm
was six. His mother held the family together for several years, until she was
confined to a mental hospital. Malcolm was thirteen at the time, and like
most of the other children in the family, was placed in a foster home.

Things went well in foster care for a while and he was very popular in
an all-white school. One day he understood the reality of his situation,
however, when his favorite teacher urged him not to consider becoming a
lawyer because "niggers" should instead find a trade like carpentry. At the
end of eighth grade he arranged to move in with his sister in Boston, but he
soon dropped out of school and became a hustler of drugs and other items
in the underworld of Boston and New York. In February 1946 he was sentenced to ten years in prison for burglary.

In prison Malcolm was converted to the Nation of Islam, led by Elijah
Muhammad, and turned his life around. He became obsessed with reading,
and the history of injustices he read about seemed to confirm Muhammad's
teachings of the evil nature of whites and the need to create a separate
nation, freed from the poisons of alcohol, drugs, and hopelessness. When
Malcolm was released in 1952, he replaced Little, his slave-heritage surname, with an X. Muhammad assigned him as minister of Temple Seven in
Harlem in 1954, where he stayed for nine years. Malcolm married Betty X
on January 14, 1958.

Malcolm's abilities elevated him into a media figure, lecturing and de-
bating on college campuses, radio, and television. In 1963 Muhammad made
Malcolm the organization's first national minister, but Malcolm faced opposition within the group. The problem came to a head after the assassination of President John F. Kennedy on November 22, 1963, when Muhammad
placed a three-day moratorium on any Muslim comments on the event.
However, when reporters asked Malcolm for comments, he said the assassination was a case of the "chickens coming home to roost." This was interpreted negatively by the press, and Muhammad silenced him for ninety
days. Malcolm obeyed, but eventually decided that his personal safety was
at risk in the organization, and left.

On March 8, 1964, he founded the Muslim Mosque, Inc. as a new
spiritual aid to end the oppression of blacks. After only a few weeks of
initial work on the group, he felt it important to make a pilgrimage to Mecca
(a "Hajj"), and left for Egypt on April 13, 1964. There, Malcolm was impressed by the easy relationships among people of all colors and nationalities, and was also struck by the distance between the beliefs and practices of

the Nation of Islam and those of mainstream Islam. He felt compelled to rethink many things, and wrote his famous "Letter from Mecca" describing how he no longer believed that all white people were evil. In Mecca he took the name El-Hajj Malik El-Shabazz, "Shabazz" referring to a legendary black tribe.

He returned to the United States in May 1964 and founded the Organization of Afro-American Unity (OAAU) as a secular organization to improve the lives of African Americans. He made contact with several African states and in late 1964 spoke at the Second Organization of African Unity Conference in Africa. On February 21, 1965, during a speech at the Audubon Ballroom in Harlem, he was assassinated, and three members of the Nation of Islam were later convicted. Although the OAAU and the Muslim Mosque, Inc. shut down soon after his death, the power of Malcolm's life and work continues to affect a broad spectrum of American people. In addition to his autobiography, there have been numerous books about him and a major motion picture, "X" was released in 1992.

Marden, Orison Swett: Orison Marden (1848-1924), one of the most popular New Thought authors in history, was born on a New England farm. He graduated from Boston University in 1871, received an M.D. from Harvard University in 1881, then stayed for the LL.B. in 1882. When he graduated he had about $20,000 saved up from successful catering and hotel management jobs he had pursued on the side. He developed a resort area near Newport, Rhode Island, then bought a chain of hotels in Nebraska. In 1892 his businesses failed and by 1894 he was back in Boston.

By this time he had become interested in the writings of Samuel Smiles, British author of *Self-Help* and numerous other such works. He determined to become the American version of Smiles and succeeded very well. His first book, *Pushing to the Front* (1894), went through twelve printings the first year, was translated into 25 languages, and sold one million copies in Japan alone. In December 1897 he founded *Success Magazine* and built a huge subscription list, for that time, of almost 500,000. Despite such a following the magazine foundered in December 1911 and was absorbed into a generalist periodical called *The Circle*. In 1918 he began the *New Success* magazine, which had healthy growth until his death ended the run.

Although Marden rarely used the term New Thought, his was a thoroughly New Thought faith. For some years he was president of the League for a Higher Life, a New Thought organization in New York City. He wrote over fifty books, most of them popular sellers, and most of them covering his favorite topics of optimism and confidence—typical New

Thought themes. He believed that Jesus showed that all people have the power of God within them, if they could only learn to direct it toward the achievement of their goals.

Martello, Leo Louis: Leo Martello (b. September 26, 1931), founder of Witches International Craft Associates (W.I.C.A.) and of the Witches Anti-Defamation League, was born in Dudley, Massachusetts. He attended Assumption College and Hunter College and then became a professional medium. He received a Doctor of Divinity degree from the National Council of Spiritual Consultants, which group also ordained him in 1955.

For several years, in addition to his own spiritualist work, he was a national officer of the American Graphological Society and wrote for the spiritualist magazine *Psychic Observer*. In 1961 he published *Your Pen Personality* and in 1964 he published *It's In the Cards*. In the 1960s he founded the International Guidance Temple of Bible Spiritual Independents, headquartered in New York City.

In 1969 he changed the entire course of his career by publishing a book on witchcraft, then in 1970 publicly declaring himself to be a witch and founding Witches International Craft Associates (W.I.C.A.). He has claimed that he had been a witch all along, since initiation into a traditional Sicilian family of witches on September 26, 1949. It was not until he visited the family roots in Sicily in the 1960s, however, and reestablished contact with those witches, that he decided to pursue the craft publicly.

For Halloween of 1970 he planned a "Witch-In" for Central Park and was at first refused a permit by the parks department, until he threatened to file suit with the American Civil Liberties Union. The event was a success, with plenty of media coverage, and Martello's reputation as a leading Wiccan was set. In the years since then he has published hundreds of articles and several books on the craft. He founded two periodicals, *Witchcraft Digest* and the *W.I.C.A. Newsletter*, and Hero Press. He has also founded several organizations serving the Wiccan community, including Witches Encounter Bureau, the Witches Liberation Movement, and the Witches Antidefamation League.

Mason, Charles Harrison: Charles Mason (September 8, 1866-November 17, 1961), founder of the Church of God in Christ, was born near Memphis, Tennessee. His parents, former slaves, were active in the Missionary Baptist Church. When he was twelve the family moved to Arkansas and he experienced conversion. The next year, 1879, a yellow fever epidemic killed his father. Mason then also caught the illness, and only a miraculous recovery in September 1880 saved his life. He celebrated by beginning to preach.

Mason was ordained in 1891, but his then-fiancée did not want to be married to a preacher, and kept him out of full-time ministry. After she divorced him in 1893 he went into a period of spiritual crisis. This ended when he read the autobiography of Holiness preacher Amanda Smith and he embraced the sanctification message, a message not eagerly received by most Baptists. He paired up with another Baptist minister of like mind, Charles Price Jones, and after they were expelled from Baptist fellowship they founded in Mississippi what became the Church of God in Christ in 1894. In 1903 he remarried, this time to Lelia Washington, and they had several children.

In 1907 Mason was among the early visitors to the Pentecostal revival at the Azusa Street Mission in Los Angeles, and began speaking in tongues himself. When he brought this new blessing back to the Mississippi congregation it split the church. Jones led those opposed to Pentecostalism into a new body, the Church of Christ (Holiness). Mason's church grew rapidly across racial boundaries. Before the Assemblies of God attracted many white Pentecostals at its formation in 1914, there were as many white as black congregations in the Church of God in Christ.

Mason, as permanent General Overseer, continued to lead the church for the rest of his life. His second wife died in 1936 and in 1943 he married Elsie Washington. By the end of his life he was internationally recognized as an elder statesman of Pentecostalism, and his church today is America's largest Pentecostal church and the second largest black denomination, next to the National Baptist Convention of the U.S.A., Inc.

Sri Daya Mata
Courtesy: Self-Realization Fellowship

Mata, Sri Daya: Sri Daya Mata, president of Self-Realization Fellowship founded by Paramahansa Yogananda, was born Faye Wright in Salt Lake City, Utah, in 1914. Daya Mata first met Yogananda in 1931, when she attended a series of lectures and classes that he was giving in her hometown. Inspired by the man and his teachings, she resolved to devote herself to the spiritual way of life that he taught. Soon afterwards, she became one of the first members of the monastic Self-Realization Fellowship Order, headquartered in Los Angeles.

For more than 20 years, she was part of the small circle of Yogananda's closest disciples, serving as his confidential secretary and later assuming greater spiritual and administrative responsibilities as the scope of the society's activities grew. In the closing years of Yogananda's life, he began to speak openly of the prominent role she would play in the future.

In 1955, three years after Yogananda's passing, Daya Mata succeeded Rajarsi Janakananda as president of Self-Realization Fellowship, and she has guided the work of the society ever since. As one of the first women in recent history to be appointed spiritual head of a worldwide religious movement, she has been a forerunner of today's increasing acceptance of women in positions of spiritual authority that have traditionally been reserved for men.

Sri Daya Mata, whose name means "Mother of Compassion," has made several global speaking tours, and many of her public lectures and informal talks are now available on audiocassette. Among her published works are: *Enter the Quiet Heart: Creating a Loving Relationship with God, Only Love: Living the Spiritual Life in a Changing World*, and *Finding the Joy Within You: Personal Counsel for God-Centered Living*.

S.L. ("MacGregor") Mathers
Courtesy: American Religion Collection

Mathers, Samuel Liddell: Samuel Mathers (January 8, 1854-November 20, 1918), a founder of the Hermetic Order of the Golden Dawn, was born into a Scottish family in London, England, and later gave himself the first name of MacGregor to reflect the Scottish heritage. His father died when he was young and his mother then supported the family as a clerk in the town of Bournemouth.

Mathers remained at home, reading widely and participating in the Masonic Society and the Rosicrucian Society in Anglia, until 1885. At that time he moved to London and joined the Theosophical Society. In 1887 he published *The Kabbalah Unveiled*, establishing himself as an occult scholar. During this time he met with Wynn Westcott and others to decode and rework a number of magical manuscripts. These became the basis of the Hermetic Order of the Golden Dawn (O.G.D.), founded in 1888. Westcott soon left the group and Mathers gained complete control. In 1890 he married Mina Bergson, the daughter of famous philosopher Henri Bergson.

In 1891 or 1892 he moved to Paris and established a temple of the O.G.D., adding it to the temples in London, Edinburgh, Weston-super-Mare, and Bradford. The organizing idea of the O.G.D. was the Hermetic principle of correspondence between the microcosm (human being) and the macrocosm (the universe). Through the proper magical procedures, a person can access or make manifest any powers or characteristics present in the macrocosm.

In 1903 Mathers overrode the objections of the London officers and initiated Aleister Crowley into the higher levels of the O.G.D., an act that caused a split among the British adherents. More importantly, although Crowley soon left the O.G.D., he kept and used what he had learned in the O.G.D., a significant factor in Crowley's stimulation of what became the twentieth century revival of magick. After Mathers' death, his widow moved to London and led a temple herself, but the O.G.D. eventually became defunct.

Mathew, Arnold Harris: Arnold Mathew (August 6, 1852-December 20, 1919), founder of the Old Roman Catholic Church, was born in Montpellier, France. He was raised in the Anglican Church but as a young man decided to enter the Roman Catholic priesthood. He received his D.D. in 1877 from St. Peter's Seminary in Glasgow, Scotland. After serving as a priest in local parishes in Britain for about twelve years, he rather suddenly relinquished his vows and became a Unitarian.

After a year as a Unitarian he turned to the Anglican Church and was assigned as priest to Holy Trinity Church on Sloane Street in London. On February 22, 1892, while at that church, he married Margaret Duncan. He left that parish and the Anglican Church in 1899, still in search of a completely satisfying situation. He returned to the Roman Catholic Church, but his marriage now forced him to accept lay status. He supported his family by editing and translating books. When he once again desired to serve as a priest, he considered the Old Catholic Church, which rejected papal infallibility and allowed priests to marry. In 1907 he began corresponding with Edward Herzog of the Christkatholische Kirche der Schweiz (Old Catholic Church in Switzerland), suggesting that a number of high-church Anglicans would follow an Old Catholic bishop if there were one in England.

He was consecrated in Utrecht on April 28, 1908 by Gerard Gul of the Oud-Katholieke Kerk van Nederland (Netherlands Old Catholic Church), but found his converts few. In 1910 Mathew consecrated two excommunicated Roman Catholic priests in secret, without following the Old Catholic guidelines and was expelled. He responded by founding what became known as the Old Roman Catholic Church. Over the next several years he slowly developed a jurisdiction, but lost most of his followers in 1915 when he outlawed membership in Theosophy. He returned briefly to the Roman Catholic Church, then returned to the remains of his jurisdiction. He died in poverty, failing in his church-building goals, but achieving lasting fame as a major source of independent episcopal orders, providing the basis for dozens of independent churches all over the world.

Matthew, Wentworth Arnold: Wentworth Arnold Matthew (June 23, 1892-1973), founder of the Commandment Keepers Congregation of the Living God and an important figure in black Judaism in America, was born in Lagos, Nigeria. After the death of his father, his mother took him to live in her native West Indies. Later, like so many other young men in the West Indies at that time, he longed to go to the United States for the adventures and jobs that reputedly waited there. He managed the journey in 1913 and picked up odd jobs before becoming a minister for the Church of the Living God, the Pillar and Ground of Truth, a black Pentecostal group.

Around 1917 he encountered Marcus Garvey and his Universal Negro Improvement Association (UNIA) and enthusiastically joined. He also met Arnold Josiah Ford, who believed that all blacks had a Jewish heritage, but this knowledge had been stolen by whites through slavery. This idea intrigued Matthew, who began learning Hebrew and Jewish history and tradition, perhaps from Ford. In 1919 he founded the Commandment Keepers, Holy Church of the Living God, an interesting combination of Jewish and Christian elements, still giving homage to Jesus as a savior.

After the discovery in the early 1920s of the Ethiopian Jews called Falashas, Matthew identified with them, claiming ordination from both the chief rabbi of the Falashas and from the Ethiopian National Church (Coptic Christian). In 1930 Ford left New York for Ethiopia and turned his congregation over to Matthew, who then resettled on 131st Street in Harlem and renamed his group the Commandment Keepers Congregation of the Living God.

Over the years Matthew developed the Ethiopian Hebrew Rabbinical College and dropped references to Christianity, described as the religion of the Gentiles or whites. The congregation followed kosher food laws, kept Saturday sabbaths, and followed other traditional Jewish practices, but there were nontraditional practices as well, such as footwashing and healing. Beliefs unusual to Judaism included the idea that the biblical patriarchs were black men. In his healing ministry, Matthew used what he called "Cabalistic Science," a blend of conjuring and voodoo. Matthew's work has been maintained by his grandson, David M. Dore.

McGuire, George Alexander: George McGuire (March 26, 1866-November 10, 1934), founder of the African Orthodox Church, was born in Sweets, Antigua, West Indies. He graduated in 1886 from the Antigua branch of Mico College for teachers and entered the Moravian Theological Seminary at Nisky, St. Thomas. In so doing he followed the religious leanings of his Moravian mother rather than his Anglican father. In 1888 he began pastoring a church in St. Frederickstead in St. Croix, but was not ordained until January 17, 1893. In 1892 he married Ada Eliza Roberts.

In 1894 he moved to the United States, where he was reordained as an Episcopal priest on October 22, 1897. He served St. Andrew's Episcopal Church in Cincinnati (1897-99); in Richmond, Virginia (1899-1901); and at St. Thomas First African Protestant Episcopal Church in Philadelphia (1901-05). In 1905 he was assigned archdeacon for the Commission for Work Among the Colored People, and succeeded in increasing the number of missions from one to nine. From 1909 to 1911 he was the founding priest of St. Bartholomew's Episcopal Church in Cambridge, Massachusetts. While there, he graduated from the (non-accredited) Boston College of Physicians and Surgeons. From 1911 to 1913 he was Field Secretary of the American Church Institute for Negroes.

In 1913 McGuire returned to Antigua to see his family and think about his future. He served several parishes over the next five years, including St. Paul's in Falmouth. He returned to the United States in 1918 to support fellow West Indian Marcus Garvey and his Universal Negro Improvement Association (UNIA) in New York City. This nationalist group fueled McGuire's frustration at the Episcopal Church for its inability to let blacks gain any real power. He left that church in 1919, was named Chaplain-General of the UNIA, and formed a congregation called the Good Shepherd Independent Episcopal Church.

Over the next two years he formed similar congregations in many places, aiming at an international black church that would be the official religion of the UNIA. Toward this goal in early 1921 he published *The Universal Negro Catechism* and *The Universal Negro Ritual* for the UNIA. About this time, however, Garvey made it clear that he did not share this goal and pressed McGuire to leave the UNIA. McGuire organized the African Orthodox Church with a number of independent black clergy on September

2, 1921 and was elected its first bishop. He obtained episcopal consecration on September 28, 1921, from Joseph René Vilatte of the American Catholic Church.

Far ahead of his time, McGuire explicitly geared a Catholic/Episcopal belief system to the needs of a black audience, using, for example, pictures of a black Christ and a black Madonna. Although his clergy were rarely full-time, he emphasized the need for education and helped organize a training seminary.

McPherson, Aimee Semple: Aimee Semple McPherson (October 9, 1890–September 27, 1944), founder of the International Church of the Foursquare Gospel, was born in Ontario, Canada. She grew up a member of the Salvation Army but in 1907 was converted to Pentecostalism. The following year she married the man responsible for that conversion, Rev. Robert Semple. In 1909 she was ordained and in 1910 they went to China as missionaries. Robert soon died of malaria and she returned to the United States. She married Rolf Kennedy McPherson in 1912, but the union lasted only a few years.

After this series of troubles she did not fade away, but instead threw herself even more into her work. In 1915 she conducted a successful series of revivals in Ontario, Canada, and decided that the itinerant ministry was her calling. By 1918 she had a headquarters in Los Angeles and a magazine, *Bridal Call*. In 1923 she opened the huge Angelus Temple in Los Angeles and began to reduce her travel schedule. In 1924 she began her own radio station, KFSG, now the third-oldest station in Los Angeles. She also founded a Bible and training institute, the Lighthouse of International Evangelism, and soon branch churches were sprouting up in numerous towns. In 1927 the International Church of the Foursquare Gospel was formally incorporated as a new denomination.

McPherson had to counter much opposition to a woman minister and part of her success was the development of a colorful style that defied categorization. The Angelus Temple was the site of oratorios, dramas, and attention-getting extravaganzas. In 1926 she disappeared for a month, returning to claim that she had been kidnapped. Critics claimed that this was just another stunt and she was brought up on charges, but they were dropped for lack of evidence. In 1931 she married David L. Hutton. At her death her son by Rolf McPherson took over leadership of the organization.

Dr. Franz Anton Mesmer
Courtesy: American Religion Collection

Mesmer, Franz Anton: Franz Anton, or Friedrich Mesmer (1734-1815), was born at Iznang on Lake Constance, Germany, and studied medicine at the University of Vienna, where he put forward the theory that a magnetic fluid surrounds and links all things and beings on earth and in the heavens.

The idea of such a fluid, which has its origins in ancient times in both West and East, is the approximate equivalent of the Hindu notion of prana, the Chinese ch'i, and the Japanese ki. It was argued that through this force one person could influence the organism and psyche of another, and that the influence exerted by the fluid on living creatures was comparable to the effect produced by the common magnet, to which medicinal powers were attributed. The fluid was called animal magnetism.

Mesmer, following the ideas of the English physician Richard Mead about the power of the sun and moon on the human body, wrote *De Planetarum Influxu* in which Father Maximilian Hehl was very interested. Hehl believed in the influence of planetary magnetism on physical health, and used magnets to treat magnetic imbalances of the body and pain.

Mesmer, who started using the magnets, maintained that sickness was the result of an obstacle to the flow of the fluid through the body, which could be controlled by mesmerizing or massaging the body's magnetic poles, and, after inducing a crisis, restoring the harmony of man with nature. During his practices, Mesmer was able to induce sleep, later called hypnosis or great sleep, during which various forms of psychical phenomena occurred, such as communication with dead or distant spirits, who sent messages through the fluid to the patient's internal sixth sense. While not directly concerned with matters of the afterlife, the association of Mesmer's methods with spirit communication makes him an important figure in the birth of spiritualism.

Later, Mesmer found that the vital energy could be transmitted directly from healer to patient through touch or with the help of iron rods or wands. In 1778 he founded in Paris a fashionable hospital, which he maintained until 1789, although his fortunes declines after Louis XVI established two commissions which investigated Mesmer's practices and found no evidence to support the existence of animal magnetism. The French Revolution forced him to leave the country. He died at Lake Constance in 1815.

Metz, Christian: Christian Metz (December 30, 1794-July 27, 1867), leader of the Church of True Inspiration, also known as the Amana Society, was born in Neuwied, Germany, and grew up in the Church of True Inspiration, founded in 1714. This was a pietist group that favored personal religious experience and more radical obedience over the formalism of the state churches. It taught pacifism and respect for contemporary prophecy and other gifts of the Holy Spirit.

In his early twenties Metz, now working as a carpenter in Ronnesburg, the heart of the church, became a recognized church leader. In 1823 he became the sole head of the church and had to deal with increasing persecution of pietists. In 1826 much of the group moved to Hessen, and then near Arnsburg in 1832. In 1842 Metz received a divine message to move to the United States. They purchased the former Seneca Indian Reservation near Buffalo, New York, and in 1843 about 800 followers established Ebenezar on that land.

Not previously a communal property group, in the new circumstances communalism was adopted as a practical means of organization. Eventually outgrowing the first site, in 1855 Metz led the move to a 26,000-acre tract in Iowa he called Amana ("Believe Faithfully"). The move of 1200 faithful from New York actually took place over ten years, and a total of six Amana villages were created on the property. In 1861 the whole community of Homestead was purchased so the Amana Society could have an entry to the railroad line.

After Metz's death Barbara Heinemann led the group until her death in 1883, and after that time there was no single, inspired leader. Besides farming, the society became famous for its successful business ventures, particularly in building home appliances. In 1932 the society separated the church from the businesses and dissolved the economic communalism.

Michaux, Lightfoot Solomon: Lightfoot Michaux (November 7, 1884-October 20, 1968), founder of the Gospel Spreading Church and pioneer radio and television minister, was born near Newport News, Virginia. He followed his father into the seafood merchandising business and married Mary Eliza Pauline in 1906. They became active in the predominantly black Church of Christ (Holiness) U.S.A. denomination, and in 1917 he had a vision of founding a church. He received ordination from the Church of Christ (Holiness) U.S.A. and began Everybody's Mission. In 1921, with a successful congregation, he separated from the denomination and founded the Gospel Spreading Tabernacle Building Association.

Soon Michaux had a number of congregations aligned with his organization. In 1928 he moved the headquarters to Washington, D.C. and began the Radio Church of God on station WJSV. He developed a huge choir for the show with such future stars as Mahalia Jackson. By 1934 the show, carried by CBS, reached 25 million people every Saturday night, the largest audience of any African American in the country's history. His message was always upbeat and he was known as the "Happy Am I Evangelist" who orchestrated such festive events as the annual mass baptism on the Potomac River or in Griffith Stadium.

Michaux's organization had a major policy goal of providing social services to the needy, and that work had a tremendous impact during the Depression. Michaux found jobs for the unemployed and supported orphanages. He created the Good Neighbor League in 1933, which ran many programs, including the penny Happy News Cafe. He built the 594-unit Mayfair apartment complex in 1946, one of the largest such developments for blacks in the United States.

In 1948 he became the country's first television preacher when his sermons were broadcast over the Washington, D.C. station WTTG. By that time his fame had passed its prime and only a few radio stations carried his program. In 1964 he reorganized the church into the Gospel Spreading Church.

Militz, Annie Rix: Annie Militz (November 15, 1855-June 22, 1924), founder of the Home(s) of Truth, was born in San Francisco, California, the daughter of Hale Rix, a prominent judge. Militz became a schoolteacher and was introduced to New Thought in November 1886 trying to find comfort for her invalid mother. Militz became intrigued and in April 1887 attended the course held by the famous visiting New Thought teacher, Emma Curtis Hopkins. After the third class she was completely converted and began to heal others.

Soon thereafter she joined with another Hopkins student, Sadie Gorie, to establish the Pacific Coast Metaphysical Company in the back of Gorie's bookstore. By 1888 the group was doing well enough to found a "Christian Science Home" on Turk Street in San Francisco. Later they came up with the name "Home of Truth." Militz probably took Hopkins' theological course by mail and traveled to Chicago to be ordained by her on May 29, 1889. One month later Hopkins asked her to be professor of mathematics at the seminary. She served as a non-resident faculty member, traveling to reviews and graduations every six months.

When Gorie died in the summer of 1891, Militz left the San Francisco work in the hands of sister Harriet Hale Rix and others and moved to

Chicago, becoming professor of Scripture Revelation and vice-president of Hopkins' Christian Science Association. At the seminary she met Paul Militz and married him on November 28, 1891. In August 1893 she began writing biblical interpretation articles for *Unity* magazine and was very influential in Unity's development.

In 1894 the seminary closed and Militz moved back to California. By that time a second Home of Truth had opened in Alameda, and Militz moved to Los Angeles to open another one. In 1911 she founded *Master Mind* magazine to serve the now numerous Homes of Truth across the country, the largest New Thought organization of its time. On January 3, 1916 she opened her own seminary, the University of Christ, in Los Angeles, and established a New York branch in 1918. In her final years she thought it possible to overcome death and promised to rise three days after her death. This did not happen, and her national network was gradually reduced to the current single Home in Alameda.

Miller, William: William Miller (February 15, 1782-December 20, 1849), founder of the Adventist movement, was born in Pittsfield, Massachusetts and grew up in Low Hampton, New York. As a young adult, he identified religiously with deism. On June 29, 1803 he married Lucy Smith and moved to Poultney, Vermont, where he joined the militia. After the War of 1812 he returned to the family farm in Low Hampton, where he remained the rest of his life, when not on the road preaching.

He was converted by Baptists about 1816 and began a serious study of the Bible, particularly those sections dealing with prophecy. He came to believe that Jesus would return about 1843. His first major public address on his discoveries was in Dresden, New York, in 1831, and a revival soon followed. He received a license to preach from the Baptists in 1833 and began to travel widely with this message. He was well received and his 64-page booklet, *Evidences from Scripture and History of the Second Coming of Christ About the Year A.D. 1843* (1833), gained a wide circulation, and in 1836 became part of his first book.

In 1839, after hearing Miller speak at the Chardon Street Chapel in Boston, its pastor, Joshua V. Himes, was convinced and became Miller's close assistant. Himes, a man with promotional talent, made Miller's message national news. In March 1840, Himes began issuing a periodical, *Signs of the Times*, and in October 1840 a conference on Miller's work was held at the church. Other conferences soon followed. Excitement built when, in January 1843, Miller specified that the return would occur between March 21, 1843 and March 21, 1844.

By that time, however, formerly cooperative churches began to oppose him. Some Millerites began to leave their denominations, though Miller was against that. After March 21, 1844, a new date, October 22, 1844, was set, but still Christ failed to appear. Miller and his followers had to deal with the Great Disappointment. After a short period of despair, Miller still spoke of a near return, but argued against any further date-setting. As his health declined he lectured less and died a few years later. In his wake came many Adventist groups, such as Jehovah's Witnesses, that put the Great Disappointment behind them and created an enduring movement.

Monroe, Eugene Crosby: Eugene Monroe (May 30, 1880-March 25, 1961), founder of Shiloh Trust, was born in Sherman, New York. He completed his basic schooling through the LaSalle Correspondence School. He married Grace Marjorie Blanchard in 1902 and in 1906 began working as an engineer and draftsman. While working at the Van Dorn Iron Works in Philadelphia he was ordained in 1923 by the Apostolic Church, a British-based Pentecostal group. He began pastoring part-time on the side.

In 1928 Van Dorn downsized and Monroe lost his job. He founded the Monroe Artcraft Shop and spent most of his time restoring old furniture. In 1942 ill health forced retirement from all his activities and he bought a farm near his hometown of Sherman. He began to put his religious beliefs down on paper and over time copies of his writings began to circulate. A community of people, eventually called Shiloh Trust, began to gather around the farm as people were drawn to the source of that ministry. Shiloh Trust developed a health food distribution and other small businesses to support the work of mending spiritually broken people. In 1949, a year after the death of his first wife, Monroe married Frieda Weigand McFarland. By the time of Monroe's death Shiloh Trust was a thriving business and his son took over its operations.

Montgomery, Ruth: The American journalist Ruth Montgomery (1912-), born Ruth Schick in Princeton, Indiana, has been a highly influential new age author. She claims to be able to communicate with spirit guides via automatic writing, in her case automatic typing. She has written about reincarnation, magnetic healing, Atlantis, Lemuria, Earth changes, and visits from spirits.

After being introduced to occult in 1956 by the medium Sr. Malcolm Pantin, she started using a Ouija board, which enabled her to make contact with various spirits, including her dead father. In 1958 she met trance medium Arthur Ford, who suggested she write about life after death, and who told her that she had the ability to do automatic writing, through the help of spirit guides. In 1960, an entity appeared who announced itself as Lily who would communicate material for books from the world beyond the grave.

Among her publications are: *A Gift of Prophecy* (1965), about Jeanne Dixon; *A Search for the Truth* (1966), about her spiritual explorations; *Here and Hereafter* (1968), the result of an investigation of reincarnation undertaken with the help of her guides; *A World Beyond* (1971) a book about life after death, written after the death of Ford, who she believed joined Lily's group of guides; *Companions Along the Way* (1974), in which she maintains that she lived during the lifetime of Jesus, when she was supposedly a sister of Lazarus. The book *Strangers Among Us* (1979) includes her famous theory of walk-ins, which are supposed to be highly developed discarnate entities, taking over the body and personality of an incarnate adult in order to raise spiritual consciousness and help the humankind.

Sun Myung Moon
Courtesy: International Cultural Foundation

Moon, Sun Myung: Sun Myung Moon (b. January 6, 1920), founder of the Unification Church (the Holy Spirit Association for the Unification of World Christianity), was born Yong Myung Moon in what is now North Korea. When he was ten his family converted to Christianity and joined the Presbyterian Church. When he was sixteen he began receiving heavenly visitations indicating he had been chosen to lead God's forces on earth. This came during a time when Korean Pentecostal Christians were popularly predicting a Korean messiah.

After attending Waseda University in Japan he married and began to preach. About this time he changed his name to Sun Myung Moon, meaning someone who has clarified the Word or Truth. In 1946 he founded the Broad Sea Church in Pyongyang in today's North Korea, but his anti-communist activities made him a target for government authorities and he was imprisoned from 1946 until he was expelled from the country in 1950. After some time in Pusan, he moved to Seoul in today's South Korea and in 1954 founded the Holy Spirit Association for the Unification of World Christianity.

Moon taught that Jesus' attempt to restore humanity from its fallen condition was cut short by his crucifixion. His resurrection ensured spiritual salvation for believers, but the completion of heaven on earth requires the messiah to be born again, and Moon is this messiah. By 1957 a Korean edition of the *Divine Principle*, the church's major statement of faith, was in print. He was divorced by his first wife and in 1960 married Hak Ja Han, with whom he has had 14 children.

After brief visits to the United States in 1965 and 1969, Moon made a permanent move there in December 1971, settling in the New York area. Most of the converted members were young and made the church their full-time occupation. Anti-cult groups accused the church of brainwashing and deceitful practices, but Moon suffered a major setback from a conviction of tax evasion, for which he served 13 months in prison in 1984-85. He acquired the *Washington Times* in 1985 and control of the University of Bridgeport in Connecticut in 1991. In 1996 he launched the Family Federation for World Peace as a broad umbrella for his cultural activities. In the mid-1990s, he shifted his focus to South America and began working to develop a model community on a tract of land in Brazil.

Morris, Joseph: Joseph Morris (December 15, 1824-June 15, 1862), founder of the Church of Jesus Christ of the Most High, was born in Cheshire, England. He had little education and went to work at an early age to help his poverty-stricken family. In 1848 he married Mary Thorpe and converted to the Church of Jesus Christ of Latter-day Saints (the Mormons). They then moved to St. Louis, Missouri, where he gained employment on a river boat and joined a Mormon splinter group, the Congregation of the Presbytery of Zion. After a few years he moved on to Pittsburgh, and then in 1853 moved to Salt Lake City, Utah, headquarters for the church.

This was a difficult time for him. He had no stable income, his first wife left him, and his second marriage in 1855 lasted only about a year. He married for a third time in 1857 to Elizabeth Jones, and tried schoolteaching, but was dismissed for his excessive piety. Shortly thereafter he received a revelation that informed him he was a chosen prophet. After failing to receive Brigham Young's support, he moved in 1860 to South Weber, Utah, to form his own group. He and seventeen followers were excommunicated in February 1861 and that April they formally organized the Church of Jesus Christ of the Most High. Soon there were more than 300 adherents.

Morris had several distinctive elements in his teaching. He believed in reincarnation and thought that he was the reincarnation of the biblical Seth and Moses. He taught monogamous marriage, rather than plural marriage, and communal ownership of property. Overarching everything else was a belief in the imminent return of Jesus Christ. In 1862 the group captured three people (Mormons) who were trying to force a Morrisite to leave. Morris refused to release the prisoners and the Utah militia was sent to force the issue. During the battle Morris and many others were killed. His followers were scattered, some joining with other prophets like George Dove or George Williams.

John Morton
Courtesy: Movement for Spiritual Inner

Morton, John: John Morton is a spiritual leader of the Movement of Spiritual Inner Awareness (MSIA), second only to John-Roger Hinkins, MSIA's founder. Morton is regarded as the "anchor" in the physical plane for an intelligent spiritual energy referred to in the movement as the Mystical Traveler Consciousness (MTC). The MTC has the function of guiding aspirants along the path to Soul Transcendence, which is the ultimate goal of MSIA's spiritual practices.

Morton has traveled and lectured around the world for over fifteen years with the purpose of assisting people in discovering the divinity within themselves. He has been a licensed counselor, a park ranger, and a workshop facilitator.

In 1988, he joined John-Roger's Movement of Spiritual Inner Awareness in order to study Soul Transcendence, the realization of oneself as a soul and as one with the Divine. Besides having been an ordained minister and president of MSIA, Morton has worked with several organizations, such as the University of Santa Monica, as a member of the Board. He is also a member of the Board of Directors at the Institute for Individual and World Peace, which is establishing a peace retreat in Santa Barbara, California, where people can study peace as a way of living "without againstness." In 1993 the Good Works Foundation, dedicated to philantropical support of charity, was founded by John Morton and his wife Laura.

Moses, Rev. William Stainton: The medium William Stainton Moses (1839-1892), born in Donnington, Lincolnshire, England, was a prominent British Spiritualist. After graduating at Exeter College, Oxford, he

Rev. William Stainton Moses
Courtesy: American Religion Collection

was ordained as a minister of the Church of England at the age of 24 and was sent to Kirk Maughold, near Ramsey, on the Isle of Man.

In 1872 Dr. Stanhope Templeman Speer, who had taken care of him when he fell seriously ill, induced him to attend seances, although Moses was not very interested in spiritualism at that time. However, his interest in communicating with the spirit world increased after the seance, and within about six months he started showing astonishing paranormal abilities. Among the phenomena attributed to him are levitations of himself, apports, telekinesis, table tiltings, mysterious lights, sounds, and scents of varying description. These phenomena, which also included materializations of luminous hands and columns of lights with human shape, continued till 1881.

He began to do automatic writing in 1872 when, with the guide of a group of spirits headed by "Imperator," he started recording a series of scripts which became the basis of the newspaper *The Spiritualist,* that he published under the pseudonym "M.A. Oxon," and of his works, *Psychography* (1878), *Spirit Identity* (1879), *Higher Aspects of Spiritualism* (1880), *Ghostly Visitors* (1882) and *Spirit Teachings* (1883), a book that became known as the Spiritualists' Bible.

He joined, for a short time, the Society for Psychical Research, which was established in 1882 by a group of researchers and Spiritualists in order to investigate mediumship. The critical attitude displayed by the researchers, however, induced him to quit the Society and to dedicate himself to the London Spiritualist Alliance, which he had founded in 1884 and which had its own journal, *Light.* This journal is still published today by what became the successor to the LSA, the *College for Psychic Studies.* Moses died in 1892, of complications brought on by Bright's disease, and after his death he allegedly joined the "Imperator" group, with whom he communicated through the American trance medium Leonora E. Piper.

Muhammad, Elijah: Elijah Muhammad (October 7, 1897-February 25, 1975), leader of the Nation of Islam, was born in Sandersville, Georgia. His father was a sharecropper and part-time Baptist preacher. Muhammad had no formal schooling beyond age nine, and at age sixteen he left home, supporting himself mostly as a railroad worker. He married Clara Evans in 1919 and after a few years they made their way to Detroit, where he found a job on a Chevrolet plant assembly line. During the Depression years, beginning in 1929, Muhammad was laid off and had difficulty finding steady employment. His wife helped support the eight children as a domestic.

About 1930 Muhammad encountered Wallace D. Fard, founder of Temple No. 1 in Detroit of the Nation of Islam, a group similar to Noble Drew Ali's defunct Moorish Science Temple of America. Fard taught that Islam was the real religious heritage of blacks, that whites were the result of unfortunate scientific experiments by blacks (the original humans), and that blacks would once again rule society beginning in 1984. Fard replaced Muhammad's original surname of Poole with the Muslim name of Muhammad.

Muhammad founded Temple No. 2 in Chicago in 1932, and when Fard disappeared in 1934, claimed right of succession as his chief assistant. In 1942 he was charged with sedition—sympathizing with the Japanese and urging black men not to serve in the military. He was ultimately jailed, not for those charges, but for not being himself registered according to the Selective Service Act. He served over four years in prison and gained through that experience a martyr status that assured his status in the organization.

Muhammad enforced strict discipline relating to dress, food, and behavior, established parochial schools, and promoted black capitalism. Muhammad was critical of the civil rights movement, feeling that the ultimate goal of blacks should be the creation of a separate nation rather than integration. The two biggest boosts to the group were the conversions of Malcolm X in 1952 and heavyweight boxing champion Muhammad Ali (Cassius Clay) in the 1960s. By 1975 the Nation of Islam was a truly significant organization, with about 100,000 members in 70 temples.

Muktananda, Paramahansa: Paramahansa Muktananda (May 16, 1908-October 2, 1982), founder of the Siddha Yoga Dham, was born in Dharmasthala, India. At age 15 he left home to seek enlightenment. In 1947 he encountered Bhagawan Sri Nityananda, whom he took as his guru. Over the following years of training Muktananda claimed to have achieved total enlightenment. When Nityananda died in 1961 Muktananda established the Shri Gurudev Ashram in his honor in Ganeshpuri, India, a center that became headquarters for his own work as leader of Siddha Yoga Dham. During the 1960s the first western visitors began to arrive.

In 1970 Muktananda went on a world tour accompanied by Richard Alpert (AKA Baba Ram Dass). This was greatly successful and led to the foundation of hundreds of siddha yoga centers internationally. Siddha yoga, like many forms of yoga, focuses on awakening the kundalini energy at the base of the spine. What is distinctive about siddha yoga is the role of the guru, who does not just provide guidance, but actively intervenes in the efforts to activate the kundalini.

In 1974 Werner Erhart, founder of est, sponsored another visit by Muktananda to the United States. Besides Erhart and Richard Alpert, he was a strong influence on two others who became famous gurus. Both Swami Rudrananda and Franklin Jones (Bubba Free John; Da Love Ananda) were former disciples of his. In 1975 the Siddha Yoga Dham Associates was formally established to facilitate the coordination of Muktananda-related centers.

Murray, William John: William Murray (?-c.1924), founder of one of the largest New Thought churches in America, has had surprisingly little written about him, thus many details of his life and work are unavailable. He established the Church of the Healing Christ in New York City in 1906. By 1917 it was the largest New Thought organization in that city, and that year he affiliated the previously independent congregation with Divine Science, led at that time by Nona Brooks.

His congregation of about 1,000 met in the ballroom of the Waldorf-Astoria Hotel, and his Astor Lectures were widely read. Murray's success led to the famous ministry of Emmet Fox, who further built the congregation into the largest in New York City and possibly the largest in the United States during the 1940s.

Musser, Joseph White: Joseph Musser (March 8, 1872-March 19, 1954), founder of the Apostolic United Brethren, was born in Salt Lake City, Utah. He grew up in a polygamy-practicing family of the Church of Jesus Christ of Latter-day Saints, and was a young adult when that church issued its 1890 statement disavowing that practice. He worked as a court stenographer and married Rose Selms Borquist in 1892. From 1895 to 1898 he did mission service in the southern United States.

Musser later reported that upon his return to Utah the president of the church (1898-1901), Lorenzo Snow, told him that, despite the church's public pronouncement about polygamy, he had been selected for plural marriage. By the time he married a second wife (Mary Caroline Hill) in 1901 the church's attitude had changed sufficiently that he needed to join a group of fundamentalists near Forestdale, Utah, to feel comfortable. In 1910 he was personally named by the church as among those working against church authority, and he eventually left the church.

In 1929 he claimed that he had been commissioned to see that each year children were born from polygamous marriages, and soon joined the United Order Effort led by like-minded Lorien Woolley. In the ensuing years Musser became a major spokesperson for the Mormon fundamentalists. He ran Truth Publishing Company in Salt Lake City and edited a magazine called *The Truth*. In 1951 he succeeded John Barlow as head of the United Order Effort and immediately created controversy by the changes he implemented. In 1953 he suffered an incapacitating stroke and relations among members worsened. After he appointed all new leaders, including Rulon C. Allred, the group split, with only a minority of members following Musser. After his death the following year Allred became leader of the group, eventually called the Apostolic United Brethren.

F.W.H. Myers
Courtesy: American Religion Collection

Myers, Frederic William Henry: Frederic W.H. Myers (1843-1901), a founding and leading member of the Society for Psychical Research, was born in Keswick, Cumberland, England, of a religious family. During the years he spent at Trinity College, Cambridge, studying classical literature, he experienced a deep religious crisis which led him to the loss of faith.

In the summer of 1871, he and Henry Sidgwick had a profound discussion about the possibility of achieving valid knowledge of the Unseen World through the study of psychical phenomena. In 1872 he began to attend numerous seances, the most important of which was the one presided by William Stainton Moses in 1874. After this event, Myers, Sidgwick and Edmund Gurney established a group to investigate the phenomenon of mediumship, and they founded the Society for Psychical Research in 1882. Myers participated to important investigatory commitees, such as the Literary Committe, and among the most important investigations in which he participated were the cases of Leonora Piper and of Eusapia Palladino.

He developed the concept of the "subliminal consciousness," conceived as the ground from which conscious thought sprang. According to Myers, who anticipated Sigmund Freud's idea of the "unconscious," the subliminal consciousness receives extrasensory inputs and survives physical death. He was convinced that there was survival after death, and this belief was strengthened by the mediumistic communications he had received from the woman he had passionately loved in his youth, his cousin's wife Annie Hall Marshall, who committed suicide in 1876 and who inspired his *Fragments of an Inner Life*.

In the classic book *Human Personality and Its Survival of Bodily Death* (1903), which was completed and published after his death, he systematized the findings of psychical research. His other books include *Phantasms of the Living*, written in 1886 with Gurney and Frank Podmore to collect accounts of apparitional experiences, *St. Paul* (1867), *Essays, Classical and Modern* (1885) and *Science and a Future Life* (1893).

N

Nachman of Bratslav, Rabbi: Rabbi Nachman (Nisan 1, 5532 [April 4, 1772]-Succos 4, 5570 [October 15, 1810]), an important Hasidic leader, was born in Medzhibozh in the Ukraine. His mother was the granddaughter of the Baal Shem Tov, the founder of Hasidism. Very little is known of his early life. In 1785, shortly after his bar mitzvah, he married Sosia and went to live, according to custom, at her father's house.

About 1790 they moved to Medvedevka where he, as a zadik (mystic teacher), began to attract Hasidim (pious followers). Much of our information about Nachman comes from his faithful disciple, Nathan. In 1798 Nachman rather suddenly left his wife and three daughters to visit the Holy Land and was gone about a year. Upon his return he declared that he was the leader of all zadikim, and proceeded to alienate most of his colleagues. In 1802 he moved to Bratslav, now with both a major reputation and isolation. His Hasidim were fiercely loyal, and believed him to be God's chosen zadik.

In 1803 or 1804 he began to yearn for the coming of the Messiah, and apparently came to believe that he was that Messiah. In 1806 he experienced a deep disappointment that his various messianic expectations had not come to pass. Further, in 1807 his wife died and he contracted tuberculosis. During this period of turmoil, he began to tell stories, stories unlike any others in Hasidic history. These stories were enigmatic and did not rely on biblical or Talmudic references. They have been described as mystical autobiography set in a folk-tale framework.

He remarried and continued producing homilies and stories in the face of his disease. In May 1810 he moved to Uman, the site of a famous massacre of Jews. He said that after his death he would be able to help the troubled Uman souls to heaven. He did not appoint a successor, and followers interpreted some of his last words—"My light will glow till the days of the Messiah"—to mean that he would continue, in death, to be the only needful zadik. The Bratslaver movement continued, and is a major Hasidic group in the United States today.

Nakayama, Miki Maegawa: Miki Nakayama (June 2, 1798-January 26, 1887), founder of Tenrikyo, largest of the "New Religions" of Japan, was born Miki Maegawa in Yomato Province, Japan. As a child, she was an exceedingly devout Buddhist, offering prayers twice daily to Amida Buddha and attending the local temple. Her arranged marriage to Zembei Nakayama was completed in 1811, when she was thirteen. She continued her devotions such that, about 1817, she was initiated into the service of deliverance, Gojusoden.

Her life suddenly changed in October 1838, when she fell into a trance and a voice identified as Ten no Shogun ("the Heavenly General") spoke through her, saying that she was now a mediator between humans and God the Parent. The change in her life from that point was gradual; she continued to be a wife and mother, but she began to give away household items to the poor. After her husband's death in 1853 she felt free to give away all her other possessions and moved to a two-room cottage next to two of her children.

Nakayama also practiced spiritual healing. Izo Iburi, her eventual successor, joined in 1853 after Nakayama healed his wife of miscarriage-related problems. In 1864 he opened a small worship center next to her cottage and slowly the worship patterns distinctive to Tenrikyo were introduced. Nakayama taught that in order to be cleansed of the greed, arrogance, and other things that cloud our being, we must follow a path of self-reflection, prayer, and tsutome, or sacred service, such as building orphanages and libraries. Prayers are often short and repeated in mantra-like fashion.

In 1875 she had a revelation that her garden was the place where humanity was first created, and had a column built with a large cup at the top to catch the dew from heaven that creates wisdom and happiness. Before her death she had written seventeen volumes of Ofudesaki, the Tenrikyo scriptures. She and her followers endured many persecutions and imprisonments. Tenrikyo was not recognized by the government until 1908, when it became an approved Shinto sect.

Nee, Watchman: Watchman Nee (November 4, 1903-June 1, 1972), founder of the Local Church, was born Ni Shu-tsu (Henry Nee) in Swatow, People's

Republic of China. His grandfather was a Congregationalist minister and he was raised as a Methodist. He rejected religion in college, but experienced conversion and rededication to the church in 1920 through Methodist evangelist Dora Yu. After studying at Yu's Bible school in Shanghai for about a year, he moved to Fuchow to begin his own ministry.

Using the name To-Sheng, or Watchman, signifying his role in alerting people to live for God, he formulated a new kind of church organization based upon his ideas of early Christian communities. Gathering like-minded people, he began to establish autonomous congregations, one per city, each run by a committee of elders. He established no separate order of clergy, though a few leaders did full-time evangelism for what came to be called the Local Church. He placed great emphasis on church life, with members expected to meet several times each week.

Nee discovered a great similarity to the approach of John Nelson Darby (1800-1883), founder of the Plymouth Brethren who was also a fundamentalist and against denominationalism. In 1933 Nee went to England to visit a branch of the Plymouth Brethren headed by James Taylor, but that relationship was short-lived. During the 1930s Nee traveled widely, nurturing congregations, which flourished particularly in China. He also wrote a number of books. During World War II he took a job in a factory owned by his brother, as church resources were very meager at the time. That factory was later given to the church, as were a number of other businesses.

In 1949 the Chinese revolution ended with the formation of the People's Republic of China, which accused Nee of being a spy for the United States and the Nationalist government. Nee was at first ejected from Shanghai and then placed in prison, where he spent the rest of his life. The Local Church has since spread around the world.

Newbrough, John Ballou: John Newbrough (June 5, 1828-April 22, 1891), founder of the Faithists of Kosmon movement and channel for *Oahspe: A New Bible,* was born near Springfield, Ohio. He graduated from Cincinnati Medical College in 1849 and also learned dentistry from a Cincinnati dentist. After graduation he set up a dental and medical practice in New York City. At one point he invented a dental plate formula that broke the monopoly on dental plates held by the Goodyear Rubber Company.

In 1849 he followed the Gold Rush to California and struck it rich. He then went to Australia to mine gold and struck it rich there as well. In 1859 he married Rachel Turnbull and returned to his practice in New York City. His interest in Spiritualism grew such that he became a trustee of the New York Spiritualist Association. His wife did not share that interest, and the marriage broke up in the 1870s. For two years he lived at Domain, a Spiritualist colony in Jamestown, New York, but became frustrated at the low level of discussions with the spirits. He wanted some basic metaphysical issues addressed.

In 1881 he purchased a typewriter, and one morning he began channeling a book from some angelic beings. The automatic writing took place every morning for one hour for almost a year and the result was *Oahspe: A New Bible* (1882). This large book, written in a King James Bible style, tells the story of humanity beginning on the lost continent of Pan in the Pacific. Religion evolved through a number of prophets, including Jesus, and directed by angels towards the Kosmon Era, which began in the nineteenth century. In this era the world will be transformed into a paradise.

In 1883 a group called "Faithists of the Seed of Abraham," a title inspired from the book, took shape in New York. According to a vision in the book, they decided to found a colony and orphanage. They bought property near Las Cruces, New Mexico, and in 1885 began to build Shalam. Newbrough moved there and married Frances Van de Water Sweet on September 28, 1887. Shalam eventually housed about fifty children, but only lasted until 1900. Newbrough and some children were killed by a flu epidemic in 1891. Various Faithist groups have continued following the inspirations of *Oahspe* until the present time.

Newman, Hugh George de Willmott: Hugh Newman (January 17, 1905-February 28, 1979), leader of the Catholic Apostolic Church (also known as the Catholicate of the West), grew up in the Catholic Apostolic Church (Irvingite). By his thirties he was general manager and secretary of the National Association of Cycle Traders and edited the association's magazine, *The National Journal.* He married Lola Ina del Carpio Barnardo in 1937 and about that time began thinking about getting ordained. His own church no longer had priests, so he looked elsewhere. He was ordained on October 23, 1938 by James Columba McFall of the Old Roman Catholic Church, but was unable to find a stable ministry.

In 1941 Arthur Wolfort Brooks of the Apostolic Episcopal Church in America, created a British branch (on paper) of his group, to be called the Old Catholic Orthodox Church, and named Newman its head. On April 10, 1944 William Bernard Crow of the Ancient British Church consecrated Newman, on the authorization of Brooks, and Newman took the religious name of Mar Georgius. On March 23, 1944 the Ancient British Church, the British Orthodox Catholic Church and the Old Catholic Orthodox Church semi-merged to form the ecumenical Western Orthodox

Catholic Church, soon renamed the Catholicate of the West. Crow headed this new organization and Newman became the first Catholicos of the West. The following year the Catholicate of the West became autonomous, with Newman as its patriarch. That year he also became head of the Ancient British Church.

The Catholicate of the West, also called the Catholic Apostolic Church, never became much of a force. Newman, however, in his desire to form ecumenical ties and create a rock-solid episcopal pedigree, epitomized the tendency of independent bishops towards multiple consecrations, and achieved some fame for this. He was consecrated at least 14 times and in turn consecrated at least 37 people.

Ngo-Dinh-Thuc, Pierre Martin: Pierre Mgo-Dinh-Thuc (October 6, 1897-December 13, 1984), episcopal source behind the Latin-Rite Catholic Church, was born in Phu Cam, Vietnam. He was ordained a Roman Catholic priest in 1925 and was consecrated bishop on May 4, 1938. He was part of a very powerful family; his brother, Diem, was president of Vietnam during the Vietnam War. Ngo-Dinh-Thuc became Archbishop of Hue, Vietnam, on November 24, 1960.

He retired to Italy during the 1960s, leaving the conflict of war behind. When Vatican II finished its deliberations in 1965, he was very much opposed to its liberalizing edicts, and became a spokesperson for many traditionalists. In the early 1970s he became impressed by the traditionalist Catholic organization formed around the visions of the Virgin Mary experienced by Clemente Gómez in Spain. On December 31, 1975, he traveled to Spain and ordained Gómez and some others, later consecrating Gómez on January 11, 1976. These actions earned him excommunication from the Roman Catholic Church, but he repented and was reinstated later that year.

For a number of years the Roman Catholic Church and Ngo-Dinh-Thuc lived an uneasy truce, until he performed more consecrations and was excommunicated again on February 1, 1983. He was reconciled again in July 1984, some six months before his death, but by that time he was more well-known for his schismatic actions than for his pre-retirement career. He and Bishop Marcel Lefebvre have been the two greatest forces in the late 20th century in the growth of movements around an independent episcopacy.

Nichols, L. T.: L.T. Nichols (October 1, 1844-February 28, 1912), founder of the Meggido Mission Church, was born in Elkhart, Indiana and grew up in rural Wisconsin. He had no first name beyond the initials inherited from his father. He had little formal schooling, but became a student of the Bible. As a young man he began preaching, accepting no money for his ministries and affiliating with no denomination.

In 1874 he moved to Oregon with a small group of followers, and by 1880 had fully developed his most distinctive teachings. He denied the existence of the Devil, hell, the trinity, the "fall" with Adam and Eve, and the immortality of the soul. He taught that Jesus was God's son and the Holy Spirit is not a person, but a force. He believed that each person is responsible for their own salvation, which is gained by keeping the commandments of God. The ultimate reward for a faithful life is immortality, whereas sinners simply die.

In 1883 he moved to Dodge City, Minnesota and entered the manufacturing industry. He continued to build and develop congregations in his spare time, gaining a number of churches in the Midwest. In 1901 he bought a steamboat and named it "Megiddo," the biblical name of a town and valley in Palestine and part of the term "Armageddon," the final battle between good and evil. Nichols believed that the "end time" was near. About 30 families joined him on the boat, and they evangelized along the Mississippi and Ohio Rivers until 1903, when the boat was sold and the group moved to some land at Rochester, New York. Although the boat was gone, its name remained as the group's name. In his final years he passed the torch of leadership to Maud Hembree, a former Roman Catholic nun. The group is still active in Rochester.

Nikkyo Niwano
Courtesy: Rissho Kosei-Kai

Niwano, Nikkyo: Nikkyo Niwano was the founder of Rissho Kosei Kai, a popular Nichiren Buddhist group that emerged from Reiyukai in 1938. Niwano was an ambitious, self-educated farmer's son who formed the group in part to satisfy his desire to propagate the teachings of the Lotus Sutra. His movement generally follows in the footsteps of Nichiren. The Muryogi Sutra, the Lotus Sutra, and the Kanfugen Sutra are emphasized, and the Daimoku is integral. The laws of cause and effect are seen to apply universally and the only means of avoiding the consequences of those laws (and the laws of reincarnation) is by repentance and holy living. Faith and repentance lead to the final goal, pefect Buddhahood.

Like many other Buddhist organizations, groups meet in instruction halls for Dharma worship. The Lotus Sutra and Daimoku are chanted, followed by a homily. Niwano's success in transforming his organization into a major Japanese religion was at least partially attributable to the institution of *hoza*. After the formal worship concludes, the assembly disperses into smaller groups for *hoza* (group counselling). During *hoza* the groups enagage in discussions of the more complex issues of faith. Personal problems may also be discussed in *hoza*. There are presently about 6,000,000 adherents to Rissho Kosei Kai in the world, mostly in Japan.

Ruth Norman (Uriel)
Courtesy: Unarius Academy of Science

Norman, Ruth: Ruth Norman was the leader, with her husband Ernest, of the Unarius Academy of Science, a UFO movement based on the expectation that interplanetary spaceships will land in San Diego, California, in 2001. For this purpose, sixty-seven acres of land in the mountains of San Diego were purchased. The group defines the situation of contact with beings from outer space as a benevolent one.

She was known as Uriel, standing for Universal Radiant Infinite Eternal Light, and played the role of a divine being, and participated in the work of spiritual hierarchy presiding over a ccnfederation of planets. She has been variously designated as the "Magical Madonna" and a "Mother Goddess."

Ruth claimed over two hundred previous reincarnations, two of which are recognized mother goddess figures, Kuan Yin, the Chinese Goddess of Peace, and Isis, the Great Mother Goddess of Egypt. In 1973, she announced that she had progressed in her evolution to become a healing archangel, and in 1974 she claimed to have received knowledge from the inner worlds that she was the "Spirit of beauty, Goddess of Love." In 1981, she declared that her powers and duties had increased, and at a ceremony at the Unarius Center, she appeared as the Cosmic Generator, that is the direct supplier of the "Light-Force Energies into the earth worlds."

Ruth met Ernest, who had previously worked with several spiritualist churches, at a psychic convention in 1954. At the time of their first meeting, he informed her that she had once been the pharaoh's daughter who had found Moses in the bulrushes.

He clairvoyantly received transmissions from such planets as Mars and Venus, Eros, Orion, Muse, Elysium, Unarius, and Herems, through which beings on these planets—most notably great teachers and ascended masters—described their cities. Descriptions of such channelings are contained in a set of books known as the *Pulse of Creation Series*.

The Normans began having a modest following during the fifties and the sixties, and in the early years of Unarius they published their teachings in the book *The Infinite Concept of Cosmic Creation*, in which they asserted that everything is energy: atoms, higher knowledge, human body, and human experiences. Through scientific understanding of this energy, that vibrates in frequencies and wave forms, individuals can be in contact with such things as higher intelligence, the advanced teaching centers, and even past lives.

The Normans moved to several cities in California, and eventually settled in Escondido. In 1965 they got in touch with their past lives as Jesus and Mary Magdalene.

After Ernest's death in 1971, Ruth began to excel as a visionary, and increased the number of messages from outer space and from the spiritual planets. In 1973, higher energies led to the appearance of ascended beings before Ruth, who related her story to her student Antares, with whom she began to view the happenings in the city Parhelion on the planet Eros. These channellings are described in the book called the *Conclave of Light Beings* (1973), whereas more channelings were included in the *Tesla Speaks* series.

The Unarian prophecy started to emerge in 1974. According to this prophecy, the landing of the starships will usher in a new golden age of logic and reason, bringing higher knowledge and gifts of technology to earth. The flying saucers are described as extremely large, and each of them is believed to bring one thousand scientists to earth. They will become visible only after having stabilized the consciousness of Earth. They will be responsible for such benevolent acts as recovering the libraries of Atlantis and Lemuria, and opening a university and a medical center, that will be free of charge. However, the most important gift of the starships will be the Space Brothers, powerful healers who will help human beings to change their own societies, by emanating complete love and peace.

Uriel opened a center on February 15, 1975, which attracted new students. Her role as cosmic emissary expanded, and since then Unarius has attracted the attention of the media. During the late seventies, Unarius, whose use of past-life regression and readings as a regular process of intersubjectivity became unique, also started making films and videos.

Among other practices of the Unarius Center are the psychology of consciousness, and art therapy. Among the several celebrations performed by the center throughout the year is Interplanetary Confederation Day, held around October 12th each year in order to commemorate the union of the planets under the guidance of Uriel.

Unarius reached its heyday in the eighties, when Uriel was still strong despite her advanced age. However, by 1989 her health began to slip, because of her age and osteoporosis. She died on July 12, 1993.

Norris, John Frank: John Norris (September 18, 1877-August 20, 1952), founder of the World Baptist Fellowship, was born in Dadeville, Alabama, and shortly thereafter moved to Texas. Despite growing up in a poor, sharecropping family, after his call to the ministry he managed to work his way through Baylor University and the Southern Baptist Theological Seminary in Louisville, Kentucky.

From his very first pastorate, he showed unusual ability. He built a tiny congregation in Texas to a membership of 1,000 in just a few years. He also gained the editorship of *The Baptist Standard*, the official organ of Texas Southern Baptists. In 1909 he accepted the pastorate of the First Baptist Church in Fort Worth, where he stayed for the rest of his life, boosting its membership past 28,000. He began another magazine, the *Fence-Rail* (later *The Fundamentalist*).

Despite his success as a church leader, Norris's extreme fundamentalism and other conservative views made him a controversial figure. He initiated an anti-Catholic campaign in Fort Worth that ended with Norris shooting and killing a Catholic businessman in 1926. Although the charges were dropped on the basis of self-defense, Norris's name was dropped from the Baptist Bible Union officiary, effectively isolating him.

He left the Southern Baptist Convention in 1931 and founded the World Baptist Fellowship. He expanded his ministry into Detroit, and from 1934 to 1948 was pastor of both the Temple Baptist Church in Detroit and the Fort Worth congregation. In 1939 he began the Bible Baptist Institute, which eventually became the Arlington Baptist College in Arlington, Texas. In 1952, while at a youth rally in Florida, Norris died of a heart attack.

Noyes, John Humphrey: John Humphrey Noyes (September 3, 1811-April 13, 1886), founder of the Oneida Community, was born in Brattleboro, Vermont. His father was a wealthy businessman. In 1826, at age fifteen, Noyes entered Dartmouth University, anticipating a law career, but experienced conversion in 1831 and entered seminary. He graduated from Yale Divinity School in 1834 and associated with the Free Church.

He became an itinerant preacher of perfectionism, teaching that the second coming had already occurred, and thus people can attain a measure of perfection. In 1836 he settled in Putney, Vermont, and worked on his ideas via his magazines, *The Witness* (1837-43) and *The Perfectionist* (1843-44). He gathered a small group of disciples and in 1841 formed them into a covenant group. In 1844 a formal incorporation of the communal life of 28 adults was set up.

In 1846 Noyes began experimenting with his most famous doctrine, that of complex marriage. He believed that standard monogamy unduly limited love, and decided that every male in the group should be considered married to every female in the group. This did not mean wild orgies, but a carefully regulated system where each encounter was arranged ahead of time by a third party and records were kept to avoid exclusive relationships from forming. Noyes's small-scale experiments with this leaked to the community and he was forced to leave.

The group reassembled at Oneida, New York, where Noyes's ideas gained full blossom. At its height, almost 300 people lived at Oneida and several branch communities. Its various industries, particularly the making of silverware, kept it prosperous. Oneida was very successful until a combination of Noyes's failing health, outside harassment, and a critical younger generation led to a crisis, and Noyes moved to Canada in June 1879. Soon thereafter the community abandoned complex marriage, and in 1880 communalism in general was dissolved in favor of a joint-stock company.

O

Oberholtzer, John H.: John Oberhotzer (January 10, 1809-February 15, 1895), one of the founders of the General Conference Mennonite Church, was born on a farm in Clayton, Pennsylvania. For a while he was a schoolteacher, but most of his secular career was spent as a locksmith. He married Mary Riehn in the 1830s and they joined the Great Swamp Mennonite Church near Germantown, Pennsylvania.

In 1842 he was chosen by lot as his congregation's new minister and over the next five years introduced a number of innovations that in particular pleased the younger members. He accepted as members those who had married outside the community, wrote a constitution for the congregation, preached in non-Mennonite churches, and organized the first Mennonite Sunday school in America. Opposition to these changes came to a head in 1847, when he wanted to give the general membership a voice in church decisions and to keep minutes of church meetings.

Oberholtzer and his followers soon felt compelled to leave the church and begin a new congregation. In 1860 he arranged a merger with three other like-minded congregations in Iowa, thus forming the General Conference Mennonite Church. He served as the church's first chairman and began its first mission project of evangelizing the Native Americans. He retired in 1872 but maintained editorship of the periodical he had begun in 1852, the *Religioser Botschafer (Religious Messenger)*.

Ofiesh, Abdullah: Abdullah Ofiesh (October 22, 1880-July 24, 1966), founder of the Holy Eastern Orthodox Catholic and Apostolic Church in North America, was born in Mohiedathet, Lebanon. In 1902 he was ordained a priest in the Syrian Orthodox Patriarchate of Antioch, and was often known by his religious name of Aftimios. Over the next several years Ofiesh became involved in church administrative reform efforts, a delicate issue that placed him in considerable political turmoil. He requested a transfer to the United States, where the Russian Orthodox Church had charge of Orthodox ministries to all nationalities. In 1905 he began work under Raphael Hawawenny in New York City, leader of the Russian Orthodox ministries to the Lebanese and Syrians. After Hawawenny passed away in 1914, Ofiesh was elected to succeed him as Bishop of Brooklyn, and was consecrated on May 13, 1917, becoming archbishop in 1923.

During the 1920s the Russian Orthodox Church underwent great changes as a result of the Russian Revolution, causing unrest among the Orthodox ethnic groups in the United States, who demanded release from Russian control. In 1926 Ofiesh suggested the creation of a new, non-ethnic-based, American form of Orthodoxy, and the following year received permission from the Russian hierarchy to create the Holy Eastern Orthodox Catholic and Apostolic Church in North America, usually shortened to the American Orthodox Catholic Church.

Unfortunately, he received opposition from many of the other Orthodox leaders around the world and from the Episcopal Church, which considered itself the American form of Orthodoxy and at that time was paying many of the bills of the Russian Orthodox Church's work in America. Within two years the Russian church pulled all support from Ofiesh, but he did not want to see his dream of a united American orthodoxy die, and responded by declaring independent status. In 1932 he lost the court battle to keep the Brooklyn cathedral, leaving him with only a handful of parishes. On April 29, 1933 he married, in opposition to Orthodox tradition and canon law, and his following further eroded. He was excommunicated on October 4, 1933, and he retired to Pennsylvania, leaving the warring factions in his church to find their own way.

Okada, Kotama: Kotama Okada (February 27, 1901-June 23, 1974), founder of Sekai Mahikari Bunmei Kyodan (Church of World True Light Children), was born Yoshikazu Okada in Tokyo, Japan. Born into a samurai family, his father was a major general in the army. Okada in turn graduated from Rikugun Shikan Gakko, a military academy, and became one of the emperor's imperial guards. Early in World War II he injured his back, developed spinal tuberculosis, and was given only a few years to live. He then put all of his money into four factories with air force contracts, only to see all four destroyed later in the war.

After the war, his back somehow healed, Okada joined the Church of

World Messianity, which taught the obtaining of healing and happiness through the reception of *johrei*, or God's Light. By 1959 he had rid himself of debt. On February 27, 1959 he had a revelation from Su-God (the Lord God) to change his name to Kotama ("Jewel of Light") and from that point began an independent healing mission with some variations on the teachings of the Church of World Messianity. He taught followers how to gain access to God's Light (Mahikari), even how to radiate it through the palm of one's hand, a process known as Mahikari no Waza. Members also make use of an Omitama, a pendant used to focus the Light.

Over time Okada assumed the titles of Sukuinushisama (Master of Salvation) and Oshienushisama (Spiritual Leader), and taught that he was the incarnation of the Shinto deity Yonimasu-o-amatsu. The movement grew to international proportions and in 1973 he had an audience with Pope Paul VI. After Okada's death he was succeeded by his daughter, Seishu Okada, but through a court battle with a rival leader the headquarters was lost. Seishu Okada created a new headquarters and renamed the group Sukyo Mahikari (True Light Supra-Religious Organization).

Okada, Mokichi (Meishu-sama): Mokichi Okada (December 23, 1882–February 10, 1955), founder of the Church of World Messianity (Sekai Kyusei Kyo), was born in Tokyo, Japan. His family never had much money and he was troubled by ill health growing up. In 1906 he managed to open a small store, which became very successful. In June 1907 he married Taka Aihara. In 1917 he patented an artificial diamond, enhancing his growing wealth. Still bothered by poor health, he visited a religious healer and got better, not, he thought, because of the healer so much as that he stopped taking the medication.

Just when things seemed to fall into place, his wife died in 1919 (he married Yosiko Ota later that year), he lost the bulk of his fortune in the 1920 stock market crash, and in 1923 his store was destroyed in an earthquake. Seeking consolation, he joined Omoto, a new Japanese religion. In 1926 he began receiving revelations that led him to sell his business and become a healer. He saw himself as a transmitter of *johrei*, that is, moving God's Direct Light into the spiritual body to create harmony, prosperity, and peace. On June 15, 1931 he declared the beginning of the Daylight Age in the realm of the spirit.

In 1934 he left the Omoto religion and founded Dai Nihon Kannon Kai (Japan Kannon Society). During World War II his group was suppressed by the government along with many others, but it grew even so. He taught that the final judgment was near, to be followed by paradise on earth, and that enlightened ones should try to create anticipatory paradises now. Thus after the war he built a paradise on his Hakone estate and later another one at his Atami estate.

In 1950 he changed the name of his movement to the Church of World Messianity (Sekai Kyusei Kyo). Later that year he faced tax evasion charges and went to jail for a time. He lived to see the first centers outside Japan established in Hawaii (1953) and Los Angeles (1954). Since then it has spread around the world.

O'Kelly, James: James O'Kelly (c.1735-October 16, 1826), founder of the Republican Methodist Church, was probably born in Ireland and married Elizabeth Meeks in 1759. He migrated to America about 1778. Most of his biographical records have been lost. Probably converted to Methodism while still in Ireland, he entered the Methodist ministry in 1779 at New Hope, North Carolina.

At that time Methodists were still members of the Anglican Church and constituted a revival movement within it. As a lay member, O'Kelly could not perform the sacramental functions of an ordained priest. He was part of an attempt by some Methodist preachers in 1780 to ordain each other and was temporarily dropped from the Methodist preacher list. When the Methodist Episcopal Church was formed as a separate entity in December 1784, Bishop Francis Asbury ordained O'Kelly, who functioned as a presiding elder in Virginia for the next ten years.

O'Kelly remained very independent-minded. When founder John Wesley sent Richard Whatcoat to America in 1787 to function as a bishop, O'Kelly and others felt it as an imposition and for several years the church thus refused to officially put him in that office. In 1789 Asbury included O'Kelly in a small group designed to run the church at the national level, but O'Kelly thought it too easily controlled by Asbury and led a campaign against the council. Bishop Coke and Jesse Lee also were against it and so the first General Conference met in 1792. At that meeting, O'Kelly continued his critique of the powers of the bishop's office by trying to limit the bishop's appointment powers. This effort was defeated and ultimately led to formation of the Republican Methodist Church on August 4, 1794. In Virginia alone almost 4,000 Methodists followed O'Kelly in this move.

O'Kelly participated in the more egalitarian leadership of the Republican Methodist Church for the rest of his life, engaging for many years in pamphlet arguments with the leadership of the Methodist Episcopal Church. O'Kelly's church eventually merged with the Christian Church, which later became part of the United Church of Christ.

Olazabal, Francisco: Francisco Olazabal (October 12, 1886-June 9, 1937), founder of the Latin American Council of Christian Churches, was born in El Verano, Mexico, where his father was mayor and his mother a lay missionary for the Methodist Episcopal Church, South. Olazabal was not interested in religion and left home at age eighteen. In San Francisco he was converted to Christianity by members of the Christian and Missionary Alliance.

He returned to Mexico, graduated from Wesleyan College in San Luis, Poposi, in 1910, and began pastoring a church in El Paso, Texas. In 1911 he entered Moody Bible College in Chicago but left within a few months to serve as a Methodist missionary in California. After some time in Compton (1911-13) and Pasadena (1913-16), he moved to San Francisco, where he was ordained elder for the Methodist Episcopal Church, South.

In San Francisco he was converted to Pentecostalism and joined the Assemblies of God. He returned to El Paso and built the first of several Assemblies of God Spanish-speaking congregations. In 1922 he led most of those believers out of the Assemblies of God over the issue of wanting a Latino in charge of the mission to Spanish-speakers. Olazabal helped found the Latin American Council of Christian Churches and held the post of its president for the rest of his life.

Over the remainder of his career Olazabal deepened his importance as the introducer of Pentecostalism among Spanish-speakers. His church work spread across the United States, Mexico, and Puerto Rico. He seriously considered a merger with the Church of God, led by Ambrose Tomlinson, but was killed in a car accident before the culmination of negotiations, and his successors decided against the move.

Col. Henry Steel Olcott
Courtesy: American Religion Collection

Olcott, Henry Steel: Henry S. Olcott (August 2, 1832-February 17, 1907), a founder of the Theosophical Society, was born in Orange, New Jersey and grew up in New York City. He attended New York University briefly in 1847-48, but financial reverses in the family forced him to leave school and work on a farm in Elvira, Ohio, with relatives. There he learned both farming and Spiritualism. In 1853 he went to New Jersey to study agricultural chemistry on the farm of Professor J. J.

Mapes. In 1855 he tried running his own school, but it failed after a few years.

About 1859 he became assistant agricultural editor for the *New York Tribune,* and on April 26, 1860 he married Mary Eplee Morgan. At the beginning of the Civil War Olcott joined the Army, eventually becoming a colonel successful in special criminal investigations. He was part of the team that investigated President Lincoln's assassination and made the first arrest in the case, Ned Spangler. In 1868 Olcott was admitted to the New York bar and entered a career in law.

His life changed in 1874 when he met Helena Blavatsky in Vermont, while investigating Spiritualist activity. He became part of the inner circle that discussed her occult ideas, and in 1875 helped her and William Q. Judge found the Theosophical Society. He was elected president and held that position for the rest of his life. In 1876 he shared an apartment with her while she wrote *Isis Unveiled.* About this time he and his wife divorced.

In 1876 Olcott and Blavatsky moved to India to establish a new headquarters, and Olcott ran an import-export business for support. By 1880 their new magazine, *The Theosophist,* was providing enough support for Olcott to travel. In Ceylon he formally became a Buddhist, and the rest of his career was spent supporting both Buddhism and Theosophy. His book, *Buddhist Catechism* (1947), became a popular English-language introduction to Buddhism. He founded branches of the Theosophical Society in various parts of Asia and Australia. In 1895 he could not prevent the schism of most of the American branches under William Judge, but his organizational and promotional skills helped maintain the general success of the society.

Owen, Robert Dale: (November 9, 1801-June 17, 1877), a leading spokesperson for communalism, free thought, and spiritualism, was born in Glasgow, Scotland. He was the eldest son of Robert Owen, wealthy industrialist and social radical, who in 1825 had founded the (non-religiously based) communitarian experiment of New Harmony, in Indiana. Robert Dale Owen completed his education in Europe and arrived in New Harmony in January 1826. There he served as teacher and editor of *The New Harmony Gazette.*

In the spring of 1827 he traveled to Nashoba, Tennessee, where some months before, Frances Wright had put the ideals of New Harmony to practice in a community of both blacks and whites, adding the doctrine of free sexual love. These communitarian practices, however, were given up in February 1828. Owen left in March and embarked on a lecture tour, reuniting the following year with Wright in New York, where they continued the New Harmony newspaper as *The Free Enquirer*. Owen's father left America in the summer of 1829, signalling the end of New Harmony's experiment.

In 1830 Owen published *Moral Physiology*, one of the earliest books available to the public on birth control. He married Mary Jane Robinson on April 12, 1832 and soon thereafter resettled in New Harmony, now a town much like any other. He served five years in the Indiana House of Representatives and one term in the U.S. House of Representatives. In 1853 he was appointed consul to the Kingdom of the Two Sicilies (Naples) and lived there until 1858.

In Naples he was converted to Spiritualism and once back in the United States became a leading promoter of that movement. His books, *Footfalls on the Boundary of Another World* (1860) and *Debatable Land Between This World and the Next* (1871) were introductions to Spiritualism for many thousands. In 1874 he wrote his last book, *Twenty-Seven Years of Autobiography, Threading My Way*. His first wife died in 1871 and on June 23, 1876 he married Lottie Walton Kellogg.

P

Pagtakhan, Francisco de Jesus: Francisco Pagtakhan (b. 1916), a major force in contemporary independent episcopal movements, grew up in the Philippines. He was ordained a priest in the Iglesia Filipina Independiente (Philippine Independent Catholic Church) in 1937, served a number of parishes, and rose through the ranks. He was consecrated bishop on September 22, 1957 and for some years was Performance Officer in the church headquarters. In 1974 he was named Archbishop Secretary for Missions, Ecumenical Relations, and Foreign Affairs.

By means of the ecumenical ties he gained through this office, Pagtakhan became involved in the traditionalist Anglican movement. He assisted in the several consecrations that helped found the Anglican Catholic Church, a schism from the Episcopal Church. He was very close to Macario V. Ga, head of the Philippine Independent Catholic Church, who was also very traditionalist and sympathetic to those concerned about the "liberalism" of the Episcopal Church. At the time, the Episcopal Church was in communion with the Philippine church and there was great tension with Ga, fueled by Pagtakhan's actions. In March 1980 Pagtakhan went so far as to incorporate in Texas the Holy Catholic Church, Anglican Rite Jurisdiction of the Americas, as an umbrella group for the independent Anglicans, in an effort to avoid further splintering.

In 1981 Ga led about half of his church, including Pagtakhan, in a split away from the Episcopal Church. This meant Pagtakhan was more free to pursue his traditionalist agenda. In 1982 he rejected the Holy Catholic Church, Anglican Rite Jurisdiction of the Americas, and began the rival Anglican Rite Diocese of Texas. Because of his activity on behalf of traditionalist Anglicans/Episcopalians, and having consecrated at least 17 persons, Pagtakhan has become a significant figure in the world of independent bishops.

Palmer, Phoebe Worrall: (December 18, 1807-November 2, 1874), a founder of the nineteenth century holiness movement, was born in New York City and raised in a particularly pious Methodist family. She married Walter C. Palmer on September 28, 1827 and in the following years suffered through the early deaths of each of their three children.

In 1832 the Allen Street Methodist Church began a series of revival meetings that resulted in a weekday prayer meeting for women. In 1837 the Tuesday afternoon meetings, by that time meeting in the Palmer home, produced an experience of sanctification among several women, including Palmer. Sanctification refers to holiness, a work of grace in which the recipient becomes perfect in Christian love. In 1839 the men were invited to join, and the group was renamed the Tuesday Afternoon Union Meeting for the Promotion of Holiness.

This concept of holiness or sanctification had been a part of Methodism since its founder, John Wesley, wrote *A Plain Account of Christian Perfection*. It had, however, not previously been highlighted as an instantaneous, rather than progressive, event. In the 1840s, at the time that the Palmers began traveling to promote holiness, it also began to be promoted independently by evangelist Charles G. Finney, a Congregationalist minister who had read Wesley, and thus it moved to other denominations.

Phoebe Palmer became a well-known evangelist in her own right, stretching the accepted leadership roles for women. She founded the New York Female Assistance Society for the Relief and Religious Instruction of the Sick Poor and helped found a number of Methodist churches. Her books, such as *The Way of Holiness* (1845) and *Faith and Its Effects* (1848), helped make the holiness movement take on national proportions.

In 1859 the Palmers began an extended trip to England and Ireland and toward the close of the Civil War returned to revive the war-weary holiness movement. They bought the major holiness periodical, *Guide to Holiness*, and within a decade had expanded its readership more than fivefold, to 40,000. She wrote more books and was a prominent leader in independent camp meetings, though she never left the Methodist Episcopal Church.

Paramananda, Swami: Paramananda was born Suresh Chandra Guha Thakurta in 1884 in India. He was initiated into Sannyas at the age of 17 by Swami Vivekananda, becoming his youngest monastic disciple. He came to the United States in 1906 to assist Swami Abhedananda at the New York Vedanta Society, the first U.S. center. In 1909 Paramananda opened the Vedanta Centre in Boston and established a monastic community of

H.H. Swami Paramananda
Courtesy: Vedanta Center

American women. Like his teacher, he believed in the equality of men and women. He ordained Sister Devamata to teach Vedanta from the platform. During his lifetime, women monastics carried major responsibility in every area of the work.

In 1931, Swami Paramananda founded work in India for destitute women and children. Two ashramas, which include schools, an orphanage, shelter and training for women in need, continue to flourish in Calcutta.

Until his death in 1940, all of the centers founded by Swami Paramananda were part of the Ramakrishna Math (monastery) and Mission whose headquarters were at Belur, Calcutta, India. At his death, his centers were excommunicated from Ramakrishna Math and Mission because he left as his designated spiritual successor Srimata Gayatri Devi, an Indian woman of his monastic community. The beliefs, traditions and practices of the Vedanta Centre and Ananda Ashrama remain identical with those of the Ramakrishna Order, the break between the two being purely administrative. Those beliefs include the view that the true nature of each individual is Divine and that the purpose of human life is to realize the Divine within one's own soul.

Parham, Charles Fox: Charles Parham (June 4, 1873-January 29, 1929), modern-day originator of Pentecostalism and founder of the Apostolic Faith Church, was born in Muscatine, Iowa and grew up in rural Kansas. He experienced conversion at age 13 and by the time he entered Southwestern Kansas College was a licensed preacher for the Methodist Episcopal Church. In college he came down with rheumatic fever and was expected to die. A faith healing, however, convinced him of a call to the ministry, which he began full-time immediately.

In 1894, after two years of circuit pastoring for the Methodists he turned independent. He married Sarah Thislethwaite in 1896 and in 1898 they opened a healing house in Topeka, Kansas. There he began a periodical, *The Apostolic Faith*, teaching reliance upon God's power. In 1900 he opened a new center, still in Topeka, and worked with Bible students on interpreting biblical verses on the baptism of the Holy Spirit. They decided that this appeared to mean speaking in tongues and they began to pray for this blessing to occur. It happened first to Agnes Ozman, who remained unable to speak English for three days. Soon it came to Parham and the other students, and preaching this baptism of the Holy Spirit, this Pentecostal experience, occupied Parham for the rest of his life.

He opened a Bible school in Houston, Texas in 1905, and among the students was William J. Seymour, who then introduced Pentecostalism to his Azusa Street Mission in Los Angeles with astonishing success. Parham visited that church, but disliked what he saw. He came to realize that he had no control over the rapid spread of the movement, and even opposed attempts to organize it. In 1911 he settled in Baxter Springs, Kansas, as evangelist and Bible school teacher. The loose grouping of congregations that followed his teachings became known as the Apostolic Faith Church.

Parker, Daniel: (April 6, 1781-December 3, 1844), founder of the Two-Seed-in-the-Spirit Predestinarian Baptist churches, was born in Culpepper County, Virginia and grew up in poverty on the Georgia frontier. In 1802 he joined the Nails Creek Baptist Church in Franklin, Georgia and was soon licensed to preach. In 1803 he moved with his wife and parents to Tennessee, where they joined the Trumbull Baptist Church in Dickson County. That congregation ordained him in 1806 and in the following years he pastored a number of churches.

In 1810 Parker became acquainted with a particular brand of predestinationism, was convinced of its truth, and began to promote it so forcefully that ever since it has been identified with his name. This "two-seed" doctrine is partly an interpretation of Genesis 3:15, where God says to the serpent, "I will put enmity between you and the woman, and between your seed and her seed; he shall bruise your head, and you shall bruise his heel." The belief is that Satan (the serpent) placed an evil seed in Eve, accounting for the murderous Cain. Thenceforth, each person is born either of the good seed and thus belongs to God both in this life and the next, or is of the bad seed, belonging to Satan. Such predestinarian theology was designed to counter the growing evangelical and missions movement among Baptists. No amount of mission work can change the nature of one's "seed."

In 1815 Parker was elected moderator of the Concord Baptist Association in Tennessee, giving him a further platform from which to condemn mission societies, theological education, Bible societies, and such. From 1817 to 1832 he lived in Illinois, where he founded the Lamatte Baptist Church in Crawford County, published several pamphlets, served in the Illinois senate (1826-27), and edited the *Church Advocate* periodical (1829-30).

In 1833-34 he established the Pilgrim Predestinarian Regular Baptist Church of Jesus Christ in Texas and worked the rest of his life to expand the Texas work. By 1890 those in various states who followed his views numbered almost 13,000, but by 1945 had dwindled to about 200, and the movement is now virtually defunct.

Parker, Quanah: Quanah Parker (c.1845-February 23, 1911), a founder of the Native American Church, was born in Texas. His father was Peta Nocona, a Comanche chief and spiritual leader, and his mother, Cynthia Anne Parker, was a white woman, taken captive at age twelve, who lived with the tribe for 25 years, until 1860. Three years after she left, his father died, and he was orphaned.

In 1874 he was in a group that trapped some white buffalo hunters. They believed the battle would end in their favor because magical shirts provided by the medicine man would turn away the bullets. This did not happen, and Parker was thrown into a period of spiritual questioning. The following year his Kwahadi group of Comanches arrived at their assigned reservation in Oklahoma. After some years he visited his mother's family in south Texas and apparently while there encountered the ceremonial use of peyote, a psychedelic cactus drug that had long been used for medicinal purposes.

Parker helped spread the practice of peyote religion into the Comanche, Kiowa, and other tribes. After the demise of the Ghost Dance with the 1890 massacre at Wounded Knee, South Dakota, the peyote religion became the major unifying force among the diverse tribal groups. Parker became a popular leader and the United States government related to him as Chief of the Comanches. He encouraged the integration of peyote practice with Christian beliefs and symbolism, although he kept several wives. With great diplomacy he was able to cope with an Oklahoma law against peyote passed in 1899 and keep at bay initial federal efforts to ban peyote use.

In 1909 those following the peyote ceremony adopted the name Union Church (changed to the Native American Church in 1918). Today the church is one of the largest pan-Indian religious groups and in 1966, thanks partly to Parker's early efforts, a federal law was passed that clearly allowed the religious use of peyote by that church.

Pathfinder, Peter: Peter Pathfinder (b. March 22, 1937), founder of the Aquarian Tabernacle Church, was born in Jersey City, New Jersey. Also known as Pierre (or Peter) C. Davis, he served for many years in Jersey City variously as councilman, mayor, constable, and police commissioner. In the 1970s he moved to Seattle, Washington as branch manager for the electronic security division of the William J. Burns International Detective Agency.

For many years he studied with a number of Neo-Pagan teachers and was thereby known by many in the Neo-Pagan community. In 1975 the Covenant of the Goddess was formed by Alison Harlow, Gwydion Pendderwen, and Aidan A. Kelly as an ecumenical organization fostering communication and cooperation among Neo-Pagan groups. Pathfinder (Davis) was chosen as its first Public Information Officer and in that capacity wrote and produced its first information brochures.

In 1979 he founded the Aquarian Tabernacle Church, which has sought recognition on a par with other established churches, incorporating in 1983 and achieving tax exempt status in 1991. It participates in the Washington State Interfaith Council. Pathfinder has served in many ways as a consultant, including for law enforcement agencies on occult-related crimes and for the Washington State Department of Corrections Religious Program.

Patterson, Charles Brodie: Charles Patterson (1854-1917), well-known author and editor, was also the founder of the Alliance of Divine Unity, among the first of the larger New Thought groups. Little is known of his early life. He began an independent New Thought healing ministry in Hartford, Connecticut, in 1887. This saw enough success that he was able to establish his following as a congregation. He founded the Alliance (or Church) of Divine Unity in Hartford in 1894, and a second Alliance of Divine Unity was later founded in New York City. Worship services in the former were held on Sunday evenings and in the latter were on Thursday evenings.

In 1897 Patterson founded *Mind* magazine and the Alliance Publishing Company (with John Emery McLean) as an outgrowth of the success of these groups. He edited *Mind* until 1906, during which time it became one of the most respected New Thought journals. He also edited *Arena*, a popular cultural review magazine, from November 1900 to March 1904. About 1900 he founded the Alliance School of Applied Metaphysics in New York City and brought Helen Van Anderson, founder of the Church of the Higher Life, on board as vice-president. During the summers he was a popular leader at a New Thought retreat center in Oscawana-on-Hudson, New York, a center he helped organize in 1902.

Patterson was a high-profile figure in the early New Thought ecumenical efforts, and was the first president of the International Metaphysical League in 1899. He was named an honorary president of the International New Thought Congress in Chicago in 1916. He wrote about a dozen books, his most productive period being between 1909 and 1915.

Paxson, Diana: Diana Paxson (b. February 20, 1943), founder of the Fellowship of the Spiral Path, was born in Detroit, Michigan, but grew up in California. She received her B.A. in 1964 from Mills College and her M.A. in literature in 1968 from the University of California. For the next ten years she taught school and developed educational materials.

During the 1970s she was initiated into the Aquarian Order of the Restoration, a group based on the work of British magician Dion Fortune. She became particularly interested in studying the Kabbalah and various aspects of ritual. In 1979 she helped found Dark Moon Circle, a women's mystery group, and was ordained as a priestess in 1982. By then, based in the San Francisco area, she had gained another source of income through her novels and short stories, many with Pagan themes and settings.

From 1981 to 1986 she was president of the Center for Non-Traditional Religions, and when that disbanded in 1986 she founded the Fellowship of the Spiral Path, also intended as something of an umbrella organization for a number of small Neo-Pagan groups. Among other things, it sponsors the Clergy Collegium for Neo-Pagan leaders, and the monthly presentation of the Liturgy of the Lady, written in 1981 by Paxson. In 1986 she founded a co-ed group, the Equinox Circle, and in 1988 began Hrafnir, a specialized group for investigation of the Norse magical heritage. From 1987 to 1989 she served as first officer of the international ecumenical group, Covenant of the Goddess.

Pelley, William Dudley: William Dudley Pelley (March 12, 1890–June 1965), founder of Soulcraft, Inc., was born in Lynn, Massachusetts. His father was a stern minister of the Methodist Episcopal Church. The family's poor financial status required Pelley to leave school at age 14 and begin working in the mills. His childhood was not pleasant, and as a young adult he encountered problems with his journalism career, a failed marriage, and the death of his first daughter.

Despite nurturing a private agnosticism, he served in 1918 as a reporter for the Methodist Episcopal Church on foreign missions in Asia, and then reported on the Russian Revolution for the Young Men's Christian Association (Y.M.C.A.). During the 1920s he wrote motion picture scores and wrote successfully for magazines. In 1928 he had a spontaneous out-of-body experience, which transformed him religiously into an occult orientation. He reported receiving messages thereafter from ethereal entities called "mentors." They informed him that every human spirit is part of the Godhead and that life on earth is a classroom where spirits are to become more aware of themselves, others, and God.

Despite this lofty worldview, Pelley was active throughout the 1930s and early 1940s in various hate campaigns against the New Deal, communism, and the Jews. In 1933 he organized the Silver Shirts, modeled after Hitler's Brown Shirts. He was finally arrested on sedition charges in 1942 and was sentenced to 15 years in prison, but after serving seven years was released by an act of the Supreme Court.

He spent his remaining years writing books and lessons describing his Soulcraft philosophy. He refused to found a church out of concern that the philosophy would turn dogmatic. Fellowship Press, run by his daughter and son-in-law, keeps his ideas in circulation.

Percival, Harold Waldwin: Harold Percival (April 15, 1868-March 6, 1953), founder of the Word Foundation and co-founder of the Theosophical Society of New York, was born to a British family in Bridgetown, Barbados. His father died when he was ten and he then moved with his mother to the United States. In 1892 he joined the Theosophical Society, then led in the United States by William Q. Judge. After Judge's death in 1896, Percival joined with some others to form the independent Theosophical Society of New York and the Theosophical Publishing House.

Over the following years, Percival wrote extensively. He founded *The Word* magazine in 1904 and edited it until 1917. He published such books as *The Zodiac* (1906) and *Karma, the Law of Life* (1910). Gradually he put together his own belief system based on a mystical experience in 1893. He believed that by focusing his "Conscious Light" upon a subject he could gain complete knowledge of it. About 1912 he began dictating material gained while in such a state of concentration and the results were finally released in 1950 as *Thinking and Destiny*. That book stated that as humans become ever more conscious, they gain more control over the destiny created by one's thinking. In 1950 he established the Word Foundation to spread his ideas, a work the foundation has continued since his death in 1953.

Pike, Bishop James Albert: The Episcopal Bishop of California James Albert Pike (1913-1969), well known for his unorthodox theological views, became a Spiritualist when his son Jim killed himself in 1966 after experimenting with hallucinogenic drugs. Pike began his journey toward spiritualism as a result of poltergeist phenomena, which occurred in at least two different places: in Christ Church rectory in Poughkeepsie, New York, where he heard books being moved and found candles mysteriously extinguished, and in the library of the Cathedral of St. John the Divine in New York City, where he heard shuffling feet and footsteps on the floor and stairs.

Beginning February 20, 1966, Bishop Pike felt that his son might be trying to communicate with him when other poltergeist phenomena occured in his apartment. He sat in seances with a London medium, Mrs Ena Twigg, who, after examining a passport belonging to Jim Jr., became very distressed and reported that he was trying to get through to his father in order to ask forgiveness for the suicide and to express his love. During another seance, Twigg went into trance allowing Jim Jr. to speak through her and to prophesy that his father would leave his post very soon and would be going to Virginia. Both events happened.

In America, he sat with mediums Arthur Ford and George Daisley, through whom he received detailed messages from his son about his standing fast against the charges of doctrinal heresy, which Pike countered with the publication of his *If This Be Heresy*. Pike published his communications with Jim Jr. in the book *The Other Side* in 1968. He died in the Israeli desert in 1969, during a trip to the Holy Land that he took with his wife Diane Kennedy. Three days before his body was discovered, he communicated with Mrs Twigg. In a long and painful message, Pike told her what had happened, how he had struggled against death and the transition to the Other Side, and that his body would be found on a cliff in the Judaean desert near the Dead Sea (which it was).

Plummer, George Winslow: George Plummer (August 25, 1876-January 23, 1944), co-founder of the Holy Orthodox Church in America and co-founder of the Societas Rosicruciana in America, was born in Boston, Massachusetts. After college he moved to New York City, where he worked as art director for several magazines and joined the Masons. In 1907 he and Sylvester C. Gould created the Societas Rosicruciana in America as a Rosicrucian group that would allow non-Masons as members. After Gould's death in 1909, Plummer succeeded him as head of the group. Over the years, Plummer founded (1916) a magazine for the society, *Mercury*, established a number of schools, and wrote most of the study material.

Plummer's interests were also directed toward leading a specifically religious group. He was ordained by Manuel Ferrando of the Reformed Episcopal Church and was also consecrated by him on November 17, 1918. In the 1920s he founded the Seminary of Biblical Research, through which he issued lessons in Christian mysticism. In 1924 he co-founded with Arthur W. Brooks the Anglican Universal Church of Christ in the United States of America (Chaldean). In 1934 he left that group and joined William Albert Nichols, an heir to Aftimios Ofiesh's American Orthodox Apostolic Church, in founding (on March 16) the Holy Orthodox Church in America to carry on Ofiesh's work. He was reconsecrated by Nichols on May 8, 1934.

The Holy Orthodox Church in America kept close ties with Plummer's Rosicrucian organization, sharing many leaders. In 1935 Plummer's first wife died and in 1937 he married his long-time secretary, Gladys Emily Müller. She later succeeded him as head of the Societas Rosicruciana in America and in 1950 married Stanislaus De Witow, his successor in the Holy Orthodox Church in America.

Srila Prabhupuda leads devotees chanting (1976)
Photo: Vishakha Dasi
Courtesy: Bhaktivedanta Book Trust

Prabhupada, Abhay Charan De Bhaktivedanta: A. C. Bhaktivedanta Prabhupada (September 1, 1896–November 14, 1977), founder of the International Society for Krishna Consciousness, was born Abhay Charan De, in Calcutta, India. His father, a cloth merchant, took him often to Hindu worship at the temple across the street from their home. While in Scottish Churches College he accepted an arranged marriage to 11-year-old Padharani Satta. In 1920 he refused his college degree in solidarity with Mahatma Gandhi's call to avoid British goods.

He found work in a pharmaceutical company and over the following years became increasingly dissatisfied with family and work life and correspondingly interested in the religious quest. He became a disciple of Sri Srimad Bhaktisiddhanta Saraswati Goswami, the head of an old devotional group called Guadiya Math. He wrote a number of religious books and became a favorite of his teacher, who in 1936 told him he would soon take the worship of Krishna to the West.

In 1956 he separated himself from his secular life, took holy vows, and took the name A. C. Bhaktivedanta Swami Prabhupada. In 1965 he made the prophesied trip to the United States and opened a center in New York

City, publishing a magazine called *Back to Godhead*. He founded the International Society for Krishna Consciousness (ISKCON) in 1966 and opened a center in San Francisco in 1967. Over the next decade he attracted several thousand core (full-time, live-in) members and over 200,000 lay constituents. Devotees showed devotion to Krishna through chanting the Hare Krishna mantra, public dancing, and other activities.

Prabhupada weathered a storm of criticism over the movement, which many took to be a cult. He spent much of his time preparing the organization for the future. He arranged for the orderly transition of authority and committed as many of his thoughts to paper as possible. Over 60 volumes of his works were published prior to his death and more have been put together since then.

Elizabeth Clare Prophet
Courtesy: Kali Productions

Prophet, Elizabeth Clare: Elizabeth Clare Prophet (b. April 8, 1940), spiritual leader of the Church Universal and Triumphant, was born in Red Bank, New Jersey as Elizabeth Clare Wulf. She was a student at Boston University when she met Mark L. Prophet on April 22, 1961. He had founded the Summit Lighthouse to publish the messages of the masters. By the time of this meeting, Elizabeth Prophet had already moved away from her Christian Science upbringing and was interested in the I AM movement. They were married in 1963.

Together they ran the Summit Lighthouse, first out of their house in Beacons Head, Virginia, then in 1966 from Colorado Springs, Colorado. Mark Prophet provided the teaching material for the membership by way of dictated messages from the Ascended Masters, primarily Saint Germain and El Morya. The Masters are those saints and mystics of the past who have achieved freedom and enlightenment and are now involved in guiding the destiny of earth. The I AM is the God-presence within each person, and the goal is to more and more clearly access that wisdom and power.

After Mark Prophet's death in 1973, she received the mantle of Messenger from Saint Germain and continued the transmittal of messages from the Ascended Masters, including her deceased husband, now known as Lanello. In 1974 she incorporated the group as the Church Universal and

Triumphant and in 1978 moved the headquarters to Malibu, California. In 1986 they moved again to a 28,000-acre parcel near Yellowstone Park in Montana.

Mark Prophet
Courtesy: Church Universal and Triumphant

Prophet, Mark L.: Mark Prophet (December 24, 1918-February 26, 1973), founder of the Summit Lighthouse, which later became the Church Universal and Triumphant, was born in Chippewa Falls, Wisconsin. Before Air Force duty in World War II he worked for the Soo Line Railroad. After the war he was a salesman and during the 1950s became involved with the teachings of the Ascended Masters, a tradition initially related to the I AM Religious Activity of Guy and Edna Ballard in the 1930s and since carried by numerous other groups as well.

Francis K. Ekey had an independent group, the Lighthouse of Freedom, in Philadelphia, and Prophet founded a branch of that in Washington, D.C. In 1958 Prophet's group went independent as the Summit Lighthouse and began publishing the *Ashram Notes* newsletter. In 1963 he married Elizabeth Clare Wulf, who helped run the church out of their new home in Beacons Head, Virginia. The following year Prophet established an inner group for serious students, the Keepers of the Flame Fraternity. In 1966 the headquarters were moved to Colorado Springs, Colorado.

During most of these years Prophet spent much time dictating messages from the Ascended Masters, mostly Saint Germain and El Morya, into teaching material. Some, such as *The Overcoming of Fear Through Decrees* (1966), were published in book form during Prophet's lifetime, and other dictations have since been collected into various posthumous books. He taught the I AM presence as the God-power in each person and the use of the spoken word, particularly decrees, to call forth that power. The soul's goal through numerous incarnations is to become one with Christ while still in physical embodiment. After Prophet's death the group was led by Elizabeth Prophet and in 1974 was incorporated as the Church Universal and Triumphant.

Benjamin and Mary Purnell (1907)
Courtesy: The Israelite House of David as
Reorganized by Mary Purnell

Purnell, Benjamin: Benjamin Purnell (1861-1927) was the founder of the House of David, and was the most well-known American leader deriving from the lineage of British prophetess Joanna Southcott. At the age of sixteen he married Angelina Brown, but they soon separated and remarried without being divorced. In 1880 he married Mary Stoddard, with whom he began moving from town to town.

After having obtained a copy of Southcottite prophet James J. Jazreel's *The Flying Roll*, the Purnells joined a Jazreelite commune in 1882 in Detroit, where the year before the leader "Prince" Michael Mills had proclaimed himself the Seventh Angel of Revelation 8:6. Purnell was received at the community and was made a "Pillar"—leader—by Prince Michael. Soon, after denouncing Prince Michael as an imposter, Purnell proclaimed himself the Seventh Angel and was expelled from the Detroit colony.

After a period of itinerant preaching, Purnell settled in Fosteria, Ohio, where he published his first book, *Star of Bethlehem*, in 1902. In the same period, he joined a group of Jazreelites in Benton Harbor, Michigan, but after few years he decided to establish a new colony in Australia, where he founded the House of David among the followers of John Wroe, another Southcottite prophet.

When he returned to the United States in 1905, he brought eighty converts with him and purchased land outside Benton Harbor, where he began establishing the House of David. The House of David, which became a strong self-supporting community, had an amusement park, as well as a band and a famous baseball team. Members of the community, who accepted Purnell as the Seventh Angel, took Nazarite vows. They did not cut their hair, were vegetarian, and adopted a celibate life, although Purnell continually faced charges of sexual immorality with the many female members of the community.

In 1922 Purnell made his last public appearance, and in 1926 was arrested after having been caught in his night clothes with four female group members. One year later the colony was declared a public nuisance. Five weeks after a judicial decision excluding the Purnells from further association with the colony, Purnell died and H.T. Dewhist took control of the House of David. He did this against the will of Mary Purnell, who in 1930 reorganized a new colony with her supporters. Both colonies still exist and continue to circulate the books of Benjamin Purnell, such as his *Book of Wisdom*, *The Ball of Fire*, and the *Book of Dialogues*.

Pursel, Jach: Jach Pursel famous New Age channel for the disembodied entity Lazaris, was born in Lansing, Michigan. After attending the University of Michigan he began a career with State Farm Insurance. In 1972, with his wife, Peny, he learned to meditate, and in 1974 began receiving messages from a spirit called Lazaris. Soon he was regularly channeling Lazaris while in a trance state.

Lazaris, who claimed never to have taken human form, discoursed at length on cosmic and spiritual matters, covering most of the standard New Age themes. Pursel was able to leave his job in 1976 and devote himself full-time to channeling. In addition to lectures and workshops, he distributed tapes and videos, and Lazaris became one of the most well-known entities in New Age circles. Pursel founded Concept: Synergy to coordinate his work, and is presently headquartered in Florida.

Q

Quimby, Phineas Parkhurst:

Phineas P. Quimby
Courtesy: American Religion Collection

Phineas Quimby (February 16, 1802–January 16, 1866), seminal figure in the rise of the New Thought movement, was born in Lebanon, New Hampshire. Not much is known of his early life; he began his adult life as an obscure clockmaker in Belfast, Maine. In 1836 mesmerism was introduced to America by Charles Poyen, who traveled the lecture circuit giving demonstrations. Quimby attended some of these lectures and was fascinated. Desiring to replicate the lecture demonstrations on his own, Quimby found a local man, Lucius Burkmar, who could easily be placed in a trance. In the trance state, Burkmar showed what seemed to be mind-reading and clairvoyant abilities.

Quimby and Burkmar turned professional and toured the Northeast from about 1842 to 1847, highlighting Burkmar as a diagnostician and healer of disease. The standard belief about mesmerism was that it was accomplished by means of an invisible fluid called "ether" or "animal magnetism" and could be affected by electricity. Quimby came to believe that only the mind, or one's belief system, was at work. He decided that the only reason people were cured by Burkmar is that they believed he could cure them.

After working out his new healing system on his own for several years, Quimby set up an office in Portland, Maine, in 1859. Although the details of how he dealt with individual patients are sketchy, he apparently focused on explaining how their false ideas created what they thought were illnesses. He claimed to use the power of his own thoughts to help set things right. This was an entirely new approach to disease. The fledgling psychoanalytic profession eventually agreed with him that "hypnotism" was a purely mental process, but stated that only some illnesses were mental in origin and therefore amenable to a mental cure. Quimby claimed that all bodily disorders were the product of wrong thinking, and this is the basic idea he gave to posterity, particularly to all who followed him in metaphysical religion.

From 1859 until his death in 1866, Quimby treated an estimated 12,000 patients. A small group of these were interested in the philosophy behind the cures and became his inner circle of students. His most important student was Mary Baker Eddy, founder of Christian Science, the source organization for most of the splinter groups that became New Thought. Other important students were Warren Felt Evans, author of the first book on this metaphysical perspective, and Julius and Annetta Dresser, who became New Thought leaders in the Boston area. Quimby founded no organization and provided for no successor. His manuscripts, privately held by his family for many years, were not publicly available until an edition was published by the Dressers' son, Horatio Dresser, in 1921. In 1988 a three-volume edition of his writings became available.

R

Swami Sivananda Radha
Courtesy: Yasodhara Ashram

Radha, Swami Sivananda: Sylvia Hellman traveled to India after having had a vision of Swami Sivananda Saraswati during a meditation session. There Sivananda initiated her into the Sanyasa Order and she acquired the name of Swami Sivananda Radha. Upon her return to Canada she founded Yasodhara Ashram in Vancouver, Canada, in 1956 and moved it to Kootenay Bay in 1963.

While in India she also learned the Divine Light Invocation from guru Babaji; this technique allows one to visualize a healing white light which emanates from divine energy. In her teachings Swami Radha blends together the yogic techniques she learned in India with western psychological and symbolic concepts, her aim being a better understanding between East and West. A Temple of Divine Light Dedicated to All Religions has been constructed. Swami Radha also created a publishing company named Timeless Books, and in Idaho she established the Association for the Development of Human Potential, which is connected with the ashram.

Rael: Born Claude Vorilhon in 1946, French race-car driver and journalist Rael was the founder of the Raelian movement. On December 13, 1973 he was contacted by an advanced extraterrestrial civilization dur-

Rael
Courtesy: Raelian Movement

ing a walking tour of the Clermont-Ferrand volcanic mountain range in France. He received a message that he understood to be destined for the whole world. He subsequently wrote two books, in 1974 and 1975, that were published in English in one volume as *Space Aliens Took Me to Their Planet: The Most Important Revelation in the History of Mankind* (1978). In addition to informing the public about the message he received, the other part of his mission was to build an embassy for the extraterrestrials.

Rael described the aliens of his encounter as small human-shaped beings with pale green skin and almond eyes. He asserted that these aliens entrusted him with a message concerning humans' true identity. According to this message, human beings were "implanted" on Earth by superior extraterrestrial scientists, the Elohim, who created man from DNA in their laboratories. Rael's doctrine claiming that a renegade group of aliens gave early humans knowledge that was forbidden by the other extraterrestrials reflects the myth of Prometheus, according to which he stole fire from the gods for the benefit of humankind. Rael is also "the last of forty prophets" whose mission is to warn humankind that since 1945 and Hiroshima we have entered the "Age of Apocalypse."

Rael denies the existence of God or the soul. He claims that the only hope of immortality is represented by a regeneration through science. Rael, whose version of free love resembles that of Fourier, John Humphrey Noyes, and Rajneesh, encourages members of his movement not to marry, nor to maintain a long-term relationship, but rather to commune with others by exploring sexuality with the opposite sex, the same sex, and any other life form. An annual sensual meditation workshop features fasting, nudity, sensory awareness exercises, and sexual experimentation, in order for the participants to achieve the "cosmic orgasm." According to Rael, these sexual customs reflect those of the space aliens that he observed.

Rajneesh, Osho (Bhagwan) Shree: Bhagwan Rajnessh (December 11, 1931-January 19, 1990), founder of the Rajneesh Foundation International and the Osho Commune International, was born Rajneesh Chandra

Mohan in Kuchwada, India. On March 21, 1953, during his early college days, he announced an experience of samadhi, or enlightenment. He went on to receive his M.A. in philosophy in 1957 and took a professorship at Jabalpur University. Over the following years the tensions between his work as scholar and his position as unorthodox spiritual teacher became too great and he resigned from the university in 1966.

In 1970 he founded a congregation in Bombay and the next year adopted the title Bhagwan, or God. He intended this to signify his method of direct, soul-to-soul teaching, rather than an intellectualized experience. In 1974 his following had grown sufficiently to support the purchase of six acres in Poona, which became his headquarters. Drawing from sources as diverse as humanistic psychology and Sufism, he believed that releasing emotions and developing self-expression in freedom were key elements in the process towards enlightenment. He taught "dynamic meditation," which activated the body through various means, including regulated breathing, chanting, and screaming. He encouraged indulgence in sex as liberating and consciousness-raising. Initiates took vows, not to renounce life, but to embrace it with abandon.

His following became almost entirely European and American as Indians abandoned his teachings as immoral. Seeking a more conducive environment, Rajneesh moved to the United States in 1981 and moved to a 64,000 acre ranch near Antelope, Oregon. As his unusual teachings and lavish life-style (93 Rolls-Royces) became known in the area, and particularly after he proposed building a communal village to be called Rajneeshpuram, opposition became as intense there as in India. In 1985 he was charged with immigration fraud and deported back to India, where he reactivated the Poona compound. In 1988 he dropped "Bhagwan" from his name in favor of "Osho," meaning "one upon whom the heavens shower flowers," and the organization was renamed Osho Commune International. Osho died in Poona in 1990.

Rama, Swami: Swami Rama, founder of the Himalayan International Institute of Yoga Science and Philosophy, was born in Uttar Pradesh, India. He was orphaned at a young age and Sri Madhavananda Bharati raised him, not only as a parent, but as a spiritual master, instructing him in the Hindu scriptures and traditions. Rama's general schooling was extensive, and he received a medical degree from Darbhanga Medical School in 1945.

In 1949 Rama became one of the four Shankaracharya's, making him one of Hinduism's most important living authorities, but after three years

Swami Rama
Courtesy: Himalayan International Institute

he left to pursue studies of western philosophy and pyschology. He became a well-known instructor of yoga and taught at several universities. In 1970 he participated in experiments at the Menninger Clinic in the United States on voluntary control of the autonomic functions in the body. His surprising ability to affect his brainwaves, body temperature, and blood flow helped establish the elements of biofeedback therapy and gave yoga a new philosophical and scientific legitimacy in the West.

In 1971 Rama founded the Himalayan Institute in Glenview, Illinois, near Chicago, and over the years it gained numerous branch institutes. By 1978 the headquarters had moved to Honesdale, Pennsylvania, and served not only as an ashram but as a full research center on yoga-related subjects. Rama continued to develop the work of the institute both in the United States and abroad, particularly India. The Glenview location is famous for its annual yoga congress, which attracts yoga practitioners of all persuasions. Swami Rama passed away in 1996.

Sri Ramakrishna
Courtesy: American Religion Collection

Ramakrishna, Sri: Sri Ramakrishna (February 18, 1836-August 16, 1886), famous Hindu priest and teacher of Swami Vivekananda, was born in Kamarpukur, India. His birth name was Gadagkar Chattopadhyay, the son of poor parents in a rural village. In his youth he moved to Calcutta to assist his brother in the operation of a Sanskrit school. Already he showed signs of unusual religious interest and ability, particularly in the practice of meditation. In 1855 he became a priest in a temple dedicated to the goddess Kali.

Ramakrishna's meditation became more and more intense and he began to have visions of Kali. This was so unusual that his friends and colleagues were concerned for him and decided that marriage would be good for him. He reluctantly agreed to leave the temple for a time for more secular pursuits, and married the five-year-old child, Saradamani Devi, arranged for him. In 1861 he returned to the temple and in 1865 began a quest for complete unity with the divine. At one point he reportedly was in a trance for six months and was in danger of losing his life. Kali appeared to him again and told him to be satisfied with a more normal state of consciousness.

Over time Ramakrishna gathered disciples who believed that his life showed evidence, not of an unbalanced mind, but rather of spiritual gifts. In 1872 his wife joined him again for a more adult, though apparently platonic, relationship. After his death, one of his disciples, later known as Swami Vivekananda, organized a Ramakrishna Order and eventually helped found the Vedanta Society in the United States.

Paschal Beverly Randolph
Courtesy: American Religion Collection

Randolph, Paschal Beverly: Paschal Randolph (October 8, 1825-July 29, 1875), founder of the Fraternitas Rosae Crucis, was born in New York City. His father was from a prominent Virginia family and his mother was a former slave from Madagascar. Randolph, concerned about his heritage, claimed that his mother was a member of Madagascan royalty. He did not see himself as a black man. After she died of smallpox he was raised by a family friend.

In 1841 he ran away from home and sailed the seas for five years until an injury forced him to stay on land. He became a barber and by 1850 had learned enough medicine to practice as a naturopath, specializing in sexual problems. That year he is supposed to have traveled to Europe, where he found and joined the Rosicrucian Fraternity in Germany before returning to America. In 1854 he is supposed to have returned to Europe and studied with Eliphas Levi and others for several years. In Paris in 1858 he reportedly was made Supreme Grand Master of the Western World and a Knight of L'Ordre du Lis.

Back in the United States he began speaking on behalf of Rosicrucianism and in 1861 founded the first Rosicrucian lodge in nineteenth-century America, in San Francisco. In 1862 he reportedly spent some time in the

Middle and Far East. Upon his return he worked as a recruiter for black soldiers in Boston for the Union Army. In 1864, at the request of President Lincoln, he went to Louisiana to educate the newly-freed slaves. After Lincoln was assassinated, Randolph was the only African-American to accompany his body back to Illinois, though his color caused him to be removed from the train.

After the war, Randolph returned to his medical practice, hanging out a shingle in Boston, and in 1871 he organized a new Rosicrucian lodge. In 1872 he was arrested for circulating literature on free love, on the basis of such books he had written as *The Grand Secret; or, Physical Love in Health and Disease* (1862) and *Love and the Master Passion* (1870). The charges made for a well-attended and well-publicized trial in which he successfully defended himself. Issues of sexuality were certainly key to his work and teaching. In 1874 he published *Eulis, the History of Love*, in which he discussed his idea that the ancient Eleusinian Mysteries were about the sexual act. He believed that the same mystic sexual elements were at the base of Rosicrucian teachings, though he advocated that sex-magick be practiced only by married couples.

The Boston fire of November 1872 destroyed Randolph's home and he moved to Toledo, Ohio. He married in 1874 and had a son, but committed suicide the following year after discovering his wife in adultery. The Fraternitas Rosae Crucis went into a period of near-extinction until it was resurrected by R. Swinburne Clymer in 1895. Randolph's teachings on sex magick in particular would later be picked up by occult magician Aleister Crowley.

Rapp, George: (November 1, 1757–August 7, 1847), founder of the Rappite community of New Harmony, Indiana and Economy, Pennsylvania, was born in Iptingen, Württemberg, Germany. He had only a basic schooling before following his father into the farming and vine-dressing business. In 1783 he married Christine Benzinger, with whom he had two children.

In the following several years, he began to read the Bible more seriously and developed a severe critique of the prevailing church standards as not adhering to the radical demands of scripture. In 1787 he began to preach, but persecution was a constant obstacle. In 1804 his followers, numbering some 600, moved to Zelienople (near Evansville), Pennsylvania and created a communitarian village. Rapp came to believe that Adam was originally androgynous and that the separation into male and female was the true "fall." He also believed that Jesus was androgynous, part of the work of his restoration. Rapp decided that celibacy was the most biblically appropriate lifestyle, and in 1807 the whole community took a vow of celibacy.

In 1814 the group moved to New Harmony, Indiana. There they continued the practices that made them among the most successful communal groups in American history. They had a diversified economy, making items ranging from wagons to cultivated silk. They were the first to develop prefabricated houses. Rapp's son, the economic genius of the community, helped write Indiana's first state constitution. New Harmony became Indiana's largest city. When success seemed to threaten the group, they sold the property and built a new town, Economy, near Pittsburgh, Pennsylvania.

Regardie, Francis Israel: Israel Regardie (November 17, 1907-March 10, 1985), influential ritual magician, was born Israel Regardie, of an orthodox Jewish family in London, England. When he was fourteen the family moved to Washington, D.C., where he discovered the writings of Madame Blavatsky, founder of the Theosophical Society. He read widely in the occult and Asian religions and eventually met Karl Germer, a disciple of Aleister Crowley.

In 1928, after some time at the Philadelphia School of Art, Regardie went to Paris to meet Crowley personally. He ended up staying with Crowley several years as his secretary, at some point adding Francis as his first name. After this apprenticeship he published two books that established him among the leaders of the field, *The Garden of Pomegranets* (1932) and *The Tree of Life: A Study in Magic* (1932). He spent several years with a branch of the Hermetic Order of the Golden Dawn, but became disenchanted with the leadership, leading him to break his oath of secrecy and publish the group's inner workings and rituals in *My Rosicrucian Adventure* (1935) and four volumes of *The Golden Dawn* (1938-40).

He had moved to New York City to put together *The Golden Dawn* volumes, and there decided to change his career orientation altogether. He graduated from the Chiropractic College of New York in 1941, and after military service during World War II (1942-45) earned a degree in psychology, a follower of Nandor Fordor and later, Wilhelm Reich. He established a chiropractic/psychoanalytic office in Los Angeles and worked quietly there for twenty-five years.

In 1969 his *Tree of Life* book was reprinted and the following year *The Garden of Pomegranets* was reprinted. With the occult revival of the 1970s he once again was a sought-after ritual magician. At his retirement home in Arizona he wrote several more books and taught a number of serious students, some of whom have tried to resurrect the Golden Dawn tradition.

Remey, Charles Mason: Charles Remey (May 15, 1874-February 4, 1974), founder of the Orthodox Abha World Faith, was born in Burlington, Iowa. While in Paris studying architecture, he discovered the Baha'i Faith and joined a local group. In 1901 he met Abdu'l-Baha, then leader of the Baha'i Faith, with whom he formed an ongoing relationship.

After teaching for a few years at George Washington University in Washington, D.C. Remey became a commercial architect. After settling into that career he set aside time to visit various Baha'i groups in the Middle East. Abdu'l-Baha asked him to put an account of his tour in writing, which became *Observations of a Baha'i Traveller* (1914). Over the years Remey wrote a number of other books introducing the public to the Baha'i Faith, at a time when there was very little in English on that group. At the request of Abdu'l-Baha, Remey was the architect for the Baha'i temple on Mount Carmel in Israel, and he designed a number of other temples for the faith as well.

When Shoghi Effendi took over the movement in 1921, he also looked to Remey as a key western convert. In 1951 Effendi formed the International Baha'i Council and appointed Remey president. Remey was also a member of the Hands of the Cause, a group that Effendi shaped into a formal ruling body. Nine members of the Hands of the Cause, including Remey, led the Baha'i Faith after Effendi's death in 1957, until the Universal House of Justice was elected in 1963. During that time, at the Baha'i headquarters in Haifa, Israel, Remey came to believe that Effendi had intended him to continue the role of individual leader (guardian) of the faith. Remey was unable to convince other leading Baha'is of this, however, and in 1960 was expelled from the organization.

Remey continued to press for reconsideration until 1968, when he founded a rival group, the Orthodox Abha World Faith. Soon afterward he retired to Florence, Italy, and left the organization in other hands. After his death in 1974 the group splintered into three new organizations, each claiming a different successor to Remey.

Reyes, Benito: Benito F. Reyes, the author of over twenty books about philosophy, psychology, religious studies, and Oriental culture, graduated from the University of the Philippines. Before founding the Uni-

Benito F. Reyes meets the Pope
Courtesy: World University of America

versity of the City of Manila in 1967, he was professor at the Far Eastern University in Manila, taught at Boston University in 1951-52 as a Fulbright-Smith-Mundt professor and at the State University of New York in 1965 as a Fulbright-Hays philosophy professor. In 1975 he founded, with his wife Dominga, the World University of America in Ojai, California, which is an institution dedicated to the promotion of world peace through education, and to the liberation of consciousness of the human being.

His interest in *out-of-body experiences* and the nature of human consciousness after life had its beginning in an experience he had at the age of sixteen, when he first went consciously out of the body. At the age of twelve, he began accompanying his mother who helped people to die as a *Pho-O,* that is, one who helps the spirit release the body, and rejoices with it at its conscious departure. Conscious out-of-body experiences (COOBEs), as well as near-death experiences, which he experienced at least twice around the Second World War, represented an integral part of his life. He argued that he experienced COOBE every night, consciously and with full control, and sometimes without having to first allow his body to sleep.

In his *Scientific Evidence of the Existence of the Soul,* written in 1949, Reyes postulates that the soul exists and that it constitutes a nonphysical element in the human being. In the works *Conscious Dying,* and *Practice of Conscious Dying,* Reyes deals with the psychology of conscious dying, based on the phenomenology of near-death-experiences. Conscious dying, which is also among the themes of the Bardo Thodol or the Tibetan Book of the Dead, is claimed to be the key that will unlock the door of Immortality. This state is achieved by going through death consciously, through birth consciously, and between death and rebirth consciously.

Richmond, Olney: Olney H. Richmond (1844-1920) is most remembered as the founder of the Order of the Magi in Chicago in1889, one of the new astrological religions (like Thomas Burgoyne's Brotherhood of Light and Hiram Butler's Esoteric Fraternity) founded in America in the nineteenth century. What has not been known was that the Order of the Magi was the "outer court" (as it would now be called) for a coven of Witches. This Tradition of "the Magus Olney Richmond" was passed on by Arlene Richmond to Donald Nelson, a Chicago bookseller and publisher, who recruited Thomas Giles into the Tradition. Giles, who was initiated by a Priestess, reports that the initiation was sexual. Giles, in turn, became one of the founders of the American Tradition and of the Pagan Way. This "Magi" Tradition is one of the few known pre-Gardnerian Witchcraft traditions in America. Richmond was also the author of a set of "Temple Lectures" on the exoteric practices of the Order.

—Aidan A. Kelly

Roberts, Benjamin Titus: Benjamin Titus Scott (1823-1893) was the founder and first general superintendent of the Free Methodist Church. He was born at Cattaraugus, New York, and grew up in the famous "Burned-Over District" of Western New York. Shortly after moving to Little Falls in order to study law, he returned to his hometown and redirected his life into the ministry. He entered Wesleyan University, and taught Sunday school at a black church, which influenced his opinions on slavery considerably.

In 1848 he was admitted to the Genesee Conference of the Methodist Episcopal Church, and married Ellen L. Stowe. He successively served a series of appointments. During one of them, at Pike, he experienced sanctification, that is the second work of grace believed to make one perfect in love. He soon began to oppose innovations within the Methodist church, such as the pew rentals, the wearing of gold and costly apparel, as well as the use of organs. Thus, besides the reformers who wished to return to old standards, a larger group that favored change emerged in the conference.

In 1857 Roberts' article "New School Methodism" appeared on the *Northern Independent*, attacking all of the innovations that he felt were sapping Methodism. In the same year he was publicly censured by the bishop for immoral and un-Christian conduct in condemning his fellow ministers, and in 1858 he was tried and expelled.

In the following years he traveled and spoke to audiences whenever he was allowed, while some of his followers organized meetings to protest the Genesee Conference's action. They finally met and formed the Free Methodist church in August 1860, and elected Roberts general superintendent. He established the first society three days later at Pekin, New York, and wrote the constitution as well as the *Discipline* for the new church. He also wrote an apology, *Why Another Sect*, and became the editor of the monthly periodical *Earnest Christian*. His farm at North Chili, New York, became the site of the church's first school, that he directed for the next twenty years.

Roberts, Jane: Jane Roberts (May 8, 1929-September 5, 1984), pioneer New Age channel, was born in Albany, New York. She attended Skidmore College from 1947 to 1950 and held a variety of jobs. She married Robert Butts in 1954, but for her later publishing purposes used her maiden name of Roberts.

She and her husband began receiving messages from Seth in 1963, while experimenting with a Ouija board. Soon Seth conversed through Roberts while she was in a complete trance. His messages were recorded and collected into books, such as *The Coming of Seth* (1966). Roberts was something of a recluse and rarely appeared as a public figure, but the Seth books became extremely popular.

The Seth phenomenon is credited with being the starting point for New Age channeling. The spirits contacted by the nineteenth century mediums were generally deceased friends or family members who brought comfort to the bereaved. If more famous deceased persons were contacted, the purpose was usually to "prove" the continuance of life after death. Two exceptions were Andrew Jackson Davis (1826-1910) and Edgar Cayce (1877-1945), whose primary experience in spirit contact was the retrieval of knowledge, particularly health knowledge, though there was also significant metaphysical content. New Age channeling deals with spirit entities that may or may not have lived human lives, and emphasizes discourses on metaphysical and life meaning issues. Normally a New Age channel will channel only one entity and do traveling presentations.

During Roberts' lifetime other people appeared who claimed they were channeling Seth, claims that Roberts denied. She believed that Seth was not the spirit of a deceased person, but rather an activity of the unconscious. Several Seth newsletters appeared, along with the Austin Seth Center, all independent of Roberts.

Robinson, Frank B.: Frank Robinson (July 5, 1886-October 19, 1948), the founder of Psychiana, one of the first mail-order religions, was born in New York City. He attended the Baptist Bible Training School in Toronto and became a Baptist minister like his father, but that did not last long. He later wrote that several events conspired to turn him against traditional Christianity and he began a long road toward finding another career and another religious home.

He finally settled on New Thought after attending the College of Divine Metaphysics in Indianapolis in 1915-16. He continued studies on his own and after becoming a pharmacy manager in Moscow, Idaho, in 1928, he began holding New Thought classes on the side. The following year he founded Psychiana and built it as a mail-order religion. He discouraged the formation of Psychiana groups in favor of followers connected only by correspondence courses and the *Psychiana Quarterly*.

His teachings were fairly standard New Thought fare, identifying God with natural law and asserting that by understanding this law people could rid themselves of poverty, sickness, and unhappiness. Psychiana became one of the most successful New Thought groups, developing students in all 50 states and 70 other countries. At one point he reportedly received as much as 1,000 letters a day. After a time he assumed the title of archbishop and eventually assigned four bishops to help administrate the organization. Psychiana became defunct only a few years after his death.

Roerich, Nicolas Konstantinovitch: Nicolas Roerich (October 9, 1874-December 13, 1947), co-founder of the Agni Yoga Society, was born in St. Petersburg, Russia. He began in his father's footsteps as a lawyer, but his real interests as an artist eventually came to the fore and he became internationally renowned for his work. He was elected to the Russian Imperial Academy of the Fine Arts in 1909.

He and his wife, Helena, left Russia at the time of the Revolution and moved to Europe. In 1920 the Art Institute of Chicago invited them to visit. After a national tour, they settled in New York, where he founded the Master Institute of the United Arts. About that time they joined the Theosophical Society, founded by Helena P. Blavatsky, and became very involved. Helena translated Blavatsky's *The Secret Doctrine* into Russian and soon claimed to receive messages from one of Theosophy's spiritual masters, Master Morya.

She published the first volume of *Leaves of M's Garden* in 1924, and together with Nicolas organized what was at first an informal discussion group into the Agni Yoga Society. The Roerichs began traveling and in 1929 settled in the Punjab, India. He founded the Himalayan Research Institute to carry out archaeological digs and other research and she continued to publish books from Master Morya. Nicolas also published numerous books on art, spirituality, and peace. He established the Roerich Pact and Banner of Peace, an agreement that warring countries would not harm centers of education and culture. A museum of his work in New York also houses the continuing work of the Agni Yoga Society.

Rudhyar, Dane: Dane Rudhyar (1895-1985) is known for having reoriented astrology from prediction of events to its present emphasis on the analysis of personality. He was born Daniel Chennevierre in Paris, where he spent the first 20 years of his life. He started developing his mind at age 12, when he became seriously ill, and at age 16 he passed his baccalaureate in philosophy at the Sorbonne. He was introduced to the artistic and musical world of Paris, and to the thought of such philosophers as Friedrich Nietzsche, whose concept that all existence is cyclic in character had a significant impact on him.

After writing *Claude Debussy*, and the *Cycle of Musical Civilization*, describing Western civilization as having reached an autumnal state, Rudhyar refocused his attention on music and the piano, and studied with Pessard at the Paris Conservatoire until the beginning of World War I. Having been exempted from military service for health problems, in 1916 he left for New York, in order to perform the dance-drama *Metachory*, for which he had written some music. In 1917, he performed his pieces *Poemes Ironiques* and *Vision Vegetale*, which were the first polytonal music heard in America.

In New York, Rudhyar met the Zen teacher Sasaki Roshi, and became interested in Oriental music and philosophy as well as Western occultism. After spending some months in Canada, he moved to Philadelphia, where he wrote the orchestral work *Soul Fire*, and the pieces *Mosaics*, *Ravishments*, and *Tres Poemes Tragique*. Among his writings were also essays on the Baha'i movement and social organization, as well as plans for a world city. He was introduced to Christine Wetherill Stevenson, founder of the Philadelphia Art Alliance and initiator of the Little Theatre Movement, who ha been producing a play about the life of the Buddha. She asked Rudhyar to compose scenic music for a play about the life of Christ, that was produced in the summer of 1920.

In 1920-21, his interest in Oriental philosophy deepened, and in it he found confirmation of his beliefs about the cyclic nature of civilization. After leaving motion picture work in 1927, he began giving lecture-recitals, composing music, and writing many articles on music and philosophy, such as his *Rebirth of Hindu Music* (1928) published in Madras, India.

In 1929, Rudhyar moved to Carmel, California, where he composed music, a poetic novel, and a booklet entitled *Education, Instruction, Initiation*. In 1930, he married Malya Contento, through whom he met Marc Edmund Jones, who introduced him to astrology in terms of what was then an unprecedented philosophical approach. Rudhyar became also interested into the depth psychology of Carl Jung, and in 1931-32 he wrote a series of seven pamphlets under the general title *Harmonic Astrology*. In 1932, he started a collaboration with Paul Clancy, founder of successful magazine *American Astrology*. During the summer of 1933, he was able to read through all of Jung's works that had been translated into English, and he decided to "develop a series of connections between Jung's concepts and a reformulated type of astrology." In *The Astrology of Personality* (1936), Rudhyar developed and unified a series of articles that he had previously written on such topics as politics, philosophy, psychology, esoteric traditions, by using his new approach.

A series of personal problems and marriage difficulties led him to question several things he had accepted on faith, and he wrote the unpublished books "Man, Maker of Universes" (1940), and "The Age of Plenitude" (1942). His marriage eventually broke down completely, and in 1945 he married Eya Fechin, with whom Rudhyar left for Colorado and New Mexico, where he did most of his paintings and wrote *The Moon: The Cycles and Fortunes of Life* (1946), and *Modern Man's Conflicts* (1946). He then moved back to New York, where his renewed interest in music led him to perform again. After his second marriage collapsed (1954), Rudhyar returned to California, where he began rebuilding his life at age 60, completing his orchestral work *Thresholds*, and writing astrology booklets that were published under the series title *Seeds for Greater Living*.

After another painful crisis in 1957-58, Rudhyar left for Switzerland, where he completed and translated into French *Fire Out of the Stone*. He lectured in Paris for few months, spent another year in California, and then decided to return to Europe, where he began to publish his works on astrology again through the Verhulst's Service Press.

In 1963, he returned to America, where he married Gale Tana Whitall in 1964. They settled in San Jacinto, California, where they lived for the next 10 years, during which Rudhyar finally received recognition and respect for his work. His books became acceptable to such New York publishers as Penguin, Doubleday, and Harper & Row. During these years he wrote such books as *The Practice of Astrology* (1966), *Astrological Study of Psychological Complexes and Emotional Problems* (1966), *The Rhythm of Human Fulfillment* (1966), *Of Vibrance and Peace* (1967), *Astrological Triptych* (1968), and *Astrological Timing: The Transition to the New Age* (1968). In March

1969, Rudhyar founded the International Committee for Humanistic Astrology, and about the same time he was invited to speak at Esalen, a human potentials institute.

Several books followed, and of these Rudhyar considered *The Planetarization of Consciousness* (1970) to be his most basic work, condensing all his thought into an integrated statement.

His marriage to Tana ended in 1976, and he eventually married Leyla Rasle in 1977. During the last years of his life he wrote *Astrology and the Modern Psyche* (1977), *Astrological Triptych* (1978), *Beyond Individualism* (1979), *Astrological Insights* (1979), *Astrology of Transformation* (1980), and *Rhythm of Wholeness* (1983). He died in California on September 13, 1985.

—Aidan A. Kelly

Russell, Charles Taze: Charles Russel (February 16, 1852-October 31, 1916), founder of the Watch Tower Bible and Tract Society (which later became better known as Jehovah's Witnesses), was born in Pittsburgh, Pennsylvania. Raised as a Scotch-Irish Presbyterian, he showed more interest in his father's retail clothing business than in religion until he ran across Jonas Wendall. Wendall, an Adventist preacher in the line of William Miller, was predicting the end of the world in 1874.

Russell thought this was important enough to start his own group and study the Bible seriously. He eventually developed his own interpretations of various Bible passages. He decided that the human soul is mortal, not immortal, and thus what happens to evil souls is not eternal torment, but simple annihilation by not being resurrected at Judgment Day. Further, the Kingdom of God, he thought, would be a heavenly government run by Jesus and 144,000 helpers to rule over the earth.

The 1874 date came and went, but this was not a problem for Russell, who decided that Christ's spiritual presence had arrived at that time, indeed initiating the new millennium, and that God's more visible rule would begin in 1914; thus the famous Russellite slogan: "Millions now living will never die." In 1879 he founded the magazine *Watch Tower and Herald of Christ's Presence* and began also issuing a number of pamphlets describing his doctrinal positions. The movement grew steadily, fueled by Russell's frequent debates with other clergy. In 1909 world headquarters was established in Henry Ward Beecher's former parsonage in Brooklyn, New York. The most complete statement of his mature ideas is in the six-volume *Millennial Dawn* that he wrote over a dozen years (the series was later renamed *Studies in the Scriptures*).

When 1914 came and went without the advent of God's rule, Russell suggested that World War I was caused by Satan being expelled from heaven and that Jesus did begin his heavenly rule at that time. Joseph Franklin Rutherford, Russell's successor, was less interested in setting specific dates.

Rutherford, Joseph Franklin: Joseph Rutherford (November 8, 1869-January 8, 1942), leader of the Jehovah's Witnesses, was born in Morgan County, Missouri. Two years after being admitted to the Missouri bar as a lawyer in 1892, Rutherford encountered Charles Taze Russell's Watch Tower Society. After several years of study Rutherford was finally baptized into the group in 1906. He showed early evidence of his commitment to his new faith by that same year publishing *Man's Salvation from a Lawyer's Viewpoint* (1906).

A few months after Russell died, Rutherford was elected president of the society on January 6, 1917. During World War I the group encountered much hostility because of their pacifist stance, and in 1918 Rutherford and several others were arrested on sedition charges. They served less than a year before being released, and eventually the sentence was reversed. Rutherford had to deal with this kind of persecution his entire tenure. In 1940, for example, the group lost a Supreme Court case over a school requirement to salute the flag and recite the Pledge of Allegiance (though this ruling was effectively reversed in 1943).

Russell thoroughly reorganized the group, which had originally not expected to function after 1914, when God was to have begun ruling the earth. Russell helped reform millennial expectations on a less date-bound basis, rewrote the hand-out literature, established literature distribution campaigns, wrote numerous books, and introduced a new magazine, *The Golden Age* (now *Awake!*). In 1931, at his suggestion, the organization adopted the name Jehovah's Witnesses. His monumental work led many to call him the "second founder" of the Jehovah's Witnesses.

S

Sai Baba, Sathya: Sai Baba (b. November 23, 1926), spiritual leader of the Sathya Sai Baba movement, was born in Puttaparthi, India. His birth name was Satyanarayana because his mother experienced birth pains while performing the Hindu devotions called Satyanarayana Puja. Stories abound concerning his extreme religious devotions even as a child and of his miraculous abilities to create objects out of thin air. When he was fourteen he fell into a coma that lasted two months. When he awakened, on May 23, 1940, he suddenly announced, "I am Sai Baba of Shirdi," a holy man who had died in 1918. From that point he took the name Sathya Sai Baba and encouraged worship of himself every Thursday. On October 20, 1940 he claimed to have achieved release from maya (ignorance of the true nature of reality).

Over time Sai Baba gained a large following in India that expanded internationally. The movement took hold in the United States in 1967 after a series of lectures by Indra Devi, a recent visitor to his headquarters, Prasantha Nilayam (Home of the Supreme Peace). Sai Baba is considered by followers to be an avatar, or divine incarnation, and stories of his miracles, particularly materializations, continue to augment his veneration. The content of his teaching concerns his mission to reestablish dharma (cosmic moral order). He has provided support for a number of social outreach programs, particularly in the areas of health and education. His books include commentaries on Hindu scriptures and transcriptions of his public lectures.

Sandford, Frank Weston: Frank Sandford (October 2, 1862-March 4, 1948), founder of Kingdom, Inc., was born on a farm in Bowdoinham,

Maine. After briefly trying out teaching and law he entered the ministry and pastored a number of Free Baptist congregations in Topsham and Somersworth, Maine. After receiving what he interpreted as messages from God, he left the Free Baptists and moved to Maine. There he attracted enough followers to help him build the Shiloh community, complete with a Bible school, residence center, children's building, hospital, and post office.

Sandford continued to receive revelations and under their guidance he incorporated the community as the Kingdom, in reference to the phrase "Thy Kingdom come" in the Lord's Prayer, and proclaimed himself Elijah, returned to help see in the new era. He also proclaimed himself King David and began ruling the community in dictatorial fashion. This led to various defections and the conviction of Sandford of cruelty to a minor with a fine of $100.

After this incident Sandford traveled to Palestine and then sailed on a missionary tour of the world. That tour, however, did not go well either, with the death of six crew members, and he was convicted of manslaughter. He served a ten-year sentence in prison, during which time he conducted Bible studies and maintained contact with the Kingdom community. He returned to Maine in 1921 but disbanded the village in 1923 and created a new headquarters in Boston. After his death in 1948 the Kingdom survived for a time in several scattered congregations, and was sometimes known as Church of the Living God or as The Holy Ghost and Us Society.

Sasaki, Shigetsu: Shigetsu Sasaki (1882-May 17, 1945), founder of the First Zen Institute of America, was born in Japan. He became a successful artist and joined a lay Zen Buddhist movement called Ryomoko-Kai. Part of that group, including Sasaki and his wife, went to America in 1906 to evangelize. The venture was not successful, but he decided to stay in New York as an artist. His wife returned to Japan in 1914, placing a strain on the relationship.

In 1919 Sasaki returned to Japan to reunite his marriage and complete his Zen training. He continued occasional visits to New York and after becoming a Zen master in 1928 returned there to settle down. He founded the Buddhist Society of America in 1930, later (1944) renamed the First Zen Institute of America, and was popularly known by the name Sokei-an. He gained many disciples, including the popular Zen author Alan Watts.

During World War II Sasaki was a victim of anti-Japanese sentiment and was placed in a prison camp for 13 months in 1942-43. This displacement contributed to his already failing health. One of his former students, a Navy commander, testified on his behalf and he was finally released. In 1944 he married Ruth Fuller Everett, Watts's mother-in-law and editor of *Cat's Yawn*, the institute's periodical. He passed away the following year, naming his wife as his successor.

Swami Satchidananda
Courtesy: Satchidananda Ashram

Satchidananda, Swami:
Swami Satchidananda was born in southern India on December 22, 1914. He married and started a family at the age of 23. However, a mere five years later his wife died, leaving Satchidananda with two young sons. Placing his sons in the care of his parents, in 1946 Satchidananda entered the Ramakrishna Mission and was initiated into the life of intentional celibacy, study and service. In May 1949, Satchidananda met Swami Sivananda at his ashram in Rishikesh on the banks of the Ganges River. Two months later, Swami Sivananda initiated Satchidananda into the Holy Order of Sannyas. Swami Sivananda gave him the name Satchidananda. Three years later, he added the title of Yogiraj, Master of Yoga.

In 1953 Sivananda instructed Satchidananda to go to Sri Lanka and serve that island's people by opening a branch of the Divine Life Society. Satchidananda found Sri Lanka to be divided by differences in caste, language and religion. He transformed the traditional July festival in honor of the guru into an All Prophets Day that honored masters from all religions. He worked for peace and interreligious understanding between the Tamil and Singhalese populations. Satchidananda and his followers built temples and conducted services for those in prison. He became one of the best-known people in Sri Lanka.

As the guest of artist Peter Max, Satchidananda came to New York city in 1966. Within two months, his following had grown from a few friends of Max to the founding membership of the Integral Yoga Institute. Due to the extraordinary interest in his teaching in America, Satchidananda decided to work in the United States. On July 25, 1968, Satchidananda received the first permanent resident visa ever issued for the entry of a "Minister of Divine Words" into the United States. Swami Satchidananda was present at the opening of the Woodstock festival in 1969. In 1975 Swami Satchidananda initiated 28 disciples into the Holy Order of Sannyas.

Integral Yoga International purchased 750 acres of land along the James River in Virginia in 1979 as a permanent home for the Satchidananda Ashram and an extended residential community called Yogaville. The Integral Yoga Ministry was established in 1980. In 1986 the Light of Truth Universal Shrine (LOTUS) was dedicated to honor all the world religions at the Virginia ashram. The LOTUS symbolizes the unity in diversity of all religions and reflects Satchidananda's teaching that "Truth is One—Paths are Many."

Scott, Orange: Orange Scott (1800-1847) was the co-founder of the Wesleyan Methodist Church. Born into a poor family in rural New England, he had little education and never attended church. His religious consciousness was awakened in 1820 when, in an effort to find God, he began to read the Bible and to attend Church. In the same year he experienced a conversion at a Methodist camp in Barre, Vermont, and he eventually joined the Methodist Episcopal Church.

He became a class leader and a preacher, and was admitted into the New England conference in 1822. He served several charges, during which he was able to educate himself. He became a delegate to the General Conference in 1832, and in 1836 and 1840 he chaired the delegation.

His troubles with the church began when he was introduced to abolitionism and the issue of slavery, which he considered a moral evil. At that time the Methodists were pursuing a mild policy that simply opposed slavery. By circulating copies of the periodical *The Liberator*, he won his fellow ministers of New England to his position.

He championed the cause of abolitionism at the 1836 Methodist General Conference, which unfortunately adopted a resolution opposing the abolitionist position. Thus Scott started the abolitionist periodical *The Wesleyan Quarterly Review*, and began to call for reform of the church's government. He was eventually released from his post as presiding elder and assigned to the church at Lowell.

From 1837 to 1839 he lectured for the Anti-Slavery Society. After the 1849 General Conference again took a position against abolitionism, Scott moved to Newbury, Vermont, and founded *The True Wesleyan* as a forum for his position. He finally left the church altogether on November 8,

1842, just months after the New Hampshire Conference.

Since he lost hope of the Methodists' accepting reform, in 1842 Scott decided to organize a new church, that was founded in June 1843 at Utica, New York. The Wesleyan Methodist Connection of America, later named the Wesleyan Methodist Church, was an abolitionist nonepiscopal Methodist denomination, and Scott was its first president, and the *True Wesleyan* became its periodical.

In 1846 Scott, who was sick with tuberculosis, moved to Newark, New Jersey, where he died in 1847. His church eventually merged with the Pilgrim Holiness Church in 1968 to form the Wesleyan Church, which became a strong supporter of the holiness movement in the late nineteenth century.

Sears, Julia Seton: Julia Sears (December 27, 1862-April 25, 1950), founder of the Church and School of the New Civilization, was born into a Catholic family in Schuyler, Illinois. She was a sickly child and developed tuberculosis, though she managed to maintain her activities. She taught in the Ohio public schools for five years and on December 7, 1882 married S. S. Kapp, with whom she had one daughter.

As her marriage broke up around 1890 she moved to Colorado for her health and in 1898 received an M.D. from Gross Medical School in Denver. After several years of working mostly among poor mountain people she took post-graduate work at Tufts Medical College (1902-03) in Boston. She returned to Denver, married Franklin Warren Sears on November 16, 1903, then the two moved to Boston where she established a new practice. She also began teaching New Thought classes on the side.

How Sears learned New Thought is unknown. She may have been inspired by the heavy metaphysical activity in Boston during her time at Tufts. In any case, in 1905 she left her medical practice and taught New Thought full-time. She moved to New York City in 1906 and by 1910 was able to open a spacious headquarters in the New York American Building. That year she traveled to England and founded a center that eventually was called the First New Thought Church and School of London. On September 14, 1911 she founded the New Thought Church and School in Denver and the next month established its periodical, *The Column*. In 1912 she changed the name of her work to the Church and School of the New Civilization.

About 1913 she returned to New York to pastor the original church there. Over the years she brought in a number of other branch churches in several states. Everything went well for her except her marriage, which ended in divorce in 1914. She wrote some fifty books and in one year reportedly made $30,000 just in royalties. In 1937 she founded a new headquarters near Ocala, Florida, but most of the bungalows burned in 1945 and were never rebuilt. Her churches did not long survive her passing.

Nyogen Senzaki
Courtesy: American Religion Collection

Senzaki, Nyogen: Nyogen Senzaki (1876-May 7, 1958), Zen Buddhist teacher and founder of the Mentorgarten Meditation Hall, was discovered as an infant beside his frozen mother in Siberia. A shipwright adopted him, gave him the name Senzaki, and boarded him with a Buddhist scholar. In 1896 he entered Soyen Shaku's Engakuji monastery in Kamakura, Japan, and was a roommate of D. T. Suzuki. In 1901 he left the monastery to found a mentorgarten, or nursery school, but soon found the society's increasing militarism and decreasing interest in Zen incompatible with his interests.

In 1905 he moved to the United States and became a servant in the household of Alexander Russell in San Francisco. Russell was a Zen convert and at the time was hosting Soyen Shaku in his home. Shaku encouraged Senzaki to teach Zen, but Senzaki had no American sponsor and limited resources. After working a variety of jobs he finally was able, beginning in 1922, to rent halls from time to time for teaching and lecturing. In 1928 he established a following in Los Angeles as well. He did not gain a stable location until 1931 when he founded the Mentorgarten Meditation Hall in Los Angeles.

During World War II Senzaki was placed with other Japanese-Americans in an internment camp in Wyoming and made the best of it by continuing his teaching in that location. He was released in 1945 and reestablished his career in Los Angeles, writing a number of books in addition to his teaching. Although he did not personally become very famous, he was a vital link in the development of American interest in Buddhism and was often host to other Zen teachers who were passing through the area.

Seymour, William Joseph: William Seymour (May 2, 1870-September 28, 1922), founder of the Azusa Street Apostolic Faith Mission, was born in Centerville, Louisiana. His upbringing was in poverty; both his parents had been slaves. After moving to the midwest he joined the Church of God (Anderson, Indiana) and decided to enter the ministry after surviving smallpox with only scarring and blindness in one eye. He was ordained with the Church of God (Anderson, Indiana) in 1902.

In 1905 he attended classes in Houston, Texas, taught by Charles Fox Parham, founder of the modern-day Pentecostal movement. Seymour converted to Pentecostalism, though he did not immediately receive the baptism of the Holy Spirit (the Pentecostal term for speaking in tongues). Through another Parham student he was invited to pastor a church of disaffected Holiness believers in Los Angeles, but he was locked out of the church within a week. Only a few of them welcomed his Pentecostal teachings. This small group began home meetings and in April 1906 the group began to experience speaking in tongues. Seymour himself began speaking in tongues on April 12. From this point the group grew very fast and took over a former Methodist church on Azusa Street for their home.

The San Francisco earthquake of April 18, 1906 was considered by many to be one of the signs of the end times and the Azusa Street Mission printed thousands of pamphlets that correlated these signs with the rise of Pentecostalism. Interest in the Azusa Street phenomenon reached a fever pitch and under Seymour's direction it became the major force in spreading Pentecostalism across the United States and beyond.

On May 13, 1908 he married Jennie Evans Moore and a jealous assistant stole the church's mailing list for the periodical, *The Apostolic Faith*, reducing the group's national influence. In 1913 Seymour lost most of his following to the anti-trinitarian, "Jesus Only" theology. In his remaining years he struggled to put together a new following, but the mission became defunct about ten years after his death.

Shaku, Soyen: Soyen Shaku (1859-1919), famous Rinzai Zen Buddhist teacher, was born in Japan and was ordained a monk at the age of 12. Under the direction of his master, Imakita Kosen Roshi, he attended Keio University for several years, then went to Ceylon (today's Sri Lanka) to study Sanskrit and Theravada Buddhism. He received the dharma transmission from Imakita Kosen Roshi in 1884, marking him as a legitimate successor. When Kosen died in 1892, Shaku took over his Engakuji monastery in Kamakura, Japan.

Soyen Shaku
Courtesy: American Religion Collection

Shaku was an important speaker for Buddhism at the 1893 World Parliament of Religions held in conjunction with the Chicago World's Fair. He did not know English and had his presentations read for him. At that event he met publisher and editor Paul Carus, who became an important American supporter of Buddhism. Shaku arranged for his pupil Daisetz Teitaro Suzuki to go to America in 1897 and Suzuki stayed with Carus for a number of years.

In 1905 Shaku returned to the United States and stayed near San Francisco with American converts Alexander Russell and his wife. He gave many lectures with D. T. Suzuki serving as interpreter and after nine months returned to Japan. Shaku was a key figure in the early spread of Buddhism in the United States, not only through his own activity, but also through the work of such influential disciples as D. T. Suzuki and Nyogen Senzaki.

Henry Sidgwick
Courtesy: American Religion Collection

Sidgwick, Henry: The philosopher Henry Sidgwick (1838-1900) was a founding member and first president of the Society for Psychical Research. He was born in Skipton, Yorkshire, England, and raised by his mother after his father, the Reverend William Sidgwick, died when he was three years old. His interest in psychical research began when he was undergraduate student in classics and mathematics at Trinity College, where he graduated in 1859. In 1883 he became Knightbridge professor of moral philosophy and among his students were Arthur Balfour, Edmund Gurney and Frederic W.H. Myers.

On a starlight walk in the summer of 1871, he had an important conversation with Fredrick Myers about the possibility of achieving some form of knowledge of the Unseen World by observing psychical phenomena. In 1874 they both joined a group formed by Balfour, Gurney and others, whose purpose was the study of mediumship. He attended numerous seances, most of which had discouraging results, because of detected or strongly suspected trickery. However, his interest in psychical research continued to occupy a central role in his life, especially after Sir William Barrett's successful experiments on telepathy.

In 1882 he was elected president of the Society for Psychical Research, which he established with Myers and Gurney, as well as other members of the former group that had been studying psychical phenomena. Among his most important investigations are the cases of Helena P. Blavatsky, founder of the Theosophical Society, and of the medium Eusapia Palladino. This last case and the sittings he had at the end of his life with the medium Leonora Piper confirmed his earlier distrust of mediumship.

He played a major part in the organization of the Census of Hallucinations, conducted between 1889 and 1894. His works include *The Methods of Ethics* (1874), *Principles of Political Economy* (1883), *Phantasms of the Living* (1886), written with other members of the Society, and *Practical Ethics* (1898).

Simons, Menno: Menno Simons (1496-1561), born at Witmarsum, Friesland in the Netherlands, was an Anabaptist leader after whom the Mennonite Church was named. Little information has survived about his early years. He was ordained a priest in 1524, and served as vicar in Pingjum, not far from his birthplace.

Shortly after assuming his duties as priest, he began to doubt the bread and wine actually became Christ's body and blood (the doctrine of transubstantiation a key tenet of the Catholic faith), perhaps as a result of contact with the Sacramentists, a group of Dutch religious reformers who viewed the Sacraments as symbolic. He also began to read Zwingli, Luther, and other reformation writers. His study of Luther convinced him that the Bible was a higher authority than the Church. In response to contemporaneous Anabaptist teaching, he also became convinced that the biblical model for baptism was the baptism of adult believers rather than the infant baptism practiced by the Church.

However, in spite of his ideological conversion to Protestantism, he remained within the Catholic fold until the suppression of the Anabaptist community at Munster in 1535. After the leaders of this community were tortured to death, Menno left his church and joined the Anabaptist underground as an itinerant evangelist. By the 1540s he had become a recognized leader of the movement. In 1554 he helped to compose the Wismar Articles, which was an agreement among Anabaptists on proper belief and practice. The Anabaptists in northern Germany and Holland became known as Mennonites in recognition of the decisive influence of Menno's leadership.

Simpson, Albert Benjamin: Albert Benjamin Simpson (1843-1919) was the founder of the Christian and Missionary Alliance. Born in Canada's Maritime Provinces, he grew up on a farm, and at the age of fourteen decided to be a minister in the Presbyterian Church where he had been raised. He experienced salvation while reading the book *Gospel Mystery of Salvation*, and at the age of sixteen he began teaching school in order to support his college study. He attended Knox College, and after his graduation he was ordained and accepted a call to Knox Church in Hamilton.

In 1873 he moved to Louisville, Kentucky, where, as a pastor of a Presbyterian church, he came to know the holiness movement, and led the congregation in the building of the Broadway Tabernacle. In 1889 he moved to New York City, where he was pastor of Thirteenth Street Presbyterian Church for two years, during which he was sanctified and openly identified with the holiness movement. He also emerged as a strong advocate of spiritual healing after experiencing a physical healing at a summer resort at Old Orchard, Maine.

Because of his new convictions, which included belief in adult baptism by immersion, he withdrew and formed in 1882 an independent congregation that embodied Simpson's ideal of a missionary-oriented church. Among his activities were the organization of a missionary training college, a ministry to "fallen women," two rescue missions, an orphanage, a mission to sailors, and a medical clinic for the poor.

The first national convention was held in 1886 at Old Orchard, where the members of the church decided to organize a mission to Tibet and other places that did not have any Christian witness. This plan was formalized by the organization of the Evangelical Missionary Alliance, as well as the International Missionary Alliance, and the Christian and Missionary Alliance. The alliance had missionaries in twelve fields by 1893, when Simpson took his first international mission tour.

Among Simpson's works are the periodical *Word, Work, and World*, which continues today as the *Alliance Weekly*, as well as more than seventy books that include *The King's Business* (1886); *The Fullness of Jesus* (1886); *Christ in the Bible* (1889); *The Fullness of Jesus*, 2nd ed. (1890); *The Four-Fold*

Gospel; *Hymns of the Christian Life* (1891); and *Millenial Chimes* (1894). Simpson's movement became a strong body in America, supporting several schools to train missionaries and having stations around the world.

Singh, Darshan: Darshan Singh (September 14, 1921-May 20, 1989), founder of the Sawan Kirpal Ruhani Mission, was born in Kountrilla, India. His father was Kirpal Singh, founder of Ruhani Satsang, a very successful Sikh (Sant Mat) group. His father's guru, Sawan Singh, also became his guru, and under Sawan Singh's guidance Darshan Singh studied literature and poetry at the Government College in Lahore. Afterwards he entered government service, rising to the position of Deputy Secretary of India.

After Sawn Singh's death in 1948 Kirpal Singh went independent, founding Ruhani Satsang in 1951, and Darshan Singh had an active role in that. When his father died in 1974, Darshan Singh was ready to take over, and most members were in agreement, but the board of directors refused to acknowledge any successor. Thus, the following year, while maintaining his secular job, Darshan Singh founded his own organization, Sawan Kirpal Ruhani Mission. On November 20, 1977, the headquarters near the University of Delhi was formally dedicated and in 1978 Singh made his first world tour. He retired from the government position in 1979 and thereafter was able to devote himself completely to his religious work.

Among other ecumenical activities, in 1981 he presided over the Sixth World Fellowship of Religions Conference. He opened a free kitchen and medical dispensary at his headquarters. He wrote a number of books and oversaw the publication of the magazine *Sat Sandesh: The Message of the Masters*.

Singh, Kirpal: Kirpal Singh (February 6, 1894-August 21, 1974), founder of Ruhani Satsang, one of the Sikh (Sant Mat) groups with the most success in North America, was born in Sayyad Kasran, Pakistan. His secular career was spent in the India military services department, from which he retired in 1947. During those years Singh was also deeply involved in the spiritual quest. In 1917 he had a vision of a "Radiant Form" that he took to be Guru Nanak, the founder of Sikhism. Later, when he met Sawan Singh in 1924, leader of the Radhasoami Satsang in Beas, India, he recognized him as the figure in the vision. Kirpal Singh then stayed as a disciple of Sawan Singh for the next 24 years.

In 1948 Sawan Singh died and Kirpal Singh claimed the guru's lineage. This was disputed, and Kirpal Singh founded a new organization, Ruhani Satsang. Following his master, he taught surat shabd yoga, a means of attuning oneself to the divine emanations, sometimes pictured as like a sound current. Kirpal Singh made visits to the United States in 1955 and 1963, where initial work had already been done by disciples such as T. S. Khanna. Singh founded the World Fellowship of Religions as an ecumenical venture and published a number of books. At Kirpal Singh's death the organization split into several groups.

Sant Thakar Signh
Courtesy: Kirpal Light Satsang

Singh, Sant Thakar: Sant Thakar Singh (b. March 26, 1929), founder of Kirpal Light Satsang, was born in India. His father was a carpenter and both parents were very pious. When Singh was 11 his father died and circumstances forced him to work full-time when not in school. Even so, he managed to finish at the top of his class and then go on to receive an engineering degree. As per Indian tradition, he entered an arranged marriage. His secular career was as an officer in the Irrigation Branch of the Punjab Public Works Department.

Wherever he went he organized or participated in religious study groups of various kinds, but always felt that they did not quite match his inner need. In 1965 he went to hear Kirpal Singh, founder of the Ruhani Satsang, and after some initial hesitation was initiated as a disciple. The training in meditation he received from Kirpal Singh turned out to be exactly what he was looking for, and he worked assiduously to promote Kirpal Singh's work.

When Kirpal Singh died in 1974, Thakar Singh felt that he was the appropriate choice for successor. The American directors followed Darshan Singh, Kirpal's son, but Madam Hardevi, leader of the Sawan Ashram and the Ruhani Satsang in India, supported Thakar. After a period of meditation and retreat, Thakar Singh took the reins of leadership on February 5, 1976. Those in America who chose to follow him organized as the Kirpal Light Satsang, with headquarters in Kinderhook, NY. He has since made several trips to the U. S. to support the fledgling group.

Singh, Sawan: Sawan Singh (July 27, 1858-April 2, 1948), the second leader of Radhasoami Satsang Beas, was born in Mehmansinghwala, India. His family was part of the agricultural caste in the Punjab. He received a degree from the Thompson College of Engineering and found a position with the army corps of engineers in Murree. About that time he became a disciple of Jaimal Singh, founder of Radhasoami Satsang Beas. This was a reformist Sikh sect that sits apart from the Sikh mainstream largely because it follows a living guru rather than accepting the Sikh scriptures and community as the contemporary gurus.

When Jaimal Singh died in 1903, Sawan Singh succeeded him as leader, though, following his master's wishes, he remained in his secular career until retirement in 1911. At that point he was able to devote his full attention to the group, which correspondingly flourished. It is said that in his many travels across India he initiated more than 125,000 disciples, building the Radhasoami Satsang Beas into the largest of the Radha Soami movements. Although he never visited the West, he nevertheless had an indirect impact there. A disciple, Dr. Julian P. Johnson, wrote *The Path of the Masters* (1953), a popular Radhasoami book in the West. Another disciple, Kehar Singh Sasmus, initiated a couple in Washington state, who in turn initiated others. Still another disciple, Kirpal Singh, began a highly successful work in the United States, though under different auspices.

Sivananda, Swami Saraswati: Swami Sivananda (September 8, 1887-July 14, 1963), founder of the Divine Life Society, was born in Patamadai, India. His birth name was Kuppuswami Iyer. As the son of a government official he grew up in a relatively privileged environment and was able to attain a medical degree. He did not settle down as a physician, however, but felt called to a religious path. He became a student of Swami Viswananda Saraswati in the city of Rishikish, and was initiated into the life of an ascetic holy man.

In 1934 Sivananda founded his own ashram and two years later founded the Divine Life Trust (Society). His vision of the divine life was a combination of yogic discipline and service to other human beings. His ashram included a medical dispensary that eventually grew into a full hospital with outreach to a leper colony. Sivananda wrote over 200 books and gained many followers. He planned a trip to western countries but was prevented by poor health. He still managed to make a significant impact in the West through several students. Beginning in the 1960s, disciples such as Swami Vishnu Devananda and Swami Satchidananda became very well known in North America and helped popularize hatha yoga.

Slocum, John: John Slocum (c.1841-c.1897), founder of the Indian Shaker Movement, led an obscure early life. He may have been born among the Squaxin in the state of Washington. As a young man he married Mary Thompson, with whom he had many children, and lived around Olympia, Washington. Although he had received some Roman Catholic missionary instruction as a child, he was known as an adult for living a rough life.

In 1881 he became sick and apparently died, but just before the funeral he woke up, shocking everyone present. He claimed that he had in fact died and had been sent back to help make amends for his sinful life. Soon a church was built and he was regularly preaching, but enthusiasm among the people faded. Slocum fell ill again, and his wife, fearful he would finally die this time, began sobbing, praying, and shaking uncontrollably. When he improved, she reported that it was due to her shaking.

Thus did shaking become a part of the community's worship, and the church began to grow again, both with members and with visitors who were intrigued by the activity. The Slocums led the church into the 1890s, but then they returned to obscurity, leaving remnants of the Indian Shaker Movement that reportedly continue today.

Smohalla: Smohalla (c.1815-1907), founder of the Washani, or Dreamer Religion, was born into the Wanapan (or Solulk) tribe in Wallula, Washington. Little is known about his early life. He did odd jobs around the Catholic mission near his home, but did not convert. Because of his abilities as a warrior, visionary, and medicine man, he became a tribal leader.

In the 1850s he was left for dead after a fight with the chief of a neighboring tribe. He did not die, but managed to leave the area and eventually settled in Mexico. After a number of years he returned home and created great excitement as a man back from the dead. He said that he returned to them to bring a message from the spirit world. The message was a prophecy that the white men would disappear and everything would return to the paradise of the time before.

Smohalla's speaking abilities lent power to his message and soon he had many followers. By the 1870s the Washani or Dreamer Religion had fully developed, with rituals and ceremonies. Among his converts was Tuekakas (Old Joseph), a Nez Perce chief, and this was an important influence in the Nez Perce revolt of 1877. Smohalla lived to see the religion spread particularly among the Pacific Northwest tribes. Followers believed him to be a messiah figure and continued to carry his message for several decades after his death.

Joanna Southcott
Courtesy: The Israelite House of David as Reorganized by Mary Purnell

Southcott, Joanna: The apocalyptic prophetess Joanna Southcott (1750-1815) was born at Tarford, Devonshire, in rural England. She was raised as an Anglican, and she learned upholstery trade. She led a mundane life until the age of forty-two, when suddenly she began to hear a voice that she claimed was that of God. Through "automatic writing" she could write down what the voice said, as well as other material that warned that the time of the end was near and that Jesus Christ would soon return. She tried to convince people of the truth of her prophecies, in particular the Rev. Joseph Pomroy, whom she believed could be her voice to convince the church of her communications.

In 1794, Joanna began portraying herself as the bride mentioned in Revelation 19, and in 1800 she began publishing some of her communications. At the time, she had made no converts. Her first work was a series of pamphlets, *The Strange Effects of Faith*, the publication of which produced the response that she was expecting, and attracted the attention of some clergymen. In 1802 she moved to London with some followers, where she met the wealthy philanthropist Elias Carpenter. Owner of a papermill, Carpenter gave her a ream of paper, with which Joanna began to prepare seals by cutting the paper into small squares and by putting a brief message and the signature onto each of them. Then she gave these seals to followers as a sign of their renunciation of the devil. She claimed that the world was controlled by Satan and that this condition could be changed only if a sufficient number of people were sealed.

More than eight thousand seals were given out between 1803 and 1804, although most of the people that received the seals were among the followers of fallen apocalyptic leader Richard Brothers. Among her followers there were also a number of would-be leaders who threatened to divide her movement by offering their own prophecies. In response, some of her closest followers opened chapels, such as those in London, Leeds, Stockport, Bath, Bristol, and Exeter. In 1807 she gave out fourteen thousand seals.

In 1814 her voice told her that the following year she would bear a child, and that her baby would be identical with the one called Shiloh, a biblical figure generally identified with Jesus. She was pronounced pregnant by many physicians, but her pregnancy was eventually proclaimed hysteric in origin. Thus no baby was born, and Joanna, who was very disappointed, died before the end of the year.

The movement was thrown into chaos, and most supporters finally gathered around George Turner who saved the movement by asserting that Joanna had given birth but the child had immediately been taken up into heaven. In the United States the Southcottites gave origin to three groups: the Christian Israelite Church, the House of David, and the House of David Reorganized.

Spangler, David: David Spangler (b. January 7, 1945), New Age theoretician and founder of the Lorian Association, was born in Columbus, Ohio, and grew up in Phoenix, Arizona. As a teenager he was interested in theosophical groups and psychic phenomena. After attending college briefly he moved to Los Angeles in 1965 and began a traveling lecture and counseling service with Myrtle Glines. He discovered a channeling ability with an entity named John and in 1967 published his first ruminations about the New Age, *The Christ and the New Age*.

In 1970 he visited the Findhorn Community in northern Scotland, founded by Peter Caddy, and ended up staying for three years as its co-director. There he met Julia Manchester, whom he eventually married. The Findhorn Community has vied with the Universal Link as the most important group bringing the New Age movement into being, and through it Spangler became a major spokesperson.

Upon returning to the United States in 1973, Spangler founded the Lorian Association in Belmont, California, for those dedicated to bringing in the New Age. He traveled widely as a popular lecturer and began writing his most important books, such as *Revelation, the Birth of a New Age* (1976) and *Towards a Planetary Vision* (1977), viewed by many as definitive New Age statements. He has been quick to oppose New Age elements he sees as unauthentic or problematic, particularly apocalyptic visions that may prevent people from working to actively manifest the New Age. He published an autobiography, *Emergence, the Rebirth of the Sacred*, in 1984. The Lorian Association was disbanded in the late 1980s.

Spurling, Richard G., Jr.: Richard Spurling (1858-May 24, 1935), a founder of the Church of God (Cleveland, Tennessee), was born in Germany. The family soon thereafter moved to Kentucky, then Tennessee. His father built a lumber mill and was a Baptist preacher on the side. When he became dissatisfied with the Baptists he founded the Christian Union in 1886. Spurling, Jr. took over both the lumber mill and the church when his father died later in 1886.

In 1896 Spurling moved his congregation to Camp Creek, North Carolina, the site of a holiness revival, and united with the congregation there, taking the new name Holiness Church of Camp Creek. This church occasionally was witness to speaking in tongues, but did not develop a theology based upon that experience. Later in 1896 Ambrose Jessup Tomlinson, an agent for the American Bible Society, found the church and eventually joined it in 1903. He worked together with Spurling to bring a couple of other congregations into association, forming the Church of God in 1907. In 1908 the church became Pentecostal, finding the transition an easy and natural one. Over the following years Tomlinson became the dominant personality of the church, but Spurling remained an important figure.

Starhawk (Miriam Simos): Starhawk is perhaps the best known of the current leaders of the Neopagan movement, and is especially noted for having provided the movement with a theory of political action that is, in its way, comparable to the "Social Gospel" movement in American Christianity. She was born Miriam Simos on June 17, 1951, in St. Paul, Minnesota; daughter of Jack Simos and Bertha Simos; married Edwin W. Rahsman January 22, 1977. She pursued her undergraduate education at the University of California, Los Angeles, receiving a B.A. (cum laude) in 1972, with a major in Art, and did graduate study at UCLA in 1973. While in Los Angeles, she studied witchcraft with Sara Cunningham and Z. Budapest.

Arriving in the San Francisco area in 1973, she gave workshops for women in photography, writing, poetry, and feminist thought, 1973-74; and studied Fairy Tradition witchcraft with Victor Anderson, who is the source of almost all the information in her first book, *The Spiral Dance*. She founded the Compost Coven, which was one of the original signers of the Covenant of the Goddess in 1975; Starhawk was elected national First Officer (President) for the term 1976-77, Alison Harlow having held that position during the first year of the organization's existence. Starhawk taught adults at the Bay Area Center for Alternative Education, 1975-77, and was a free-lance film writer for industrial training films, 1978-80.

On October 31, 1979, *The Spiral Dance* was published in California on the same day that Margot Adler's *Drawing Down the Moon* was published in New York.

In about 1980, Starhawk was one of the founders of Reclaiming: A Center for Feminist Spirituality and Counseling, in Berkeley, Calif., which is a feminist collective that offers classes, workshops, public rituals, and private counseling in the tradition of Goddess religion, and she has served as a director, teacher, and counselor for the collective since then. She returned to graduate study at Antioch West University, 1980-82, received her M.A. in the feminist therapy program, which combined women's studies and psychology. Matthew Fox appointed her as a faculty member of his Institute for Culture and Creation Spirituality at Holy Names College in Oakland.

Starhawk described her first book, *The Spiral Dance: A Rebirth of the Ancient Religion of the Great Goddess*, as "an overview of the growth, suppression, and modern-day reemergence of the Old Religion of the Goddess, the pre-Christian tradition known as paganism, Wicca, or witchcraft. The book presents the history, philosophy, theology, and practice of this serious and much misunderstood religion, and explores its growing influence on the feminist and ecology movements." It is evident from this statement that she subscribes to the Gardnerian myth of the Craft as a survival from the witchcraft of medieval times; however, she does not mention Gerald B. Gardner in her book, except in the bibliography, and generally fails to give credit where it is due to him or to the other sources of her information.

She has also said, "*Dreaming the Dark* is a further exploration of the Goddess as a catalyzing symbol of the immanent consciousness that challenges the present social order. My motivation in most of my work has been the integration of a strong feminist vision and commitment to social justice with a strong spiritual search. I was born and raised Jewish, with a strong Hebrew education. Presently, I am a leader of the religion of the Great Goddess, the life force manifest in nature, human beings, and the world. To me the Goddess is a symbol that evokes women's strength and men's nurturing capabilities, and restores deep value to nature, sexuality, and the ecological balance."

— Aidan A. Kelly

Rudolf Steiner
Courtesy: American Religion Collection

Steiner, Rudolf: Rudolf Steiner (February 27, 1861-March 30, 1925), founder of the Anthroposophical Society, was born in Kraljevic, Austria, the son of a railroad worker. Attending the Technical University in Vienna he became interested in the works of writer Johann Wolfgang Goethe. He eventually became well-known as a Goethe scholar; he wrote the introduction to the standard edition of Goethe's scientific works and gained a position at the Goethe Archives in Weimar.

He was interested in mystical and occult spirituality. He moved to Berlin in 1897 to edit a literary magazine and there discovered the Theosophical Society. In 1902 he was elected head of the German Section of the society. From the beginning he had a number of disagreements with the society, particularly concerning the position of Jesus Christ. He thought Jesus was pivotal in history whereas Theosophy relegated him to the status of one of many incarnations of God.

In 1909 these disagreements came to a head when the Theosophical Society announced Jiddu Krishnamurti as the new Christ for this age. In 1912 Steiner took most of the German Theosophists into the Anthroposophical Society, which developed as a sort of Christian Theosophy. Headquarters were moved near Basel, Switzerland, where Steiner designed the Goetheanum center. He later created Eurythmy, a form of rhythm movement, and in 1919 the Waldorf schools were begun to show the application of Anthroposophy in education. In 1922 he created the Christian Community to provide a more familiar congregational form and liturgy. Since his death Anthroposophy has gained a following in the United States and has expanded internationally.

Storrs, George: George Storrs (1796-1879) was one of the founders and the first president of the Life and Advent Union. He was born at Lebanon, New Hampshire, in a community of Congregationalists that he joined at the age of nineteen. During the illness of his wife, who lived only six and a half years after their marraige, he was befriended by a Methodist Episcopal Church minister and joined that church. In 1825 he was admitted to the New England Conference, and in 1826 he was accepted into full connection. Successively he served a series of appointments in various towns of New Hampshire, which was set off as a separate Conference in 1832.

Storrs, who had become an active abolitionist, was arrested in 1835 at a meeting of the Sanbornton Bridge Anti-slavery Society. Both his abolitionist sentiments and his health led to his withdrawal from the church in 1840.

Storrs was convinced that immortality was conditional upon faith in Christ and that the wicked would not exist in hell but rather would be totally destroyed after the final judgment. He published his ideas in *An Inquiry: Are the Souls of the Wicked Immortal? In Three Letters*, the year after he left the Methodists. In 1842 he became pastor of a small independent congregation in Albany, New York. *An Inquiry; Are the Souls of the Wicked Immortal? In Six Sermons* contained a series of six sermons on conditional immortality that he preached in that period. In the same year, he was introduced to William Miller's Adventism by Calvin French, and he eventually became an Adventist evangelist. Storrs and conditional immortality became then the focus of controversy through Adventism.

In 1843 he started the Adventist periodical *The Bible Examiner*, authored the book *The Second Advent*, and became an advocate of the seventh-month expectation which looked for the return of Christ in 1844. However, after the Great Disappointment of 1844, he refused to set any further date. In 1845 Storrs aligned himself with the discouraged Adventists who reorganized at a conference held in Albany, and who eventually formed the Advent Christian Church.

Besides conditional immortality, Storrs introduced the issue known as "life-theory," according to which there would be no general resurrection, but only the righteous would be raised. This theory led to the formation in 1863 of the Life and Advent Union, of which Storrs was president and an active minister for the rest of his life, continuing to publish the *Bible Examiner*. The Life and Advent Union merged again with the Advent Christian Church in 1964.

Sun Bear: Sun Bear (1929-1991), founder of the Bear Tribe, was born on the White Earth Indian Reservation in Michigan. The son of Louis and Judith LaDuke, he spent the first part of his life going by the name Vincent LaDuke. At age 15 he left the reservation and traveled the country, working a number of jobs and visiting other Native American groups. In 1952 he joined the Army, but deserted shortly after basic training, and continued his absorption of various traditional Indian practices.

Over the next ten years he spent time with the Pomo Indians and the Washone Indians of Lake Tahoe, settling with the Reno-Sparks Indian colony in Nevada. He also spent some time in Hollywood as an Indian actor, but was finally arrested as a deserter and spent six months at the Lompoc Federal Correctional Institute in Lompoc, California. After a time back in Reno he returned to Hollywood and acted in a number of major films.

In 1961 he founded *Many Smokes* (later renamed *Wildfire*), a newspaper with national Indian news. In 1965 he met his future partner, Annie Ross (later called Nimimosha) and the following year the two of them and two other non-Indians moved from Los Angeles to Reno, founding the Bear Tribe. The Bear Tribe slowly grew, teaching survival skills, shamanic practices, and other Native American traditions. It has become very popular in New Age circles and sponsors the well-known Medicine Wheel gatherings. Sun Bear was also controversial among some Native Americans who were concerned about the implications of New Age appropriation of their culture.

Suzuki, Daisetz Teitaro: D. T. Suzuki (October 18, 1870-July 12, 1966), one of the best-known Buddhist authors and teachers in the Western world, was born into a Samurai family in Kanazawa, Japan. As a young man he entered the teaching profession, but soon moved to Tokyo to attend the Imperial University and undertake Zen training at the Engakuji monastery in Kamakura under Soyen Shaku.

In 1897 Shaku sent him to work with Paul Carus of the Open Court Publishing Company in Chicago. Until 1909 Suzuki and Carus worked on a number of translations and editions of important religious scriptures, including the *Tao Te Ching* and Ashvoghosho's *The Awakening of Faith*. When Shaku visited California in 1905-06, Suzuki served as his translator. In 1909 Suzuki returned to Japan and two years later married Beatrice Erskine Lane. In 1919 he accepted a position teaching philosophy of religion at Otani University in Tokyo, the major school of the Hompa Hongwanji sect of Shin Buddhism. Over the next thirty years he published most of his important works on Buddhism and edited *The Eastern Buddhist*.

In 1949 he spent a year at the University of Hawaii as visiting professor, then spent a year at Claremont Graduate School in California. At that point 80 years old, he accepted a position at Columbia University, where he stayed for six years. His presence there was a major impetus to the popularity of Zen in the "beat" generation, and the Zen Studies Society was founded to continue bringing Buddhism to the attention of

Americans. After about a year in Cambridge, Massachusetts, he retired to Japan in 1958.

Suzuki, Shunryu: Shunryu Suzuki (1904-December 4, 1971), founder of the Zen Center of San Francisco, was born in Japan. He followed in the footsteps of his father, who was a Soto Zen priest. He graduated from Komazawa Buddhist University and then continued his training at Eiheiji monastery. He eventually became priest of the Zounji temple and then of the Rinso-in temple. He married, but became a widower during the 1930s.

He was distressed by the growing militarism in Japan and during World War II was openly critical of the war effort. After the war he rebuilt the Rinso-in temple and helped restore two kindergartens. He married the principal of one of the kindergartens, Mitsu Matsuno. In the following years he gained a solid reputation for his administrative and priestly skills.

In 1959 he was appointed to head the San Francisco Soto Zen temple, Sokoji. In a period of only a few years he oversaw the transition of the temple from an almost exclusively Asian-American enclave to a center that was also popular among other Americans, particularly those of the young, "hippie" generation. He was open to this expanded work, but did not "dilute" the teachings for the new audience. He emphasized the importance of disciplined sitting, the traditional *zazen* (Zen meditation).

In 1967 the classes at Sokoji were so popular that expansion into other facilities was both possible and necessary. The Tassajara Springs property near Carmel Valley was purchased and rebuilt as Zen Mountain Center, Zenshinji Monastery. This began to serve, not only the San Francisco community, but growing affiliate centers in other parts of northern California. In 1970 Suzuki published his major writing effort, *Zen Mind, Beginner's Mind*, which gained a wide readership.

Swedenborg, Emanuel: Emanuel Swedenborg (1688-1772) was a Swedish mystic who became famous for his visions of higher spiritual realms, and for his travels to these realms. Swedenborg did not begin to have visionary experiences until later in life, after a modestly accomplished career as a scientist. He was special assessor to the Royal College of Mines. He had little interest in religious matters until 1743, at the age of 56, when he had a remarkable dream about the spiritual realm. Then followed a whole series of visions and dreams in which he met Jesus,

Emanuel Swedenborg
Courtesy: American Religion Collection

God and some of the great figures of history, visited the spirt realms, and conversed with the dead. He was instructed in the true nature of the universe. He also had clairvoyant experiences, including, in 1759, an incident in which he was able to perceive a fire in Stockholm (three hundred miles distance).

Swedenborg began to think of himself as a divinely appointed messenger, and started communicating the information he was receiving to other people. Letting go of his career, he shut himself away from other people so that he could work on receiving and recording visionary information. Many of his friends feared that he had gone crazy, and the Church opposed him. He learned how to self-induce his ecstatic states, as well as how to become a medium for communication in the form of automatic writing. He died at the ripe old age of 84 in London in 1774. A Swedenborgian church was not formed until after he had passed away, at first in England in 1778, and later in America in 1792. In 1810, the Swedenborg Society was founded for the purpose of publishing and disseminating Swedenborg's works. His most popular book, *Heaven and Hell*, offers a description of the afterlife. The Spiritualist movement of the 19th century adopted certain Swedenborgian notions, especially as these were reformulated and expressed in the writings of Andrew Jackson Davis.

T

Teish, Luisah: Luisah Teish (b. c.1948), Yoruban priest, was born Catherine Allen in New Orleans, Louisiana. Her parents named her after her grandmother, Catherine Mason Allen, who actually did most of her parenting. Her mother was Roman Catholic and her father was African Methodist Episcopal, but Teish generally attended the local Sanctified Church.

She moved to Los Angeles about 1963 and in 1966 graduated from Manual Arts High School with interests in journalism and dance. In 1967 she attended Pacific University in Forest Grove, Oregon, and was radicalized by racist encounters there. The next year was spent at Reed College in Portland, Oregon, and then in 1969 she received a scholarship to study dance with Katherine Dunham at the Performing Arts Training Center in East St. Louis, Illinois.

It was in St. Louis that she got in touch with her African heritage, learning African and Haitian dances. She joined the Fahamme Temple of Amun-Ra, where she was given her current name, meaning "adventurous spirit," and learned about Voudou (or Voodoo) and African mystery schools. She found a position as choreographer for the Black Artists Group in St. Louis, but her personal life was filled with difficulties. In 1973 she lost a baby and moved to Oakland, California, to live with her younger sister, Safi. After a suicide attempt in 1974 she found comfort with Voudou groups and a Yoruban priest helped her connect with a spirit guide. She joined the dance group Bata-koto, which emphasized Haitian dances and dances of the orishas (Yoruban deities).

In the late 1970s she discovered that her grandmother's house in New Orleans was on the site of the home of Marie LaVeau, known in the 1800s as the Voudou Queen of New Orleans. This brought meaning to some childhood psychic experiences and enabled a deeper connection to Voudou. Soon she began leading classes at the Berkeley Women's Center on African goddesses and Voudou traditions. About 1982 she was ordained priest of the Lucumi branch of the Yoruba tradition and in 1985 she published *Jambalaya: The Natural Woman's Book of Personal Charms and Practical Rituals*.

Tenskwatawa: Tenskwatawa (literally "The Open Door") was the Shawnee Prophet who helped forge a pan-Indian alliance opposed to Euroamerican intrusions in the years leading up to the War of 1812. He was one of three male triplets born in early 1775; his more famous brother Tecumseh was seven years older. Tenskwatawa's father died at the Battle of Point Pleasant prior to his birth, and after his mother abandoned him while still a small child, he was raised by his older sister Tecumpease, her husband Black Fish, and other Shawnee. And while still a child, he lost an eye playing with a bow and arrows. Perhaps as a consequence of this unfortunate childhood, he grew up to be a boastful alcoholic, acquiring the derogatory nickname Lalawethika ("noisemaker" or "rattle"). As a young man, he took a wife and fathered several children.

In early 1805, Lalawethika was a less than successful medicine man for a group of Shawnee living in eastern Indiana. In the wake of military defeat and an unfavorable treaty that had been imposed a decade earlier, many of the midwestern tribes had slid into a state of social and cultural demoralization. Lalawethika the alcoholic fully embodied this demoralized state. In the wake of an epidemic of a European disease on which the healer's ministrations had little impact, he unexpected fell into a comalike state that the Shawnee interpreted as death. However, before the funeral arrangements could be completed, Lalawethika revived, to the amazement of his fellow tribesmen. Considerably more amazing were the revelations he had received during his deathlike trance.

Lalawethika had been permitted to view heaven, "a rich, fertile country, abounding in game, fish, pleasant hunting grounds and fine corn fields." But he had also witnessed sinful Shawnee spirits being tortured according to the degree of their wickedness, with drunkards being forced to swallow molten lead. Overwhelmed by the power of his vision, Lalawethika—who now declared himself Tenskwatawa, the "Open Door" (leading to paradise)—abandoned his old ways. More revelations followed in the succeeding months—revelations that eventually added up to a coherent new vision of religion and society.

Although the new revelation departed from tradition on many points (e.g., new songs and dances were introduced), its central thrust was a nativistic exhortation to abandon Euroamerican ways for the lifestyle of earlier generations. Tenskwatawa successfully extended his religion to other tribes, particularly the Kickapoos, Winnebagos, Sacs, and Miamis. New rituals that reflected the Shawnee's contact with Catholicism evolved to formalize conversions.

While the new movement experienced its share of ups and downs, the promise of restored greatness was overwhelmingly appealing. Consequently, the religious leadership of the prophet remained strong until Tenskwatawa's prophecy of victory failed at the battle of Tippecanoe on November 7, 1811. Although from a purely military angle the battle was indecisive, Tenskwatawa's status as a leader was irreparably damaged. The hopes that Tenskwatawa's vision addressed were then transferred to the more secular efforts of his brother Tecumseh to unite the tribes in opposition to Euroamericans.

Following the Battle of the Thames in 1813, Tenskwatawa fled to Canada where he remained for a decade. He returned to the United States after agreeing to lead the remaining Shawnees out of the mid-West to Kansas. Subsequently, in and around 1828, tribal bands founded villages along the Kansas River. There the celebrated Western artist George Catlin painted a portrait of Tenskwatawa, in 1832. He died in November 1836 in what is now Kansas City.

Thorn, Michael: Michael Thorn (b. February 21, 1956), founder of Witches & Pagans for Gay Rights and founder of the Kathexis Coven, was born in Rockville Centre, New York. He received a B.A. in psychology in 1978 from the State University of New York at Stony Brook and an A.S. degree in nursing from the State University Agricultural and Technical College at Farmingdale in 1980.

In 1974, just out of high school, he was initiated into the Gardnerian Wicca Tradition, and in 1978 was initiated into the Faerie Tradition, founded by Victor H. Anderson. He was a charter member of the North East Local Council of the Covenant of the Goddess. The Covenant of the Goddess was founded in 1975 as an ecumenical organization dedicated to improving communication and cooperation among Neo-Pagan groups, and Thorn has held local and national offices within it. Sometimes known as Michael Harismedes, he founded Witches & Pagans for Gay Rights in 1983 and the Kathexis Coven in 1984.

Tomlinson, Ambrose Jessup: Ambrose Tomlinson (September 22, 1865-October 2, 1943), a founder of the Church of God (Cleveland, Tennessee) and founder of the Church of God of Prophecy, was born in Westfield, IM. In 1889 he married Mary Jane Taylor, a devout Quaker through whom he reactivated his own Quaker background. He became a traveling agent for the American Bible Society.

In 1896 he became entranced with a small Holiness Church of Camp Creek, North Carolina, led by Richard G. Spurling, Jr. He arranged for his family to move there and he joined the church in 1903. After receiving ordination from the church he moved to Cleveland, Tennessee, where he persuaded an independent congregation to affiliate with Spurling's church. In 1906 a convention was held with these two churches and a third, with Tomlinson as moderator. The following year they adopted the name Church of God.

In 1908 Tomlinson had the Pentecostal experience of speaking in tongues and led the Church of God into accepting that orientation. He was elected general moderator in 1909 and general overseer in 1910, a position he held until 1922. During those years he led the church into national and international prominence. In 1922 he was accused of misappropriating church funds and was impeached. (Interpretations of the events of 1922 vary greatly between competing churches.) He then formed another Church of God (the suffix "of Prophecy" was added in 1952 to avoid confusion), which upon his death was led by a son, Milton A. Tomlinson.

Tomlinson, Homer Aubrey: H. A. Tomlinson (October 25, 1893-December 4, 1968), founder of the Church of God (World Headquarters), was born in Westfield, Indiana. His father, Ambrose Jessup Tomlinson, was a founder and leader of the Church of God (Cleveland, Tennessee). Homer Tomlinson went into the advertising business, but was brought into church work when his father began the Church of God of Prophecy. To help the new denomination, Tomlinson began a congregation in Jamaica, New York, and evangelized around the Northeast.

When A. J. Tomlinson died in 1943 his other son, Milton, was elected general overseer. Homer objected, stating that his father had chosen him as successor, but Milton eventually won the case in court. Homer Tomlinson then founded the Church of God (World Headquarters) in New York City. Perhaps due to his advertising training, Tomlinson displayed great talent for attracting attention to his church. He believed that his church's mission included getting its members elected to public office to help usher in the kingdom of God. To this end he founded the Theocratic Party and ran as candidate for president of the United States. At the church's 1954 convention he was crowned "King of All Nations of Men in Righteousness." His international travels gained the church mission congregations in numerous countries, and by the time of his death the church was a significant, well-established organization.

Torres, Penny: Penny Torres, the popular New Age channel of the entity Mafu and leader of the Foundation for the Realization of Inner Divinity, was raised as a Roman Catholic. At age 13 she went into a brief coma due to pituitary cancer and was diagnosed as terminal. She struggled with pain over the next several years, eventually learning to cope with it through self-hypnosis. About the time of her marriage to Los Angeles policeman Tony Torres the cancer had somehow disappeared.

In 1986 she attended a channeling session on a whim and was told that an entity named Mafu wanted to channel through her. Not knowing what to make of this new part of her life, she went to the Spiritual Sciences Institute in Santa Barbara, California, for help, and soon learned how to go into a trance and contact Mafu. She began offering public channeling sessions and then weekend workshops, becoming a major West Coast attraction. Mafu Seminars was founded to organize the work and distribute tapes and videos. In 1987 the magazine *Reflections* was initiated.

In late 1989 Torres traveled to Hardiwar, India and took the vows of a sannyassi (akin to a monk) from Swamis Nityananda Paramahansa and Sivananda Giri. Upon return to the United States in 1990 she dismantled Mafu Seminars and established the Foundation for the Realization of Inner Divinity. She also took the name of Swami Paramanada Saraswatti. A subsidiary of the foundation, the Center for God Realization, continues to distribute Mafu's materials and organizes the seminars.

Towne, Elizabeth Lois Jones: Elizabeth Towne (May 11, 1865-June 1, 1960), editor of *The Nautilus*, one of the longest-running New Thought periodicals in the United States, was born into a Methodist family in Portland, Oregon. She left school at age fourteen and a half to be married to Joseph Struble on April 10, 1880, with whom she had two children.

At some point she learned about New Thought, perhaps through Lucy Mallory, editor of *World's Advance Thought*, based in Portland. She reportedly was acquainted with the teachings of Paul Militz and T. J.

Shelton. About 1894 she began supplementing the family income as a free-lance teacher of religion and healer. This became her means of support after she separated from her husband in 1899 (the divorce was finalized in 1900). Crucial to her independence was *The Nautilus* magazine that she began in October 1898 and quickly gained an audience.

After a brief time in South Dakota in late 1899 she moved to Holyoke, Massachusetts, where her fiance, William Towne, known to her only through correspondence, was living. They married on May 26, 1900 and he became a real partner in her publishing efforts, when not at his job at the American Writing Paper Company. By November 1904 *The Nautilus* had 12,000 paying subscribers and was the backbone of the Elizabeth Towne Publishing Company, which issued books by many authors on New Thought topics, including at least fifteen of her own books.

Towne was known for her frequent use of the term "I AM," one of the biblical names for God (Exodus 3:14), as a tool to enable people to connect with their all-powerful selves. Along with New Thought themes, she promoted vegetarianism and the "Gospel of Fresh Air," urging people to take 50-100 deep breaths of outdoor air each day with an appropriate affirmation. She was president of the International New Thought Alliance in 1924-25 and about that time was ordained a minister of the Church of the Truth, though generally she was not church oriented. She was a staunch feminist and in 1926 was the first female alderman-at-large ever elected in Holyoke. She continued to issue *The Nautilus* until August 1951.

Trine, Ralph Waldo: Ralph Waldo Trine (September 9, 1866-February 21, 1958), perhaps the most popular New Thought author in American history, was born in Mt. Morris, Illinois. From Knox College he received a B.A. in 1891 and an M.A. in 1893, studying history and political science. About that time he married Grace Steele Hyde.

After college Trine moved to Boston, worked a number of jobs, and discovered New Thought. In 1896 he published *What All the World's A-Seeking*, which found a wide readership. His 1897 book, however, *In Tune with the Infinite*, broke just about every sales record and eventually was translated into twenty languages. From that point he made his full-time living from his writing. His many books presented the standard New Thought idea that the material world is the manifestation of the spiritual world, the locus of reality and power. Thus the more humans are able to place themselves in harmony with the activity of the spiritual world, the more they can achieve their goals and potential.

A key to Trine's success was that he focused on Jesus and used God-language much more than some other New Thought writers. Further, his overall vocabulary raised few difficulties for most Christians. They read his books without concern for his New Thought orientation, thus making some aspects of the New Thought worldview a standard part of the cultural fabric. In the 1920s he met Henry Ford, the auto pioneer, who credited Trine's books for some of his great success.

Trungpa Rinpoche, Chogyam: Chogyam Trungpa Rinpoche (1939-1987), the eleventh Trungpa Tulks, can be considered the first Tibetan Buddhist teacher to have an important repercussion on Western society. He was regarded as a controversial figure, since he appreciated alcohol and women.

His teachings on Tibetan Buddhism, a complex blend of Mahayana Buddhism with Indian Tantrism and Tibetan shamanism, were adapted to a Western environment, and constituted the basis for the establishment of succeeding Tibetan teachers.

Trungpa arrived in the United States in 1970, where he founded Karme Choling, a center in Vermont. During the following years he traveled throughout the country, and established a number of centers, which were incorporated into the national organization known as Vajradhatu. The educational institution behind the movement was the Naropa Institute, that was opened in Boulder, Colorado.

Trungpa is also known for his contributions to the vocabulary of the New Age with such concepts as "spiritual materialism." In his *Cutting Through Spiritual Materialism*, he described this term as the acquisitive impulse in spiritual seeking, a preoccupation with "collecting" spiritual experiences, artifacts, and initiations. He died at the movement's international headquarters in Halifax, Nova Scotia.

Twitchell, John Paul: Paul Twitchell (October 22, 1908?-September 17, 1971), founder of ECKANKAR, was born in Paducah, Kentucky. After serving with the Navy in World War II he became a freelance journalist, especially as a correspondent for *Our Navy*. In 1950 he joined Swami Premananda's Self-Revelation Church of Absolute Monism, originally founded by Swami Paramahansa Yogananda (founder of the Self-Realization Fellowship). Twitchell settled on the headquarter grounds in Washington, D.C. with his wife and edited the group's magazine, *The Mystic Cross*.

Paul Twitchell
Courtesy: ECKANKAR

The year 1955 was a major one for Twitchell. Premananda asked him to leave the church, he broke up with his wife, and was accepted into the teachings of Kirpal Singh, founder of Ruhani Satsang. About the same time he became involved with the Church of Scientology and was one of the first graduates of its program. He met his second wife, Gail Atkinson, in Seattle and they moved to San Francisco in 1964. No longer associated with either Scientology or Ruhani Satsany, by May 1965 he was conducting Soul Travel workshops at the California Parapsychology Foundation in San Diego. His teachings emphasized "soul travel" as a direct path to God, distinguished from the lower, psychic experience of "astral projection."

In 1965 Twitchell became "the Mahanta, the Living ECK Master," and founded ECKANKAR as a modern-day religion. ECK, the Light and Sound of God, is the life current emanating from the Godhead, and enlightenment is gained by tapping into that current and moving with it back into the divine realms. In this basic schema it strongly resembles the standard shabd yoga cosmology, though other aspects of ECKANKAR just as strongly differ from it. Twitchell led the group to worldwide success. He passed away in 1971.

V

Van Anderson, Helen: Helen Van Anderson (1859-?) was founder of the Church of the Higher Life and among the first non-Christian Science trained ministers of New Thought. Her work was forgotten for many years and there is still little known about her life, especially her youth. She is said to have accepted New Thought about 1885 after being healed of a severe eye affliction.

In 1886 Emma Curtis Hopkins, a former student of Mary Baker Eddy (founder of Christian Science), founded the independent Hopkins College of Christian Science in downtown Chicago. Helen ("Nellie") Van Anderson became one of her most dedicated students. In September 1888 she left Chicago to do missionary work in Iowa and Colorado for the Hopkins Student Association and returned to report on her work at the October meeting of the Chicago Hopkins Student Association. By that time Hopkins had transformed her school into the Hopkins Theological Seminary and Van Anderson was in the first graduating class. Commencement exercises were performed on January 10, 1889, at which time the graduates were ordained by Hopkins.

After working as an independent healer in Chicago for a while, Van Anderson moved to Boston about December 1893. She felt it was the place to go, even though she knew no one there. In February 1894 she founded the Church of the Higher Life with Sunday services. Its only creed was the phrase attributed to Jesus—"Love is the fulfilling of the Law." Church activities included mothers' meetings, the Emerson Study Club, spiritual training classes, and a healing service every Sunday. She was ordained again on December 15, 1895 by three ministers who were either Unitarian or Universalist—Revs. Minot J. Savage, Frances E. Kollock, and Antoinette B. Blackwell.

She pastored that church for five years, then turned it over to William J. Leonard and in 1900 became vice-president of the Alliance School of Applied Metaphysics in New York, led by Charles Brodie Patterson. Little is known of her life after that point. She may have stayed with the Alliance School until retirement. Her next-to-last known published book was in New York in 1906 and her last known published book was back in Chicago in 1912.

Venta, Krishna: Krishna Venta (1911-December 10, 1958), founder of W.F.L.K. Fountain of the World, was born Francis Heindswaltzer Pencovic in San Francisco, California. He was orphaned at the age of eight and had a troubled youth. His first marriage failed after a few years and several children, and his wife sued for divorce on the basis of nonsupport. He had difficulties with the law more than once and in 1942 was jailed for writing bad checks. During his prison sentence he spent some time on the road gang and some time in the State Mental Hospital in Stockton, California, where he was diagnosed as a delusional paranoid, telling people he was the True Christ.

After this episode he spent some time in Utah, where he studied Mormonism and its founder, Joseph Smith. There he also married Ruth, his second wife, with whom he had six children. This relationship was more successful, and with Ruth's support he founded WFLK Fountain of the World, a blending of Hindu and Christian elements. He took the name Krishna Venta and claimed that he was the reincarnation of Christ. As per Mormon belief he had worked among the American Indians almost 150 years previously, then spent time in the Himalayas. He (Christ) teleported to America on March 29, 1932 and took over the body of Francis Pencovic.

Venta attracted a group of committed followers who believed in him as a world savior. They lived communally, sharing all their worldly goods and practicing Wisdom, Faith, Love, and Knowledge (W.F.L.K.). In the late 1940s the group moved to Box Canyon near Chatsworth, California, where they settled on 26 acres. Venta gained a local reputation for a promiscuous sex life and for a penchant for Las Vegas gambling. In 1958 two former members complained to the authorities that he was a fraud and guilty of statutory rape. Not waiting for the authorities to act, they then went to the group's main building, confronted Venta, and blew up the building, killing themselves, Venta, and seven others. The group managed to last another twenty years, however, before finally disbanding.

Vilatte, Joseph René: Joseph Vilatte (January 24, 1854-July 8, 1929), the first Old Catholic priest in the United States and founder of the American Catholic Church, was born in Paris, France. He was raised as a Roman Catholic and as a young man began studies in Canada towards the priesthood. In 1879, after three years in seminary, he was influenced to leave the Roman Catholic Church by Charles Chiniquy, a former priest-turned-Presbyterian. After a period of exploration he became an independent Presbyterian missionary among Belgians in Green Bay, Wisconsin, and was ordained for this work by a Presbyterian minister on July 15, 1884.

The Belgians he worked with had left the Roman Catholic Church but were not interested in becoming Protestants, so Vilatte sought connections with the Old Catholics in Europe, most of whom had left the Roman Catholic Church after its 1870 proclamation of papal infallibility. He was ordained in June 1885 in Switzerland by Eduard Herzog of the Old Catholic Church of Switzerland, and became the first Old Catholic priest in the United States. His work in Wisconsin proceeded successfully and soon he had three small congregations working in ecumenical concert with the local Episcopal bishop. Soon, however, he felt he needed episcopal status to carry on the work properly, but the Old Catholics would not consecrate him. He finally was consecrated in Sri Lanka on May 29, 1892 by Antonio F. X. Alvarez of the Malankara Orthodox Syrian Church.

Upon his return to Wisconsin the congregations were faring poorly and in 1898 he left them in the hands of an assistant and moved to the east coast to work with Stanislas Kaminski among Polish immigrants. In 1915 he incorporated the American Catholic Church in the state of Illinois. He continued working with various ethnic immigrant groups dissatisfied with their treatment in the Roman Catholic Church, but the number of converts was small. In 1920 he retired, leaving the work in the hands of Frederick E. J. Lloyd. On June 1, 1925 he submitted to the Vatican and was allowed to live out his days in a monastery near Versailles, France.

Vivekananda, Swami: Swami Vivekananda (January 12, 1863-July 4, 1902), founder of the Vedanta Society, was born in Calcutta, India. His birth name was Narendranath Datta, and as part of a high-caste family he had access to British education. He grew up part of the Brahmo Samaj, a group of Western-influenced, Hindu reformers, but eventually became dissatisfied with it.

Swami Vivekananda (1900)
Courtesy: American Religion Collection

As a young man he encountered Sri Ramakrishna in Calcutta, a mystic priest in the service of the goddess Kali. While remaining in college he became a disciple of Ramakrishna and after his death in 1886 organized the other followers into what became the Ramakrishna Order. As a monk, he took the name Swami Vivekananda. He arranged to be a speaker at the 1893 World's Parliament of Religions in Chicago. His cultured presentation of Hinduism, along with the exotic appeal of the Far East, made him extraordinarily popular. After the parliament he conducted a major lecture tour, laying the foundations for the creation in 1894 of the Vedanta Society, the first Hindu mission in the United States. After only a few years branches in San Francisco and Boston were added to the one in New York City.

Vivekananda's successes in the West also made him a popular figure back in India, where the Ramakrishna Order gained a solid standing after his return in 1897. Although Ramakrishna worshiped God as Universal Mother (via Kali), Vivekananda emphasized a more philosophic brand of Hinduism, wherein insight into the underlying unity of all things is the goal. Vivekananda's influence on the development of appreciation of Hinduism in the West would be hard to overestimate.

Voigt, Valerie: Valerie Voight (b. October 10, 1953), prominent West Coast Neo-Pagan leader, was born in Selma, Alabama. At age sixteen, after several years as a "born-again" Christian, she realized she was actually a Pagan. Not knowing any other Pagans personally and in fact not knowing that there were any other Pagans in the United States, she kept the matter to herself.

She received a B.A. in classical languages from the University of Kansas, studying world religions along the way. In 1975, about the time of her graduation, she found an ad for the Church of All Worlds, founded by Otter Zell and at that time headquartered in St. Louis, Missouri. This led her to knowledge of other groups, and in 1978 she moved to San Francisco, California, a major center of Neo-Paganism.

In the Bay Area she joined the New Reformed Orthodox Order of the Golden Dawn and began her own coven. Mensa, an organization for highly intelligent people, had a Witchcraft/Occult/Pagan Special Interest Group (SIG), of which she soon became coordinator. About that time she also began a newsletter, *Pagana*. In 1982 she was initiated into both Gardnerian witchcraft and the Faerie Tradition of Victor H. Anderson. That year she co-founded the Centre of Divine Ishtar, for which she taught an introductory class on witchcraft.

In the years since then she has taught numerous classes and workshops and has been a prominent contact point between the Neo-Pagan community and the media, law enforcement, and the general public. In 1987 she helped found the South Bay Circles, an ecumenical association of covens that hosts the eight Sabbat festivals for the South Bay area.

W

Donald Walters
Courtesy: Ananda Village

Walters, James Donald: James Donald Walters (b. May 19, 1926), founder of the Ananda Church of God-Realization (Ananda Cooperative Community), was born in Toleajen, Romania. His father was an American oil geologist and Walter was raised an Episcopalian in the Anglo-American transplanted community. At age nine he was sent to a boarding school in Switzerland and at age eleven to another one in England. The family moved to the United States in 1939 and in 1943 he entered Haverford College.

He never finished his college degree, but in 1946 settled in Charleston, South Carolina as a playwright. There he ran across a copy of the *Bhagavad Gita*, part of the Hindu scriptures, and felt at home with it. He also found Paramahansa Yogananda's *Autobiography of a Yogi* and was very impressed. In 1948 he moved to Los Angeles and became a disciple of Yogananda. After Yogananda's death in 1952 he took the vows of the holy life and became Swami Kriyananda. From 1955 to 1958 he was the head priest at the Hollywood center and from 1960 to 1962 he was a member of the board of directors and vice-president of the Self-Realization Fellowship.

At that point he left to lecture and write. He eventually decided to pursue one of Yogananda's interests, that of creating small, economically independent communities. In 1967 he bought 750 acres of land near

Nevada City in northern California and the following year founded Ananda Village. The community became very successful, with members, representing many nationalities and ethnic groups, owning their own homes and some of the businesses. The group even survived a forest fire in 1976 that destroyed almost all of the buildings.

In the 1980s he renounced his monastic vows, shaved his beard, began wearing western clothes, and stopped using the name Kriyananda in favor of his birth name. In 1990 he founded the Ananda Church of God-Realization, open to both community and non-community members. Walters has written dozens of books and some musical compositions and has overseen the creation of five other communities and some 50 other centers around the world.

Warner, Daniel Sidney: Daniel Sidney Warner (1842-1895) was the founder of the Church of God. Born in rural Ohio, he served as a private in the Union Army, and at the end of his military career was a self-professed infidel. His conversion occurred in 1865 at a Methodist meeting, and he preached his first sermon at a Methodist gathering on Easter Sunday of 1866.

However, he decided not to join the Methodist Episcopal Church, and in 1867 he was licensed to preach by the Church of God founded by John Winebrenner, characterized by a disavowal of all sectarianism. He spent the next six years in a pastorate in northwest Ohio, and then he moved to Nebraska as a general missionary. In 1875 he eventually moved back to Ohio as the pastor of a church.

In July 1877 he experienced sanctification, and joined the National Association for the Promotion of Holiness. Despite opposition from his fellow ministers of the Church of God, he was assigned a circuit in the area of Canton, Ohio, which he eventually resigned in order to preach sanctification and holiness. He was finally tried and expelled from the Church of God, and became a full-time holiness evangelist. In 1878 he became associated with the Northern Indiana Eldership of the Church of God, which had previously broken with Warner's Church of God, and was appointed the assistant editor of the periodical *Herald of Gospel Freedom* (later called the *Gospel Trumpet*), becoming the sole editor in 1880.

In 1881 he withdrew from both the National Holiness Association and the Northern Indiana Eldership because of the recognition of "sects" in their constitutions, and formed the Church of God ("Anderson, Indiana") at Beaver Dam, Indiana. Warner, who was financially strapped for many years and who had been left by his wife Frankie Miller, devoted himself to evangelistic work, and introduced the practice of using an evangelistic team. He toured the churches with a group of musicians, and eventually married one of them. Some of his songs are included in an early Church of God publication titled *Anthems from the Throne*. He died in 1895 at Grand Junction, Michigan.

Watts, Alan Wilson: Alan Watts (January 6, 1915-November 16, 1973), author and popularizer of Buddhism in America, was born in Chilehurst, England. As a young man he became interested in Asian religions. He read as much material as was available and developed a correspondence with Christmas Humphreys, leader of the Buddhist Lodge in England. Watts wrote many articles for the periodical published by the Buddhist Lodge and developed his own spirituality, focused on Zen but including also aspects of Taoism and yoga.

In 1935 he published his first book, *The Spirit of Zen*, based on D. T. Suzuki's work. Watts was able to meet Suzuki in person at the 1936 World Congress of Faiths in London. In 1938 he married Eleanor Everett and moved to the United States. Deciding to pursue his religious interests through more conventional means, he entered Seabury-Western Theological Seminary in Evanston, Illinois, and was ordained an Episcopal priest in 1945. By that time a naturalized citizen of the United States, he served for five years as Episcopal chaplain at Northwestern University in Evanston.

In 1950 his life completely changed. His marriage dissolved, he resigned from the ministry, and he married Dorothy DeWitt. The following year he moved to San Francisco to teach at the American Academy of Asian Studies. On the West Coast he gained a reputation as a "beat" philosopher and associated with other figures of that movement, including Jack Kerouac, Gary Snyder, and Richard Alpert (Baba Ram Dass). His many books helped popularize Buddhism, particularly Zen Buddhism, by connecting its world view with that of the emerging youthful counterculture.

Between 1951 and 1961 Watts wrote five books, including *The Way of Zen* (1957) and *Psychotherapy, East and West* (1961). In 1962 followers of his work organized the Society for Comparative Philosophy to help promote his thinking. Through it the *Alan Watts Journal* was published. His final book was his autobiography, *In My Own Way* (1972). While critics have suggested that Watts popularized Asian thought to the point of misconception, his work greatly contributed to Western interest in and dialogue with the East.

Webb, Muhammad Alexander Russell: Alexander Webb (November 18, 1846-October 1, 1916), founder of the Moslem Mosque, was born in Hudson, New York. He grew up as a Presbyterian, but left the church when he was twenty. He became a newspaper journalist and for a time owned his own newspaper. In 1876 he moved to Missouri to work at the *St. Joseph Day Gazette* and then later at the *Missouri Republican*.

In 1887 Webb became United States consul to the Philippines and in Manila discovered Islam. Despite having become a hard-bitten, secularized news reporter, he was immediately drawn to the faith, and became a convert in 1888. He resigned his position in 1892 and upon returning to the United States began lecturing on Islam. In 1893 he founded the Oriental Publishing Company and the periodical *Moslem World*.

At the World's Parliament of Religions, held as part of the 1893 Chicago World's Fair, Webb was the lone advocate for Islam and defender against its critics. Soon thereafter he opened a mosque in New York, the first mosque in the United States, and supervised the Islamic Propaganda Mission in the U.S.A. New York City at that time was receiving much of the first significant immigration wave from predominantly Muslim countries around the eastern Mediterranean, so there was much need of a public Muslim presence. Webb also wrote a number of books to bring Islam to the attention of the American public. In honor of Webb's pioneering service on behalf of Islam, the sultan of Turkey named Webb the honorary Turkish Consul of New York.

The Rt. Rev. James Ingall Wedgewood
Courtesy: Liberal Catholic church

Wedgwood, James Ingall:
James Wedgwood (May 24, 1883-March 13, 1951), co-founder of the Liberal Catholic Church, was born in England. As a young man he belonged to the Confraternity of the Blessed Sacrament, an Anglo-Catholic group within the Anglican Church. He became an analytical chemist at York.

At one point he heard Annie Besant speak and was converted to Theosophy, in which he became very active. In 1911 he moved to London and worked as General Secretary of the English section of the Theosophical Society. In 1912 he founded the

Temple of the Rosy Cross, a cabalistic body within Theosophy. He wanted to be ordained and was pleased to discover Arnold Harris Mathew's Old Roman Catholic Church in 1913. Mathew ordained him on July 22, 1913 and soon ordained a number of other Theosophists. When competing loyalties with Theosophy became a problem for Mathew, he ordered all of his followers to sever their ties with Theosophy. Instead he lost much of his jurisdiction.

Wedgwood joined with Frederick Samuel Willoughby of the Old Roman Catholic Church to create the Liberal Catholic Church. Willoughby consecrated him on February 13, 1916 and assigned him as Regionary Bishop for Great Britain and Ireland for the Liberal Catholic Church. Wedgwood then sailed to Australia where he consecrated Charles Leadbeater, and soon continued his travels on an around-the-world tour promoting Theosophy. At the first organizing synod for the church in London on September 6, 1918, Wedgwood was named presiding bishop, a position he held until 1923. He was the author of several books and was instrumental in placing the Liberal Catholic Church on a firm foundation.

Weltmer, Sidney Abram: Sidney Weltmer (July 7, 1858-December 5, 1930), founder of the Weltmer School of Magnetic Healing, was born in Wooster, Ohio, but the family later moved to Missouri. Functioning public schools were scarce and he received his education at home. Afflicted in his teens by tuberculosis and faced with death, he prayed for a cure and began to recover. At age nineteen, when he was well, he became a preacher for the Southern Baptist Convention, while also teaching school in Atkinsville, Missouri.

He did not continue in church work; by 1893 he was city librarian in Sedalia and teaching at a local business college. Religiously, he decided to pursue his own path. Fascinated by stories of healing in the Bible and elsewhere, he decided that the crucial element in healing was the belief that it could or would be done. He tried his hand at healing others, activating their own faith through suggestion and other techniques, and found such great success that in 1897 he and his brother, Ernest Weltmer, founded the Weltmer School of Magnetic Healing (also sometimes called the Institute of Suggestive Therapeutics) in Nevada, Missouri.

Weltmer had three main teaching tenets, gained by transforming religious terms into psychological terms: the counterpart of forgiveness was intention, the counterpart of agreement or obedience was suggestion, and the counterpart of prayer was concentration. He believed that working through these principles could activate the divine power within each human to overcome all obstacles. From 1901 to 1909 he edited *Weltmer's Magazine*, which gained a wide readership, and he also authored a number of books in his career.

Weltmer's institute became hugely successful. At its height, as many as 400 patients a day were treated and daily income was over $3,500. This success had a backlash, however. He was sued for fraud and the case went to the Supreme Court, which ruled in 1901 that his system was legal. The school did not long survive his death in 1930.

White, Alma Birdwell: Alma White (June 16, 1862-June 26, 1946), founder of the Pillar of Fire, was born in Louis County, Kentucky. She worked in a tannery with her father and at age sixteen experienced conversion and joined the Methodist Episcopal Church. She felt called at that time to be a minister, but that was not an option for women in the church at that time. Instead she became a teacher and in 1882 moved to Montana, where she married a Methodist minister, Arthur Kent White.

She tried to be content in the role of minister's assistant, but could not, and began to run her own, very popular, revival meetings. The Methodist hierarchy countered with strong opposition and White left the church in 1901. In 1902 she founded the Methodist Pentecostal Union, renamed the Pillar of Fire in 1917. She was among the first women in modern times to serve in the role of bishop. Her husband functioned as *her* assistant for a time before exiting from the marriage. Following the donation of a suitable tract of land, she moved the headquarters of the church from Denver, Colorado to Zarephath, New Jersey.

White was a prolific speaker and author and successfully established a stable organization. She championed many causes, including vegetarianism, healing, pacifism, premillennialism, and women's rights. One of the church's periodicals was pointedly called *Woman's Chains*. She also supported the Ku Klux Klan, primarily because of their anti-Catholicism, but the denomination later dropped that aspect of her teaching. After her death her two sons led the organization for many years.

White, Ellen Gould Harmon: Ellen White (November 26, 1827-July 16, 1915), co-founder of the Seventh-day Adventist Church, was born in Gorham, Maine, the daughter of Eunice Gould and Robert Harmon, a hat-maker. Her formal schooling ended at age nine after a head injury, from which she never fully recovered, made her subject to dizzy spells.

In 1842 she was baptized into the Methodist Episcopal Church, but the following year her family joined the Adventist movement, led by William Miller, and the Methodists expelled them. In 1844, when Miller's prediction of Christ's Second Coming failed, White rallied many of the disappointed followers to keep their faith. She believed that the prediction had validity in that Christ had arrived to prepare the heavenly temple for his eventual earthly reign.

She married James White in 1846 and the following year, through the influence of a member of the Seventh Day Baptist Church, accepted Saturday as the day of worship. Through their Bible study group, writing, and speaking engagements, they began to have a significant impact, and by the time they moved to Battle Creek, Michigan in 1855, there was a real following. She gained a reputation as a prophetess whose visions of Christ and heavenly Adventists renewed the confidence of many. White's most important theological work, *The Great Controversy between Christ and His Angels and Satan and His Angels*, was published in 1858.

In 1860 the Whites decided on the name for their group, the Seventh-day Adventist Church, and its organizing conference was held in 1863. Over the next fifty years Ellen White, as its leader shaped the church into a stable, international body, known by many for its hospitals and health consciousness. White authored over 25 books and 200 shorter works.

Wierwille, Victor Paul: The Way International was founded by Victor Paul Wierwille (1916-1985), originally a minister in the Evangelical and Reformed Church. A Pentecostal, ultradispensational Christian group, the Way has its roots in a 1942 radio ministry called "Vesper Chimes." It assumed its present name in 1974, after being renamed the Chimes Hour in 1944, and the Chimes Hour Youth Caravan in 1947.

While a student at Mission House College, Wierwille decided to enter the ministry. He earned his B.D. at Mission House Seminary, in Minnesota, and did graduate work at the University of Chicago and Princeton Theological Seminary, earning a M.Th. in 1941. After being ordained in 1942, he became pastor of the Church at Paine, from which he moved to Van Wert, Ohio, two years later, to become pastor of St. Peter's E. & R. Church.

During his stay in Van Wert he became an avid student of the Bible, concentrating upon the doctrine of the Holy Spirit. In 1948, he was awarded a Ph.D. by the Pikes Peak Bible College and Seminary, in Manitou Spring, Colorado, and in 1951 he manifested the reception of God's holy spirit and spoke in tongues for the first time.

The first "Power for Abundant Living" (PFAL) class, given in 1953, contained the initial results of his research on biblical truth. After one year, he began to study Aramaic under the influence of Dr. George M. Lamsa, translator of the Lamsa Bible, and began to accept a view of Biblical doctrine which departed more and more from that of his Denomination. In 1957 he resigned his ministry from the Evangelical and Reformed Church in order to devote himself full-time to his work. He led his ministry, which was chartered as The Way, Inc. in 1955, and then changed to The Way International in 1975. The headquarters of The Way was established on the family farm outside New Knoxville, Ohio. He retired from leading the ministry full time in 1983, and passed away two years later.

Wilmans, Helen: Helen Wilmans (c.1832-c.October 1907), founder of Mental Science, was one of the most successful early New Thought leaders. In her first marriage she lived in Soda Spring Valley, California, and was a schoolteacher. She became a widow about 1875 and moved to San Francisco to support herself and her two daughters as a journalist, eventually becoming editor of the *Pacific Greenbacker*.

In 1881 she moved to Chicago to join the editorial staff of *The Chicago Express*, where she became well-known for muckraking articles. She married Colonel Charles C. Post on July 28, 1883. In 1886 she left the newspaper to found *The Woman's World*, a reformist journal dedicated to socialism. In June 1886 she took a course from touring New Thought teacher Emma Curtis Hopkins, and was reportedly converted in the fifth lesson. She began healing and teaching on her own. By the end of the year she sold her journal and moved to Douglasville, Georgia, where her husband had already moved to cope with tuberculosis. She reportedly cured him and continued to develop what she called her "mental science" teaching.

In 1889 she began *Wilman's Express* and about that time began her trademark practice of using the mails for absent treatments of patients. In 1892 Wilmans moved to a tract just north of Sea Breeze, Florida, and began building what she hoped would become a major retreat and healing center. Indeed, she was able to build a 120-room hotel, a mental science college, paved streets, and much more because of her spectacular success. She had as many as 10,000 patients each year, each sending in $3 to $5 per week for absent treatments. Her many books sold well, too. Her *Conquest of Poverty* (1899), reflecting her business/prosperity emphasis, sold 40,000 copies in three months.

Wilmans also began a new denomination. By the end of 1901 there were about a dozen Mental Science Temples spread across North America. That year Wilmans began a protracted battle against the charge of mail fraud. The U.S. Circuit Court of Appeals, on February 27, 1905, stated that her mental healing practice was lawful, but by that time, having been denied much use of the mails for several years, she was almost broke, and never recovered. The Mental Science Temples disappeared after her death.

Winebrenner, John: John Winebrenner (1797-1860) was the founder of the Churches of God of North America (General Eldership). Born on a farm in rural Maryland and raised in the German Reformed Church, he developed an early inclination for the ministry. After attending Dickinson College, he moved to Philadelphia to study theology with Dr. Samuel Helffenstein, the pastor of Race Street Reformed Church. During his brief stay in Philadelphia, he experienced regeneration, and in 1820 he was ordained by the Reformed Synod meeting at Hagerstown, Maryland, from where he moved to Harrisburg, Pennsylvania, to become pastor of the Salem Reformed Church.

His first book, *A Compendium of the Heidelberg Catechism*, appeared in 1922. Some leading members opposed Winnebrenner's use of the so-called "new measures," the revivalistic techniques popularized by Charles G. Finney that involved women praying in public, praying for individuals by name in meetings, protracted meetings, the use of an anxious bench, and letting ministers from other denominations preach in the church's Sunday services. This tension resulted in the denial of his entry into the church in April 1823, and in the subsequent split in the congregation.

In 1825 Winebrenner erected in Harrisburg the Union Bethel Church, from which the Churches of God were formed. The main purpose of the formation of Union Bethel and other congregations was represented by the opportunity to restore true primitive Christianity, conforming to the biblical model. Thus the true name, the Church of God, was adopted. This church was to be congregational in government, with elders and deacons designated as leaders. The practice of immersion was adopted as well as foot washing, and by 1830 the "Eldership," formed by the elders of the Church of God, became an advisory body facilitating cooperation among the Churches.

In 1830 Winebrenner resigned the pastorate of Union Bethel, and spent the rest of his life as a preacher-at-large for the growing movement, and as a writer. Among his publications is his single most popular work, *A Prayer Meeting and Revival Hymn Book*.

Wood, Henry: Henry Wood (January 16, 1834-March 28, 1909), popular early New Thought author, was born in Barre, Vermont. He attended Barre Academy from 1848 to 1852, then graduated from Commercial College in Boston in 1854. He married Margaret Osborne Baker in 1860 and became a successful businessman.

In 1887, at age 54, he published *Natural Law in the Business World*, wherein he indicated how his success had come at the price of his health. He suffered from the typical neurasthenic symptoms of the time, including insomnia and "dyspepsia," until he was cured by the mental philosophy of New Thought. From that point on, he devoted himself to spreading New Thought through books and articles, as well as running a private sanitarium.

He was one of the founding members of the influential Metaphysical Club of Boston in 1895 and was elected president in 1899. He has been described as the first New Thought philanthropist, endowing the "Silence Room" of the Metaphysical Club and occasionally espousing aspects of socialism, though his overall political and social philosophy was not consistent. He wrote about 15 books and was active into his last years. His final book and one of his most important, *The New Old Healing*, was published in 1908.

Wovoka: Wovoka (c.1856-September 20, 1932), originator of the Ghost Dance, was born in a Paiute village in Mason Valley, Nevada. His father, Tavibo, was a tribal leader and "dreamer," who thought there might come a time when divine intervention would cause the whites to disappear and restore the Indian ways of life. Wovoka was trained in the healing arts and other things befitting the son of a leader, including the analysis of dreams.

At age 14 his father died and he went to live and work at the Wilson ranch in Pine Grove, Nevada, where he was known as Jack Wilson. In the 1880s he began to have dreams and visions elaborating on his father's earlier vision. On January 1, 1889, after a solar eclipse, he had a vision lasting three days, during which he gained most of the content, including songs and dances, for the Ghost Dance, or more accurately, Spirit Dance. Within a year it had spread throughout the Midwest. It was believed that the Ghost Dance ceremonies would invoke the great ancestral spiritual powers for the destruction of the invading white society. The Sioux added the use of a "Ghost Shirt" to the ceremonies, which was supposed to provide its wearers with invulnerability to bullets or other harm.

White authorities believed the Ghost Dance to be a dangerous influence and were anxious to shut it down. The tensions climaxed with the massacre by federal troops of some 200 Sioux at Wounded Knee, South Dakota, on December 29, 1890. The inability of the shirts to protect from harm, plus the continuing encroachment of white society, led to the quick demise of the Ghost Dance, thereafter practiced only in isolated areas. Wovoka continued to lead the Walker River Paiutes, but not as a Ghost Dance visionary.

Wroe, John: John Wroe (September 19, 1782--February 5, 1863) was the founder of the Christian Israelites. His father was a worsted manufacturer and John was apparently physically abused by his father and brothers. He had a humpback as a result of injuries he sustained, and was deaf for many years after almost drowning. He was eventually cured. His formal schooling lasted only one year, and he taught himself how to write. He married rather young, and went into business with his father.

Wroe became extremely sick in 1819, so sick that he thought he might die. This confrontation with his own mortality prompted him to reflect seriously on his spiritual state. On November 11, 1819, Wroe began speaking with angels in a series of visions. After one set of these experiences, he felt a desire to convert to Judaism. He unsuccessfully sought out rabbis in both Manchester and London.

He also had a vision in which he conversed with Joanna Southcott, the founder of a small sect. He interpreted the vision to mean that he should join the Southcotties, and he became affiliated with a group at Bradford. Having experienced other people who had asserted that they were prophets, this group resisted Wroe's claims to leadership after the death of their leader, George Turner, in 1821. It was not until October 1822 that a majority of the Church's ruling committee accepted Wroe.

Wroe rapidly consolidated his leadership. He traveled to other Southcott congregations in north England, and succeeded in bringing many into his fold. He also made trips to Europe in 1823. In 1824 Ashton became the new headquarters for the movement he was to pastor for four decades.

Wroe named the movement Christian Israelites, and required that they adopt certain "Jewish" regulations, such as fully observing the Mosaic laws. They adopted a particular mode of dress, and males grew their hair and beards. Everyone abstained from alcohol and tobacco and learned Hebrew. The movement slowly grew slowly until 1830-31 when Wroe was accused of having sexual encounters with a number of young females. He responded to these accusations by moving his headquarters to Wrenthrope and cutting off his relationship with the group at Ashton.

Wroe then focused his attention on building a worldwide movement. His first missionaries to the United States arrived in 1844, where they established a congregation in New York City. John L. Bishop arrived several years afterwards, and established what came to be called the Christian Israelite Church. The movement expanded across the country, from Massachusetts to Minnesota. Wroe visited North America four times on various world tours. Australia, however, was where he found his greatest success, and he died there at the ripe old age of eighty.

The only congregation of the Christian Israelite church left in the United States is in Indianapolis, Indiana. The balance of Wroe's movement left to become affiliated with the House of Israel led by Benjamin Purnell, another Southcott prophet.

Y

Paramahansa Yogananda
Courtesy: Self-Realization Fellowship

Yogananda, Swami Paramahansa:
Yogananda (January 5, 1893-March 7, 1952), founder of the Self-Realization Fellowship, was born Mukunda Lal Ghosh in Gorakhpur, India. His father, a railroad executive, was a practitioner of Kriya Yoga and a student of Lahiri Mahayasa. Yogananda followed the religious interests of his father. After high school he went to Benares and became the disciple of Sri Yukteswar Giri, another student of Mahasaya.

Under the direction of Yukteswar, Yogananda went to college, and upon graduation in 1914 took holy vows in the Swami Order and the monastic name of Yogananda, meaning "bliss through yoga." In 1916 he discovered the techniques of Yogoda, a yoga-based system of life-energy control. In 1917 he founded the Yogoda Satsanga Society of India and began a school for boys in which the regular curriculum included courses on yoga and meditation.

In 1920 he was invited to speak to the International Congress of Religious Liberals in Boston. This provided the long-awaited opportunity to introduce the West to yoga, and he stayed to tour and lecture rather than returning to India. That same year he founded Self-Realization Fellowship, and later (in 1925) established the international headquarters in Los Angeles. In 1924 the United States tightened its Asian immigration laws and Yogananda was the last major Indian spiritual leader to enter the country until the laws were changed in the mid-1960s.

Yogananda taught Kriya Yoga, an ancient science of meditation that focuses upon awakening higher spiritual perceptions by drawing energy to the subtle centers in the spine and brain. For a long time his Self-Realization Fellowship and Vivekananda's Vedanta Society constituted almost the sum total of Indian-based religious societies in America. Yogananda's *Autobiography of a Yogi* (1946) has been influential among many who have not taken up the practice of yoga or adopted its philosophy but were fascinated by the opportunity to see inside his spiritual journey.

Yogi, Maharishi Mahesh: Maharishi Mahesh Yogi (b. 1918?), popularizer of Transcendental Meditation (TM), was born in India. Little is known of his early life other than his graduation from Allahabad University about 1940 with a degree in physics. From 1940 to 1953 he spent in seclusion with Guru Brahamananda Saraswati, generally known as Guru Dev, whose specialty was meditation. After Guru Dev's death in 1953 he spent two years in the Himalayas before beginning to teach in Karala. On January 1, 1958, he founded the Spiritual Regeneration Movement to organize the spread of TM around the world and thus regenerate humanity.

Maharishi spent the next several years touring around the world establishing TM centers and writing his first major books. In the United States such personalities as Mia Farrow, Jane Fonda, and the Beatles embraced TM, contributing to its rapid growth. In 1972 he announced the organization of the World Plan Executive Council as the new coordinator of the movement. He also announced the World Plan, a detailed strategy for spreading TM and the Science of Creative Intelligence through the whole world. In 1976 he announced the World Government of the Age of Enlightenment as a means of finding answers to various world problems.

Maharishi has encouraged the study of TM in scientific circles and some of those studies have supported TM's claims to improve health, athletic abilities, cure addictions, and so on. Claims that advanced practitioners, including Maharishi, can levitate or become invisible have elicited widespread criticism. TM has generally been marketed as a secular discipline, but in 1978 the courts ruled that it was religious in nature and could not therefore be taught in public schools or otherwise receive public money. Despite such setbacks, Maharishi has continued to advance the aims of his organization.

Z

Zalman of Ladi, Rabbi Shneur: Rabbi Shneur Zalman of Ladi (1745-1813) was the founder of Chabad-Lubavitch Hasidism. Born in Byelorussia from a long line of distinguished rabbis, he studied the Torah, Talmud, and Kabbalah, and was recognized as a child prodigy. When he was twelve he was sent to the center of Talmudic scholarship at Vitebsk, and three years after he married the daughter of Rabbi Judah Leib Segal.

At the age of twenty he went to the Hasidic Center of Meseretz in Poland in order to study for two years under Rabbi Dovber, the head of the Baal Shem Tov movement. He became the *maggid*, or preacher, in 1767 in Liozna, where he spent ten years developing his particular perspective on Hasidism that was to distinguish the Lubavitch movement. Rabbi Zalman's first major work was the revision of the handbook of Jewish law known as the *Shulchan Aruch*, which was originally compiled by Rabbi Joseph Caro two centuries earlier.

In 1773 he headed to Liozna, and after ten years he transferred his headquarters to Ladi, the major center for the spreading of Chabad Hasidism. The term Chabad, referred to his systematic approach to the study of Hasidism—as pointed out in his main publication, the *Tanya*—is an acronym formed from the words *chockmath*, *binah*, and *daath*, the names of the first three realms, or *sephirot*, emanating from God according to the Kabbalah. Zalman's approach included the preservation of the traditional Jewish approach to God through study and learning.

The Chabad's theology emphasized God's individual providence over all creation, expounded the notion of God's continuous creation, and opposed the notion of God's self-limitation in place of which God's omnipresence was proposed. The reality of evil was appreciated as well, and evil was regarded as being real and placed in the world by God in order to test humans for their ultimate good.

When Rabbi Dovber died in 1772, the Hasidic community was afflicted by major problems given to the emergence of strong and organized opposition from the traditional non-Kabbalistic Jewish rabbis known as the Mitnagdim. In 1798 Zalman was denounced as a traitor to the Russian government, and imprisoned in St. Petersburg, from where he was released on express orders of the Czar, after impressing those placed in charge of his case.

Zalman, who died in the small village of Piena, near Kurst, was succeeded by his son, Rabbi Dovber (1778-1827), and the lineage of leadership of the Lubavitch movement has been passed through the family to the present day. A Lubavitcher community had been in existence in New York since the 1920s. When Rabbi Joseph Isaac Schneersohn moved to the United States in 1940, he took direct leadership of that small community, which was the only one across North America. The aggressive approach towards the Jewish community resulted in a spectacular growth of the Lubavitch movement since World War II.

Zeiger, Robert Gerald John Schuyler: Robert Zeiger (b. January 1, 1929), head of the Apostolic Catholic Church of the Americas, was born in Denver, Colorado. In the early 1950s he attended the Roman Catholic St. Thomas Seminary in Denver, but in 1954 he married and gave up (for a time) becoming a priest, remaining in his job with the Colorado Employment Service. He became disillusioned with the Roman Catholic Church after learning more about its history and when he discovered Old Catholicism, which allowed married priests, it seemed like a perfect fit.

He was ordained on February 22, 1959 by William H. F. Brothers of the Old Catholic Church in America and was consecrated on July 1, 1961 by Peter A. Zhurawetsky of the Orthodox Catholic Patriarchate of America. That year Zeiger founded the American Orthodox Catholic Church as a means of enacting his own particular vision of ministry and built his following from the headquarters in Denver. He was consecrated again in 1976 by Joseph John Skureth of the Western Orthodox Catholic Church. That year Zeiger's church associated with Gordon Albert Da Costa's Anglican Church of the Americas and became known as the Apostolic Catholic Church of the Americas.

In 1977 Zeiger returned to the Roman Catholic Church as a layperon in a Uniate Ruthenian congregation. In 1981 he left Roman Catholicism again and associated with a new group, the Holy Synod of Denver. When this did not work out he returned in 1986 to the Apostolic Catholic

Church of the Americas. Since that time he has been arrested twice for "pro-life" activities.

Zell, Morning Glory: Morning Glory Zell (b. May 27, 1948), priestess of the Church of All Worlds, was born Diana Moore in Long Beach, California. She attended Methodist and Pentecostal churches as a youth, but grew dissatisfied with the sexism of the Christian tradition. She had similar difficulties with Zen Buddhism and the Vedanta Society, though through the latter she discovered Goddess worship. In high school she read Sybil Leek's *Diary of a Witch* and decided that was the path for her.

In 1968 she participated in a vision quest, changed her name, and began exploring Celtic shamanism. In 1969 she married a man she met on the way to join a commune in Oregon. In 1973 she met Timothy (now Otter) Zell at the Gnosticon festival in Minneapolis. She obtained a divorce that year and moved to St. Louis to join Zell, and married him in 1974. He ordained her a priestess for his Church of All Worlds and made her co-editor of the church's famous periodical, *Green Egg*.

In 1976 the Zells left St. Louis and began a period of travel and exploring some religious issues. They settled on some land in Mendocino County, California, owned by the prominent pagan, Alison Harlow. In 1977 Morning Glory founded the Ecosophical Research Association to explore history, mythology, and natural science. Its first big project was looking into the possibility that the legendary unicorn had actually been artificially produced by Middle Eastern people. A young goat's horns were surgically altered, and when the goat matured in 1980 it was presented to the media and eventually travelled with the Ringling Brothers/Barnum & Bailey Circus. Other projects have included the New Guinea Mermaid expedition and a Peruvian Pilgrimage.

In 1985 the Zells moved to some land willed to them in Ukiah, California, and rejuvenated the Church of All Worlds. In 1988 the *Green Egg* was also reintroduced, and she has resumed her position as coeditor.

Zell, Oberon: Oberon (formerly "Otter") Zell (b. November 30, 1942), founder of the Church of All Worlds, was born Timothy Zell in St. Louis, Missouri, but grew up in Clark Summit, Pennsylvania. While at Westminster College in Fulton, Missouri, he met Richard Lance Christie, who was interested in psychic phenomena and alternative religious expressions. On April 7, 1962, they founded a "water-brotherhood," called "Atl." Zell had a marriage that lasted from 1963 to 1971, and he briefly was in the

Oberon Zell (1996)
Courtesy: Church of All Worlds

graduate clinical psychology program at Washington State.

In 1968 Zell moved to St. Louis, Missouri, and legally incorporated the Church of All Worlds, one of the first Neo-Pagan groups to incorporate and the first to achieve tax exempt status, granted in 1971 after a court battle. The church took much inspiration from Robert Heinlein's book *Stranger in a Strange Land* (1961), in which a Church of All Worlds was created around small groups called nests. It focuses on personal and interpersonal development in the context of a magical worldview and reverence for Mother Earth. In the early 1970s Zell formulated the Gaia (Gaea) Hypothesis, that the earth is a single, living organism. This idea has since become very important in New Age and other circles. From 1968 to 1976 the church's periodical, *Green Egg*, was one of the most significant Neo-Pagan (a term coined by Zell) publications in the nation. In 1974 he married Diana Moore, already known as Morning Glory.

In 1976 the Zells left the church and publications in the hands of others and went into a period of travel, retreat, and research. The church soon dissolved. The Zells eventually settled on some land in northern California owned by Alison Harlow, and slowly attracted followers. They created a unicorn through surgery on a young goat, which was presented to the world in 1979. That year, after a vision quest, Zell changed his name to Otter G'Zell, then later to Otter Zell and finally Oberon Zell. In 1985 the Zells moved to some land in Ukiah, California, willed to them by Gwydion Pendderwen, and reactivated the Church of All Worlds. In 1988 the *Green Egg* periodical was reestablished, and the Zells have since renewed their leadership within the larger Neo-Pagan world.

Bibliography

Abbas Amanat, *Resurrection and Renewal: The Making of the Babi Movement in Iran, 1844-1850.* Ithaca: Cornell University Press, 1989.

Abd-ru-shin. *Awake! Selected Lectures.* Vomperberg, Tyrol, Austria: Maria Bernhardt Publishing Co., n.d.

Abd-ru-shin. *In the Light of Truth.* Vomperberg, Tyrol, Austria: Maria Bernhardt Publishing Co., 1954.

'Abdu'l-Bahá, *Selections from the Writings of 'Abdu'l-Bahá.* Haifa:Bahá World Centre Publications, 1978.

Abehsera, Michael. *Zen Macrobiotic Cooking.* New York: Avon, 1970.

Aberle, David F. *The Peyote Religion Among the Navaho.* New York: Wenner-Glen Foundation for Anthropological Research, 1966.

Acharya, Pundit. *A Strange Language.* Nyack, NY: Yoga Research School, 1939.

Acharya Sushil Kumar, *Song of the Soul.* Blairstown, NJ: Siddhachalan Publishers 1987.

"The Acid Test of Accountability" *Cornerstone* 22. 102/103 (1994).

Adams, Evangeline. *The Bowl of Heaven.* New York: Dodd, Mead & Co., 1924.

Adamski, George. *Pioneers of Space: A Trip to the Moon, Mars, and Venus.* Los Angeles: Leonard-Freefield Co., 1949.

Adamski, George. *Questions and Answers by the Royal Order of Tibet.* n.p.: Royal Order of Tibet, 1936.

Adefunmi I, Oba Efuntola Oseijeman Adelabu. *Olorisha, A Guidebook into Yoruba Religion.* Sheldon, SC: The Author, 1982.

Adefunmi, Baba Oseijeman. *Ancestors of the Afro-Americans.* Long Island City, NY: Aims of Modzawe, 1973.

Adkin, Clare E. *Brother Benjamin: A History of the Israelite House of David*. Berrien Springs, MI: Andrews University Press, 1990.

Adler, Felix. *Creed and Deed: A Series of Discourses*. New York: Putnam, 1877.

Adler, Jacob, and Robert M. Kamins. *The Fantastic Life of Walter Murray Gibson: Hawaii's Minister of Everything*. Honolulu: University of Hawaii Press, 1986.

Adler, Margot. *Drawing Down the Moon*. New York: Viking Press, 1979. Rev. ed. Boston: Beacon Press, 1986.

Adler, Margot. *Drawing Down the Moon: Witches, Druids, Goddess-Worshippers, and Other Pagans in America Today*, 2nd ed. Boston:Beacon Press, 1989.

Adolph Ernst Knoch, 1874-1965. Saugus, California: Concordant Publishing Concern, 1965.

Aetherius Society. *Temple Degree Study Courses*. Hollywood, CA: The Aetherius Society, 1982.

Age, Mark. *How to Do All Things: Your Use of Divine Power*. Ft. Lauderdale, FL: Mark-Age, 1988.

Ahmad, Hazrat Mirza Bashiruddin Mahmud. *Ahmadiyyat or the True Islam*. Washington, DC: American Fazl Mosque. 1951.

Ahmad, Hazrat Mirza Bashiruddin Mahmud. *Invitation*. Rabwah, Pakistan: Ahmadiyya Muslim Foreign Missions, 1968.

Ahmad, Mirza Ghulam Hazrat. *Our Teaching*. Rabwah, West Pakistan: Ahmadiyya Muslim Foreign Missions Office, 1962.

Aho, James. *The Politics of Righteousness: Idaho Christian Patriotism*. Seattle, WA: University of Washington Press, 1990.

Ahrens, Frank. "A Krishna Clan's Chants for Survival." *Washington Post*. Sept. 8, 1991, F1.

Aitken, Robert. *A Zen Wave*. New York: Weatherhill, 1978.

Aitken, Robert. *The Mind of Clover*. San Francisco, CA: North Point Press, 1984.

Aivanhov, Omraam M. *Love and Sexuality*. Frejus, France: Editions Prosveta, 1976.

Aivanhov, Omraam M. *The Universal White Brotherhood Is Not a Sect*. Frejus, France: Editions Prosveta, 1982.

Ajaya, Swami. *Living with the Himalayan Masters: Spiritual Experiences of Swami Rama*. Honesdale, Pennsylvania: Himalayan Institute, 1978.

al-'Arabi, Ibn. *Sufis of Andalucia*. Berkeley and Los Angeles: University of California Press, 1971.

al-'Arabi, Ibn. *The Bezels of Wisdom*. New York: Paulist Press, 1980.

Alan, Jim, and Selena Fox. *Circle Magick Songs*. Madison, WI: Circle Publications, 1977.

Albert, Mimi. "Out of Africa: Luisah Teish." *Yoga Journal* (January-February 1987): 32-35, 63-66.

Ali, Nobel Drew. *Moorish Literature*. The Author, 1928.

Ali, Noble Drew. *Timothy Drew, The Holy Koran of the Moorish Science Temple of America*. [Baltimore, MD]: Moorish Science Temple of America, 1978.

Allard, William Albert. "The Hutterites, Plain People of the West." *National Geographic* 138, no. 1 (July 1970): 98-125.

Allen, A.A. and Walter Wagner. *Born to Loose, Bound to Win*. Garden City, NY: Doubleday, 1970.

Allen, A.A. *My Cross*. Miracle Valley, AZ: A.A.Allen Revivals, n.d.

Allen, James B. and Glen M. Leonard. *The Story of the Latter-day Saints*. Salt Lake City: Deseret Book Company, 1992.

Allen, Paul M., ed. *A Christian Rosenkreutz Anthology*. Blauvelt, NY: Rudolph Steiner Publications, 1968.

Allen, Steve. *Beloved Son*. Indianapolis: Bobbs-Merrill Company, 1982.

Allred, Rulon C. *Treasures of Knowledge*. 2 vols. Hamilton, MT: Bitteroot Publishing Col, 1982.

Alper, Frank. *Exploring Atlantis*. Farmingdale, NY: Coleman Publishing, 1982.

Althma, Leh Rheadia. *The Garden of the Soul*. Newberry Springs, CA: AUM Temple of Universal Truth, 1943.

Altman, Nathaniel. *Eating for Life*. Wheaton, IL: Theosophical Publishing House, 1977.

Ambrose, G., and G. Newbold. *A Handbook of Medical Hypnosis*. New York: Macmillan, 1980.

The American Buddhist Directory. New York: American Buddhist Movement, 1985.

Amipa, Lama Sherab Gyaltsen. *The Opening of the Lotus*. London: Wisdom Publications, 1987.

Amish Life in a Changing World. York, PA: York Graphic Services, 1978.

Amma. *Swami Muktananda Paramahansa*. Ganeshpuri, India: Shree Gurudev Ashram, 1969.

Amrit Desai, *Guru and Disciple*. Sumneytown, PA: Kripalu Yoga Ashram (1975).

Amritanandamayi, Mataji. *Awaken Children!* 2 vols., Vallickavu, Kerala, India: Mata Amritanandamayi Mission Trust, 1989-90.

Anandamurti, Shrii Shrii. *Baba's Grace*. Denver, CO: Amrit Publications, 1973.

Anandamurti, Shrii Shrii. *Baba's Grace*. Los Altos Hills, CA: Ananda Marga Publications, 1973.

Anandamurti, Shrii Shrii. *The Great Universe: Discourses on Society*. Los Altos Hills, CA: Ananda Marga publications, 1973.

Anandamurti, Shrii Shrii. *The Spiritual Philosophy of Shrii Shrii Anandamurti*. Denver, CO: Ananda Marga Publications, 1981.

The Ancient Wisdom School. A Collection of Teachings from Ramtha. Ed. by Diane Munoz. Yelm, WA: Diane Munoz, 1992.

The Aquarian Academy. Eureka, CA: Sirius Books, 1978.

The Awakened. Los Angeles: Awakened, 1933.

Anderson, Alan. *Horatio W. Dresser and the Philosophy of New Thought*. Boston: Boston University, Ph.D. dissertation, 1963.

Anderson, Arthur M., ed. *For the Defense of the Gospel*. New York: Church of Christ Pub. Co., 1972.

Anderson, C. Alan. *Horatio W. Dresser and the Philosophy of the New Thought*. Boston: University of Boston, Ph.D. dissertation, 1963.

Anderson, C. LeRoy. *For Christ Will Come Tomorrow: The Saga of the Morrisites*. Logan, UT: Utah State University Press, 1981.

Anderson, Max J. *The Polygamy Story: Fiction or Fact*. Salt Lake City: Publishers Press, 1979.

Anderson, Victor H. *Thorns of the Blood Rose*. Privately published, 1960. Rpt. Redwood Valley, CA: Nemeton, 1970.

Andrews, Edward Deming. *The Gift To Be Simple*. New York: Dover, 1962.

Andrews, Lynn. *Medicine Woman*. New York: Harper & Row, 1981.

Andrews, Sherry. "Maranatha Ministries." *Charisma* 7, no. 9 (May 1982).

Angel Power Newsletter. Carmel, CA: First Church of Angels.

Anka, Darryl. *Bashar: Blue Print for Change, A Message from Our Future*. Simi Valley, CA: New Solutions Publishing, 1990.

Anka, Darryl. *Orion and the Black League*. Encino, CA: Interplanetary Connections, 1978.

Apocalypse (magazine) Bulletin de Liaison du Mouvement Raelian, n.d..

The Aquarian Academy. Eureka, CA: Sirius Books, 1978.

Aquino, Michael A. *The Church of Satan*. n.p.: The Author, 1989.

Arbaugh, George Bartholemew. *Revelation in Mormonism*. Chicago: University of Chicago Press, 1932.

Arboo, Madam, as told to Harold Preece. "What 'Voodoo' Really Is." *Exploring the Unknown* 4, no. 6 (April 1964): 6-19.

Arcana: Inner Dimensions of Spirituality 1:1. Bryn Athyn, PA: Swedenborg Association, 1994.

Arguelles, Jose. *The Transformative Vision: Reflections on the Nature and History of Human Expression*. Berkeley, CA: Shambhala. 1988.

Arleen Lorrance and Diane Kennedy Pike, *The Love Project Way*. San Diego: Love Project Publications, 1980.

Armor, Reginald. *Ernest Holmes, the Man*. Los Angeles: Science of Mind Publications, 1977.

Armstrong, Herbert W. *The United States and the British Commonwealth in Prophecy*. Pasadena,CA: Worldwide Church of God, 1980.

Arndt, Karl J. R. *George Rapp's Successors and Material Heirs*. Cranbury, NJ: Fairleigh Dickinson, 1972.

Arnold, Eberhard, and Emmy Arnold. *Seeking for the Kingdom of God*. Rifton, NY: Plough Publishing House, 1974.

Arnold, Eberhard. *Foundation and Orders of Sannerz and the Rhoen Bruderhof*. Rifton, NY: Plough Publishing Company, 1976.

Arnold, Eberhard. *The Early Christians*. Rifton, NY: Plough Publishing House, 1970.

Arnold, Eberhard. *Why We Live Communally*. Rifton, NY: Plough Publishing House, 1976.

Arnold, Eberhard. *Why We Live in Community*. Rifton, New York: Plough Publishing House, 1967.

Arnold, Emmy. *Torches Together*. Rifton, NY: Plough Publishing House, 1971.

Arrington, Juanita R. *A Brief History of the Apostolic Overcoming Holy Church of God, Inc. and Its Founder*. Birmingham, AL: Forniss Printing Company, 1984.

Articles of Faith and Doctrine. Schell City, MO: Church of God at Schell City, 1982.

Articles of Faith of the Associated Brotherhood of Christians. Hot Springs, AR: Gosless Printing, n.d.

Ashlag, Yehuda. *Kabbalah: A Gift of the Bible*. Jerusalem, Israel: Research Centre of Kabbalah, 1994.

Ashmore, Lewis. *The Modesto Messiah*. Bakersfield, CA: Universal Press, 1977.

Astrological Research and Reference Encyclopedia. 2 vols. Los Angeles: Church of Light, 1972.

Atkinson, William Walker [Yogi Ramacharaka, pseud.]. *The Hindu-Yogi Science of Breath*. Chicago: The Yogi Publication Society, 1903.

Atkinson, William Walker. *The Law of the New Thought*. Chicago: The Psychic Research Co., 1902.

Atlantis: Fact or Fiction. Virginia Beach: ARE Press, 1962.

Aurobindo, Sri. *Sri Aurobindo Birth Centenary Library*. 30 vols. Pondicherry, India: Sri Aurobindo Ashram, 1970-72.

Austin-Sparks, Theodore. *The Centrality and Supremacy of the Lord Jesus Christ*. Washington, DC: Testimony Book Ministry, n.d.

Austin-Sparks, Theodore. *The Work of God at the End of Time*. Washington, DC: Testimony Book Ministry, n.d.

Avenell, Bruce. *A Reason for Being*. La Grange, TX: Eureka Society, 1983.

The Awakened. Los Angeles: Awakened, 1933.

Awbrey, Scott. *Path of Discovery*. Los Angeles: United Church of Religious Science, 1987.

Baba Premanand Bharati, *Krishan* New York: Krishna Samaj, 1904.

Bach, Marcus. *He Talked With God*. Portland, Oregon: Metropolitan Press, 1951.

Bach, Richard. *The Bridge Across Forever*. New York: Dell, 1984.

Badham, Paul and Linda, eds. *Death and Immortality in the Religions of the World*. New York: Paragon House, 1987.

Baer, Hans A. "Black Spiritual Israelites in a Small Southern City." *Southern Quarterly* 23. 1985. pp. 103-24.

Baer, Hans A. *The Black Spiritual Movement: A Religious Response to Racism*. Knoxville, TN: University of Tennessee Press, 1984.

Baer, Hans A. *The Black Spiritual Movement: A Religious Response to Racism*. Knoxville, TN: University of Tennessee Press, 1984.

Baer, Hans A. *The Black Spiritual Movement: A Religious Response to Racism*. Knoxville, TN: University of Tennessee Press, 1984.

Bahá'u'lláha, *Writings of Bahá'u'lláha: A Compilation*. New Delhi: Bahá Publishing Trust, 1986.

Bailey, Alice A. *The Unfinished Autobiography*. New York: Lucis Publishing Company, 1951.

Bailey, Dorothy A. *The Light of Ivah Bergh Whitten*. Southampton: A.M.I.C.A., n.d.

Bailey, Paul. *Wovoka: The Indian Messiah*. Los Angeles: Westernlore Press, 1957.

Bainton, Roland H. *The Reformation of the Sixteenth Century*. Boston: Beacon, 1952.

"Baker Roshi Forms New Group." *Vajradhatu Sun* (March 1985): 4.

Baker, Charles F. *Bible Truth*. Grand Rapids, MI: Grace Bible College, Grace Gospel Fellowship, Grace Mission, 1956.

Baker, Charles F. *Dispensational Relations*. Grand Rapids, MI: Grace Line Bible Lessons, n.d.

Baker, Charles F. *God's Clock of the Ages*. Grand Rapids, MI: Grace Line Bible Lessons, 1937.

Baker, Martha. *Sermonettes in Rhyme*. Little Rock, AK: Allison Press, 1960.

Baker, Robert E. *As It Was in the Days of Noah*. Independence, MO: Old Path Publishers, 1985.

Balagopal. *The Mother of Sweet Bliss*. Vallickavu, Kerala, India: Mata Amritanandamayi Mission Trust, 1985.

Ball, John. *Ananda: Where Yoga Lives*. Bowling Green, OH: Bowling Green University Popular Press, 1982.

Ballard, Guy W. *The "I AM" Discourses*. 4th ed. Chicago: St. Germain Press, 1935, 1982.

Ballard, Guy W. *Unveiled Mysteries*. 4th ed. Chicago: St. Germain Press, 1934, 1982.

Balleine, G. R. *Past Finding Out*. New York: 1956.

Ballou, Adin. *Autobiography of Adin Ballou, 1803-1890*. Lowell, MA: 1896.

Balsekar, Ramesh S. *Experiencing the Teachings*. Redondo Beach, CA: Advaita Press, 1988.

Balsekar, Ramesh S. *From Consciousness to Consciousness*. Redondo Beach, CA: Advaita Press, 1989.

Balyoz, Harold. *Three Remarkable Women*. Flagstaff, AZ: Altai Publishers, 1986.

Balyuzi, Hasan M. *Bahá'u'lláha: King of Glory*. Oxford: George Ronald, 1980.

Band, Arnold J., ed. *Nahman of Bratslav: The Tales*. New York: Paulist Press, 1978.

Banerjee, H. N. and W. C. Oursler. *Lives Unlimited: Reincarnation East and West*. New York: Doubleday, 1974.

Barbour, Hugh. *The Quakers in Puritan England*. New Haven, CT: Yale University Press, 1964.

Barker, Eileen. 1989. *New Religious Movements*. London, Her Majesty's Stationary Office.

Barker, Eileen. *The Making of a Moonie: Choice or Brainwashing?* New York: Basil Blackwell, 1984.

Barkun, Michael. *Religion and the Racist Right: The Origins of the Christian Identity Movement*. Chapel Hill, NC: University of North Carolina Press, 1994.

Barnett, H. G. *Indian Shakers: A Messianic Cult of the Pacific Northwest*. Carbondale, IL: Southern Illinois University Press, 1957.

Barnouw, Victor. "Siberian Shamanism and Western Spiritualism." Journal of the Society of Psychical Research 36 (1942):140-68.

Barrett, H.D. *Life Work of Cora L. V. Richmond*. Chicago: Hack & Anderson, 1895.

Barrett, L. E. *The Dreadlocks of Jamaica*. London: Heinemann, 1977.

Barthel, Diane L. *Amana, From Pietist Sect to American Community*. Lincoln: University of Nebraska Press, 1984.

Bartleman, Frank. *Another Wave Rolls In!* Northridge, California: Voice Publications, 1962.

Bartley, William Warren III. *Werner Erhard: The Transformation of a Man, the Founding of est.* Clarkson N. Potter, Inc., New York: 1978.

Basham, Don. *A Handbook on Holy Spirit Baptism.* Monroeville, PA: Whitaker Books, 1969.

Basham, Don. *Ministering the Baptism of the Holy Spirit.* Monroeville, PA: Whitaker Books, 1971.

A Basic Introduction of the Teachings and Practices of the Hohm Community. Prescott Valley, AZ: Hohm Community, n.d.

Baumann, Louis S. *The Faith.* Winona Lake, IN: Brethren Missionary Helard Co., 1960.

Bayard, Jean-Pierre. *La Guide des sociétés secrètes.* Paris: Philippe Lebaud, 1989.

Beacham, A. D., Jr. *A Brief History of the Pentecostal Holiness Church.* Franklin Springs, GA: Advocate Press, 1983.

Beall, Myrtle. *The Plumb Line.* Detroit, MI: Latter Rain Evangel, 1951.

Bear, Robert. *Delivered Unto Satan.* Carlisle, PA: The Author, 1974.

Beasley, Norman. *The Cross and the Crown.* Boston: Little, Brown, and Co., 1952.

Becker, Robert O., M.D., and Gary Selden. *The Body Electric: Electromagnetism and the Foundation of Life.* New York: William Morrow, 1985.

Bedell, Clyde. *Concordex to the URANTIA Book.* Laguna Hills, CA: The Author, 1980.

Bednaroski, Mary Farrell. 1989. *New Religions and the Theological Imagination in America.* Bloomington: Indiana University Press.

Beebe, Charles S. *Spirits in Rebellion.* Dallas: Southern Methodist University Press, 1977.

Beeston, Blanche W. *Now My Servant.* Caldwell, ID: Caxton Printers, 1987.

Beeston, Blanche W. *Purified as Gold and Silver.* Idaho Falls, ID: The Author, 1966.

Begg, W. D. *The Holy biography of Hazrat Khwaja Muinuddin Chishti.* Tucson, AZ: Chishti Mission of America, 1977.

Beissel, Johann Conrad. *Mysterion Anomias.* Philadelphia: 1728.

The Beliefs and Practices of the Local Church. Anaheim, CA: Living Stream Ministry, 1978.

Bell, Jessie W. *The Grimoire of Lady Sheba.* Llewellyn, 1972.

Bender, D. Wayne. *From Wilderness to Wilderness: Celestia.* Dushore, PA: Sullivan Review, 1980.

Bender, H.S. and John Harsch, *Menno Simons' Life and Writings.* Scottdale, PA: 1936.

Benedict, F. W., and William F. Rushby. "Christ's Assembly: A Unique Brethren Movement." *Brethren Life and Thought* 18 (1973): 33-42.

Benjamine Elbert. *Astrological Lore of All Ages.* Chicago: Aries Press, 1945.

Benner, Joseph S. *The Impersonal Life.* San Gabriel, CA: Willing Publishing Company, 1971.

Bennett, John G. *Creative Thinking.* Sherborne, England: Coombe Springs Press, 1964.

Bennett, John G. *Enneagram Studies.* York Beach, ME: Samuel Weiser, 1983.

Bennett, John G. *Gurdjieff, Making a New World.* New York: Harper & Row, 1973.

Bennett, John G. *Is There "Life" on Earth?* New York: Stonehill Publishing Company, 1973.

Bennett, John G. *Witness.* Tucson, AZ: Omen Press, 1974.

Bennett, John. *Witness: The Autobiography of John Bennett.* London: Turnstone Books, 1974.

Berg, Philip, ed. *An Entrance to the Zohar.* Jerusalem, Israel: Research Centre of Kabbalah, 1994.

Berg, Philip, ed. *Kabbalah for the Layman*, 3 vols. Jerusalem, Israel: Research Centre of Kabbalah.

Berg, Philip, ed. *The Wheel of the Soul.* Jerusalem, Israel: Research Centre of Kabbalah, 1984.

Berkeley Holistic Health Center. *The Holistic Health Lifebook.* And/Or Press, 1979.

Bernard, Pierre. "In Re Fifth Veda." *International Journal of the Tantrik Order.* New York: Tantrik Order in America, [1909].

Bernard, Raymond. *Messages from the Celestial Sanctum.* San Jose, CA: Supreme Grand Lodge of AMORC, 1980.

Besant, Annie. *Autobiographical Sketches.* London: Freethought Publishing Co., 1885.

Beskow, Per. *Strange Tales About Jesus.* Philadelphia: Fortress Press, 1983.

Bestor, Arthur. *Backwoods Utopias.* Philadelphia: University of Pennsylvania Press, 1950.

Bethards, Betty. *Relationships in the New Age of AIDS.* Novato, CA: Inner Light Foundation, 1988.

Bethards, Betty. *Sex and Psychic Energy.* Novato, CA: Inner Light Foundation, 1977.

Bethards, Betty. *The Dream Book: Symbols for Self-Understanding.* Petaluma, CA: Inner Light Foundation, 1983.

Bethards, Betty. *The Sacred Sword.* Novato, CA: Inner Light Foundation, 1972.

Bethards, Betty. *There Is No Death.* Novato, CA: Inner Light Foundation, 1975.

Between Pleasure and Pain: The Way of Conscious Living. Sumas, WA: Dharma Sara Publications, 1976.

Bey, Hamid. *My Experiences Preceding 5000 Burials*. Los Angeles: Coptic Fellowship of America, 1951.

Bhagavad Gita. Juan Mascaro, transl. Baltimore, MD: Penguin, 1970.

Bill, Annie C. *The Universal Design of Life*. Boston: A. A. Beauchamp, 1924.

Billington, Ray Allen. *The Protestant Crusade 1800-1860: A Study of the Origins of American Nativism*. New York: Macmillan, 1938.

Biography, the Sublime Maestre, Sat Guru, Dr. Serge Raynaud de la Ferriere. St. Luois, MO: Educational Publications of the IES, 1976.

Birdsong, Robert E. *Mission to Mankind: A Cosmic Autobiography*. Eureka, CA: Sirius Books, 1975.

Bishop, Rufus. *Testimonies of the Life, Character, Revelation and Doctrines of Our Blessed Mother Ann Lee and the Elders with Her*. Albany, New York: 1888.

Bjorling, Joel. *The Churches of God, Seventh Day, A Bibliography*. NY: Garland Publishing, 1987.

Blacksun. *The Elements of Beginning Ritual Construction*. Madison, WI: Circle, 1982.

Blavatsky, H.P. *Isis Unveiled*. Wheaton, IL: Theosophical Publishing House, 1972.

Blavatsky, Helena P. *Collected Writings*. 16 vols. Wheaton, IL: Theosophical Publishing House, 1950-1987.

Blavatsky, Helena Petrovna. *The Secret Doctrine*. 1889.

Blessing, William Lester. *Hallowed Be Thy Name*. Denver, CO: House of Prayer for All People, 1955.

Blessing, William Lester. *More About Jesus*. Denver, CO: House of Prayer for All People, 1952.

Blessing, William Lester. *The Supreme Architect of the Universe*. Denver, CO: House of Prayer for All People, 1956.

Blessing, William Lester. *The Trial of Jesus*. Denver, CO: House of Prayer for All People, 1955.

Blessing, William Lester. *VOTSA*. Denver, CO: House of Prayer for All People, 1965.

Bletzer, June G. *The Donning International Encyclopedic Psychic Dictionary*. Norfolk, VA: Donning, 1986.

Bliss, Sylvester. *Memoirs of William Miller*. Boston: Joshua V. Himes, 1853.

Block, Marguerite Beck. *The New Church in the New World*. New York: Henry Holt and Company, 1932. 464 pp.

Blofeld, John. *Taoism, The Road to Immortality*. Boulder: Shambhala, 1978.

Bloom, William. *Devas, Fairies and Angels: A Modern Approach*. Glastonbury, Somerset, UK: Gothic Image Publications, 1986.

Blumhofer, Edith. "The Finished Work of Calvary." *Assemblies of God Heritage* 3 (Fall 1983): 9-11.

Bokser, Ben Zion. *The Jewish Mystical Tradition*. New York: Pilgrim Press, 1981.

Bolen, Jean Shinoda, *Goddesses in Everywoman: A New Psychology of Women*. Harper and Row, 1984.

Bolen, Jean Shinoda, *Gods in Everyman: A New Psychology of Men's Lives and Loves*. Harper and Row, 1989.

Bonewits, Isaac. *Authentic Thaumaturgy*. Albany, CA: The CHAOSium, 1978.

Bonewits, P. E. I. *Real Magic*. Weiser, 3d ed., 1988.

The Book of Books. East Rutherford, NJ: Dawn Bible Students Association, 1962.

A Book of Commandments for the Government of the Church of Christ. Independence, MO: Church of Christ (Temple Lot), 1960.

Book of Doctrines, 1903-1970. Huntsville, AL: Church of God Publishing House, 1970.

The Book of the Lord's Commandments, three vols. Independence, MO: Restored Church of Jesus Christ, n.d.

Book of Worship, The Church of the Brethren. Elgin, IL: Brethren Press, 1964.

The Book of Yahweh. Abilene, TX: House of Yahweh, 1987.

Books of Azrael. 4 vols., Santa Barbara, CA: J.F. Rowny Press, 1965-67.

Borowski, Karol. *Attempting an Alternative Society*. Norwood, PA: Norwood Editions, 1984.

Bosheke (van), André, with Jean-Pierre de Staercke. *Chevaliers du vingtième siècle. Enquête sur les sociétés occultes et les ordres de chevalerie contemporains*. Anvers: EPO, 1988.

Boswell, Charles. "The Great Fume and Fuss Over the Omnipotent Oom." *True* (January 1965): 31-33, 86-91.

Bouchard, Alain (1989) "Mouvement Raelian" in *Nouvel Age... Nouvelles Croyances*. Montreal: Editions Paulines & Mediaspaul.

Boucher, Mark T. *J. Roswell Flower*. Springfield, MO: The Author, 1983.

Bowden, Henry Warner. *Dictionary of American Religious Biography*. Westport, CT: Greenwood Press, 1977.

Bozeman, John. "A Preliminary Assessment of Women's Conversion Narratives at New Vrindaban." *Syzygy* 3. 1994.

Bozeman, John. "Jesus People USA after Twenty Years: Balancing Sectarianism and Assimilation." Paper read before the Communal Studies Society, New Harmony, IN, October 16, 1993.

Bozeman, John. "Jesus People USA: An Examination of an Urban Communitarian Religious Group." M.A. thesis, Florida State University, Fall, 1990.

Bozeman, John. "The Interfaith Mission of New Vrindaban." Paper read before the Communal Studies Association, Nauvoo, IL, October 16, 1992.

Bracelin, J. L. *Gerald Gardner: Witch.* London: Octagon Press, 1960.

Braden, Charles S. "Gestefeld, Ursula Newell." In *Notable American Women*, edited by Edward T. James, Janet Wilson James, and Paul S. Boyer, vol. 2, 27-28. Cambridge, MA.: The Belknap Press of Harvard University Press, 1971.

Braden, Charles S. "Hopkins, Emma Curtis." In *Notable American Women*, edited by Edward T. James, Janet Wilson James, and Paul S. Boyer, vol. 2, 219-20. Cambridge, Mass.: The Belknap Press of Harvard University Press, 1971.

Braden, Charles S. *Spirits in Rebellion.* Dallas: Southern Methodist University Press, 1963.

Braden, Charles Samuel. *These Also Believe.* New York: Macmillan, 1949.

Bradlee, Ben, Jr., and Dale Van Atta. *Prophet of Blood.* New York: G. P. Putnam's Sons, 1981.

Brahma Baba—The Corporeal Medium of Shiva Baba. Mount Abu, India: Prajapita Brahma Kumaris Ishwariya Vishwa Vidyalaya, n.d.

Brahmavidya, Swami. *Transcendent-Science or the Science of Self Knowledge.* Chicago: Transcendent-Science Society, 1922.

Brandon, Ruth. *The Spiritualists.* New York: Alfred A. Knopf, 1983.

Branham, William Marrion. *Conduct, Order, Doctrine of the Church.* Jeffersonville, IN: Spoken Word Publications, 1974.

Branham, William. *Footprints on the Sands of Time.* Jeffersonville, IN: Spoken Word Publications, n.d.

Braude, Ann. *Radical Spirits.* Boston: Beacon Press, 1989.

Breese-Whiting, Kathryn. *The Phoenix Rises.* San Diego: Protal Publications, 1971.

Brent, Peter. *The Godmen of India.* Chicago: Quadrangle Books, 1972.

Brickley, Donald P. *Man of the Morning.* Kansas City, MO: Nazarene Publishing House, 1960.

A Brief Biography of Darshan Singh. Bowling Green, VA: Sawan Kirpal Publications, 1983.

Brief Life Sketch of Param Sant Kirpal Singh Ji Maharaj. Wembly, England: Kirpal Bhavan, 1976.

Briggs, Katharine. *An Encyclopedia of Fairies.* New York: Pantheon, 1976.

Brinton, Ellen Star. "The Rogerenes." *New England Quarterly.* 16 (March 1943):3-19.

Brinton, Howard. *Friends for Three Hundred Years.* New York: Harpers, 1952.

Britten, Emma Hardinge. *Modern American Spiritualism.* New York, 1870. Rpt. New Hyde Park, NY: University Books, 1970.

Britten, Emma Hardinge. *Nineteenth Century Miracles*. New York: William Britten, 1884.

Brock, Peter. *The Quaker Peace Testimony, 1660-1914*. York: Sessions, 1991.

Bromage, Bernard. *Tibetan Yoga*. Wellingborough, Northamptonshire, England: The Aquarian Press, 1979. First published 1952.

Bromley, David G. and James T. Richardson. *The Brainwashing/Deprogramming Controversy*. New York: Edwin Mellen, 1983.

Bromley, David G., and Anson D. Shupe, Jr. *Moonies in America: Cult, Church, Crusade*. Beverly Hills, CA: Sage, 1979.

Brooke, Anthony. *The Universal Link Revelations*. London: Universal Foundation, 1967.

Brooks, John P. *The Divine Church*. El Dorado Springs, MO: Witt Printing Company, 1960.

Brooks, Louise McNamara. *Early History of Divine Science*. Denver, CO: First Divine Science Church, 1963.

Brooks, Nona L. *Short Lessons in Divine Science*. Denver: The Author, 1928.

Brooks, Nona L. *The Prayer That Never Fails*. Denver: Divine Science Church and College, 1935.

Brooks, Tal. *Avatar of Night*. New Delhi: Tarang Paperbacks, 1984.

Brooks, Tal. *Planetary Influence*. New York: The Author, 1898.

Brotz, Howard M. *The Black Jews of Harlem*. New York: Schocken Books, 1970.

Broughton, Luke Dennis. *The Elements of Astrology*. New York: The Author, 1898.

Brown, Charles E. *When the Trumpet Sounded*. Anderson, IN: 1951.

Brown, Gordon. *Christian Science Nonsectarian* Haslemere, Surrey, England: Gordon and Estelle Brown 1966.

Brown, Henry Harrison. *Dollars Want Me*. San Francisco: "Now" Folk, 1903.

Brown, Henry Harrison. *Man's Greatest Discovery*. San Francisco: "Now" Folk, 1901.

Brown, Kingdon L. *The Metaphysical Lessons of Saint Timothy's Abbey Church*. Grosse Pointe, Michigan: St. Timothy's Abbey Church, 1966.

Brown, Raymond S. *The Community of the Beloved Disciple*. Paulist Press.

Brown, Slater. *The Heyday of Spiritualism*. New York: Hawthorn Books, 1970.

Browne, Robert T. *Introduction to Hermetic Science and Philosophy*. Hermetic Society, n.d. 4-page tract.

Browning, Clyde. *Amish in Illinois*. The Author, 1971.

Brownlow, Lerow. *Why I Am A Member of the Church of Christ*. Fort Worth, TX, n.d.

Brumback, Carl. *Suddenly from Heaven*. Springfield, MO: Gospel Publishing House, 1961.

Brunier, Nina. *The Path to Illumination*. Highway Highlands, CA: The Author, 1941.

Brunton, Paul. *A Message from Arunchala*. New York: Samuel Weiser, 1971.

Bryan, Gerald B. *Psychic Dictatorship in America*. Burbank, CA: The New Era Press, 1940.

Buber, Martin. *The Origin and Meaning of Hassidism*. New York: Horizon Press, 1960.

Buchman, Frank N. *Remaking the World*. London, England: Blandford Press, 1961.

Buckland, Raymond. *Buckland's Complete Book of Witchcraft*. St. Paul, MN: Llewellyn Publications, 1986.

Buckland, Raymond. *The Tree: The Book of Shadows of Seax-Wica*. Samuel Weiser, 1974.

Buckley, Tim. "History of the Zen Meditation Center of Rochester." *Wind Bell* 8 (Fall 1969): 51-3.

Buczynski, Edmund M. *Witchcraft Fact Book*. NY: Magickal Childe, 1969.

Budapest, Zsuzsanna . *The Feminist Book of Lights and Shadows*. Venice, CA: Luna Publications, 1976.

Budapest, Zsuzsanna E. *The Holy Book of Women's Mysteries*. Berkeley: Wingbow Press, 1989.

Budapest, Zsuzsanna. *The Rise of the Fates*. Los Angeles: Susan B. Anthony Coven No. 1, 1976.

Buddhist Churches of America, 75 Year History, 1899-1974. 2 vols. Chicago: Norbert, 1974.

Buddhist Handbook for Shin-shu Followers. Tokyo: Hokuseido Press, 1969.

Buehrens, John A. and F. Forrester Church. *Our Chosen Faith*. Boston: Beacon Press, 1989.

Bullinger, E. W. *The Book of Job*. Atascadero, CA: Scripture Research, 1983.

Bunger, Fred S. and Hans N. Von Koerber. *A New Light Shines Out of the Present Darkness*. Philadelphia: Dorrance Company, 1971.

Burgess, Stanley M., and Gary B. McGee, eds. *Dictionary of Pentecostal and Charismatic Movements*. Grand Rapids, MI: Zondervan Publishing House, 1988.

Burgoyne, Thomas H. *Celestial Dynamics*. Denver, CO: Astro-Philosophical Publishing Co., 1896.

Burgoyne, Thomas H. *The Light of Eqypt*. 2 vols. Albuquerque, NM: Sun Publishing Company, 1980.

Burham, Kenneth E. *God Comes to America*. Boston: Lambeth Press, 1979.

Burke, George. *Faith Speaks*. Oklahoma City, OK: Rexist Press, 1975.

Burke, George. *Magnetic Healing*. Oklahoma City, OK: Saint George Press, 1980.

Burkett, R. K. . *Garveyism as a religious movement: The institutionalization of a black civil religion*. London: Scarecrow, Press, 1878.

Burkett, Randall. *Garveyism as a Religious Movement*. Metuchen, New Jersey: Scarecrow Press, 1978.

Burkhardt, Frederic, and Fredson Bowers, eds. *The Works of William James: Essays in Psychical Research*. Cambridge, MA: Harvard University Press, 1986.

Bussell, D. J. *Chirothesia*. Los Angeles: Chirothesian Church of Faith, n.d.

Bussell, D. J. *Co-Ordinating Knowledge*. Los Angeles: National Academy of Metaphysics, n.d.

Bussell, D. J. *First Steps in Metaphysics*. Los Angeles: National Academy of Metaphysics, n.d.

Butler, Hiram E. *Special Instructions for Women*. Applegate, CA: Esoteric Fraternity, 1942.

Butler, Hiram E. *The Goal of Life*. Applegate, CA: Esoteric Publishing Company, 1908.

Butler, Hiram E. *The Narrow Way of Attainment*. Applegate, CA: Esoteric Publishing Company, 1901.

Butler, Hiram E. *The Seven Creative Principles*. Applegate, CA: Esoteric Publishing Company, 1950.

Buzzard, Anthony. *The Kingdom of God—When & Whence?* Oregon, IL: Restoration Fellowship, 1980.

Buzzard, Anthony. *What Happens When We Die?: A biblical View of Death and Resurrection*. Oregon, IL: Restoration Fellowship, 1986.

Buzzard, Anthony. *Who Is Jesus?: A Plea for a Return to Belief in Jesus, the Messiah*. Oregon, IL: Restoration Fellowship, n.d.

Byers, Andrew L. *Birth of a Reformation*. Anderson, IN: 1921.

Cabot, Laurie. *Power of the Witch: The Earth, the Moon, and the Magical Path to Enlightenment*. New York: Delacorte Press, 1989.

Caddy, Eileen. *Flight Into Freedom*. Longmead, Dorset: Element Books, 1988.

Cady, H. Emilie. *Lessons in Truth*. Kansas City, MO: Unity School of Christianity, 1919.

Cady, H. Emilie. *Miscellaneous Writings*. Rev. ed. as *How I Used Truth*. Lee's Summit, MO: Unity School of Christianity, 1934.

Cain, Nellie B. *Exploring the Mysteries of Life*. Grand Rapids, MI: Spiritual Research Society, 1972.

Cain, Nellie B. *Gems of Truth from the Masters*. Grand Rapids, MI: Spiritual Research Society, 1965.

Callen, Barry L., ed. *The First Century*. 2 vols. Anderson, IN: Warner Press, 1979.

Cambridge Buddhist Assocation. Cambridge, MA: Cambridge Buddhist Association, 1960.

Cameron, Charles, ed. *Who Is Guru Maharaj Ji?* New York: Bantam Books, 1973.

Cammell, C. R. *Aleister Crowley*. London: New English Library, 1969.

Campbell, Bruce F. *Ancient Wisdom Revived: A History of the Theosophical Movement*. Berkeley: University of California Press, 1980.

Campbell, Joseph with Bill Moyers. *The Power of Myth*. New York: Doublday, 1988.

Campbell, Joseph. *The Hero With a Thousand Faces*. Princeton, NJ: Princeton University Press, 1949.

Campion, Anita Montero. *My Guru from South America: Sat Arhat Manuel Estrada*. St. Louis: The Author, 1976.

Canet, Carlos. *Oyotunji*. Miami, FL: Editorial AIP, n.d.

Canizares, Raul. "Epiphany and Cuban Santeria." *Journal of Dharma* 15:4. Oct-Dec 1990. pp. 309-313.

Canizares, Raul. "Palo: An Afro-Cuban Cult Often Confused with Santeria." *Syzygy: Journal of Alternative Religion and Culture* 2:1-2. Winter/Spring 1993. pp. 89-96.

Cannon, Hana. "Waking Up in Russia" *Gate Way* April-May 1992: 39-45.

Carden, Karen W., and Robert W. Pelton. *The Persecuted Prophets*. New York: A. S. Barnes, 1976.

Carden, Maren L. *Utopian Community to Modern Corporation*. Baltimore: John Hopkins University Press, 1969.

Carden, Maren Lockwood. *Oneida, Utopian Community to Modern Corporation*. Baltimore, MD: 1969.

Carl McIntire's 50 Years, 1933-1983. Collingswood, NJ: Bible Presbyterian Church, 1983.

Carlsen, C. J. *Elling Eielsen, Pioneer Lay Preacher and First Norwegian Pastor in America*. Master's thesis, Minneapolis: University of Minnesota , 1932.

Carlson, G. Raymond. *Our Faith and Fellowship*. Springfield, MO: Gospel Publishing House, 1977.

Carre, John. *An Island of Hope*. Mariposa, CA: House of Light, 1975.

Carter, Ben Ammi. *God, the Black Man, and Truth*. Chicago: Communicators Press, 1982.

Carter, Paul A. "The Reformed Episcopal Schism of 1873: An Ecumenical Perspective." *Historical Magazine of the Protestant Episcopal Church* 33 (September 1964): 225-238.

Carus, Paul. *The Dawn of a New Religious Era*. Chicago: Open Court Publishing Co., 1913.

Carus, Paul. *The Gospel of Buddha*. Chicago: Open Court Publishing Co., 1894.

Case, Paul Foster. *The Tarot*. 2nd ed. Los Angeles, CA. Builders of the Adytum, Ltd. Temple of Tarot and Holy Quabalah, 1990.

Case, Paul Foster. *The True and Invisible Rosicrucian Order*. The Author, 1928.

Casewit, Curtis W. *Graphology Handbook*. Para Research, 1980.

Cat's Yawn. New York: First Zen Institute in America, 1947.

Cavendish, Richard, ed. *Encyclopedia of The Unexplained. Magic, Occultism and Parapsychology*. London: Arkana Penguin Books, 1989.

Cavendish, Richard. *A History of Magic*. London: Weidenfeld and Nicolson, 1977.

Cayce, Edgar. *What I Believe*. Virginia Beach, VA: Edgar Cayce Publishing Company, 1946.

Cayce, Hugh Lynn. *Venture Inward*. New York: Harper and Row, 1964.

Chadda, H. C., ed. *Seeing Is Above All: Sant Darshan's First Indian Tour*. Bowling Green, VA: Sawan Kirpal Publications, 1978.

Chadwick, Henry. *The Early Church*. New York: Penguin, 1967.

Chaffanjon, Arnaud, - Bertrand Galimard Flavigny, *Ordres & contre-ordres de chevalerie*, Paris: Mercure de France, 1982.

Chainey, George. *Deus Homo*. Boston, MA: Christopher Publishing House, 1927.

Chainey, George. *The Unsealed Bible*. London: Kegan Paul, Trench, Truebner & Co., 1902.

Challenge. London: Lubavitch Foundation of Great Britain, 1970.

Chaney, Earlyne, and William L. Messick. *Kundalini and the Third Eye*. Upland, CA: Astara's Library of Mystical Classics, 1980.

Chaney, Earlyne. *Beyond Tomorrow*. Upland, CA: Astara, 1985.

Chaney, Earlyne. *Remembering*. Los Angeles: Astara's Library of Mystical Classics, 1974.

Chaney, Earlyne. *Shining Moments of a Mystic*. Upland, CA: Astara, 1976.

Chaney, Earlyne. *The Book of Beginning Again*. Upland, CA: Astara, 1981.

Chaney, Robert G. *"Hear My Prayer."* Eaton Rapids, MI: The Library, Spiritualist Episcopal Church, 1942.

Chaney, Robert G. "Hear My Prayer." Eaton Rapids, MI: The Library, The Spiritualist Episcopal Church, 1942.

Chaney, Robert G. *Mediums and the Development of Mediumship*. Freeport, N.Y.: Books for Libraries Press, 1972.

Chaney, Robert Galen. *The Inner Way*. Los Angeles, CA: DeVorss & Co., 1962.

Chaney, Robert. *Mysticism, the Journey Within*. Upland, CA: Astra's Library of Mystical Classics, 1979.

Chang, Carsun. *The Development of Neo-Confucian Thought*. New York: Twayne Publishers, 1957.

Chapman, A.H. *What TM Can and Cannot Do for You*. New York: Berkeley Publishing Corporation, 1976.

Chapman, Paul, ed. *Clusters*. Greensboro, NC: Alternative, 1975.

Chen, James. *Meet Brother Nee*. Hong Kong: The Christian Publishers, 1976.

Chesham, Sallie. *Born to Battle*. Chicago: Rand McNally & Co., 1965.

Chia, Mantak, and Maneewan Chia. *Healing Love Through the Tao: Cultivating Female Sexual Energy*. Huntington, NY: Healing Tao Books, 1986.

Chia, Mantak, with Michael Winn. *Taoist Secrets of Love: Cultivating Male Sexual Energy*. New York: Aurora Press, 1984.

Chia, Mantak. *Awaken Healing Energy Through the Tao*. New York: Aurora Press, 1983.

Chia, Mantak. *Taoist Ways to Transform Stress into Vitality: The Inner Smile/Six Healing Sounds*. New York: Aurora Press, 1985.

Chinmayananda, Swami. *A Manual for Self-Unfoldment*. Napa, CA: Chinmaya Publications (West), 1975.

Chinmayananda, Swami. *Kindle Life*. Madra: Chinmaya Publications Trust, n.d.

Chinmayananda, Swami. *Meditation (Hasten Slowly)*. Napa, CA: Family Press, 1974.

Chinmayananda, Swami. *The Way to SElf-Perfection*. Napa, CA: Chinmaya Publications (West), 1976.

Chinmoy, Sri. *My Lord's Secrets Revealed*. New York: Herder & Herder, 1971.

Christ, Carol P. *Diving Deep and Surfacing*. Boston, MA: Beacon Press, 1980.

The Christ (Through Virginia Essene). *New Teachings for an Awakened Humanity*. 1986.

The Christian Mystery School. Pelhan, NH: Homebringing Mission of Jesus Christ, 1983.

Chryssides, George D. *The Advent of Sun Myung Moon: The Origins, Beliefs and Practices of the Unification Church*. New York: St. Martin's, 1991

Church, Connie. *Crystal Clear*. New York: Villard Books, 1987.

Church History 50, no. 2 (June 1981): 182-92.

"Church of Aphrodite, Goddess of Love is chartered in New York." *Life* (December 4, 1939).

"Church of Christ Restored." *Restoration* 4, no. 3 (July 1985): 7.

Church of God, Body of Christ Manual. Mocksville, NC: Church of God, Body of Christ, 1969.

The Church of Light Quarterly 50 (Spring-Summer 1975): ii-vi.

"The Church of the Higher Life." *Journal of Practical Metaphysics* 1 (December 1896): 76-77.

Churches of Christ Around the World. Nashville: Gospel Advocate Company, 1990.

Churches of Christ in the United States. Compiled by Lynn Mac. Nashville: Gospel Advocate Company, 1990.

Circle Guide to Pagan Resources. Mt. Horeb, WI: Circle, 1987.

"*Clarion Call*, a Classy New Journal from S. F. Gaudiyas." *Hinduism Today* 10, 9 (September 1988): 1, 17.

Clark, Jerome. "Life in a Pyramid." *Fate* 36:6. June 1983. Pp33-44.

Clark, Jerome. "UFOs in the 1980s," in *The UFO Encyclopedia*, Volume 1. Detroit, MI: Apogee Books, 1990.

Clark, Walter Houston. *Chemical Ecstasy: Psychedelic Drugs and Religion.* New York: Sheed & Ward, 1969.

Clark, Walter Houston. "What Light Do Drugs Throw on the Spiritual and the Transpersonal?" *The Journal of Religion and Psychical Research* 4, no. 2 (April 1981): 131-37.

Clymer, R. Swinburne. *The Age of Treason.* Quakertown, PA: Humanitarian Society, 1959.

Clymer, R. Swinburne. *The Rose Cross Order.* Allentown, PA: Philosophical Publishing Co., 1916.

Clymer, R. Swinburne. *The Rosicrucian Fraternity in America.* 2 vols. Quakertown, PA: Rosicrucian Foundation, 1935.

Clymer, R. Swinburne. *The Rosy Cross, Its Teachings.* Quakertown, PA: Beverly Hall Corporation, 1965.

Coad, Roy. *A History of the Brethren Movement.* Exeter: The Paternoster Press, 1968.

Coates, James. *Armed and Dangerous.* New York: Hill and Wang, 1987.

Cobb, Douglas S. "The Jamesville Bruderhof: A Hutterian Agricultural Colony." *Journal of the West* 9, no. 1 (January 1970): 60-77.

Coble, Margaret. *Self-Abidance.* Port Louis, Mauritius: Standard Printing Establishment, 1973.

Cohen, Andrew. *Autobiography of an Awakening.* Corte Madera, CA: Moksha Foundation, 1992.

Cohen, Andrew. *My Master is Myself.* Moksha Foundation, 1989.

Cohn, Norman. *Cosmos, Chaos and the World to Come: The Ancient Roots of Apocalyptic Faith.* New Haven: Yale University Press, 1993.

Cohn, Norman. *Cosmos, Chaos and the World to Come:The Ancient Roots of Apocalyptic Faith.* New Haven: Yale University Press, 1993.

Cohn, Norman. *The Pursuit of the Millennium.* London: Oxford University Press, 1957.

Cole, W. Owen, and Piara Singh Sambhi. *The Sikhs*. London: Routledge & Kegan Paul, 1978.

Cole-Whitaker, Terry. *How to Have More in a Have-Not World*. New York: Fawcett Crest, 1983.

Cole-Whitaker, Terry. *Love and Power in a World Without Limits: A Woman's Guide to the Goddess Within*. San Francisco: Harper & Row, 1989.

Cole-Whitaker, Terry. *The Inner Path from Where You Are to Where You Want to Be*. New York: Rawson Assocs., 1986.

Cole-Whitaker, Terry. *What You Think of Me Is None of My Business*. New York: Rawson Assocs., 1983.

Colemon, Johnnie. *It Works If You Work It*. 2 vols. Chicago: Universal Foundation for Better Living, n.d.

Colemon, Johnnie. *The Best Messages from the Founder's Desk*. Chicago: Universal Foundation for Better Living, 1987.

Coll, Francisco. *Discovering Your True Identity leadership Training Manual*. Osceola, IA: American Leadership College, 1972.

Coll, Francisco. *The Gifts of Intuition, Vision, Prophecy and Feeling in the Seven-Year Cycles*. Washington, DC: American Leadership College, 1981.

Collier, Sophia. *Soul Rush: The Odyssey of a Young Woman in the '70s*. New York: William Morrow and Co., 1978.

Collins, J. B. *Tennessee Snake Handlers*. Chattanooga: The Author, 1947.

Collins, William. *Bibliography of English-Language Works on the Báb and Bahá Faiths, 1844-1985*. Oxford: George Ronald, 1990.

Coloquhoun, Ithell. *Sword of Wisdom: MacGregor Mathers and the Golden Dawn*. New York: G. P. Putnam's Sons, 1975.

Communities of the Past and Present. Newllano, LA: Llano Cooperative Colony, 1924.

Companion of God. London: Brahman Kumaries World Spiritual University, 1996.

Condron, Daniel. *Dreams of the Soul: the Yogi Sutras of Patanjali*. Windyville, MO: SOM Publishing, 1992.

Conlan, Barnett D. *Nicolas Roerich: A Master of the Mountains*. Liberty, IN: FLAMMA, Association for the Advancement of Culture, 1938.

Conn, Charles W. *Like a Mighty Army*. Cleveland, TN: Church of God Publishing House, 1955.

Conn, Charles W. *Pillars of Pentecost*. Cleveland, TN: Pathway Press, 1956.

Constitution and By-Law of the Full Gospel Truth, Inc. East Jordan, MI: Full Gospel Truth, n.d.

Constitution and By-Laws. Long Beach, CA: California Evangelistic Association, 1939.

Constitution of Churches Organized as Independent Methodist Churches by the Association of Independent Methodists. Jackson, MS: Association of Independent Methodists, n.d.

Conze, Edward. *Buddhist Thought in India.* Ann Arbor: University of Michigan Press, 1967. Rpt. of 1962.

Cook, Lewis E., Jr. *Goldot: Guidebook of Life and Doctrine of Truth.* Oceanside, CA: Doctrine of Truth Foundation, 1976. Unpaged.

Cook, Philip L. *Zion City, Illinois: John Alexander Dowie's Theocracy.* Zion, IL: Zion Historical Society, 1970.

Cooke, Grace. *The Illuniated Ones.* Liss, Hampshire, England: White Eagle Publishing Trust, 1966.

Cooke, Ivan, ed. *The Return of Arthur Conan Doyle.* Liss, Hampshire, England: White Eagle publishing Trust, 1956.

Coon, Michael. "Swami Rama of the Himalayas." *Yoga Journal* (September-October 1976): 8-11.

Copeland, Gloria. *God's Will for You.* Fort Worth, TX: Kenneth Copeland Publications, 1972.

Coray, Henry W. *J. Gresham Machen, A Silhouette.* Grand Rapids, MI: Kregel Publications, 1981.

Corbett, Cynthia L. *Power Trips.* Santa Fe, NM: Timewindow Publications, 1988.

Corliss, William R., ed. *The Unfathomed Mind: A Handbook of Unusual Mental Phenomena.* Glen Arm, MD: The Sourcebook Project, 1982.

Cornelius, Lucille J. *The Pioneer History of the Church of God in Christ.* The Author, 1975.

Correspondence Between Israel Smith and Pauline Hancock on Baptism for the Dead. Independence, MO: Church of Christ, 1955.

Cosby, Gordon. *Handbook for Mission Groups.* Washington, DC: Potter's House, 1973.

Cosmic Awareness Speaks. Olympia, WA: Servants of Awreness, n.d. Vol. II & III. Olympia, WA: Cosmic Awareness Communications, 1977, 1983.

Couch, Edward T. *Evidences of Inspiration.* Bay Springs, DI: The Author, 1980.

Couch, Edward T. *The Sabbath and the Restitution.* Bay Springs, MI: The Author, 1891.

A Course in Miracles. 3 vols., New York: Foundation for Inner Peace, 1975.

Courts, James, ed. *The History and Life Work of Elder C. H. Mason, Chief Apostle, and His Co-Laborers.* Memphis, TN: Howe Printing Dept., 1920.

The Comforter Speaks. Potomac, MD: Cosmic Study Center, 1977.

The Concordant Version in the Critic's Den. Los Angeles: n.d.

The Congregational Church of Practical Theology. Springfield, LA: Congregational Church, 1970.

The Constitution: Abiding Laws or Empty Words? Island Pond, VT: Island Pond Freepaper, 1987.

The Constitution, Government and General Decree Book. Chattanooga, TN: New and Living Way Publishing Co., n.d.

The Constitution of the Bible Presbyterian Church. Collingswood, NJ: Independent Board of Presbyterian Foreign Missions, 1959.

Covenant of the Goddess Newsletter (published eight times a year, available by subscription from Covenant of the Goddess, Box 1226, Berkeley, CA 94704).

The Covenant People. Merrimac, MA: Destiny Publishers, 1966.

Cowen, Clarence Eugene. *A History of the Church of God (Holiness).* The Author, 1948.

Cox, Raymond L. *The Verdict Is In.* Los Angeles: Research Publishers, 1983.

Cox, Raymond L., ed. *The Foursquare Gospel.* Los Angeles, Foursquare Publication, 1969.

Cramer, Malinda E. *Lessons in the Science of Infinite Spirit.* San Francisco: The Author, 1890.

Cramer, Malinda E. "My Spiritual Experience." *Mind* 10 (August 1902): 321.

Cranston, Sylvia. *HPB: The Extraordinary Life and Influence of Helena Blavatsky, Founder of the Modern Theosophical Movement.* New York: Jeremy P. Tarcher/Putnam Book/ G. P. Putnam's Sons, 1993.

The Creator's Grand Design. East Rutherford, NJ: Dawn Bible Students Association, 1969.

The Creed. London: Christian Community Press, 1962.

Creme, Benjamin. *Maitreya's Mission.* Amsterdam, The Netherlands: Share International, 1986.

Creme, Benjamin. *The Reappearance of Christ and the Masters of Wisdom.* Los Angeles: Tara Center, 1980.

Crenshaw, James. *Telephone Between Two Worlds.* Los Angeles: DeVorss & Co., 1950.

Crim, Keith. Ed. *The Perennial Dictionary of World Religions.* 1981; New York: Harper & Row, 1989.

Cronon, Edmund David. *Black Moses: The Story of Marcus Garvey and the U.N.I.A.* Madison, WI: University of Wisconsin Press, 1969.

Crowell, Rodney J. *The Checkbook Bible: The Teachings of Hobard E. Freeman and Faith Assembly.* Miamisburg, OH: The Author, 1981.

Crowley, Aleister Edward. *Confessions.* New York: Hill and Wang, 1969.

Cryer, Newman. "Laboratory for Tomorrow's Church." *Together* 10, no. 3 (March 1966).

Culpepper, Emily. "The Spiritual Movement of Radical Feminist Consciousness." In Needleman, Jacob, and George Baker, eds., *Understanding the New Religions.*

New York: Seabury, 1978. Pp. 220-234.

Curtiss, Harriette A., and Homer F. Curtiss. *Letters from the Teacher* 2 vols. Hollywood, CA: Curtiss Philosophic Book Co., 1918.

Curtiss, Harriette A., and Homer F. Curtiss. *The Message of Aquaria*. San Francisco: Curtiss Philosophic Book Co., 1921.

Curtiss, Homer F. *Reincarnation*. Santa Barbara, CA: J.F. Rowney Press, 1946.

Cushing, Margaret. "Emma Curtis Hopkins, The Teacher of Teachers." *New Thought Bulletin* 28 (Spring 1945): 5-7.

Cyrus R. Teed, *The Alchemical Laboratory of the Brain* Chicago: The Eta Company, n.d.

D'Andrade, Hugh. *Charles Fillmore*. New York, Harper & Row, 1974.

Dahl, Mikkel. *God's Master Plan of Love for Man*. Windsor, Ont.: Dawn of Truth, 1961.

Dahl, Mikkel. *Have You Heard, the Great Pyramid Speaks*. Fulton, MO: Shepherdsfield, 1986.

Dahl, Mikkel. *The Coming New Society*. Windsor, Ont.: Dawn of Truth, n.d.

Daley, Yvonne. "Praise the Lord." *Vermont Sunday Magazine* (June 19, 1994).

Dallimore, Arnold. *Forerunner of the Charismatic Movement: The Life of Edward Irving*. Chicago: Moody Press, 1983.

Daniel, William A. *Rediscovering the Messages*. n.p., n.d.

Darby, John Nelson. *The Collected Works*. 34 vols. Oak Park, IL: 1971.

Dard, A. R. *Life of Ahmad*. Lahore, Pakistan: Tabshir Publications, 1948.

Darnton, Robert. *Mesmerism and the End of the Enlightenment in France.* New York: Schocken Books, 1970.

Darshan, Matri. *Ein Photo-Album Über Sri Ananda Ma*. Seegarten, Germany: Mangalam Verlag S. Schang, 1983.

Dass, Baba Hari. *Ashtanga, a Yoga Primer*. Santa Cruz, CA: Sri Rama Publishing, 1981.

Dass, Baba Ram. *Grist for the Mill*. Santa Cruz, CA: Unity Press, 1977.

Dass, Baba Ram. *Miracle of Love*. New York: E. P. Dutton, 1979.

Dass, Baba Ram. *Remember, Be Here Now*. San Christobal, NM: Lama Foundation, 1971.

Dass, Baba Ram. *The Only Dance There Is*. New York: Jason Aaronson, 1976.

Dave, H. T. *Life and Philosophy of Shree Swaminarayan*. London: George Allen & Unwin, 1974.

Davenport, Rowland A. *Albury Apostles*. England, 1970.

Davidson, C. T. *Upon This Rock*, 3 vols. Cleveland, TN: White Wing Press, 1973-76.

Davidson, Gustav. *A Dictionary of Angels Including the Fallen Angels*. New York: The Free Press, 1967.

Davies, John D. *Phrenology, Fad and Science: A Nineteenth Century American Crusade*. New Haven, CT: Yale University Press, 1955.

Davis, Andrew Jackson. *Events in the Life of a Seer*.

Davis, Andrew Jackson. *The Magic Staff*. New York: J. S. Brown & Co., 1857.

Davis, Roy Eugene. *An Easy Guide to Meditation*. Lakemont, GA: CSA Press, 1978.

Davis, Roy Eugene. *God Has Given Us Every Good Thing*. Lakemont, GA: CSA Press, 1986.

Davis, Roy Eugene. *The Path of Soul Liberation*. Lakemont, GA: CSA Press, 1975.

Davis, Roy Eugene. *The Teachings of the Masters of Perfection*. Lakemont, GA: CSA Press, 1979.

Davis, Roy Eugene. *The Way of the Initiate*. St. Petersburg, FL: New Life Worldwide, 1968.

Davis, Roy Eugene. *Yoga-Darshana*. Lakemont, GA: CSA Press, 1976.

Davis, S. and Simon, P. 1977. *Reggae bloodliness: In search of the music and culture of Jamaica*. New York: Anchor Books.

Davis, Winston. *Dojo*. Stanford, CA: Stanford University Press, 1980.

Dawn, Rose. *The Search for Happiness*. Mayan Order, 1966.

Dayton, Donald W. *Theological Roots of Pentecostalism*. Grand Rapids, MI: Zondervan Publishing House, 1987.

De Hemelsche Leer. Extracts from Issues: January 1930-1938. Organ of the General Church of New Jerusalem in Holland.

De Leon, Victor. *The Silent Pentecostals*. Taylor, SC: Faith Printing Co., 1979.

Dean, Hazel. *Powerful is the Light*. Denver, CO: Divine Science College, 1945.

Deats, Richard L. *Nationalism and Christianity in the Philippines*. Dallas: Southern Methodist University Press, 1967.

DeCharms, George. *The Distinctiveness of the New Church*. Bryn Athyn, PA: Academy Book Room, 1962.

DeCharms, George. *The Holy Supper*. Bryn Athyn, PA: General Church Publication Committee, 1961.

Dederich, Charles E. *The Tao Trip Sermon*. Marshall, CA: Synanon Publishing House, 1978

DeGroot, A. T. *New Possibilities for Disciples and Independents*. St. Louis: Bethany Press, 1963.

Delaforge, Gaetan, *The Templar Tradition in the Age of Aquarius*, Putney, VT: Threshold Books, 1987.

Dennon, Jim. *Dr. Newbrough and Oahspe*. Kingman, AZ: Faithist Journal, 1975.

Dennon, Jim. *Dr. Newbrough and Oahspe*. Kingman, AZ: Faithist Journal, 1975.

Derry, Evelyn. *Seven Sacraments in the Christian Community*. London: Christian Community Press, 1949.

DeSmet, Kate. "Return to the House of Judah." *Michigan, the Magazine of the Detroit News* (July 21, 1985).

Desroche, Henri. *The American Shakers*. Amherst: University of Massachusetts Press, 1971.

Devamata, Sister. *Swami Paramananda and His Work*, 2 vols. La Crescenta, CA: Ananda Ashrama, 1926-41.

Devi, Shri Mataji Nirmala. *Sahaja Yoga*. Delhi, India: Nirmala Yoga, 1982.

Devi, Srimata Gayatri. *One Life's Pilgrimage*. Cohasset, MA: Vedanta Centre, 1977.

Dharmapala, Anagarika. "The World's Debt to Buddha," and "Buddhism and Christianity," in J. W. Hanson, ed., *The World's Congress of Religions*. Chicago: Monarch Book Co., 1894, 377-87; 413-16.

Dhiegh, Khigh Alx. *The Eleventh Wing*. New York: Delta Books, 1973.

Dhillon, Mahinder Singh. *A History Book of the Sikhs in Canada and California*. Vancouver, BC: Shromani Akali Dal Association of Canada, 1981.

Dhiravamsa. *The Way of Non-Attachment*. New York: Schocken Books, 1977.

Dickhoff, Robert E. *Agharta*. Mokelumne Hill, CA: Health Research, 1964.

Dickhoff, Robert E. *Behold...the Venus Garuda*. New York: The Author, 1968.

Dickhoff, Robert E. *The Eternal Fountain*. Boston, MA: Bruce Humphries, 1947.

"Ding Le Mei Memorial Issue." *The Mansion Builder* (September 1972).

Dingle, Edwin John. *Borderlands of Eternity*. Los Angeles: Institute of Mentalphysics, 1939.

Dingle, Edwin John. *Breathing Your Way to Youth*. Los Angeles: Institute of Mentalphysics, 1931.

Dingle, Edwin John. *The Voice of the Logos*. Los Angeles: Institute of Mentalphysics, 1950.

Directory of Sabbath-Observing Groups. Fairview, OK: Bible Sabbath Association, 1980.

Directory. Pineland, FL: American Evangelical Christian Churches, 1988.

Discipline. Atlanta: Board of Publication of the F. B.H. Church of God of the Americas, 1962.

Divine Science, Its Principle and Practice. Denver, CO: Divine Science Church and College, 1957.

Diwakar, R. R. *Mahayogi: Life, Sadhana, and Teachings of Sri Aurobindo.* Bombay, India: Bharatiya Vidya Bhavan, 1976.

Doctrine and Discipline. Birmingham, AL: Apostolic Overcoming Holy Church of God, 1985.

The Doctrine and Discipline of the Church of Daniel's Band. n.p. 1981.

Donnelly, Ignatius. *Atlantis: The Antediluvian World.* New York: Harper's, 1882.

Donovan, Robert D. *Her Door of Faith.* Honolulu, HI: Orovan Books, 1971.

Doreal, M. *Maitreya, Lord of the World.* Sedalia, CO: Brotherhood of the White Temple, n.d.

Doreal, M. *Man and the Mystic Universe.* Denver: Brotherhood of the White Temple, n.d.

Doreal, M. *Personal Experiences Among the Masters and Great Adepts in Tibet.* Sedalia, CO: Brotherhood of the White Temple, n.d.

Doreal, M. *Secret Teachings of the Himalayan Gurus.* Denver: Brotherhood of the White Temple, n.d.

Doumette, Hanna Jacob. *After His Living Likeness.* Santa Monica, CA: Christian Institute of Spiritual Science, n.d.

Dove, James. *A Few Items in the History of the Morrisites.* San Francisco: 1892.

Dow, Lorenzo. *Life and Travels of Lorenzo Dow.* Hartford, Connecticut: 1804.

Dow, Lorenzo. *The Chains of Lorenzo.* Augusta, Georgia: 1804.

Dow, Peggy. *Vicissitudes in the Wilderness.* Liverpool: 1818.

Downton, James V., Jr. *Sacred Journeys.* New York: Columbia University Press, 1979.

Doyle, Sir Arthur Conan. *The Coming of the Fairies.* London: Hodder & Stoughton, 1922.

Doyle, Sir Arthur Conan. *The History of Spiritualism, Vol. I and II.* New York: Arno Press, 1975.

The Dream Is Upon Us and the Great Return Has Begun. Palm Springs, CA: Life Design Ministries, 1987.

Dresser, Horatio W. *History of the New Thought Movement.* New York: T. Y. Crowell, 1919.

Dresser, Horatio W., ed. *The Quimby Manuscripts.* New York: T. Y. Crowell, 1921.

Dresser, Horatio. *Spiritual Health and Healing.* New York: Thomas Y. Crowell, 1922.

Drew, Richard, ed. *Revelation to the Priesthood.* Voree, WI: Church of Jesus Christ of Latter Day Saints, 1986.

Drew, Richard, ed. *Word of Wisdom.* Voree, WI: Church of Jesus Christ of Latter Day Saints, 1986.

Driberg, Tom. *The Mystery of Moral Re-Armament*. New York: Alfred A. Knopf, 1965.

Drier, Thomas et al. *The Story of Elizabeth Towne and The Nautilus*. Holyoke, MA: E. Towne Co., 1910.

Driscoll, J. Walter. *Gurdjieff, An Annotated Bibliography*. New York: Garland Publishing, 1985.

Drummond, Andrew Landale. *Edward Irving and His Circle*. London, n.d.

Drummond, Henry. *A Narrative of the Circumstances Which Led to the Setting-Up of the Church of Christ at Albury*. n.p., 1833.

Drury, Nevill, ed. *Inner Health: The Health Benefits of Relaxation, Meditation, and Visualization*. Prism Press, 1985.

Duffield, Guy P., and Nathaniel M. Van Cleave. *Foundations of Pentecostal Theology*. Los Angeles: L.I.F.E. Bible College, 1983.

Duffy, Joseph. "The Church of bible Understanding, A Critical Expose." *Alternatives* (New York) 4, no. 6 (April/May 1977).

Dugas, Paul D., ed. *The Life and Writings of Elder G. T. Haywood*. Portland, OR: Apostolic Book Publishers, 1968.

Duggar, Lillie. *A. J. Tomlinson*. Cleveland, TN: White Wing Publishing House, 1964.

Dugger, A. N. *A Bible Reading for the Home Fireside*. Jerusalem: "Mt. Zion" Press. Reprint. Decatur, MI: Johnson Graphics, 1982.

Dugger, A. N. and C. O. Dodd. *A History of the True Religion*. Jerusalem: Mt. Zion Reporter, 1968.

Dunkard Brethren Church Manual. Bunkard Brethren Church, 1971.

Dunkard Brethren Church Polity. n.p., 1980

Dunn, Ethel and Stephen. *The Molokan Heritage Collection. I, Reprints of Articles and Translations*. Berkeley, CA: Highgate Road Social Science Research Station, 1983.

DuPree, Sherry Sherrod. *African American Holiness Pentecostal Charismatic: Annotated Bibliography*. New York: Garland Publishing, 1992.

DuPree, Sherry Sherrod. *African American Holiness Pentecostal Charismatic: Annotated Bibliography*. New York: Garland Publishing, 1992.

DuQuette, Lon Milo, and Christopher S. Hyatt. *Aleister Crowley's Illustrated Goetia: Sexual Evocation*. Phoenix, AZ: Falcon Press, 1992.

Duquette, Susan. *Sunburst Farm Family Cookbook*. Santa Barbara, CA: Woodbridge Press Publishing Company, 1978.

Durnbaugh, Donald F. *European Origins of the Brethren*. Elgin, IL: 1958.

Durnbaugh, Donald F. *The Believers' Church*. New York: 1968.

Durnbaugh, Donald F., ed. *The Brethren Encyclopedia*. 3 vols. Philadelphia, PA: Brethren Encyclopedia, 1983.

Duss, John. *The Harmonists: A Personal History,* Reprint. Philadelphia, PA: Porcupine Press, 1973.

Eardley, J. R. *Gems of Inspiration.* San Francisco, CA: Joseph A. Dove, 1899.

Easwaran, Eknath. *A Man to Math His Mountains.* Petaluma, CA: Nilgiri Press, 1984.

Easwaran, Eknath. *Dialogue with Death.* Petaluma, CA: Nilgiri Press, 1981.

Easwaran, Eknath. *Like a Thousand Suns.* Petaluma, CA: Nilgiri Press, 1979.

Easwaran, Eknath. *The Bhagavad Gita for Daily Living.* Berkeley, CA: Blue Mountain Center of Meditation, 1975.

Easwaran, Eknath. *The Mantram Handbook.* Petaluma, CA: Nilgiri Press, 1977.

Easwaran, Eknath. *The Supreme Ambition.* Petaluma, CA: Nilgiri Press, 1982.

Ebon, Martin, ed. *Maharishi, the Guru.* New York: New American Library, 1968.

Ebon, Martin. *The Devil's Bride, Exorcism: Past and Present.* New York: Harper & Row, 1974.

Eddy, Mary Baker. *Science and Health with Key to the Scriptures.* Boston: Trustees under the Will of Mary Baker G. Eddy, 1906.

Edgar Cayce on Atlantis. NY: Paperback Library, 1968.

Edminster, Clyde. *Is It Law or Grace?* Rainier, WA: Woodbrook Chapel, 1987.

Edmunds, R. David. *The Shawnee Prophet.* Lincoln: University of Nebraska Press, 1983.

Edwards, F. Henry. *Fundamentals, Enduring Convictions of the Restoration.* Independence, MO: Herald Publishing House, n.d.

Eek, Sven and Boris de Zirkoff. *William Quan Judge, 1851-1896.* Wheaton, Illinois: Theosophical Publishing House, 1969.

Egemeier, C.V., ed. *Grace Mission Story.* Grand Rapids, MI: Grace Missions, 1967.

Eggers, Ulrich. *Community for LIfe.* Scottsdale, PA: Herald Press, 1988.

Ehrman, Albert. "The Commandment Keepers: A Negro Jewish Cult in America Today." *Judaism* 8, no. 3 (Summer 1959): 266-70.

Ehrmann, Naftali Hertz. *The Rav.* New York: Feldheim Publishers, 1977.

Eikerenkoetter, Frederik. *Health, Happiness and Prosperity for You!* New York: Science of Living Publications, 1982.

Eisen, William. *Agasha, Master of Wisdom.* Marina del Rey, CA, 1968.

Eklund, Christopher. "Witches Jim Alan and Selena Fox Let Their Cauldron Bubble with Minimal Toil and Trouble." *People* (November 5, 1979): 47, 50; Fox, Selena.

Eli (Barney C. Taylor). *The First Book of Wisdom.* The Author, 1973.

Eliade, Mircea, ed. *Encyclopedia of Religion*. New York:Macmillan, 1987.

Eliade, Mircea. *Shamanism: Archaic Techniques of Ecstasy*. Princeton, NJ: Princeton University Press, 1964.

Eliade, Mircea. *Speaking in Tongues: A Cross-Cultural Study of Glossolalia*. Chicago: University of Chicago Press, 1972.

Eller, Cynthia. *Living in the Lap of the Goddess:The Feminist Spirituality Movement in America*. New York: Crossroad, 1993.

Elliott, Errol T. *Quakers on the American Frontier*. Richmond, IN: Friends United Press, 1969.

Ellwood, Robert S. and Harry B. Partin. *Religious and Spiritual Groups in Modern America*. Englewood Cliffs, NJ: Prentice-Hall, 1988.

Ellwood, Robert S. and Harry B. Partin. *Religious and Spiritual Groups in Modern America*. Englewood Cliffs, NJ: Prentice Hall, 1988.

Ellwood, Robert S., Jr. *Mysticism and Religion*. Englewood Cliffs, NJ: Prentice-Hall, 1980.

Ellwood, Robert S., Jr. *One Way*. Englewood Cliffs, NJ: Prentice-Hall, 1973.

Ellwood, Robert. *Islands of the Dawn: The Story of Alternative Spirituality in New Zealand*. Honolulu: University of Hawaii Press, 1993.

Ellwood, Robert. *Theosophy*. Wheaton, IL: Theosophical Publishing House, 1986.

Elmen, Paul. *Wheat Flour Messiah*. Carbondale, IL: 1976.

Enroth, Ronald M., and Gerald E. Jamison. *The Gay Church*. Grand Rapids, MI: William B. Eerdmans, 1974.

Enroth, Ronald, Edward E. Ericson, Jr., and C. Breakinridge Peters. *The Jesus People*. Grand Rapids: Eerdmans, 1972.

Enroth, Ronald. *Recovering from Churches that Abuse*. Grand Rapids: Zondervan, 1994.

Entwistle, Basil, and John McCook Roots. *Moral Re-Armament, What is it?* Los Angeles, CA: Pace Publications, 1967.

Erickson, Milton. *Hypnotic Realities: The Induction of Clinical Hypnosis & Forms of Indirect Suggestion*. New York: Irvington, 1976.

Erickson, Ralph D. *History and Doctrinal Development of the Order of Aaron*. Master's thesis, Brigham Young University, Provo, UT, 1969.

Ernst, James E. *Ephrata: A History*. Allentown, Penn.: 1963.

The Essence of Our Teachings. Willits, CA: Christ's Church of the Golden Rule, 1971.

Essene, Virginia. *Secret Truths for Teens & Twenties*. Santa Clara, CA: Spiritual Education Endeavors Publishing Company, 1986.

Evangel Temple's 30th Anniversary Historical Journal. Washington, DC: Evangel Temple, 1985.

Evans, Warren Felt. *Mental Medicine*. Boston: H. H. Carter & Karrick, 1872.

Evans, Warren Felt. *The Divine Law of Cure*. Boston: H. H. Carter & Co., 1884.

Evans-Wentz, W. Y., ed. *The Tibetan Book of the Dead*. 3rd ed. London: Oxford University Press, 1960.

Even, Isaac. "Chasidism in the New World." *Communal Register*. New York (1918): 341-46.

The Excellent Path Bestowing Bliss. Seattle, WA: Sakya Monastery of Tibetan Buddhism, 1987.

Fabre des Essarts, Léonce. *Les Hiérophantes. Études sur les fondateurs de religions depuis la Révolution jusqu'à nos jours*. Paris: Chacornac, 1905.

Faith and Government of the Free Will Baptist Church of the Pentecostal Faith. n.p. 1961.

Faith and Practice fo the Brotherhood of the Love of Christ. New York: Pax Christi Press, 1966.

Farajaje-Jones, Elias. *In Search of Zion: The Spiritual Significance of Africa in Black Religious Movements*. New York: P. Long, 1991.

Farkas, Mary. "Footsteps in the Invisible World." *Wind Bell* 8 (Fall 1969): 15-19.

Farquhar, J.N. *Modern Religious Movements in India*. New York: Macmillan, 1915.

Farrar, Janet and Stewart Farrar. *The Witches' God: Lord of the Dance*. London, Robert Hale, 1988. Custer, WA: Phoenix Publishing, 1989.

Farrar, Janet and Stewart Farrar. *The Witches' Goddess: The Feminine Principle of Divinity*. London: Robert Hale, 1987. Custer, WA: Phoenix Publishing, 1988.

Farrar, Stewart and Janet Farrar. *Eight Sabbats for Witches*. London: Robert Hale, 1981.

Farrar, Stewart and Janet Farrar. *The Life and Times of a Modern Witch*. London: Robert Hale: 1987. Custer, WA: Phoenix Publishing, 1988.

Farrar, Stewart and Janet Farrar. *The Witches' Way*. London: Robert Hale, 1985.

Farrar, Stewart, and Janet Farrar. *Eight Sabbats for Witches*. London:Robert Hale, 1981.

Farrar, Stewart, and Janet Farrar. *The Witches' Way*. London: Robert Hale, 1985.

Farrar, Stewart. *What Witches Do: The Modern Coven Revealed*. Coward, McCann, 1971.

Fauset, Arthur H. *Black Gods in the Metropolis*. Philadelphia, PA: University of Pennsylvania Press, 1971.

Fauset, Arthur Huff. *Black Gods of the Metropolis*. Philadelphia, PA: University of Pennsylvania Press, 1944.

Federal Court Acknowledges Christ's True Church A. Fort Worth, TX: Manney Company, 1963.

Feher, Shoshana. "Who Holds the Cards? Women and New Age Astrology." In James R. Lewis and J. Gordon Melton, eds. *Perspectives on the New Age.* Albany: State University of New York Press, 1992. pp.179-188.

Feldman, Mark, and Ron Parshley. *Theorems of Occult Magick.* Methuen, MA: P-F Publications, 1971. 10 Vols.

Ferguson, Joseph T. *Manual on Metaphysical Healing.* Birmingham, AL: Institute of Metaphysics, 1959.

Ferguson, Marilyn. *The Aquarian Conspiracy.* Los Angeles, CA: Jeremy Tarcher, 1980.

Ferguson, Marilyn. *The Brain Revolution: The Frontiers of Mind Research.* New York: Taplinger Publishing Co., Inc., 1973.

Ferguson, Robert A. *Universal Mind.* West Nyack, NY: Parker Publishing Co., 1979.

Ferguson, William. *A Message from Outer Space.* Oak Park, IL: Golden Age Press, 1955.

Ferguson, William. *My Trip to Mars.* Chicago: Cosmic Circle of Fellowship, 1954.

Ferguson, William. *Relax First.* Chicago: Bronson-Canode Printing Co., 1937.

Ferguson, William. *The New Revelation.* The Author, 1959.

Fessier, Michael, Jr. "Ervil LeBaron, the Man Who Would Be God." *New West* (January 1981): 80-84, 112-17.

Festinger, Leon, et al. *When Prophecy Fails.* New York: Harper & Row, 1964.

Festinger, Leon, Henry W. Riecken, and Stanley Schachter. *When Prophecy Fails.* New York: Harper & Row, 1956.

Fetting, Otto. *The Midnight Message.* Independence, MO: Church of Christ (Temple Lot), 1930.

Fetting, Otto. *The Word of the Lord.* Independence, MO: Church of Christ, 1938.

Feuerstein, Georg. *Encyclopedic Dictionary of Yoga.* New York: Paragon, 1990.

Feuerstein, Georg. *The Mystery of Light.* Salt Lake City, UT: Passage Press, 1992.

Field, Reshad. *I Come from Behind Kaf Mountain.* Putney, VT: Threshold Books, 1984.

Field, Reshad. *The Invisible Way.* San Francisco, CA: Harper & Row, 1979.

Fields, Rick. *How the Swans Came to the Lake.* Boulder, CO: Shambhala, 1986.

Fillmore, Charles S. *Metaphysical Bible Dictionary.* Kansas City, MO: Unity School of Christianity, 1931.

Fillmore, Charles. *Prosperity.* Kansas City, MO: Unity School of Christianity, 1938.

Fillmore, Myrtle. *The Letters of Myrtle Fillmore.* Kansas City, Missouri: Unity School of Christianity, 1936. Rpt. as *Myrtle Fillmore's Healing Letters.* Unity Village, MO: Unity Books, n.d.

Findhorn Community. *The Findhorn Garden.* New York: Harper & Row, 1975.

Fiore, Edith. *The Unquiet Dead: A Psychologist Treats Spirit Possession.* Garden City, N.Y.: Dolphin/Doubleday & Co., 1987.

Fish, H. Bashford. "Trouble Among the Children of the Prophets." *The Washington Post Magazine* (February 7, 1982).

Fisher, H. M., et.al. *Doctrinal Treatise.* Covington, OH: Little Printing Company, 1954.

Fisher, Maxine P. *The Indians of New York City.* Columbia, MO: South Asia Books, 1980.

Fitzgerald, B.J. *A New Text of Spiritual Philosophy and Religion.* San Jose, CA: Universal Church of the Master, 1954.

Flanders, Robert Bruce. *Nauvoo: Kingdom on the Mississippi.* Urbana: University of Illinois Press, 1965.

Fleer, Gedaliah. *Rabbi Nachman's Fire.* New York: 1975.

Fletcher, C.R. *Spirit in his Mind.* Victor, MT: Circle of Power Spiritual Foundation, 1984.

Fletcher, Daisy Whiting. *Alpheus Cutler and the Church of Jesus Christ.* Independence, MO: The Author, 1970.

Fletcher, Rupert J. and Daisy Whiting Fletcher. *Alpheus Cutler and the Church of Jesus Christ.* Independence, MO: Church of Jesus Christ, 1975.

Fletcher, Rupert J. *The Scattered Children of Zion.* Independence, MO: The Author, 1959.

Fletcher, Rupert J. *The Way of Deliverance.* Independence, MO: The Author, 1969.

Flint, B. C. *An Outline History of the Church of Christ (Temple Lot).* Independence, MO: Board of Publication, Church of Christ (Temple Lot), 1967.

Flint, B. C. *Autobiography.* Independence, MO: Privately printed, n.d.

Flint, B. C. *What About Israel?* Independence, MO: Board of Publication, Church of Christ (Temple Lot), 1967.

Flint, David. *The Hutterites.* Toronto: Oxford University Press, 1975.

Fodor, Nandor. *An Encyclopaedia of Psychic Science.* Secaucus, NJ: The Citadel Press, 1966. First published 1933.

Fogarty, Robert S. *"Utopian Themes with Variation": John Murray Spear and His Kiantone Domain.* Pennsylvania History, April 1962.

Fogarty, Robert S. *Dictionary of American Communal and Utopian History.* Westport, CT: Greenwood Press, 1980.

Fogarty, Robert S. *The Righteous Remnant.* Kent, OH: Kent State University Press, 1981.

Footsteps to Zion, A History of the Apostolic Christian Church of America. n.p., n.d.

For Full Moon Workers. Beverly Hills, CA: Arcana Workshops, n.d.

Forbush, Bliss. *Elias Hicks: Quaker Liberal.* New York: 1956.

Ford, Arthur. *The Life Beyond Death.* New York: G. P. Putnam's Sons, 1971.

Ford, Arthur. *Why We Survive.* Cooksburg, New York: The Gutenberg Press, 1952.

Ford, Gene. *Who is the Real Mindbender?* Anaheim, CA: The Author, 1977.

Forfreedom, Ann, and Julie Ann, eds. *Book of the Goddess.* Sacramento: Temple of the Goddess Within, 1980.

Forfreedom, Ann. *Mythology, Religion, and Woman's Heritage.* Sacramento: Sacramento City Unified School District, 1981.

Forman, Charles. "Elected Now By Time: The Unitarian Controversy, 1805-1835." In ed. Conrad Wright, *Stream of Light.* Boston: Unitarian Universalist Association, 1975. Pp. 3-32.

The Former Days. Des Moines, IA: Gospel Assembly Church, n.d.

Fornell, Earl L. *The Unhappy Medium: Spiritualism and the Life of Margaret Fox.* Austin, Texas: University of Texas Press, 1964.

Foster, Fred J. *Their Story: Twentieth Century Pentecostals.* Hazelwood, MO: World Aflame Press, 1981.

Foster, Lawrence. "James J. Strang: The Prophet Who Failed."

"Founders of the Church of Light." *The Church of Light Quarterly* 45 (February 1970): 1-3.

Fox, Emmet. *Power Through Constructive Thinking.* New York: Harper & Brothers, 1940.

Fox, Matthew. *The Coming of the Cosmic Christ.* New York: Harper & Row, 1988.

Fox, Selena. *Circle Guide to Pagan Resources.* Mt. Horeb, WI: Circle, 1987.

Franck, Ira S. *The Ephrata Story.* n.p., 1964.

Franke, E. E. *Pagan Festivals in Christian Worship.* Schenectady, NY: People's Christian Church 1963.

Frazer, Felix J. *Parallel Paths to the Unseen Worlds.* Los Angeles: Builders of the Adytum, 1967.

Frazer, James George. *The Golden Bough: A Study in Magic and Religion.* NY: Macmillan, 1922.

Free Catholic Communicant (Periodical: 1250 Grand Ave., #10, Arroyo Grande, CA 93420).

Freeman, Eileen E. "Do You Have Your Own Fravashi?—Angels in Ancient Persia," *Angel Watch*, June 1993.

Freeman, Eileen. "The Cherubim and Seraphim Society: Portrait of an African National Church." *Angel Watch* 2:3 (June 1993), p. 1 & pp. 10-11.

Freeman, Eileen. "The First Church of Angels." *Angel Watch.* November-December 1992, p. 11.

Freeman, Hobart E. *Angels of Light?* Plainfield, NJ: Logos International, 1969.

Freeman, Hobart E. *Charismatic Body Ministry.* Claypool, IN: Faith Publications, n.d.

Freeman, Hobart E. *Deeper Life in the Spirit.* Warsaw, IN: Faith Publications, 1970.

Freeman, Hobart E. *Positive Thinking & Confession.* Claypool, IN: Faith Publications, n.d.

Freeman, James D. *The Story of Unity.* Unity Village, MO: Unity Books, 1978.

Freer, Gedaliah. *Rabbi Nachman's Fire.* New York: Hermon Press, 1972.

Freer, Gedaliah. *Rabbi Nachman's Foundation.* New York: OHR MIBRESLOV, 1976.

Freud, Sigmund. *The Interpretation of Dreams.* Modern Library reprint, 1950.

Freytag, F. L. Alexander. *The Divine Revelation.* Geneva, Switzerland: Disciples of Christ, 1922.

Fripp, Peter. *The Mystic Philosophy of Sant Mat.* London: Neville, Spearman, 1964.

Frisby, Neal. *The Book of Revelation Scrolls.* Phoenix: The Author, n.d.

Froehlich, S. H. *Individual Letters and Meditations.* Syracuse, NY: Apostolic Christian Publishing Co., 1926.

Froehlich, S. H. *The Mystery of Godliness and the Mystery of Ungodliness.* Apostolic Christian Church, n.d.

Froom, Leroy Edwin. *The Prophetic Faith of Our Fathers.* Washington, D.C., 1954.

Frost, Gavin and Yvonne Frost. *The Magic Power of Witchcraft.* West Nyack, New York: Parker Publishing Co., 1976.

Frost, Gavin and Yvonne Frost. *The Witch's Bible.* New York: Berkley Publishing Co., 1975.

Frost, Gavin and Yvonne Frost. *Who Speaks for the Witch.* New Bern, NC: Godolphin House, 1991.

Frost, J. William and Bronner, Edwin. *The Quakers.* Lewiston, NY:Edwin Mellon Press, 1990.

Fry, Daniel. *A-Lan's Message: To Men of Earth.* Los Angeles, CA: New Age Publishing Co., 1954.

Fry, Daniel. *The Curve of Development.* Lakemont, GA: CSA Printers and Publishers, 1965.

Fu, Chung. *Evolution of Man.* Circle of Inner Truth, 1973.

Fujimoto, Rindo. *The Way of Zazen.* Cambridge, MA: Cambridge Buddhist Association, 1969.

The Full Moon Story. Beverly Hills, CA: Arcana Workshops, 1974.

Fuller, Laurel Jan. *Shaping Your Life: the Power of Creative Energy.* Windyville, MO: SOM Publishing, 1994.

Fulton, Gilbert A., Jr. *That Manifesto*. Kearns, UT: Deseret Publishing Co., 1974.

Fundamental Beliefs and Directory of the Davidian Seventh-Day Adventists. Waco, TX: Universal Publishing Association, 1943.

Funk, John F. *The Mennonite Church and Her Accusers*. Elkhart, PA: Mennonite Publishing Co., 1878.

Furst, Jeffrey. *Edgar Cayce's Story of Jesus*. New York: Coward-McCann, Inc., 1970.

The Gabriel Papers, Nevada City, CA: IDHHB, 1981.

Gale, Robert. *The Urgent Call*. Washington, D.C.: Review and Herald Publishing Association, 1975.

Gale, William P. *Racial and National Identity*. Glendale, CA: Ministry of Christ Church, n.d.

Gallup, George. *Adventures in Immortality*. New York: MacGraw-Hill, 1982.

Gambhrananda, Swami. *History of the Ramakrishna Math and Mission*. Calcutta: Advaita Ashrama, 1957.

Ganapati Sachchidananda, Swami. *Dattatreya the Absolute*. Trinidad: Dattatreya Yoga Centre, 1984.

Ganapati Sachchidananda, Swami. *Forty-Two Stories*. Trinidad: Dattatreya Gyana Bodha Sabha, 1984.

Ganapati Sachchidananda, Swami. *Insight Into Spiritual Music*. Mysore, India: The Author, 1986.

Ganapati Sachchidananda, Swami. *Sri Dattatreya Laghu Puja Kalpa*. Mysore, India: The Author, 1986.

Garcia, Joseph. "Peyote: a Drug or a Sacrament?" *Tucson Citizen* (January 3, 1989).

Gardner, Gerald B. *Witchcraft Today*. London: Jerrolds, 1954.

Gardner, Hugh. *The Children of Prosperity*. New York: St. Martin's Press, 1978.

Garfield, Patricia. *The Healing Power of Dreams*. New York: Fireside, 1991. 382pp.

Gargi, Balwany. *Nirankari Baba*. Delhi India: Thomson Press, 1973.

Garlichs, E. E. *The Life Beautiful*. Long Beach, CA: Aquarian Church of Chirothesia, 1946.

Garlington, Phil. "Return of the Flower Children." *California* 9 (October 1978): 81-3; 137-38.

Gaskin, Ina May. *Spiritual Midwifery*. Summertown, TN: Book Publishing Company, 1978.

Gaster, Theodore. *The Dead Sea Scriptures in English Translation*. New York: Doubleday, 1956.

Gauld, Alan. *The Founders of Psychical Research*. London: Routledge & Kegan Paul, 1968.

Gawain, Shakti. *Creative Visualization*. Mill Valley, CA: Whatever Publishing Co., 1979.

Gayer, M. H. *The Heritage of the Anglo-Saxon Race*. Haverhill, MA: Destiny Publishers, 1941.

Gayman, Dan. *Do All Races Share in Salvation?* Schell City, MO: The Author, 1985.

Gayman, Dan. *One True and Living Church*. Schell City, MO: Church of Israel, n.d.

Gayman, Dan. *The Holy Bible, the Book of Adam's Race*. Schell City, MO: Church of Israel, n.d.

Gayman, Dan. *The Two Seeds of Genesis*. Nevada, MO: Church of Our Christian Heritage, 1978.

Gaze, Harry. *Emmet Fox: The Man and His Work*. New York: Harper & Brothers, 1952.

Gedatsu Ajikan Kongozen Meditation. San Francisco: Gedatsu Church of America, 1974.

Geis, Larry, Alta P. Kelly, and Aidan A. Kelly. *The New Healers: Healing the Whole Person*. And/Or Press, 1980.

Gelberg, Steven J. "The Fading of Utopia: ISKCON in Transition." *Bulletin of the John Rylands Library of Manchester* 7 (Autumn 1988): 171-83.

Gelberg, Steven, ed. *Hare Krishna, Hare Krishna*. New York: Grove Press, 1983.

Gelberman, Joseph H. *Reaching a Mystical Experience: a Kabbalistic Encounter*. New York: Wisdom Press, 1970.

Gelberman, Joseph H. *To Be...Fully Alive*. Farmingdale, NY: Coleman Graphics, 1983.

The General Church of the New Jerusalem, A Handbook of General Information. Bryn Athyn, PA: General Church Publication Committee, 1965.

Gerber, Israel J. *The Heritage Seekers*. Middle Village, NY: Jonathan David Publishers, 1977.

Gersh, Harrym, and Sam Miller. "Satmar in Brooklyn." *Commentary* 28 (1959): 31-41.

Gersi, Douchan. *Faces in the Smoke*. Tarcher, 1992.

Gerstel, David U. *Paradise Incorporated: Synanon*. Novato, CA: Presidio Press, 1982.

Gestefeld, Ursula N. *The Builder and the Plan*. Chicago: Exodus Publishing Co., 1910.

Gibson, Luther. *History of the Church of God Mountain Assembly*. The Author, 1954.

Gibson, Walter Murry. *The Diaries of Walter Murray Gibson, 1886, 1887*. Edited by Jacob Adler and Gwynn Barrett. Honolulu: University Press of Hawaii, 1973.

Gilbert, R. A. *The Golden Dawn, Twilight of the Magicians*. Wellingborough, Northanptonshire, England: Aquarian Press, 1983.

Gilbert, Violet. *Love Is All*. Grants Pass, OR: Cosmic Star Temple, 1969.

Gilbert, Violet. *My Trip to Venus*. Grants Pass, OR: Cosmic Star Temple, 1968.

Girvin, E. A. *Phineas F. Bresee: A Prince in Israel*. Kansas City, MO: Pentecostal Nazarene Publishing House, 1916.

Gleim, Elmer Q. *Change and Challenge: A History of the Church of the Brethren in the Southern District of Pennsylvania*. Harrisburg, PA: Southern District Conference History Committee, 1973.

Gloria Lee Lives! Miami, FL: Mark-Age Meta Center, 1963.

The Gnostic Holy Eucharist. Palo Alto, CA: Sanctuary of the Holy Shekinah, 1984.

Goble, Phillip E. *Everything You Need to Grow a Messianic Synagogue*. South Pasadena, CA: William Carey Library, 1974.

Goddard, Dwight. *A Buddhist Bible*. Thetford, VT: The Author, 1938.

Goddard, Dwight. *Was Jesus Influenced by Buddhism?* Thetford, VT: The Author, 1927.

Godwin, Malcolm. *Angels. An Endangered Species*. New York: Simon and Schuster, 1990.

Goff, James R., Jr. *Fields White Unto Harvest: Charles F. Parham and the Missionary Origins of Pentecostalism*. Fayetteville, AR: University of Arkansas Press, 1988.

Gold, E.J. *Autobiography of a Sufi*. Crestline, CA: IDHHB Publications, 1976.

The Golden Years. The Mennonite Kleine Gemeinde in Russia (1812-1849). Steinbach, MN: D.F.P. Publications, 1985.

Golder, Morris E. *The Life and Works of Bishop Garfield Thomas Haywood*. Indianapolis, IN: The Author, 1977.

Goldstein, Joseph, and Jack Kornfield. *Seeking the Heart of Wisdom*. Boston, MA: Shambhala, 1987.

Goldstein, Joseph. *The Experience of Insight*. Boulder, CO: Shambhala, 1976.

Gomes, Michael. *The Dawning of the Theosophical Movement*. Wheaton, IL: The Theosophical Publishing House, 1987.

Gonzalez-Wippler, Migene. *Santeria, the Religion*. N.Y.: Harmony Books, 1989.

Goodman, Shdema. *Babaji, Meeting with Truth at Hairakhan Vishwa Mahadham*. Farmingdale, NY: Coleman Publishing Co., 1986.

Goodrick-Clarke, Nicholas. *The Occult Roots of Nazism*. Wellingborough. Northamptonshire: The Aquarian Press, 1985.

Goodwin, Lloyd L. *Prophecy Concerning the Church*. 2 vols. Des Moines, IA: Gospel Assembly Church, 1977.

Bibliography

Goodwin, Lloyd L. *Prophecy Concerning the Resurrection*. Des Moines, IA: Gospel Assembly Church, 1979.

Goodwin, Lloyd L. *Prophecy Concerning the Second Coming*. Des Moines, IA: Gospel Assembly Church, 1979.

Gordon, James S. "Holistic Health Centers in the United States." *In Salmon*, pp. 229-251.

Gordon, James S. *The Golden Guru*. Lexington, MA: Stephen Greene Press, 1987.

Goseigen, the Holy Words. Tujuna, CA: Sekai Mahikari Bunmei Kyodan, 1982.

Gospel Assembly, Twenty-Five Years, 1963-1988. Des Moines, IA: Gospel Assembly Church, 1988.

Goswami, Bhakti Raksaka Sridhara Deva. *Sri Guru and His Grace*. San Jose, CA: Guardian of Devotion Press, 1983.

Gottmann, Karl-Heinz. "The Way of the White Clouds: In Memory of Lama Anagarika Govinda." *Vajradhatu Sun* (March, 1985).

Gould, Joan. "A Village of Slaves to the Torah.'" *The Jewish Digest* (October 1967): 49-52.

Govinda, Anagarika. *Creative Meditation and Multi-Dimensional Consciousness*. Wheaton, IL: Theosophical Publishing House, 1976.

Govinda, Anagarika. *The Way of the White Clouds: A Buddhist Pilgrim in Tibet*. Berkeley, CA: Shambhala, 1966.

Graham, Aelred. *Conversations: Buddhist and Christian*. New York: Harcourt, Brace and World, 1968.

Grant, Frederick William. *The Prophetic History of the Church*. New York: Loiseaux Brothers, 1902.

Gratus, Jack. *The False Messiahs*. New York: 1975.

Graves, Samuel R. *Witchcraft: The Osirian Order*. San Francisco: JBT Marketing, 1971.

"A Great Soul Marches On." *The Church of Light Quarterly* 26 (July 1951-January 1952): 1-2.

Green, Arthur. *Nahman of Bratslav: A Critical Biography*. Alabama: 1978.

Green, Arthur. *Tormented Master*. New York: Schrocken Books, 1979.

Gregg, Irwin. *The Divine Science Way*. Denver, CO: Divine Science Federation International, 1975.

Greyson, Bruce, and Flynn, Charles P., eds. *The Near-Death Experience. Problems, Prospects, Perspectives*. Springfield, IL: Charles C Thomas, 1984.

Grier, Albert C. *Truth's Cosmology*. Spokane, WA: Church of the Truth, n.d.

Grier, Albert C., and Agnes M. Lawson. *Truth and Life*. New York: E. P. Dutton, 1921.

Grier, Gladys C. *Foundation Stones of Truth*. Los Angeles, Williang Publishing Company, 1948.

Grim, John A. *The Shaman: Patterns of Siberian and Ojibway Healing*. Norman, OK: University of Oklahoma Press, 1983.

Grimassa, Raven. *Raven's Call* (previously *Moon Shadow*), Journal of the Aridian Tradition. Moon Dragon Publications, Box 301831, Escondido, CA, 92030.

Grimassa, Raven. *The Teachings of the Holy Strega*, 2d ed., Escondido, CA: Moon Dragon Publications, 1991.

Grimassa, Raven. *Whispers: Teachings of the Old Religion of Italy; An Introduction to the Aridian Tradition*, 2d ed. Escondido, CA: Moon Dragon Publications, 1991.

Grimm, Harold J. *The Reformation Era*. New York: Macmillan, 1954.

Gross, Darwin. *Awakened Imagination*. Oak Grove, OR: SOS Publishing, 1987.

Gross, Darwin. *Be Good to Yourself*. Oak Grove, OR: The Author, 1988.

Gross, Darwin. *From Heaven to the Prairie: The Story of the 972nd Living ECK Master*. Menlo Park, California: IWP Publishing, 1980.

Gross, Darwin. *My Letter to You Discourses*. Oak Grove, OR: The Author, 1987.

Gross, Darwin. *The Golden Thread Discourses*. Oak Grove, OR: The Author, 1987.

Gross, Darwin. *Treasures*. Oak Grove, OR: The Author, 1988.

Gross, Darwin. *Your Right to Know*. Menlo Park, CA: IWP Publishing, 1979.

Gross, Paul S. *The Hutterite Way*. Saskatoon, SK: Freeman Publishing Company Limited, 1965.

Gruen, John. *The New Bohemia*. New York: Grosset & Dunlap, 1966.

Grumbine, J. C. F. *Clairvoyance*. Boston, MA: Order of the White Rose, 1911.

Grumbine, J.C.F. *Melchizedek or the Secret Doctrine of the Bible*. Boston: Order of the White Rose, 1919.

Guelzo, Allen C. *The First Thirty Years: A Historical Handbook for the Founding of the Reformed Episcopal Church, 1873-1903*. Philadelphia, PA: Reformed Episcopal Publication Society, 1986.

Guenther, Herbert, and Chögyam Trungpa. *The Dawn of Tantra*. Berkeley, CA: Shambhala, 1975.

Guiley, Rosemary E. *Encyclopedia of Witchcraft and Witches*. New York: Facts on File, 1989.

Guiley, Rosemary Ellen. *Harper's Encyclopedia of Mystical & Paranormal Experience*. San Francisco, CA: Harper Collins, 1991.

Guiley, Rosemary. *The Encyclopedia of Ghosts and Spirits*. New York: Facts on File, 1992.

Gupta, Yogi. *Yoga and Yogic Powers*. New York: Yogi Gupta New York Center, 1958.

Gurdjieff, Georges I. *Beelzebub's Tales to His Grandson*. 3 vols. New York: E. P. Dutton, 1978.

Gurdjieff, Georges I. *Life is Only Then, When "I Am."* New York: E. P. Dutton, 1982.

Gurdjieff, Georges I. *Meetings with Remarkable Men*. New York: E. P. Dutton, 1963.

Gurudev Shree Chitrabhanu, *The Psychology of Enlightenment* New York: Dodd, Mead & Co. (1979); Gurudev Shree Chitrabhanu, *Twelve Facets of Reality* New York: Dodd, Mead & Co., 1980.

Gyatso, Tenzin, the 14th Dalai Lama. *The Opening of the Wisdom-Eye*. Wheaton, IL: Theosophical Publishing House, 1972.

Gyatso, Tenzin. *The Buddhism of Tibet and the Key to the Middle Way*. New York: Harper & Row, 1975.

Haberman, Frederick. *Tracing Our White Ancestors*. Phoenix, AZ: Lord's Covenant Church, 1979.

Hagan, William T. "Quanah Parker." In R. David Edmunds, *American Indian Leaders*. Lincoln, NE: University of Nebraska Press, 1980.

Haggerty, Steve. "A Spiritual Powerhouse." *Charisma* 10, no. 10 (May 1985).

Hagin, Kenneth E. *How You Can Be Led by the Spirit of God*. Tulsa, OK: Kenneth Hagin Ministries, 1978.

Haing, Chungliang Al. *Embrace Tiger, Return to Mountain*. Moab, UT: Real People Press, 1973.

Hall, Calvin S. & Vernon J. Norby. *A Primer of Jungian Psychology*. New York: Mentor, 1973.

Hall, Franklin. *Atomic Power with God*. San Diego, CA: The Author, 1946.

Hall, Franklin. *Our Divine Healing Obligation*. Phoenix, AZ: The Author, 1964.

Hall, Franklin. *The Baptism of Fire*. San Diego, CA: The Author, 1960.

Hall, Franklin. *The Body-Felt Salvation*. Phoenix, AZ: Hall Deliverance Foundation, 1968.

Hall, James A. *Jungian Dream Interpretation*. Toronto: Inner City Books, 1983.

Hall, John R. "Afterward" to "The Apocalypse at Jonestown," pp. 290-93 in Thomas Robbins and Dick Anthony, eds., *In Gods We Trust*. New Brunswick, NJ: Transaction, 1988.

Hall, John R. *Gone from the Promised Land: Jonestown in American Cultural History*. New Brunswick, NJ: Transaction, 1987.

Hall, John R. "Public Narratives and the Apocalyptic Sect:From Jonestown to Mount Carmel." *Armageddon in Mount Carmel*, Stuart A. Wright, editor. Chicago: The University Chicago Press, n.d.

Hall, Manly Palmer. *Reincarnation: The Cycle of Necessity*. Los Angeles: The Philosophical Research Society, 1956.

Ham, F. Gerald. "The Prophet and the Mummyjums: Isaac Bullard and the Vermont Pilgrims of 1817." *Wisconsin Magazine of History*, Summer 1973.

Hamilton, Taylor J., and Kenneth G. Hamilton. *A History of the Moravian Church— The Unitas Fratrum, 1722-1957*. Bethlehem, PA: Interprovincial Board of Christian Education/Moravian Church in America, 1957.

Hamm, Thomas. *The Transformation of American Quakerism*. Indianapolis, IN: Indiana University Press, 1988.

Hancock, Pauline. *The Godhead, Is There More Than One?* Independence, MO: Church of Christ, n.d.

Hancock, Pauline. *Whence Cmae the Book of Mormon?* Independence, MO: Church of Christ, 1958.

Handbook of the Lord's New Church Which Is Nova Hierosolyma. Bryn Athyn, PA: Lord's New Church Which Is Nova Hierosolyma, 1985.

Hanish, O.Z.A. *The Power of Breath*. Los Angeles, CA: Mazdaznan Press, 1970.

Hanish, O.Z.A., and O.Rauth. *God and Man United*. Santa Fe Springs, CA: Stockton Trade Press, 1975.

Hansadutta, Swami. *The Book, What the Black Sheep Said*. Berkeley, CA: Hansa Books, 1985.

Hansen-Gates, Jan. "Growing Outdoors: The Brotherhood of the Sun." *Santa Barbara Magazine* 1, no. 3 (Winter 1975-76): 64-71.

Harden, Margaret G. *Brief History of the Bible Presbyterian Church and Its Agencies*. n.p. 1965.

Hargis, Billy James, and bill Sampson. *The National New Media, America's Fifth Column*. Tulsa, OK: Crusader Books, 1980.

Hargis, Billy James, and Jose Hernandez. *Disaster File*. Tulsa, OK: Crusader Books, 1978.

Hargis, Billy James. *Christ and His Gospel*. Tulsa, OK: Christian Crusade Publications, 1969.

Hargis, Billy James. *My Great Mistake*. Green Forest, AR: New Leaf Press, 1985.

Hargis, Billy James. *The Far Left*. Tulsa, OK: Christian Crusade, 1964.

Hari, Dass Baba. *Hariakhan Baba Known, Unknown*. Davis, CA: Sri Rama Foundation, 1975.

Harner, Michael. *The Way of the Shaman*. New York: Bantam, 1986.

Harrell, David Edwin, Jr. *All Things Are Possible*. Bloomington, IN: University of Indiana Press, 1975.

Harrell, John R. *The Golden Triangle*. Flora, IL: Christian Conservative Church, n.d.

Harrington, Walt. "The Devil in Anton LaVey." *The Washington Post Magazine* (February 23, 1986): 6-9, 12-17.

Harris, Iverson L. *Mme. Blavatsky Defended*. San Diego, CA: Point Loma Publications, 1971.

Harris, Thomas Lake. *Brotherhood of the New Life: Its Fact, Law, Method and Purpose*. Fountain Grove, CA: Fountain Grove Press, 1891.

Harris, Thomas Lake. *The Marriage of Heaven and Earth*. Glasgow, Scotland: C. W. Pearce & Co., 1903.

Harrison, J.F.C. *The Second Coming, Popular Millenarianism 1780-1850*. London, 1979.

Hatcher, William S. and J. Douglas Martin, *The Bahá" Faith: The Emerging Global Religion*. San Francisco, CA: Harper and Row, 1985.

Hate Groups in America. New York: Anti-Defamation League of B'nai B'rith, 1982.

Hawken, Paul. *The Magic of Findhorn*. New York: Harper & Row, 1985.

Hawkins, Yisrayl B. *True Stories About Christmas*. Abilene, TX: House of Yahweh, n.d.

Hayes, Norvel. *7 Ways Jesus Heals*. Tulsa, OK: Harrison House, 1982.

Haywood, Garfield Thomas. *A Trip to the Holy Land*. Indianapolis, IN: N.p., 1927.

Haywood, Garfield Thomas. *Feed My Sheep*. Indianapolis, IN: Christ Temple Book Store, n.d.

H.D. Prakashanand Saraswati, *The Philosophy of Divine Love* Auckland, NZ: International Society of Divine Love (1982).

Head, Joseph, and S. L. Cranston, eds. *Reincarnation in World Thought*. New York: Crown Pubs., Inc., Julian Press, 1967.

Healing: A Thought Away from Donato. 2 vols., Long Beach, CA: Morningland Publications, 1981.

A Healing Consciousness. Virginia Beach, VA: Master's Press, 1978.

The Heart and Wisdom of Sivananda-Valentina. 5 vols. Miami Beach, FL: The Light of Sivananda-Valentine, 1970-73.

Heidenreich, Alfred. *Growing Point*. London: Christian Community Press, 1965.

Heidrick, Bill. *Magick and Qabalah*. Berkeley, CA: Ordo Templi Orientis, 1980.

Heindel, Max. *Rosicrucian Cosmo-Conception*. Seattle, WA: Rosicrucian Fellowship, 1909.

Heindel, Mrs. Max [Augusta Foss]. *The Birth of the Rosicrucian Fellowship*. Oceanside, CA: Rosicrucian Fellowship, n.d.

Helen Kooiman Hosier. *Kathryn Kuhlman* Old Tappan, NJ: Fleming H. Revell, 1971; Kathryn Kuhlman, *I Believe in Miracles* Englewood Cliffs, NJ: Prentice-

Hall, 1962.

Heline, Corinne. *New Age Bible Interpretation,* 7 Vols. Los Angeles: New Age Press, 1938-1954.

Heller, Patrick A. *As My Spirit Beckons.* Pontiac, MI: Church of Eternal Life and Liberty, 1974.

Heller, Patrick A. *Because I Am.* Oak Park, MI: Church of Eternal Life and Liberty, 1974.

Hembree, Maud. *The Known Bible and Its Defense.* 2 vols. Rochester, NY: The Author, 1933.

Hemleben, Johannes. *Rudolf Steiner.* East Grimstead, Sussex, United Kingdom: Henry Goulden, 1975.

Henderson, A. L. *The Mystery of Yahweh.* Waynesville, NC: New Beginnings, n.d.

Hendricks, R. J. *Bethel and Aurora,* Reprint. New York: AMS Press, 1933.

Henry, James O. *For Such a Time as This.* Westchester, IL: Independent Fundamental Churches of America, 1983.

Hensley, Kirby J. *The Buffer Zone.* Modesto, CA; Universal Life Church, 1986.

The Herald of the Star. Edited by J. Krishnamurti. Vol. VI, No. 3 (March 1917).

Herbert, David Robinson. *Armstrong's Tangled Web.* Tulsa, OK: John Hadden Publishers, 1980.

Herr, John. *Complete Works.* Buffalo, NY: 1890.

H.H. Sri Sri Ganapati Sachchidananda Swamiji: A Rare Jewel in the Spiritual Galaxy of Modern Times. Mysore, India: Sri Ganapathi Sachchidananda Trust, n.d.

Hicks, Elias. *Journal of the Life and Labours of Elias Hicks, written by himself.* New York: 1832.

Hiebert, Clarence. *The Holdeman People.* South Pasadena, CA: William Carey Library, 1973.

Hinds, William Alfred. *American Communities and Cooperative Colonies.* Chicago: Charles H. Kerr & Company, 1908.

Hine, Robert V. *California's Utopian Colonies.* New Haven, CT: Yale University Press, 1966.

Hines, William Alfred. *American Communities.* New York: 1909.

"His Holiness Sakya Trizin, An Interview." *Wings* 1, no. 1 (September/October 1987): 36-38, 51-53.

Hislop, John S. *My Baba and I.* San Diego: Birth Day Publishing Co., 1985.

Historical Waymarks of the Church of God. Oregon, IL: Church of God General Conference, 1976.

History of the Megiddo Mission. Rochester, NY: Megiddo Mission Church, 1979.

Hodges, Edward Lewis. *Be Healed...A Remedy That Never Fails*. San Diego: Christian Fellowship Organization, 1949.

Hodges, Edward Lewis. *Teachings of the Secret Order of the Christian Brotherhood*. Santa Barbara, CA: J. F. Rowney Press, 1938.

Hodges, Edward Lewis. *Wealth and Riches by Divine Right*. San Diego: Christian Fellowship Organization, 1945.

Hoekstra, Raymond G. *The Latter Rain*. Portland, OR: Wings of Healing, 1950.

Hoeller, Stephan A. *The Enchanted Life*. Hollywood, CA: Gnostic Society, n.d.

Hoeller, Stephan A. *The Gnostic Jung*. Wheaton, IL: Theosophical Publishing House, 1982.

Hoeller, Stephan A. *The Royal Road*. Wheaton, IL: Theosophical Publishing House, 1975.

Hoeller, Stephan A. *The Tao of Freedom: Jung, Gnosis and a Voluntary Society*. Rolling Hills Estates, CA: Wayfarer Press, 1984.

Hoffman, Edward. "Judaism's New Renaissance." *Yoga Journal* 61 (March/April 1985).

Hoffman, Enid. *Huna, A Beginner's Guide*. Rockport, MA: Para Research, 1976.

Hogue, Wilson T. *History of the Free Methodist Church*, 2 volumes. Winona Lake, IN: 1960.

Hold Aloft the Light. La Crescenta, CA: Ananda Ashrama, 1973.

Hollenweger, Walter J. *The Pentecostals*. Minneapolis, MN: Augsberg Press, 1972.

Holliday, Robert K. *Test of Faith*. Oak Hill, WV: Fayette Tribune, 1966.

Holloway, Gilbert. *E.S.P and Your Superconcious*. Louisville, KY: Best Books, Inc. 1966.

Holloway, Mark. *Heavens on Earth: Utopian Communities in America, 1680-1880*. London: Turnstile Press, 1951.

Holmes, Donald. *The Sapiens system: The Illuminati Conspiracy*. Phoenix, AZ: Falcon Press, 1987.

Holmes, Ernest. *The Science of Mind*. New York; Dodd, Mead, and Company, 1944.

Holmes, Fenwicke L. *Ernest Holmes, His Life and Times*. New York: Dodd, Mead and Company, 1970.

Holt, Simma. *Terror in the Name of God*. New York: Crown Publishers, 1965.

The Holy Eucharist and Other Services. San Diego, CA: St. Alban Press, 1977.

The Holy Geeta with commentary by Swami Chinmayananda. Bombay: Central Chimaya Mission Trust, n.d.

Holzach, Michael. "The Christian Communists of Canada." *Geo* 1 (November 1979): 126-54.

Hooper, Robert E. *Swift Transitions: Churches of Christ in the Twentieth Century*. Compiled by Lynn Mac. West Monroe, LA: Howard Publishing Company, 1992.

Hoover, Mario G. "Origin and Structural Development of the Assemblies of God." Master's thesis, Southwest Missouri State College, 1968.

Hopkins, Budd. *Intruders*. New York: Random House, 1987.

Hopkins, Emma Curtis. *Class Lessons: 1888*. Edited by Elizabeth C. Bogart. Marina Del Rey, CA: DeVorss and Co., 1977.

Hopkins, James K. *A Woman to Deliver Her People*. Austin, TX: 1982.

Hopkins, Jeffrey. *The Tantric Distinction*. London: Wisdom Publications, 1984.

Hopkins, Joseph. *The Armstrong Empire*. Grand Rapids, MI: William B. Eerdmans Publishing Co., 1974.

Hopkins, Thomas. "Hindu Views of Death and Afterlife." In Hiroshi Obayashi, ed. *Death and Afterlife: Perspectives of World Religions*. Westport, CT: Greenwood Press, 1992, 49-64.

Horner, Jack, and J. Rey Geller. *What an Eductee Should Know*. Santa Monica, CA: Personal Creative Freedoms Foundation, 1974.

Horner, Jack. *Clearing*. Santa Monica, CA: Personal Creative Freedoms Foundation, 1982.

Horner, Jack. *Dianology*. Westwood Village, CA: Association of International Dianologists, 1970.

Horner, Jack. *Eductivism and You*. Westwood, CA: Personal Creative Freedoms Foundation, 1971.

Horsch, John. *Hutterian Brethren, 1528-1931*. Cayley, AB, Canada: 1977.

Horst, Irvin B. *A Bibliography of Menno Simons*. Nieuwkoop, 1962.

Horst, John. *The Hutterian Brethren, 1528-1931*. Cayley, B: Macmillan Colony, 1977.

Hoshor, John. *God Drives a Rolls Royce*. Philadelphia, PA: Hillman-Curl, 1936.

Hoshor, John. *God in a Rolls-Royce*. New York: Hillman, Curl, 1936.

Hosier, Helen Kooiman. *Kathryn Kuhlman*. Old Tappan, NJ: Fleming H. Revel, 1976.

Hostetler, John A. *Amish Life*. Scottsdale, PA: Herald Press, 1959.

Hostetler, John A. *Amish Society*. Baltimore, MD: Johns Hopkins University Press, 1968.

Hostetler, John A. *Hutterite Society*. Baltimore, MD: 1974.

Houriet, Robert. *Getting Back Together*. New York: Avon, 1972.

The House of Yahweh Established. Abilene, TX: House of Yahweh, n.d.

Houston, Jean. *The Search for the Beloved: Journeys in Mythology and Sacred Psychology*. Los Angeles, CA: Jeremy P. Tarcher, 1987.

Houteff, V. T. *The Great Controversy Over "The Shepherd's Rod"*. Waco, TX: Universal Publishing Association, 1954.

Houteff, V. T. *The Shepherd's Rod Series*. Salem, SC: General Association of the Davidian Seventh-Day Adventists, 1990.

Houteff, V. T. *The Shepherd's Rod*. Vol. 1. Waco, TX: Universal Publishing Association, 1945.

Houteff, Victor T. *The Shepherd's Rod Series*. Mt. Carmel:Universal Printing, 1929-35. 1990 reprint by General Association of Davidian Seventh-Day Adventists, Salem, SC.

Houteff, Victor T. *The Symbolic Code Series*. Mt. Carmel: Universal Printing, 1929-35. 1992 reprint by General Association of Davidian Seventh-Day Adventists. Tamassee, SC.

How the Forces of Love Can Overcome the Forces of Hate. Portland, OR: Universariun Foundation, n.d.

Howard, Ivan J. *What Independent Methodists Believe*. Jackson, MS: Association of Independent Methodists, n.d.

Howard, Richard P. *The Church Through the Years. 2 volumes*. Independence: Herald Publishing House, 1992, 1993.

Howell, Georgina. "The Story of K." *Vanity Fair* 51, no. 6 (June 1988): 100-108, 173-179.

Hoyt, Herman A. *Then Would My Servants Fight*. Winona Lake, IN: Brethren Missionary Herald Company, 1956.

Hua Hsuan. *The Ten Dharma-Realms Are Not Beyond a Single Thought*. San Francisco: Buddhist Text Translation Society, 1976.

Hua, Hsuan. *Buddha Root Farm*. San Francisco: Buddhist Text Translation Society, 1976.

Hubbard, L. Ron. *Dianetics: The Modern Science of Mental Health*. New York: Hermitage House, 1950.

Huffer, Alva C. *Systematic Theology*. Oregon, IL: Church of God General Conference, 1961.

Huffer, Elizabeth Louise. *Spiral to the Sun* Santa Barbara, CA: Joy Foundation 1976.

Huffer, Elizabeth Louise. *Invocations and Decrees* Santa Barbara, CA: Joy Foundation 1982.

Hugh, Paola. *I Will Arise*. 2 vols. Tacoma, WA: Amica Temple of Radiance, 1972.

Hughes, Roy H. *Church of God Distinctives*. Cleveland, TN: Pathway Press, 1968.

Hultkrantz, Ake. "A Definition of Shamanism." *Temenos* 9 (1973):25-37.

Hultkrantz, Ake. *Conceptions of the Soul Among North American Indians*. Stockholm: Ethnographic Museum of Sweden, 1953.

Humble, Floyd. *Bible Lessons*. Gardena, CA: United Spiritualist Church, 1969.

Hunt, Carl M. *Oyotunji Village*. Washington, DC: University Press of America, 1979.

Hunt, Ernest. *An Outline of Buddhism*. Honolulu, HI: Hongwanji Buddhist Temple, 1929.

Hunt, Ernest. *Gleanings from Soto Zen*. Honolulu, HI: The Author, 1953.

Hunt, Roland T. *Fragrant and Radiant Healing Symphony*. Ashingdon, Essex: C. W. Daniel Company, 1949.

Hunt, Roland T. *Man Made Clear for the Nu Clear Age*. Lakemont, GA: CSA Press, 1969.

Hunt, Roland T. *The Seven Rays to Colour Healing*. Ashingdon, Essex: C. W. Daniel Company, 1969.

Hunter, J. Melvin. *The Lyman Wight Colony in Texas*. Bandera, TX: The Author, n.d.

Hunter, Louise H. *Buddhism in Hawaii*. Honolulu: University of Hawaii Press, 1971.

The Hutterian Brethren of Montana. Augusta, MT: Privately Printed, 1965.

Hutterian Society of Brothers and John Howard Yoder, eds. *God's Revolution: The Witness of Eberhard Arnold*. New York: Paulist Press, 1984.

Hutton, Ronald. *The Pagan Religions of the Ancient British Isles: Their Nature and Legacy*, Cambridge, MA: Blackwell, 1991.

Hymns and Chants. Las Vegas, NV: Foundation Faith of God, 1977.

Hymns Old and New. Glasgow, Scotland: R.L.Allan and Son, 1951.

"I Am That." *Hinduism Today* 11, no. 3 (March 1989): 1, 5.

Ichazo, Oscar. *Arica Psycho-Calisthenics*. New York: Simon & Schuster, 1976.

Ichazo, Oscar. *The 9 Ways of Zhikr Ritual*. New York: Arica Institute, 1976.

Ichazo, Oscar. *The Human Process for Enlightenment and Freedom*. New York: Arica Institute, 1976.

Illustrations on Raja Yoga. Mount Abu, India: Prajapita Brahma Kumaris Ishwariya Vishwa Vidyalaya, 1975.

Ingle, Larry. *Quakers in Conflict: The Hicksite Reformation*. Knoxville, TN, 1986.

Inglis, Brian, and Ruth West. *The Alternative Health Guide*. New York: Alfred A. Knopf, 1983.

Inside Out. Nederland, CO: Prison-Ashram Project, Hanuman Foundation, 1976.

Inspired Thought of Swami Rama. Honesdale, PA: Himalayan International Institute of Yoga Science and Philosophy, 1983.

The International Theosophical Year Book: 1938. Adyar: The Theosophical Publishing House, 1938.

"Interview with Penny Torres." *Life Times* 1 (1987): 94-8.

Interviews with Oscar Ichazo. New York: Arica Institute Press, 1982.

Introduction to Apostles' Doctrine. Cleveland, TN: Church Publishing Company, 1984.

An Introduction to the Temple ov Psychick Youth. Brighton, Sussex, UK: Temple Press Limited, 1989.

Introductory Course of World Messianity and Joining the Church. Los Angeles, CA: Church of World Messianity, 1976.

Introvigne, Massimo, ed. *Massoneria e religioni.* Leumann (Torino): Elle Di Ci, 1994.

Introvigne, Massimo. *Il cappello del mago. I nuovi movimenti magici dallo spiritismo al satanismo,* Milan, Italy: SugarCo, 1990.

Introvigne, Massimo. *Il ritorno dello gnosticismo,* Carnago (Varese): Sugar Co., 1993.

Irving, Edward. *The Collected Works of Edward Irving.* 5 vols. London: 1864-65.

Irwin, Mabel McCoy. "Helen Wilmans." *The Nautilus* 10 (January 1908): 31-2.

Isherwood, Christopher. *Ramakrishna and His Disciples.* New York: Simon and Schuster, 1965.

Isherwood, Christopher. *Ramakrishna and His Disciples.* New York: Simon and Schuster, 1965.

Israel, Love. *Love.* Seattle, WA: Church of Armageddon, 1971.

It Does Make a Difference What You Believe! Decatur, IL: Bethel Ministerial Association, n.d.

It Shall Be Called Shiloh. North Hollywood, CA: Living Word Publications, 1975.

Itkin, Michael Francis Augustine. *The Spiritual Heritage of Port-Royal.* New York: Pax Christi Press, 1966.

Itkin, Michael Francis. *The Hymn of Jesus.* New York: Pax Christi Press, n.d.

Itkin, Mikhail. *The Radical Jesus & Gay Consciousness.* Hollywood, CA: Communiversity West, 1972.

Jackson, C. L. and G. Jackson. *Quanah Parker: The Last Chief of the Comanches.* New York: Exposition Press, 1963.

Jackson, Dave and Neta Jackson. *Living Together in a World Falling Apart.* Carol Stream, IL: Creation House, 1974.

Jackson, Richard. *Holistic Massage.* New York: Sterling Publishing Company, 1980.

Jacobs, Susan. "A New Age Jew Revisits Her Roots." *Yoga Journal* 61 (March/April 1985).

Jacques-Garvey, A. (ed.) 1967, 1969. *The philosophy and opinions of Marcus Garvey,* (1924-1926) Vol. I and Vol. II. Reprinted in New York: Arno Press.

Jade. *To Know: A Guide to Women's Magic and Spirituality.* Oak Park, IL: Delphi Press, 1991.

James, Richard. *The WIC-CAN Handbook.* Toronto: Wiccan Church of Canada, 1987.

Jamison, Wallace N. *The United Presbyterian Story.* Pittsburgh, PA: The Geneva Press, 1958.

Javad Nurbakhsh. *Masters of the Path* New York: Khaniqahi-Nimatullahi Publications 1980.

Javad Nurbakhsh, *What the Sufis Say* New York: Khaniqahi-Nimatullahi Publications, 1980.

Jayakar, Pupul. *Krishnamurti: A Biography.* San Francisco: Harper & Row, 1986.

Jefferson, William. *The Story of the Maharishi.* New York: Pocket Books, 1976.

Joesting, Edward. *Hawaii: An Uncommon History.* New York: W. W. Norton, 1972.

Johns, June. *King of the Witches: The World of Alex Sanders.* Coward McCann, 1969.

Johnson, Julian P. *With a Great Master in India.* Beas, India: Radha Soami Sat Sang, Dera Baba Jaimal Singh, 1953.

Johnson, Paul S. L. *Gershonism.* Chester Springs, PA: Layman's Home Missionary Movement, 1938.

Jolly, Raymond. *The Chart of God's Plan.* Chester Springs, PA: Layman's Home Missionary Movement, 1953.

Jonas, Hans. *Gnosis: The Message of the Alien God.* Boston, MA: Beacon, 1948.

Jonathan, Adolph and Richard Smoley. "Beverly Hills Shaman." *New Age Journal* (March/April 1989).

Jones, Franklin *The Knee of Listening.* Los Angeles: Dawn Horse Press, 1972.

Jones, Franklin [Heart-Master Da Free John]. *The Dawn Horse Testament.* San Rafael, CA: Dawn Horse Press, 1985.

Jones, Jerry. *What Does the Boston Movement Teach?* vols. 1-3. Bridgeton, MO: The Author, 1990-93.

Jones, Rufus. *Quakers in the American Colonies.* London: Macmillan, 1923.

Joseph, Alexander. *Dry Bones.* Big Water, UT: University of the Great Spirit Press, 1979.

Jouret, Luc, *Médecine et conscience,* Montreal: Louise Courteau, 1992.

The Journey Home. Santa Cruz, CA: Avadhut, 1986.

Joyti, Swami Amar. *Spirit of Himalaya.* Boulder, CO: Truth Consciousness, 1985.

Judah, J. Stillson. *Hare Krishna and the Counterculture.* New York: John Wiley & Sons, 1974.

Judah, J. Stillson. *The History and Philosophy of the Metaphysical Movements in America*. Philadelphia: Westminster Press, 1967.

Judge, William Q. *Echoes from the Orient*. New York: The Path, 1890.

Juergensmeyer, Mark, and N. Gerald Barrier, eds. *Sikh Studies*. Berkeley, CA: Graduate Theological Union, 1979.

Juergensmeyer, Mark. *Radhasoami Reality*, 1st edition. Princeton University Press, 1991.

Jung, Carl Gustav. *Flying Saucers*. Princeton, NJ: Princeton University Press, 1958.

Jung, Carl Gustav. *Memories, Dreams, Reflections*. New York: Vintage Books, 1965.

Jung, Carl Gustav. *The Archetypes and the Collective Unconscious*. 2d ed. Bollingen Series 20. Princeton: Princeton University Press, 1968.

Kagan, Paul. *New World Utopias*. Baltimore, MD: Penguin Books, 1975.

Kahn, Muhammad Zafrulla. *Ahmadiyyat, The Renaissance of Islam*. London: Tabshir publications, 1978.

Kalachakra Initiation, Madison, 1981. Madison, WI: Deer Park Books, 1981.

Kane, Margaretta Fox. *The Love-Life of Dr. Kane*. New York: Carlton, 1865.

Kaplan, Jeffrey. "The Context of American Millenarian Revolutionary Theology: The Case of the 'Identity Christian' Church of Israel." *Terrorism and Political Violence* 5 (1993) 30-82.

Kapleau, Philip. *The Three Pillars of Zen*. Boston: Beacon Press, 1965. Rev. ed. Garden City, New York: Doubleday & Co., 1980.

Kapleau, Philip. *To Cherish All Life*. San Francisco, CA: Harper and Row, 1982.

Kappeler, Max. *Animal Magnetism—Unmasked*. London: Foundational Book Company Ltd., 1975.

Kaslof, Leslie J., ed. *Wholistic Dimensions in Healing: A Resource Guide*. Doubleday, 1978.

Kaur, Sardarni Premka. *Guru for the Aquarian Age*. Albuquerque, NM: Brotherhood of Life Books, 1972.

Kawate, Bunjiro. *The Sacred Scriptures of Konkokyo*. Konko-cho, Japan: 1933.

Keegan, Marcia, ed. *The Dalai Lama's Historic Visit to North America*. New York: Clear Light Publications, 1981.

Kehoe, Alice Beck. *The Ghost Dance: Ethnohistory and Revitalization*. New York: Holt, Rinehart and Winston, 1989.

Keith, Roy, and Carol Willoughby, eds. *History and Discipline of the Faith and Practice*. Springfield, MO: Fundamental Methodist Church, 1964.

Keizer, Lewis S. *Initiation: Ancient & Modern*. San Francisco, CA: St. Thomas Press, 1981.

Keizer, Lewis S. *Love, Prayer and Meditation*. Santa Cruz, CA: The Author, n.d.

Keizer, Lewis S. *Priesthood in the New Age*. Santa Cruz, CA: the Author, 1985.

Keizer, Lewis S. *The Eight Reveal the Ninth: A New Hermetic Initiation Disclosure*. Seaside, CA: Academy of Arts and Humanities, 1974.

Kell, Wayne. "B. P. Wadia: A Life of Service to Mankind." (Unpublished.)

Kelly, Aidan A. "An Update on Neopagan Witchcraft in America." *Perspectives on the New Age*, ed. James R. Lewis. SUNY Press, 1993.

Kelly, Aidan A. and James R. Lewis. *Almanac of Magick, Witchcraft, Goddess Religions, and Satanism*. Detroit, MI: Gale Research, 1995.

Kelly, Aidan A. *Aradianic Faerie Tradition*. Los Angeles, CA: Art Magickal Publications, Book-on-Disk, 1993.

Kelly, Aidan A. *Crafting the Art of Magic, Book I: A History of Modern Witchcraft, 1939-1964*. St. Paul, MN: Llewellyn Publications, 1991.

Kelly, Aidan A. *Diana's Family: A Tuscan Lineage*. Los Angeles, CA: Art Magickal Publications, Book-on-Disk, 1993.

Kelly, Aidan A. ed. *Neo-Pagan Witchcraft*. New York: Garland, 2 vols. 1990.

Kelly, Aidan A. *Hippie Commie Beatnik Witches: A History of the Craft in California, 1967-1977*. Gardena, CA: Art Magickal Publications, 1993.

Kelly, Aidan A., ed. *The New Polygamy: The Polyamorous Lifestyle as a New Spiritual Path*. Los Angeles, CA: Art Magickal Publications, 1994.

Kelpius, Johannes. *The Diarium of Magister Johannes Kelpius*. Translated and edited by Julius F. Sachse. Lancaster, Pennsylvania: 1917.

Kemp, Russell A. "H. Emilie Cady: Physician and Metaphysician." *Unity Magazine* (August 1975): 5-9 and (September 1975): 15-20.

Kennett, Jiya. *Zen is Eternal Life*. Emeryville, CA: Dharma Publishing, 1976.

Kent, Grady R. *Sixty Lashes at Midnight*. Cleveland, Tennessee: 1963.

Kent, Grady R. *Treatise of the 1957 Reformation Stand*. Cleveland, Tennessee: Church Publishing Co., 1964.

Kent, Homer A., Sr. *Conquering Frontiers: A History of the Brethren Church*. Winona Lake, IN: BMH Books, 1972.

Kern, Richard. *John Winebrenner, 19th Century Reformer*. AHarrisburg, Penn.: 1974.

Khaalis, Hamaas Abdul. *Look and See*. Washington, DC: Hanafi Madh-hab Center Islam Faith, 1972.

Khan, Hazrat Inayat. *Biography of Pir-O-Murshid Inayat Khan*. London: East-West Publications, 1979.

Khan, Muhammad Zafrulla. *Ahmadiyyat, The Renaissance of Islam*. London: Tabshir Publications, 1978.

Khan, Pir Vilayat Inayat. *The Call of the Dervish*. New Lebanon:Omega Press, 1992.

Kilgore, Charles F. *The James O'Kelly Schism in the Methodist Episcopal Church*. Mexico City: 1963.

King, Elizabeth Delvine. *The Flashlights of Truth*. Los Angeles: AUM Temple of Universal Truth, 1918.

King, Elizabeth Delvine. *The Lotus Path*. Los Angeles: J. F. Rowny Press, 1917.

King, Francis. *Ritual Magic In England, 1887 to the Present*. Spearman, 1970.

King, Francis. *Tantra: The Way of Action: A Practical Guide to Its Teachings and Techniques*. Rochester, VT: Destiny Books, 1990.

King, Francis. *The Magical World of Aleister Crowley*. New York: Coward, McCann & Goeghegan, 1978.

King, George William. *Robert Bunger Thieme, Jr.'s Theory and Practice of Preaching*. Ph.D. diss., University of Illinois, Urbana, 1974.

King, George. *A Book of Sacred Prayers*. Hollywood, CA: Aetherius Society, 1966.

King, George. *Life on the Planets*. Hollywood, CA: Aetherius.

King, George. *The Nine Freedoms*. Los Angeles: Aetherius Society, 1963.

King, George. *The Practices of Aetherius*. Hollywood, CA: Aetherius Society, 1964.

King, George. *The Twelve Blessings*. London: Aetherius Press, 1958.

King, George. *You Are Responsible*. London: Aetherius Press, 1961.

King, Godfre Ray [Guy Ballard]. *Unveiled Mysteries*. Mount Shasta, CA: Ascended Master Teaching Foundation, 1986.

King, Godfrey Ray. *The Magic Presence*. Chicago: Saint Germain Press, 1935.

King, Joseph H. *Yet Speaketh*. Franklin Springs, Georgia: Publishing House of the Pentecostal Holiness Church, 1940.

King, Marsha. "Changing Beliefs Led Family to Rearrange Plural Union." *The Seattle Times* (October 13, 1985).

King, Serge. *The Aloha Spirit*. Kilauea, HI: Aloha International, 1990.

King, Serge. *Urban Shaman*. New York: Simon & Schuster, 1990.

Kinley, Henry Cliffor. *Elohim the Archetype (Original) Pattern of the Universe*. Los Angeles, CA: Institute of Divine Metaphysical Research, 1969.

Kinney, Jay. "Sufism Comes to America." *Gnosis Magazine* #30 (Winter 1994): 18-23.

Kirkpatrick, R. George. and Diana Tumminia. . Space Magic, Techno-Animism, and the Cult of the Goddess in a Southern Californian UFO Contactec Group: A Case Study in Millenarianism," *Syzygy: Journal of Alternative Religion and Culture*. 1(2): 159-172. 1992.

Kirkpatrick, R. George. and Diana Tumminia. "California Space Goddess: The

Mystagogue in a Flying Saucer Cult." Pp. 299-311. In *Twentieth Century World Religious Movements in Weberian Perspective*. William H. Swatos, Jr. (ed.). (Lewiston, NY: The Edwin Mellen Press, 1992).

Kishida, Eizan. *Dynamic Analysis of Illness through Gedatsu*. N.p., 1962.

Klages, Ellen. *Harbin Hot Springs: Healing Waters, Sacred Land*. Middleton, CA: Harbin Hot Springs Publishing, 1991.

Klass, Phillip. *UFO Abductions: A Dangerous Game*. Buffalo: Prometheus Books, 1988.

Klassen, Ben. *Building a Whiter and Brighter World*. Otto, NC: Church of the Creator, 1986.

Klassen, Ben. *Nature's Eternal Religion*. Lighthouse Point, FL: Church of the Creator, 1973.

Klassen, Ben. *The White Man's Bible*. Lighthouse Point, FL: Church of the Creator, 1981.

Klein, Walter C. *Johann Conrad Beissel: Mystic and Martinet (1690-1768)*, Philadelphia: 1942.

Klimo, Jon. *Channeling*. Los Angeles: Jeremy P. Tarcher, Inc., 1987.

Klinck, Carl F., ed. *Tecumseh: Fact and Fiction in Early Records*. Englewood Cliffs, NJ: Prentice-Hall, 1961.

Knight, J. Z. *A State of Mind: My Story*. New York: Warner Books, 1987.

Knisley, Alvin. *Infallible Proofs*. Independence, MO: Herald Publishing House, 1930.

Knoch, Adolph Ernst. *Spirit, Spirits, and Spirituality*. Canyon Country, California: 1977.

Kokoszka, Larry. "Time Mellows Communities Caught in Raid." *The Caledonian Record*, Vol. 156, No. 268 (Wednesday, June 22, 1994).

Konko Daijin, A Biography. San Francisco, California: 1981.

Konko Daijin: A Biography San Francisco: Konko Churches of America (1981); Yoshiaki Fukuda, *Outline of Sacred Teaching of Konko Religion* San Francisco: Konko Missions of North America, 1955.

Kornfield, Jack, and Paul Brieter. *A Still Forest Pool*. Wheaton, IL: Theosophical Publishing House, 1985.

Kornfield, Jack. *Living Buddhist Masters*. Santa Cruz, CA: Unity Press, 1977.

Koszegi, Michael M. "The Sufi Order in the West:Sufism's Encounter with the New Age," Gordon Melton, ed. *Islam in North America:A Sourcebook*. New York: Grayland, 1992.

Kotzsch, Ronald E. *Macrobiotics, Yesterday and Today*. Tokyo, Japan: Japan Publications, 1985.

Koury, Aleah G. *The Truth and the Evidence*. Independence, MO: Herald Publishing House, 1965.

Kramer, Kenneth P. *Death Dreams: Unveiling Mysteries of the Unconscious Mind.* New York: Paulist Press, 1993.

Kranzler, Gershon. *Rabbi Shneur Zalman of Ladi.* Brooklyn, NY, 1975.

Kraut, Benny. *From Reform Judaism to Ethical Culture.* Cincinnati, OH: Hebrew Union College Press, 1979.

Kraut, Ogden. *Polygamy in the Bible.* Salt Lake City, UT: Kraut's Pioneer Press, 1979.

Kraybill, Donald B. *The Puzzles of Amish Life.* Intercourse, PA: Good Books, 1990.

Krishnamurti, Jiddu. *Education and the Significance of Life.* New York: Harper & Row, 1953.

Krishnananda, Rishi. *The Mystery of Breath.* New York: Rara-Vidya Center, n.d.

Kriyananda, Goswami [Melvin Higgins]. *Pathway to God-Consciousness.* Chicago: Temple of Kriya Yoga. 1970.

Kriyananda, Goswami [Melvin Higgins]. *Yoga, Text for Teachers and Advanced Students.* Chicago: Temple of Kriya Yoga, 1976.

Kriyananda, Swami. *Cooperative Communities, How to Start Them and Why.* Nevada City, CA: Ananda Publications, 1968.

Kriyananda, Swami. *Crises in Modern Thought.* Nevada City, CA: Ananda Publications, 1972.

Kriyananda, Swami. *The Path: A Spiritual Autobiography.* Nevada City, CA: Ananda Publications, 1977.

Kueshana, Eklal [Richard Kieninger]. *The Ultimate Frontier.* Chicago: The Stelle Group, 1963.

Kuhlman, Kathryn. *I Believe in Miracles.* Englewood Cliffs, NJ: Prentice-Hall, 1962.

Kuhlman, Kathryn. *Nothing is Impossible with God.* Englewood Cliffs, NJ: Prentice-Hall, 1974.

Kummer, George. "Introduction" to *The Leatherwood God* by Richard H. Taneyhill. Gainesville, FL: 1966, vii-xv.

Kunz, Dora, ed. *Spiritual Aspects of the Healing Arts.* Theosophical Publishing, 1985.

Kushi, Michio. *Natural Healing Through Macrobiotics.* Tokyo: Japan Publications, 1978.

Kushi, Michio. *The Book of Macrobiotics.* Tokyo: Japan Publications, 1977.

LaBarre, Weston. *They Shall Take Up Serpents.* New York: Schocken Books, 1969.

Lageer, Eileen. *Merging Streams.* Elkhart, IN: Bethel Publishing Company, 1979.

Lake, John Graham. *Adventures in God.* Tulsa, OK: Harrison House, 1981.

Lake, John Graham. *The New John G. Lake Sermons.* Gordon Lindsey, ed. Dallas: Christ for the Nations, n.d.

Lama Lodru, *Attaining Enlightenmnet* San Francisco: Kagyu Droden Kunchab Publications, 1979.

Lame Deer, John and Richard Erodes. *Lame Deer Seeker of Visions: The Life of a Sioux Medicine Man*. New York: Touchstone, 1972.

Land, Gary, ed. *Adventism in America: A History*. Grand Rapids, MI: Eerdmans Publishing Company, 1986.

Landau, Ron. *The Philosophy of Ibn 'Arabi*. London: Allen and Unwin, 1959.

Landing, James E. "Cyrus R. Teed, Koreshanity, and Cellular Cosmology," *Communal Societies* 1(Autumn 1981): 1-17.

Lane, David Christopher. *The Death of Kirpal Singh*. Del Mar, CA: Del Mar Press, 1975.

Lane, David Christopher. *The Making of a Spiritual Movement: The Untold Story of Paul Twitchell and ECKANKAR*. Garland Press, 1993.

Lane, David Christopher. *The Radhasoami Tradition: A Critical History of Guru Successorship* (1st edition). New York and London: Garland Publishing, 1992.

Lanternari, Vittorio. *The Religions of the Oppressed: A Study of Modern Messianic Cults*. NY: Mentor, 1956.

Lappe, Frances Moore. *Diet for a Small Planet*. New York: Ballantine Books, 1971.

Lark, Pauline, ed. *Sparks from the Anvil of Elder Michaux*. Washington, DC: Happy New Publishing Company, 1950.

Larson, Christian D. *The Creative Power of Mind*. Los Angeles: Privately printed, 1930.

Larson, Martin A. *New Thought: A Modern Religious Approach*. New York: Philosophical Library, 1939.

Lattin, Don. 1990. "'New Age' Mysticism Strong in Bay Area." *The San Francisco Chronicle*. April 24-25, 1990.

Lattin, Don. "Journey to the East" *New Age Journal* December 1992: 70-76.

LaVey, Anton Szandor. *The Compleat Witch*. NY: Lancer Books, 1971.

LaVey, Anton Szandor. *The Satanic Bible*. NY: Avon, 1969.

LaVey, Anton Szandor. *The Satanic Rituals*. Secaucus, NJ: University Books, 1972.

"The Law of Cause and Effect as Taught by Buddha." In J. W. Hanson, ed. *The World's Parliament of Religions*. Chicago: Monarch Book Co., 1894, 388-90.

Lawson, Donna. *Brothers and Sisters All Over This Land: America's First Communes*. New York: Praeger Publishers, 1972.

Layman, Emma McCloy. *Buddhism in America*. Chicago: Nelson-Hall, 1976.

Lazaris [Jach Pursel]. *A Spark of Love*. Beverly Hills, CA: Synergy Publishing, 1987.

Lazaris [Jach Pursel]. *The Sacred Journey: You and Your Higher Self*. Beverly Hills, CA: Synergy Publishing, 1987.

Leadbeater, Charles W. *The Hidden Side of Christian Festivals*. Los Angeles, CA: St. Alban Press, 1920.

Lean, Garth. *Frank Buchman: A Life*. London, England: Constable, 1985.

LeBaron, Ervil. *An Open Letter to a Former Presiding Bishop*. San Diego, CA: The Author, 1972.

LeBaron, Ervil. *Priesthood Expounded*. Buenaventura, Mexico: Mexican Mission of the Church of the Firstborn of the Fullness of Times, 1956.

LeBaron, Ross W. *The Redemption of Zion*. Colonia LeBaron, Chihuahua, Mexico: Church of the First-Born, 1962.

LeBaron, Verlan M. *Economic Democracy Under Eternal Law*. El Paso, TX: Church of the Firstbron of the Fullness of Time, 1963.

LeBaron, Verlan M. *The LeBaron Family*. Lubbock, TX: The Author, 1981.

LeBaron, Verlan M. *The LeBaron Story*. Lubbock, TX: The Author, 1981.

Lebidoff, Florence E. *The Truth About the Doukhobors*. Crescent Valley, BC: The Author, 1948.

Lebra, Takie Sugiyama. "Logic of Salvation: The Case of a Japanese Sect in Hawaii." *The International Journal of Social Psychiatry* 16. Winter 1969/1970, pp. 45-53.

Lee, Ann. *Sound the Gospel Trumpet*. New Gloucester, ME: 1850.

Lee, Gloria. *The Changing Conditions of Your World*. Palos Verdes Estates, CA: Cosmon Research Foundation, 1962.

Lee, O. Max. *Daniel Parker's Doctrine of the Two Seeds*. Nashville, TN: 1962.

Legge, James, trans. *I Ching Book of Changes*. New Hyde Park, NY: University Books, 1964.

Leidecker, Kurt F. *History of the Washington Friends of Buddhism*. Washington, DC: United States Information Service, 1960.

Lejbovitz, Agnes. *Omraam Mikhael Aivanhov Master of the Universal White Brotherhood*. Frejus, France: Editions Prosveta, 1982.

Leland, Charles Godfrey. *Aradia: The Gospel of the Witches of Tuscany*. Scribner's, 1897. Buckland Museum reprint, 1964 (and many more recent reprints).

Lenore Friedman, *Meetings with Remarkable Women: Buddhist Teachers in America*. Boston: Shambhala, 1987.

Lenz, Frederick [Rama]. *Life-Times: True Accounts of Reincarnation*. Indianapolis, IN: The Bobbs-Merrill Co., 1979.

Lenz, Frederick [Rama]. *The Last Incarnation: Experiences with Rama in California*. Malibu, CA: Lakshmi, 1983.

Leopold, Richard William. *Robert Dale Owen, A Biography*. Cambridge, MA: 1940.

Letters to Satchakrananda. Deming, WA: Raj-Yoga Math and Retreat, 1977.

Levine, Saul. *Radical Departures: Desperate Detours to Growing Up*. New York: Harcourt Brace Javanovich, 1984.

Levinsky, Sara Ann. *A Bridge of Dreams*. West Stockbridge, MA: Inner Traditions, 1984.

Levitical Writings. Eskdale, UT: Aaronic Order, 1978.

Lewis, H. Spencer. *Cosmic Mission Fulfilled*. San Jose, CA: Supreme Gran Lodge of AMORC, 1973.

Lewis, H. Spencer. *Rosicrucian Manual*. San Jose, CA: Rosicrucian Press, 1941.

Lewis, H. Spencer. *Rosicrucian Questions and Answers*. San Jose, CA: Supreme Grand Lodge of AMORC, 1969.

Lewis, H. Spencer. *The Mystical Life of Jesus*. San Jose, CA: Rosicrucian Press, 1941.

Lewis, H. Spencer. *Yesterday Has Much to Tell*. San Jose, CA: Supreme Grand Lodge of AMORC, 1973.

Lewis, Harvey S. *Mansions of the Soul*. San Jose, California: Rosicrucian Press, 1930.

Lewis, Helen M. and Meharry H. Lewis. *75th Anniversary Yearbook*. Nashville, TN: Church of the Living God, Pillar and Ground of Truth, 1978.

Lewis, James R. "American Indian Prophets." In Timothy Miller, ed., *When Prophets Die: The Postcharismatic Fate of New Religious Movements*. Albany: SUNY Press, 1991, pp. 47-57.

Lewis, James R. and J. Gordon Melton, eds. *Church Universal and Triumphant in Scholarly Perspective* (Special issue of *Syzygy: Journal of Alternative Religion and Culture*, 1994).

Lewis, James R. and J. Gordon Melton, eds. *Perspectives on the New Age*. Albany: SUNY Press.

Lewis, James R. *Astrology Encyclopedia*. Detroit, MI: Gale Research, 1994.

Lewis, James R. "Edgar Cayce." In the *American National Biography*. New York: Oxford University Press, n.d.

Lewis, James R. *Encyclopedia of Afterlife Beliefs and Phenomena*. Detroit, MI: Gale Research, 1995.

Lewis, James R. *From the Ashes: Making Sense of Waco*. Lanham, MD: Rowman & Littlefield, 1994.

Lewis, James R. "L. Ron Hubbard." In the *American National Biography*. New York: Oxford University Press, n.d.

Lewis, James R., and J. Gordon Melton, Eds., *Sex, Slander, and Salvation: Investigating The Family/Children of God*. Stanford, CA: Center for Academic Publication, 1994.

Lewis, Samuel L. *Sufi Vision and Initiation*. San Francisco: Sufi Islamia/Prophecy Publications, 1986.

The Life of Oyasama, Foundress of Tenrikyo. Tenri, Japan: Tenrikyo Church Headquarters, 1982.

The Life That Brought Triumph. Portland, OR: Apostolic Faith Publishing House, 1955.

Lightbringer Shiloh [Harry W. Theriault]. *Holy Mizan, Supreme Paratestament of the New Song.* Bend, OR: Sacred Text Press, 1982.

The Light from the East: Mokichi Okada. Atami, Japan: MOA Productions, 1983.

Lil O'Lee and Even Eve, eds., *Polyfidelity.* San Francisco: Performing Arts Social Society, 1984.

Lincoln, C. Eric. *The Black Muslims in America.* Boston: Beacon Press, 1961.

Lind, Ingrid. *The White Eagle Inheritance.* Wellingsborough, Northamptonshire: Turnstone Press, 1984.

Lindsay, Gordon. *John Alexander Dowie.* Dallas, TX: Christ for the Nations, 1980.

Lindsay, Gordon. *The Sermons of Alexander Dowie, Champion of the Faith.* Dallas, TX: Voice of Healing Publishing Co., 1951.

Lindsey, Freda. *My Diary Secrets.* Dallas, TX: Christ for the Nations, 1976.

Lindsey, Gordon. *Bible Days Are Here Again.* Shreveport, LA: The Author, 1949.

Lindsey, Gordon. *John Alexander Dowie.* Dallas, TX: Christ for the Nations, 1980.

Lindsey, Gordon. *The Gordon Lindsey Story.* Dallas, TX: The Author, n.d.

Lindsey, Gordon. *William Branham, A Man Sent From God.* Jeffersonville, IN: William Branham, 1950.

Lindstrom, Paul. *Armageddon, The Middle East Muddle.* Mt. Prospect, IL: Christian Liberty Forum, 1967.

Lipski, Alexander. *Life and Teaching of Sri Anandamayi Ma.* Dehli, India: Motila Banaridass, 1977.

Liturgy and Hymnal. Bryn Athyn, PA: General Church of the New Jerusalem, 1966.

Living the Future. Middletown, CA: Harbin Hot Springs Publishing, n.d. Tabloid.

Living Values: A Guidebook. London: Brahma Kumaris World Spiritual University, 1995.

The Living Word of St. John. Liss, Hampshire, England: White Eagle Publishing Trust, 1985.

Lockwood, George B. *The New Harmony Movement.* New York: 1905.

Loftness, John. "A Sign for Our Times!" *People of Destiny Magazine* 3, no. 4 (July/August 1985).

Lomax, Louis E. *When the Word is Given.* Cleveland, OH: World Publishing Company, 1963.

Long, Estelle. *The Christ Family Cult.* Redondo Beach, CA: Citizens Freedom Foundation, Information Services, 1981.

Long, Max Freedom. *Introduction to Huna*. Sedona, AZ: Esoteric Publications, 1975.

Long, Max Freedom. *Recovering the Ancient Magic*. Cape Girardeau, MO: Huna Press, 1978.

Long, Max Freedom. *The Secret Science at Work*. Vista, CA: Huna Research Publications, 1953.

Long, Max Freedom. *The Secret Science Behind Miracles*. Vista, CA: Huna Research Publications, 1954.

Lorber, Jakob. *The Three-Days-Scene at the Temple of Jerusalem*. Bietigheim, Wuerttemberg, Germany: New-Salems-Society, 1932.

Lorrance, Arleen. *Why Me? How to Heal What Is Hurting You*. New York: Ranson Associates Publishers, 1977.

Lozowick, Lee. *Acting God*. Prescott Valley, AZ: Hohm Press, 1980.

Lozowick, Lee. *Beyond Release*. Tabor, NJ: Hohm Press, 1975.

Lozowick, Lee. *Book of Unenlightenment*. Prescott Valley, AZ: Hohm Press, 1980.

Lozowick, Lee. *In the Fire*. Tabor, NJ: Hohm Press, 1978.

Lozowick, Lee. *Laughter of the Stones*. Tabor, NJ: Hohm Press, n.d.

Lozowick, Lee. *The Cheating Buddha*. Tabor, NJ: Hohm Press, 1980.

Lozowick, Lee. *The Only Grace is Loving God*. Prescott Valley, AZ: Hohm Press, 1984.

Lucas, Phillip C. "From Holy Order of MANS to Christ the Savior Brotherhood: The Radical Transformation of an Esoteric Christian Order." In *America's Alternative Religions*. Timothy Miller, ed. Albany: State University of New York Press, 1995.

Lucas, Phillip C. "The Association for Research and Enlightenment: Saved by the New Age." In *America's Alternative Religions*, Timothy Miller, ed. Albany: State University of New York Press, 1995.

Lucas, Phillip C. *The Odyssey of a New Religion: The Holy Order of MANS from New Age to Orthodoxy*. Bloomington: Indiana University Press, 1995.

Lucas, Winafred B. *Regression Therapy. A Handbook for Professionals. Volume I: Past-Life Therapy*. Crest Park, CA: Deep Forest Press, 1993.

Ludlum, David M. *Social Ferment in Vermont*. New York: Columbia University Press, 1939.

Luhrmann, T. M. *Persuasions of the Witch's Craft: Ritual Magic in Contemporary England*. Cambridge, MA: Harvard University Press, 1989

Luk, A. D. K. *Law of Life*. 2 vols. Baltimore, MD: The Author, 1959-60.

Luk, A.D.K. *Law of Life*. 2 vols. Oklahoma City: A.D.K. Publications, 1959-1960.

Lutyens, Mary. *Krishnamurti, The Years of Awakening*. New York: Farrar, Straus & Giroux, 1975.

Lutyens,Mary. *Krishnamurti, The Years of Fulfillment.* London: J. Murray 1983.

Lyons, Arthur. *Satan Wants You.* New York: The Mysterious Press, 1988.

Lyra (Lucy Simms Thompson) *The Shasta Cosmic Key Message.* Long Beach, CA: Shasta Student League Foundation, 1937.

M. Okada, A Modern-Day Renaissance Man. New York: M. Okada Cultural Services Association, 1981.

Ma Jaya Sati Bhagavati. *Bones and Ash.* Sebastian, FL: Jaya Press, 1995.

Ma Jaya Sati Bhagavati. *The River.* Roseland, FL: Ganga Press, 1994. pp. 85.

Ma, Sri Anandamayi. *Sad Vani.* Calcutta, India: Shree Shree Anandamayee Charitable Society, 1981.

Macauliffe, Max Arthur. *The Sikh Religion.* New Delhi, India: S. Chand & Company, 1978.

MacGregor, Daniel. *A Marvelous Work and a Wonder.* The Author, 1911.

MacGregor, Geddes. *Angels. Ministers of Grace.* New York: Paragon House, 1988.

MacGregor, Geddes. *Images of Afterlife: Beliefs from Antiquity to Modern Times.* New York: Paragon House, 1992.

Machen, J. Gresham. *Christianity and Liberalism.* Grand Rapids, MI: W. B. Eerdmans Publishing Co., 1923.

Machen, J. Gresham. *The Virgin Birth of Christ.* New York: Harper & Row, 1930.

Mack, Alexander. *Basic Questions,* n.p., n.d.

MacKenzie, Vicki. *The Boy Lama.* San Francisco: Harper & Row, n.d.

MacLaine, Shirley. *Dancing in the Light.* New York: Bantam Books, 1985.

MacLaine, Shirley. *Out on a Limb.* New York: Bantam Books, 1983.

Madhuri [Nancy Elizabeth Sands]. *The Life of Sri Chinmoy.* Jamaica, NY: Sri Chinmoy Lighthouse, 1972.

Madhusudandasji, Dhyanyogi. *Brahmanada: Sound, Mantra and Power.* Pasadena, CA: Dhyanyoga Centers, 1979.

Mafu [Penny Torres]. *And What Be God?* Vacaville, CA: Mafu Seminars, 1989.

Mafu [Penny Torres]. *Reflections on Yeshua Ben Joseph.* Vacaville, CA: Mafu Seminars, 1989.

Mahadevan, T. M. P. *Ramana Maharshi, the Sage of Arunchala.* London: George Allen & Unwin, 1977.

Maharaj Ji, Guru. *The Living Master.* Denver, CO: Divine Light Mission, 1978.

Maharishi Mahesh Yogi. *The Science of Being and Art of Living.* London: International SRM Publications, 1963. Rev. ed. 1967.

Malaclypse the Younger (Gregory Hill), *Principia Discordia*. Mason, MI: Loompanics, 4th ed., 1978.

Mallot, Floyd E. *Studies in Brethren History*. Elgin, IL: Brethren Publishing House, 1954.

The Man [Jamshid Maani]. *Heaven*. Mariposa, CA: John Carre, 1971.

The Man [Jamshid Maani]. *The Sun of the Word of the Man*. Mariposa, CA: John Carre, 1971.

The Man [Jamshid Maani]. *Universal Order*. Mariposa, CA: John Carre, 1971.

Man, Know Thy Divinity. Auckland, NZ: Living Christ Movement, n.d.

Manaligod, Ambrosio M. *Gregorio Aglipay: Hero or Villain*. Manila: Foundation Books, 1977.

Mandal, Sant Rama. *Course of Instruction in Mystic Psychology*. Santa Monica, CA: Universal Brotherhood Temple and School of Eastern Philosophy, n.d.

Mann, John, ed. *The First Book of Sacraments of the Church of the Tree of Life*. San Francisco: Church of the Tree of Life, 1972.

Mansueto, Anthony, "Visions of Cosmopolis," *Omni* 17 (October, 1994): 64-69, 110.

Manual. New York: The Christian and Missionary Alliance, 1965.

Manual for Implementation of Gedatsu Practice. San Francisco: Gedatsu Church of America, 1961.

Manual of Apostles Doctrine and Business Procedure. Cleveland, TN: Church Publishing Company and Press, n.d.

Manual of Brotherhood Organization and Polity. Elgin, IL: Church of the Brethren, General Offices, 1965.

The Manual of the Evangelical Christian Church (Wesleyan). Birdsboro, PA: Evangelical Christian Church (Wesleyan), 1987.

Marden, Orison Swett. *Every Man a King; or, Might in Mind-Mastery*. New York: T. Y. Crowell & Co., 1906.

Marden, Orison Swett. *Pushing to the Front; or, Success Under Difficulties*. Boston and New York: Houghton, Mifflin & Co., 1894.

Margolies, Morris B. *A Gathering of Anglels: Angels in Jewish Life and Literature*. New York: Ballantine, 1994.

Marietta, Jack D. *The Reformation of American Quakerism, 1748-1783*. Philadelphia: University of Pennsylvania Press, 1984.

Marron, Kevin. *Witches, Pagans, and Magic in the New Age*. Toronto: Seal Books, 1989.

Marshall, June Clover. *A Biographical Sketch of Richard Spurling, Jr.* Cleveland, TN: Pathway Press, 1974.

Martello, Leo Louis. *Curses In Verses*. New York: Hero Press, 1971.

Martello, Leo Louis. *Weird Ways of Witchcraft*. New York: HC Publishers, 1969.

Martello, Leo Louis. *What It Means to Be a Witch*. New York: The Author, 1975.

Martin, Dorothy. *The Story of Billy McCarrell*. Chicago: Moody Press, 1983.

Martin, Edward. "The Boston Movement as a `Revitalization Movement'," D.Min. thesis, Harding Graduate School of Religion, 1990.

Martin, Rachel, as told to Bonnie Palmer Young. *Escape*. Denver, CO: Accent Books, 1979.

Martin, Tony. *Marcus Garvey, Hero: A First Biography*. Dover, MA: Majority Press, 1984.

Maryona. *Mini-Manual for Light Bearers*. Tiffin, OH: The Light of the Universe, 1987.

Maryona. *The Light of the Universe I and II*. Tiffin, OH: The Light of the Universe, 1965, 1976.

Mason, John. *Ebo Eje (Blood Sacrifice)*. New York: Yoruba Theological Archministry, 1981.

Mason, John. *Sin Egun (Ancestor Worship)*. New York: Yoruba Theological Archministry, 1981.

Mason, John. *Unje Fun Orisa (Food for the Gods)*. New York: Yoruba Theological Archministry, 1981.

Mason, John. *Usanyin*. New York: Yoruba Theological Archministry, 1983.

Mason, Mary Esther. *The History and Life Work of Elder C. H. Mason and His Co-Laborers*. Privately printed, n.d.

Master Apollonius Speaks. Los Angeles: Fellowship of Universal Guidance, 1970.

Masters, Roy. *How to Conquer Suffering Without Doctors*. Los Angeles: Foundation of Human Understanding, 1976.

Masters, Roy. *No One Has to Die!* Los Angeles: Foundation of Human Understanding, 1977.

Masters, Roy. *Sex, Sin and Salvation*. Los Angeles: Foundation of Human Understanding, 1977.

Masters, Roy. *The Satan Principle*. Los Angeles: Foundation of Human Understanding, 1979.

Masters, Roy. *Your Mind Can Keep You Well*. Los Angeles: Foundation of Human Understanding, 1968.

Mathers, S. L. MaGregor. *The Greater Key of Solomon*. Chicago: The deLaurence Co., 1914.

Mathews, Edward M. *"Freedom of Thought": An Encyclical*. Los Angeles: Liberal Catholic Church, 1959.

Mathieu, Barbara. "The Shiloh Farms Community." In Jon Wagner, ed. *Sex Roles in Contemporary American Communes*. Bloomington, IN: Indiana University Press, 1982.

Mathison, Richard. *Faiths, Cults, and Sects of America*. Indianapolis, IN: Bobbs-Merrill, 1960.

Mathur, L. P. *Indian Revolutionary Movement in the United States of America*. Delhi, India: S. Chand & Co., 1970.

Matlack, L.C. *The Life of Orange Scott*. New York: 1848.

Matthews, Edward M. "Freedom of Thought," *An Encyclical*. Los Angeles: Liberal Catholic Church, 1959.

Matthews, Edward M. *The Liberal Catholic Church and Its Place in the World*. Los Angeles: St. Alban Book Shop, n.d.

Mattison, James. *The Abrahamic Covenant and the Davidic Covenant*. Oregon, IL: Restitution Herald, 1964.

Maude, Aylmer. *A Peculiar People*. New York: Funk & Wagnalls, 1904.

Mavity, Nancy Barr. *Sister Aimee*. Garden City, NY: Doubleday, 1931.

Maxwell, C. Mervin. *Tell It To the World*. Mountain View, CA: Pacific Press, 1979.

May, Hal, ed. *Contemporary Authors*. Vol. 114. Detroit, MI: Gale Research, Inc., 1985.

Mayer, François, "Des Templiers pour l'Ere du Verseau: les Clubs Archédia (1984-1991) et l'Ordre International Chevaleresque Tradition Solaire," *Mouvements Religieux*, vol.14, n.153 (January 1993), pp.2-10.

Mazzanti, Deborah Szekely. *Secrets of the Golden Door*. New York: William Morrow & Co., 1977.

McArthur, Paul. *Test Book, Ritual, Valuable Data and Selected Poems*. Progressive Spiritualist Association of Missouri, 1908.

McClain, Alva J. *Daniel's Prophecy of the Seventy Weeks*. Grand Rapids, MI: Zondervan Publications, n.d.

McCoy, John, Ray Stanford and Rex Stanford. *Ave Sheoi...From Out of This World*. Corpus Christi, TX: The Authors, 1956.

McCoy, John. *They Shall Be Gathered Together*. Corpus Christi, TX: The Author, 1957.

McDannell, Colleen and Bernhard Lang. *Heaven: A History*. 1988; New York: Vintage, 1990.

McGrath, William R. *The Mystery of Jacob Ammann*. Carrolton, OH: Amish Mennonite Publications, 1989.

McIntire, Carl. *Modern Tower of Babel*. Collingswood, NJ: Christian Beacon Press, 1949.

McIntire, Carl. *Servants of Apostasy*. Collingswood, NJ: Christian Beacon Press,

1955.

McIntire, Carl. *Twentieth Century Reformation*. Collinswood, NJ: Christian Beacon Press, 1944.

McIntosh, Christopher. *The Rosy Cross Unveiled*. Wellingborough, Northamptonshire, United Kingdom: Aquarian Press, 1980.

McKean, Kim. "Revolution Through Restoration," *UpsideDown* 1 (April 1991):6.

McKinlay, John B., ed. *Alternative Medicines: Popular and Policy Perspectives*. New York: Tavistock Publications, 1984.

McKinley, Edward H. *Marching to Glory*. New York: Harper & Row, 1980.

McKnight, Floyd. *Rudolf Steiner and Anthroposophy*. New York: Anthroposophical Society in America, 1967.

McLeister, Ira Ford and Roy S. Nicholson. *History of the Wesleyan Methodist Church*. Marion, IN: 1959.

McLeod, Kenneth, trans., *The Chariot for Traveling the Path to Freedom* San Francisco: Kagyu Dharma, 1985.

McPhail, M. L. *The Covenants: Their Mediators and the Sin Offerings*. Chicago: The Author, 1919.

McPherson, Aimee Semple. *The Story of My Life*. Waco, TX: Word Books, 1973.

Mead, George R. S. *Fragments of a Faith Forgotten*. New Hyde Park, NY: University Books, 1960.

Meade, Marion. *Madame Blavatsky*. New York: G. P. Putnam's Sons, 1980.

Mealing, F. M. *Doukhobor Life*. Castlegar, BC: Cotinneh Books, 1975.

Meares, John L. *Bind Us Together*. Old Tappan, NJ: Chosen Books, 1987.

Meares, John L. *The Inheritance of Christ in the Saints*. Washington, DC: Evangel Temple, 1984.

Meet Our Family. Chicago: Jesus People USA, n.d.

Meiers, Michael. *Was Jonestown a CIA Medical Experiment?* Lewiston, NY: Edwin Mellen Press, 1988.

Meloon, Marion. *Ivan Spencer, Willow in the Wind*. Plainfield, NJ: Logos International, 1974.

Melton, Gordon. *Encyclopedia of American Religions*, 4th edition. Detroit, MI: Gale Research, 1993.

Melton, J. Gordon, ed. *The Peoples Temple and Jim Jones*. New York: Garland Publishing Co., 1990.

Melton, J. Gordon, Jerome Clark, and Aidan A. Kelly. *New Age Encyclopedia*. Detroit, MI: Gale Research, 1990.

Melton, J. Gordon. *Biographical Dictionary of American Cults and Sect Leaders*. New

York: Garland, 1986.

Melton, J. Gordon. *Encyclopedia of American Religions*, 4th ed. Detroit, MI: Gale Research, 1993.

Melton, J. Gordon. *Encyclopedic Handbook of Cults in America*. Revised and Updated Edition. New York & London: Garland Publishing, Inc., 1992.

Melton, J. Gordon. *New Age Enciclopedia*. Detroit, MI: Gale Reasearch, 1990.

Melton, J. Gordon. *Religious Leaders of America*. Detroit, MI: Gale Research, 1992.

Melton, J. Gordon. "The Revival of Astrology in the United States. In Stark, Rodney, ed. *Religious Movements: Genesis, Exodus, and Numbers*. New York: Paragon, 1985. pp. 279-299.

Members' Handbook. Atami, Japan: Church of World Messianity, n.d.

Memorial of Adin Ballou. Cambridge, MA, 1890.

Menzies, William W. *Anointed to Serve: The Story of the Assemblies of God*. Springfield, MO: Gospel Publishing House, 1971.

Meredith, George. *Bhagwan: The Most Godless Yet the Most Godly Man*. Poona, India: Rebel Publishing House, 1987.

Meyer, Ann, and Peter Meyer. *Being a Christ*. San Diego: Dawning Publications, 1975.

Meyer, Nancy. "Meet the Sikhs." *Los Angeles* 29:3. March 1984, pp. 174-80; pp. 241-245.

Meyers, Robert. "Khigh Dhiegh Digs I Ching." *TV Guide* (February 20, 1971): 45-48.

Michael, Allen. *ETI Space Beings Intercept Earthlings*. Stockton, CA: Starmast Publication, 1977.

Michael, Allen. *The Everlasting Gospel, God, Unlimited Mind Speaks*. Stockton, CA: Starmast Publication, 1982.

Michael, R. Blake. "Heaven, West Virginia: Legitimation Techniques of the New Vrindaban Community." In *Krishna Consciousness in the West*, ed. by David Bromley and Larry Shinn. Lewisburg, PA: Bucknell University Press, 1989.

Mickler, Michael L. *The Unification Church in America: A Bibliography and Research Guide*. New York: Garland, 1987.

Militz, Annie Rix. *Primary Lessons in Christian Living and Healing*. New York: Absolute Press, 1904.

Millennium, n.d.

Miller, J. Ivan. *History of the Conservative Mennonite Conference, 1910-1985*. Grantsville, MD: Ivan J. and Della Miller, 1985.

Miller, Milburn H. *Unto the Church of God*. Anderson, IN: Warner Press, 1968.

Miller, Rose. *The Gnostic Holy Eucharist*. Palo Alto, CA: Ecclesia Gnostica Mysteriorium, 1984.

Miller, Timothy. *American Communes 1860-1960: A Bibliography*. New York: Garland Publishing, 1990.

Miller, William. *Apology and Defense*. Boston: 1845.

Milne, Hugh. *Bhagwan, The God That Failed*. New York: St. Martin's Press, 1986.

Mindel, Nissan. *Rabbi Schneur Zalman of Ladi*. Brooklyn, NY: Chabad Research Center, Kehot Publication Society, 1973.

Ministers' Address Directory. Norfolk, VA: Gospel Assembly Ministers' Fund, 1970.

Minkin, Jacob S. *The Romance of Hasidism*. New York, 1935.

Minor, Robert Neil. *Sri Aurobindo: The Perfect and the Good*. Columbia, MO: South Asia Books, 1978.

Mintz, John and Mark Fisher. "Ex-finders Tell of Games, Complex Beliefs." *Washington Post*, 2.8.1987.

Minutes of the General Conference of the Dunkard Brethren Church from 1927 to 1975. Wauseon, OH: Glanz Lithographing Company, 1976.

Mishra, Rammurti S. *Isha Upanishad*. Dayton, OH: Yoga Society of Dayton, 1962.

Mishra, Rammurti. *Dynamics of Yoga Mudras and Five Suggestions for Meditation*. Pleasant Valley, NY: Kriya Press, 1967.

Mishra, Rammurti. *Fundamentals of Yoga*. New York: Lancer Books, 1969.

Mishra, Rammurti. *Self Analysis and Self Knowledge*. Lakemont, GA: CSA Press, 1978.

Mitchell, Robert Bryant. *Heritage & Horizons: The History of Open Bible Standard Churches*. Des Moines, IA: Open Bible Publishers, 1982.

Montgomery, Ruth. *Aliens Among Us*. New York: Putnam's, 1985.

Montgomery, Ruth. *Companions Along the Way*. New York: Coward, McCann & Geoghegan Inc., 1974.

Montgomery, Ruth. *Strangers Among Us: Enlightened Beings from a World to Come*. New York: Coward, McCann & Geoghegan, 1979.

Montgomery, Ruth. *Threshold to Tomorrow*. New York: G. P. Putnam's Sons, 1983.

Moody, Jess. *The Jesus Freaks*. Waco, TX: Word Books, 1971.

Moody, Raymond A. *Life After Life*. New York: Bantam, 1976.

Mookerjee, Ajit, and M. Khanna. *The Tantric Way: Art, Science, Ritual*. New York Graphic, 1977.

Moon, Elmer Louis. *The Pentecostal Church*. New York: Carleton Press, 1966.

Moon, Sun Myung. *God's Warning to the World*. 2 vols. New York: HSA-UWC, 1985.

Moon, Sun Myung. *The New Future of Christianity*. Washington, D.C.: Unification Church International, 1974.

Mooney, James. *The Ghost-Dance Religion and the Sioux Outbreak of 1890*. Chicago: University of Chicago Press, 1965; abridged reprint of 1896 original.

Moore, Frances Adams. *A View from the Mount*. Ojai, CA: Group for Creative Meditation, 1984.

Moore, Virginia. *The Unicorn: William Butler Yeats' Search for Reality*.

Moore, Willard B. *Molokan Oral Tradition*. Berkeley and Los Angeles: University of California Press, 1973.

Moral Values, Attitudes and Moods. Mount Abu, India: Prajapita Brahma Kumaris Ishwariya Vishwa Vidyalaya, 1975.

Moral, Herbert R. *"With God All Things Are Possible."* Norton, CT: Life Study Fellowship, 1945.

Morgan, Elsie Nevins. *Your Own Path*. Akron, OH: Sun Publishing Company, 1928.

Morgan, Harold P. *Christian Values and Principles*. 3 vols. Atascadero, CA: Ewalt Memorial Bible School, n.d.

Morris, Joseph. *Gems of Inspiration, A Collection of Sublime Thoughts by Modern Prophets*. San Francisco: 1899.

Morris, Joseph. *The Spirit Prevails*. San Francisco, CA: George S. Dove and Company, 1886.

Moses, Wilson J. *Black Messiahs and Uncle Toms: Social and Literary Manipulations of a Religious Myth*. Pennsylvania State University Press: University Park and London, 1982.

Moshier, Bud and Carmen. *Freeing the Whole Self*. Dallas, TX: The Today Church, 1971.

Moshier, Carmen. *Success Programming Songs for You!* Dallas, TX: Academy of Mind Dynamics, 1970.

The Most Holy Principle. 4 vols. Murray, UT: Gems Publishing Co., 1970-75.

Mott, Francis J. *Christ the Seed*. Boston: A. A. Beauchamp, 1939.

Mott, Francis J. *Consciousness Creative*. Boston: A. A. Beauchamp, 1937.

Mott, Francis J. *The Universal Design of Birth*. Philadelphia: David McKay Company, 1948.

Mow, Merrill. *Torches Rekindled: The Bruderhof's Struggle for Renewal*. Ulster Park, NY: Plough Publishing, 1989.

Muhaiyaddeen, M. R. Guru Bawa, Shaikh. *God, His prophets and His Children*. Philadelphia: Fellowship Press, 1978.

Muhaiyaddeen, M. R. Guru Bawa, Shaikh. *Mata Veeram, or the Forces of Illusion*. York Beach, ME: Sanuel Weiser, 1982.

Muhaiyaddeen, M. R. Guru Bawa, Shaikh. *The Guidebook*. 2 vols. Philadelphia: Fellowship Press, 1978.

Muhaiyaddeen, M. R. Guru Bawa, Shaikh. *The Truth and Unity of Man*. Philadelphia: Fellowship Press, 1980.

Muhaiyaddeen, M. R. Guru Bawa, Shaikh. *Truth and Light*. Guru Bawa Fellowship of Philadelphia, 1974.

Muhammad, Elijah. *Message to the Blackman in America*. Chicago: Muhammad Mosque of Islam, No. 2, 1965.

Muhammad, Elijah. *Our Savior Has Arrived*. Chicago: Muhammad's Temple of Islam No. 2, 1974.

Muhammad, Silis. *In the Wake of the Nation of Islam*. College Park, GA: The Author, 1985.

Muhammad, Tynnetta. *The Divine Light*. Phoenix, AZ: H.E.M.E.F., 1982.

Muhammad, W. D. *Religion on the Line*. Chicago: W. D. Muhammad Publications, 1983.

Muhammad, Wallace D. *Lectures of Elam Muhammad*. Chicago: Zakat Propagation Fund Publications, 1978.

Muhammad, Warith Deen. *As a Light Shineth from the East*. Chicago: WDM Publishing Co., 1980.

Mukerji, A. P. *The Doctrine and Practice of Yoga*. Chicago: Premel El Adaros, 1922.

Muktananda, Swami. *Guru*. New York: Harper & Row, 1981

Muktananda, Swami. *I Have Become Alive*. South Fallsburg, New York: SYDA Foundation, 1985.

Muldoon, Sylvan J. and Carrington, Hereward. *The Projection of the Astral Body*. New York: Samuel Weiser, 1970.

Mulholland, John F. *Hawaii's Religions*. Rutland, VT: Charles T. Tuttle Company, 1970.

Mulvin, Jerry. *Out-of-Body Exploration*. Marina del Rey, CA: Divine Science of Light and Sound, 1986.

Mulvin, Jerry. *The Annals of Time*. Manhattan Beach, CA: Divine Science of Light and Sound, 1982.

Mumford, Bob. *Take Another Look at Guidance*. Plainfield, NJ: Logos International, 1971.

Muncy, Raymond Lee. *Sex and Marriage in Utopian Communities*. Bloomington: Indiana University Press, 1973.

Murphy, Gardner, and Robert O. Ballou, eds. *William James on Psychical Research*. New York: Viking Press, 1960.

Murphy, Joseph M. "Santeria and Voodoo in the United States," *America's Alternative Religions*. Albany, NY: State University of New York Press, 1995.

Murphy, Larry G., J. Gordon Melton, and Gary L. Ward, eds. *Encyclopedia of African*

American Religions. New York and London: Garland Publishing Co., 1993.

Murray, William John. *The Astor Lectures*. New York: The Divine Science Publishing Association, 1917.

Mushegan, Harry A. *Water Baptism*. Atlanta, GA: Gospel Harvester World Outreach Center, n.d.

Musser, Joseph W. *Celestial or Plural Marriage*. Salt Lake City, UT: Truth Publishing Co., 1944.

Musser, Joseph W. *Michael Our Father and Our God*. Salt Lake City, UT: Truth Publishing Company, 1963.

Muzaffer Ozek Al-Jerrahi, *The Unveiling of Love* New York: Inner Traditions International, 1981.

Myers, Gustavus. *History of Bigotry in the United States*. New York: Capricorn, 1960.

Myers, John. *Voices from Beyond the Grave*. Old Tappan, NJ: Spire Books, 1971.

Nachman, Rabbi. *Azamra!* Brooklyn, NY: Breslov Research Institute, 1984.

Nada-Yolanda [Pauline Sharpe]. *Mark-Age Period and Program*. Miami, FL: Mark-Age, 1970.

Nada-Yolanda [Pauline Sharpe]. *Visitors from Other Planets*. Miami, FL: Mark-Age, 1974.

Nadwi, S. Abul Hasan Ali. *Qadianism, A Critical Study*. Lucknow, India: Islamic Research and Publications, 1974.

Nagorka, Diane S. *Spirit as Life Force*. Washington, DC: ESPress, Inc., 1983.

Nakazono, Masahilo. *Messiah's Return, The Hidden Kototama Principle*. Santa Fe, NM: Third Civilization, 1972.

Nandita and Devadatta. *Path of Bliss, Ananda Marga Yoga*. Wichita, KS: Ananda Marga Publishers, n.d.

Nanji, Azim. "The Nizari Ismaili Muslim Community in North America; Background and Development." In *The Muslim Community in North America*, edited by Earle H. Waugh, Baha Abu-Laban, and Regula B. Qureshi. Edmonton, AB: University of Alberta Press, 1983.

Narayanananda, Swami. *The Mysteries of Man Mind and Mind Functions*, n.p., n.d.

Nasr, Seyyed Hossein, ed. *Islamic Spirituality:Manifestations*. New York: Crossroad Press, 1991.

"Natural Healing in the Soviet Union." *New Scientist* August 8, 1992.

Nee, Watchman. *The Normal Christian Church Life*. Washington, D.C.: International Students Press, 1969.

Nelson, E. Clifford and Eugene L. Fevold. *The Lutheran Church Among Norwegian-Americans*. Minneapolis, MN: 1960.

Nelson, Robert. *Understanding the Crossroads Controversy*. Fort Worth, TX: Star Bible Publications, 1986.

Nethercott, Arthur H. *The First Five Lives of Annie Besant*. Chicago: University of Chicago Press, 1960.

Nethercott, Arthur H. *The Last Four Lives of Annie Besant*. Chicago: University of Chicago Press, 1963.

Nevins, William Manlius. *Alien Baptism and the Baptists*. Ashland, KY: Press of Economy Printers, 1962.

New Age Songs. Newberry Springs, CA: AUM Temple of Universal Truth, 1972.

New Catholic Encyclopedia. San Francisco: McGraw-Hill, 1967.

New Golden Dawn: Flying Roll Parts 1-15. Phoenix, AZ: Thelemic Order and Temple of Golden Dawn, 1990-91.

Newbrough, John Ballou. *Oahspe: A New Bible*, n.p., 1882.

Newcomb, Arthur. *Dowie, Anointed of the Lord*. New York: Century Company, 1930.

Nichol, John Thomas. *Pentecostalism: The Story of the Growth and Development of a Vital New Force in American Protestantism*. New York: Harper & Row, 1966.

Nichols, L. T. *The Devil and Hell of the Bible*. Rochester, New York: Megiddo Mission Church, n.d.

Nichols, Ross. *The Book of Druidry: History, Sites and Wisdom*, edited by John Matthews and Philip Carr-Gomm. London: Aquarian/Thorsons, 1990.

Nickel, Thelma. *Our Rainbow of Promise*. Tulsa, OK: Vickers Printing Co., 1950.

Nickel, Thomas R. *Azusa Street Outpouring*. Hanford, CA: Great Commission International, 1979.

Nickels, Richard D. *A History of the Seventh Day Church of God*. The Author, 1977.

Nicolas Roerich, 1874-1947. New York: Nicolas Roerich Museum, 1974.

Nielsen, Niels C., Norvin Hein, Frank E. Reynolds, Alan L. Miller, Samuel E. Karff, Alice C. Cochran, and Paul McLean. *Religions of the World*. New York: St. Martins, 1983.

Nier, Susan. *The Discovery*. Homestead, FL: OmniTouch, Inc., 1993.

Nightingale, Michael. *The Healing Power of Acupuncture*. New York: Javelin Books, 1986.

Nihle, William. *A True History of Celtic Britain*. San Diego: St. Dionysius Press, 1982; *The People's Liturgy* San Diego: Johannine Catholic Church, 1968.

Nikhilananda, Swami. *Ramakrishna: Prophet of New India*. New York: Harper & Brothers, 1948.

Nikhilananda, Swami. *Vivekananda: A Biography*. Calcutta, India: Advaita Ashrama, 1975.

Nisargadatta Maharaj, Sri. *Prior to Consciousness*. Edited by Jean Dunn. Durham, NC: Acorn Press, 1985.

Nisargadatta Maharaj, Sri. *Seeds of Consciousness*. Edited by Jean Dunn. New York: Grove Press, 1982.

Nisargaddata Maharaj, Sri. *I Am That*. Durham, NC: Acorn Press, 1983.

Nisargaddata Maharaj, Sri. *The Blissful Life*. Comp. by Robert Powell. Durham, NC: Acorn Press, 1984.

Nishiyana, Teruo. *Introduction to the Teachings of Tenrikyo*. Tenri, Japan: Tenrikyo Overseas Missionary Department, 1981.

Niwano, Nichiko. *Lifetime Beginner*. Tokyo: Kosei Publishing Co., 1978.

Niwano, Nichiko. *My Father, My Teacher*. Tokyo: Kosei Publishing Co., 1982.

Noel, Napoleon. *The History of the Brethren*. 2 vols. Denver, CO: W. F. Knapp, 1936.

Nomolos, Yaj, S.P. *The Magic Circle: Its Successful Organization and Leadership*. Toluca Lake, CA: International Imports, 1987.

Nordhoff, Charles *The Communistic Societies of the United States*, Reprint. New York: Schrocken Books, 1965.

Nordquist, Ted A. *Ananda Cooperative Village*. Upsala, Sweden: Borgstroms Tryckeri Ab, 1978.

Nordstrom, Louis, ed. *Namu Dai Bosa*. New York: Theatre Arts Books, 1976.

Nori, Don. *"Persecution at Island Pond."* Charisma 10, nr. 4, November 1984.

Norman, Ernest L. *The Voice of Venus*. Los Angeles: New Age, 1956.

Norman, Ruth E, and Vaughan Spaegel. *The Conclave of Light Beings: Or the Affair of the Millennium*. El Cajon, CA: Unarius Publishers, 1973.

Norris, Frank J. *Practical Lectures on Romans*. Forth Worth, TX: First Baptist Church, n.d.

Norwood, Frederick A. *The Story of American Methodism*. Nashville, TN: Abingdon Press, 1974.

Noyes, John Humphrey. *Confessions of John H. Noyes*. Oneida Reserve, NY: 1849.

Noyes, John Humphrey. *History of American Socialism*. (Reprinted. as *Strange Cults and Utopias of 19th-century America*. New York: Dover Publications, 1966.

Noyes, John Humphrey. *History of American Socialisms*. New York: 1966.

Nussbaum, Stan. *A History of the Evangelical Mennonite Church*. The Author, 1980.

Nyland, Wilhem. *Firefly*. Warwick, NY: The Author, 1965.

O'Connor, Elizabeth. *Call to Commitment*. New York: Harper & Row, 1963.

O'Connor, Elizabeth. *Cry Pain, Cry Hope*. Waco, TX: Word Books, 1987.

O'Connor, Elizabeth. *Eighth Day of Creation*. Waco, TX: Word Books, 1971.

O'Connor, Elizabeth. *Journey Inward, Journey Outward*. New York: Harper & Row, 1968.

O'Connor, Elizabeth. *The New Community*. New York: Harper & Row, 1976.

O'Donnell, Ken. *Pathways to Higher Consciousness*. Sydney, Australia: Eternity Ink, 1996.

O'Kelly, James. *The Author's Apology for Protesting Against the Methodist Episcopal Government*. Richmond, VA: 1798.

O'Lee, Lil, and Even Eve, eds. *Polyfidelity*. San Francisco, CA: Performing Arts Social Society, 1984.

O'Neill, Molly. "Roman Catholic Rebel Becomes a Cause Célèbre." *New York Times* (March 17, 1993): C1,8.

O.T.O. System Outline. San Francisco, CA: Stellar Visions, 1981.

Obayashi, Hiroshi, ed. *Death and Afterlife: Perspectives of World Religions*. Westport, CT: Greenwood Press, 1992, 49-64.

"Obituary [of Elizabeth Towne]." *Holyoke Daily* (June 1, 1960): 1, 16.

Odunfonda I Adaramila. *Obatala, The Yoruba God of Creation*. Sheldon, SC: Great Benin Books, n.d.

Official Directory, Rules and Regulations of the Bible Way Church of Our Lord Jesus Christ World Wide, Inc. Washington, DC: Bible Way Church of Our Lord Jesus Christ World Wide, 1973.

Ogamisama Says. Tabuse, Japan: Tensho-Kotai-Jingu-Kyo, 1963.

Olcott, Henry Steel. *Old Diary Leaves*. 6 vols. Adyar, India: 1972-75.

Omoyajowo, J. Akinyele. *The Cherubim and Seraphim Society: The History of an African Independent Church*. NY: Nok Publishers International, Ltd., 1982.

One Hundredth Anniversary of Modern American Spiritualism. Chicago: National Spiritualist Association of Churches, 1948.

Oppenheim, Janet. *The Other World: Spiritualism and Psychical Research in England, 1850-1914*. Cambridge: Cambridge University Press, 1985.

"Ordination." *Universal Truth* 8 (February 1896): 52.

Orr, Leonard [and Makhan Singh]. *Babaji*. San Francisco, CA: The Author, 1979.

Orr, Leonard, and Sondra Ray. *Rebirthing in the New Age*. Berkeley, CA: Celestial Arts, 1977.

Orrmont, Arthur. *Love Cults and Faith Healers*. New York: Ballantine, 1961.

Osborn, Arthur. *Superphysical: A Review of the Evidence for Continued Existence, Reincarnation, & Mystical States of Consciousness*. New York: Barnes & Noble, 1974.

Osborne, Arthur, ed. *The Teachings of Ramana Maharshi*. New York: Samuel Weiser, 1962.

Osborne, Arthur. *Ramana Maharshi and the Path of Self-Knowledge*. New York: Samuel Weiser, 1970.

Osteen, John H. *This Awakening Generation*. Humble, TX: The Author, 1964.

Osterhaven, M. Eugene. *The Spirit of the Reformed Tradition*. Grand Rapids, MI: William B. Eerdmans Publishing Company, 1971.

Ostrander, Sheila, and Lynn Schroeder. *Psychic Discoveries Behind the Iron Curtain*. Englewood Cliffs, NJ: Prentice-Hall, Inc., 1970.

Our Most Holy Faith. East Rutherford, NJ: Dawn Bible Students Association, 1969.

Ouspensky, P. D. *A New Model of the Universe*. New York: Alfred A. Knopf, 1931.

Ouspensky, P. D. *The Fourth Way*. New York: Alfred A. Knopf, 1957.

Owen, Robert Dale. *Footfalls on the Boundary of Another World*. Philadelphia: 1860.

Owen, Robert Dale. *Twenty-Seven Years of Autobiography, Threading My Way*. New York: 1874.

Owens, J. *Dread: The Rastafarians of Jamaica*. London: Heinemann, 1976.

Padgett, James E. *True Gospel Revealed Anew by Jesus*. 4 vols. Washington, DC: Foundation Church of the New Birth, 1958-1972.

Page, Clarence. "Deciphering Farrakhan." *Chicago* 33, no. 8 (August 1984): 130-35.

Palmer, Phoebe Worrall. *Promise of the Father: or, A Neglected Specialty of the Last Days*. New York: W. C. Palmer, 1859.

Palmer, Phoebe Worrall. *The Way of Holiness*. New York: 1845.

Palmer, Susan J. "Woman as Playmate in the Raelian Movement: Power and Pantagamy in a New Religion" in *SYZYGY: Journal of Religion and Culture* 1:3, 227-45, 1992.

Palmer, Susan J "Helpmates in the Messianic Community." *Moon Sisters, Krishna Mothers, Rajneesh Lovers: Women's Roles in New Religions*. Syracuse University Press, n.d.

Palmer, Susan J. "The Ansaaru Allah Community: Postmodernist Narrative and the Black Narrative" in Peter Clarke's (ed.) *New Islamic Movements in the West*. London, England: Curzon Press, n.d.

Paramahansa, Swami Prem. *What Is ILCC?* Hawthorne, CA: Intergalactic Lovetrance Civilization Center, [1983].

Paramananda, Swami. *The Path of Devotion*. Boston: Vedanta Center, 1907.

Paramananda, Swami. *Vedanta in Practice*. Boston: Vedanta Center, 1917.

Paranjpe, Vasant V. *Grace Alone*. Madison, VA: Fivefold Path, 1971.

Paranjpe, Vasant V. *Homa Farming, Our Last Hope*. Madison, VA: Fivefold Path, 1986.

Paranjpe, Vasant V. *Ten Commandments of Parama Sadguru*. Randallstown, MD: Agnihotra Press, 1976.

Parham, Charles Fox. *A Voice Crying in the Wilderness*. Baxter Springs, KS: Apostolic Faith Bible College, 1910.

Parham, Sarah E. *The Life of Charles F. Parham, Founder of the Apostolic Faith Movement*. Joplin, MO: Hunter Printing Co., 1930.

Parisien, Maria, ed. *Angels & Mortals: Their Co-Creative Power*. Wheaton, IL: Quest Books, 1990.

Parker, Daniel. *A Public Address to the Baptist Society of the Baptist Board of Foreign Missions*. Vincennes, IN: 1820.

Parker, Daniel. *Views on the Two Seeds; A Supplement, or Explanation of My Views*. Vandalia, IL: 1826.

Parker, Doug and Helen. *The Secret Sect*. Pandle Hill, N.S.W., Australia: The Authors, 1982.

Parker, Gail Thain. *Mind Cure in New England*. Hanover, NH: University Press of New England, 1973.

Parrish-Harra, Carol W. *Messengers of Hope*. Marina Del Ray, CA: DeVorss & Co., 1983.

Parsons, Howard L. "Religion and Politics in the USSR and Eastern Europe" in Wei-hsun, Charles and Gerhard E. Spiegler, eds. *Movements and Issues in World Religions*. New York and Westport, CT: Greenwood Press, 1987.

Pastor, David Horowitz. *Charles Taze Russell, an Early American Christian Zionist*. New York: Philosophical Library, 1986.

The Pattern of History. Merrimac, MA: Destiny Publishers, 1961.

Patterson, Charles Brodie. "Helen Van Anderson." *Mind* 10 (July 1902): 244-47.

Patterson, Charles Brodie. *In the Sunlight of Health*. New York and London: Funk & Wagnalls Co., 1913.

Patterson, J. O., German R. Ross, and Julia Mason Atkins. *History and Formative Years of the Church of God in Christ with Excerpts from the Life and Works of Its Founder—Bishop C. H. Mason*. Memphis, TN: Church of God in Christ Publishing House, 1969.

Patterson, W. A. *From the Pen of W. A. Patterson*. Memphis, TN: Deakins Typesetting Service, 1970.

Paulk, Earl. *Satan Unmasked*. Atlanta: K Dimensions Publications, 1984.

Paulk, Earl. *Ultimate Kingdom*. Atlanta: K Dimensions Publications, 1984.

Paulsen, Norman. *Sunburst, Return of the Ancients*. Goleta, CA: Sunburst Farms Publishing, 1980. Revised and retitles as *Christ Consciousness*. Salt Lake City, UT: The Builders Publishing Company, 1984.

Pavry, Jal Dastur Cursetji. *The Zoroastrian Doctrine of a Future Life*. New York: Columbia University Press, 1926.

Paxson, Diana. *The Earthstone*. New York: St. Martin's Press, 1987.

Payne, Wardell J., ed. *Directory of African American Religious Bodies: A Compendium by the Howard University School of Divinity*. Washington, DC: Howard University Press, 1991.

Pearsall, Ronald. *The Table-Rappers*. New York: St. Martin's Press, 1973.

Pearson, William Dudley. *Seven Minutes in Eternity*. Noblesville, IN: Soulcraft Chapels, 1954.

Peel, Robert. *Mary Baker Eddy: The Years of Authority*. New York: Holt, Rinehart and Winston, 1977.

Peel, Robert. *Mary Baker Eddy: The Years of Discovery*. New York: Holt, Rinehart and Winston, 1966.

Peel, Robert. *Mary Baker Eddy: The Years of Trial*. New York: Holt, Rinehart and Winston, 1971.

Pelley, William. *Road to Sunrise*. Noblesville, IN: Soulcraft Press, 1950.

Pelley, William. *The Door to Revelation*. Asheville, NC: The Foundation Fellowship, 1936.

Pelton, Robert W. *The Complete Book of Voodoo*. New York: G. P. Putnam's Sons, 1972.

Pendleton, William Frederic. *Topics from the Writings*. Bryn Athyn, PA: The Academy Book Room, 1928.

Penn, Enoch. *The Order of Melchisedek*. Applegate, CA: Esoteric Fraternity, 1961.

Percival, Harold W. *Man and Woman and Child*. New York: Word Publishing Co., 1951.

Percival, Harold W. *Thinking and Destiny*. New York: Word Publishing Co., 1950.

Perkin, Noel, and John Garlock. *Our World Witness*. Springfield, MO: Gospel Publishing House, 1963.

Pernoud, Régine. *Les Templiers*, Paris: Presses Universitaires de France, 1988.

Perry, Troy D. *The Lord Is My Sheperd and He Knows I'm Gay*. New York: Bantam Books, 1978.

Peters, Victor. *All Things Common*. New York: Harper & Row, 1971.

Peterson, Joe V. *Jesus People: Christ, Communes and the Counterculture of the late Twentieth Century in the Pacific Northwest*. Eugene, OR: M.A. thesis, Northwest Christian College, 1990.

Pfeifer, Jeffrey E. "The Psychological Framing of Cults: Schematic Representations and Cult Evaluations." *Journal of Applied Social Psychology* 22:7 (1992):531-544.

Philips, Abu Ameenah Bilal. *The Ansar Cult in America*. Sudan:Tawheed Publications, 1988.

Phylos the Tibetan [Frederick Spencer Oliver]. *A Dweller on Two Planets*. Los Angeles: Borden Publishing Co., 1899.

Pickering, Hy. *Chief Men Among the Brethren*. London: Pickering & Inglis, 1918.

Pierce, Ted M. *Healer Extraordinaire*. Yarnell, AZ: Top Publishers, 1987.

Pike, James A. and Diane Kennedy. *The Other Side*. New York: Doubleday & Co., 1968.

Pike, John M. *Preachers of Salvation*, n.p., n.d.

Pitts, Bill. "Davidians and Branch Davidians:1929-1987." In Stuart A. Wright, ed., *Armageddon in Mount Carmel*. Chicago: University of Chicago Press, 1995.

Pitcairn, Theodore. *The Beginning and Development of Doctrine in the New Church*. And, Philip N. Odhner. *Notes on the Development of Doctrine in the Church*. Bryn Athyn, PA: The Lord's New Church, 1968.

Pitcairn, Theodore. *The Bible or Word of God Uncovered and Explained*. Bryn Athyn, PA: The Lord's New Church, 1964.

Pitcairn, Theodore. *My Lord and My God*. New York: Exposition Press, 1967.

Pitts, Bill. "The Davidian Tradition," *Council of Societies for the Study of Religion Bulletin*. Vol. 22:4 (November 1993): 99-101.

Pitts, Bill. "The Mount Carmel Davidians:Adventist Reformers, 1935-1959," *Syzygy* Vol. 2: 1-2 (1993): 39-54.

Plate, Harry. "Riker: from Mechanic to Messiah" *California Today*, August 30, 1978.

Podmore, Frank. *Mediums of the 19th Century*. 2 vols. New Hyde Park, New York: University Books, 1963.

Pomeroy, Ella. "From Medicine to Metaphysics." *The New Thought Bulletin* 29 (Winter-Spring 1946): 3-5.

Ponder on This. NY: Lucis Publishing Co., 1971.

Popenoe, Cris, and Oliver Popenoe. *Seeds of Tomorrow*. San Francisco: Harper & Row, 1984.

Popoff, Irmis B. *Gurdjieff Group Work with Wilhem Nyland*. York Beach, ME: Samuel Weiser, 1983.

Portanda, Alex. "The Legacy of Harold Percival." *Psychic Guide* 4 (December 1985-January and February 1986): 26-9.

Post, Tom with Marcu Mabry, Theodore Stanger, Linda Kay and Charles S. Lee, "Suicide Cult," *Newsweek*, October 17, 1994, p.10-15.

Power for Peace of Mind. Norton, CT: Life Study Fellowship, n.d.

Power, Mary Elizabeth. M.A. Thesis, "A Study of the Seventh-Day Adventist Community, Mount Carmel Center, Waco, Texas," 1940.

Prabhupada, A. C. Bhaktivedanta Swami. *Bhagavad-Gita As It Is*. New York: Bhaktivedanta Book Trust, 1972.

Practitioner's Manual. Los Angeles: United Church of Religious Science, 1967.

Prajananda, Swami. *A Search for the Self.* Ganeshpuri, India: Gurudev Siddha Peeth, 1979.

Prather, Hugh. *A Book of Games: A Course in Spiritual Play.* Garden City, NY: Doubleday & Company, 1981.

Prather, Hugh. *Notes on How to Live in the World...and Still Be Happy.* Garden City, NY: Doubleday & Company, 1977.

"Preamble and By-Laws of the Theosophical Society" (October 30, 1875).

Pressman, Steven. *Outrageous Betrayal: The Dark Journey of Werner Erhard from est to Exile.* New York: St. Martin's Press, 1993.

Preston, H. L. *The Hell and the Heaven,* n.p., 1902.

Price, Frederick K. C. *How to Obtain Strong Faith.* Tulsa, OK: Harrison House, 1980.

Price, John Randolph. *The Planetary Commission.* Austin, TX: Quartus Foundation for Spiritual Research, 1984.

Price, Richard. *Restoration Branches Movement.* Independence, MO: Price Publishing Co., 1986.

Price, Ross E. *Nazarene Manifesto.* Kansas City, MO: Beacon Hill Press, 1968.

Priesthood Expounded. Mexican Mission of the Church of the Firstborn of the Fullness of Times, 1956.

Prince, R. (ed.). *Maroon Societies.* Garden City, NY: Anchor Press/Doubleday, 1973.

Probert, Mark. *Excerpts from the Mark Probert Seances: 1950 Series,* 3 vols. San Diego, CA: Inner Circle Press, 1950.

Probert, Mark. *The Magic Bag.* San Diego: Inner Circle Kethra E'Da Foundation, 1963.

Prophet, Elizabeth Clare. *The Great White Brotherhood in the Culture, History, and Religion of America.* Los Angeles: Summit University Press, 1976.

Prophet, Elizabeth Clare. *The Great White Brotherhood.* Malibu, CA: Summit University Press, 1983.

Prophet, Elizabeth Clare. *The Lost Teachings of Jesus.* 2 vols. Livingstone, MT: Summit University Press, 1986, 1988.

Prophet, Mark L. and Elizabeth Clare Prophet. *Climb the Highest Mountain.* Colorado Springs, CO: Summit Lighthouse, 1972.

Prophet, Mark L. and Elizabeth Clare Prophet. *The Science of the Spoken Word.* Colorado Springs, CO: Summit Lighthouse, 1974.

Prophet, Mark L. *The Overcoming of Fear Through Decrees.* Colorado Springs, CO: Summit Lighthouse, 1966.

Prophet, Mark L. *Understanding Yourself: Doorway to the Superconscious.* Los Angeles: Summit University Press, 1981.

The Prophetic Word. Revelation Number Two. Los Angeles: Fellowship of Universal Guidance, 1980.

Pruitt, Fred. *Past, Present, and Future of the Church*. Guthrie, OK: Faith Publishing House, n.d.

Pruitt, Raymond M. *Fundamentals of the Faith*. Cleveland, TN: White Wing Publishing House and Press, 1981.

Pryse, James M. *Spiritual Light*. Los Angeles: The Author, 1940.

A Public Indictment of J. J. Verigin. Krestova, BC: Christian Community of Reformed Doukhobors (Sons of Freedom), 1954.

Pugh, Liebie. *Nothing Else Matters*. St. Annes-by-the-Sea, Lancaster: The Author, 1964.

Purkiser, W. T. *Called Unto Holiness, II*. Kansas City, MO: Nazarene Publishing House, 1983.

Purnell, Benjamin. *Shiloh's Wisdom*. 4 vols. Benton Harbor, MI: Israelite House of David as Reorganized by Mary Purnell, n.d.

Purnell, Benjamin. *The Book of Dialogues*. 3 vols. Benton Harbor, MI: Israelite House of David, 1912.

Purnell, Benjamin. *The Book of Wisdom*. 7 vols. Benton Harbor, MI: Israelite House of David, n.d.

Purnell, Mary. *The Comforter, The Mother's Book*. 4 vols. Benton Harbor, MI: Israelite House of David, 1926.

Ra Un Nefer Amer [R. A. Straughn] *Metu Neter*. Vol. 1. Bronx, NY: Khamit Publishing Co., 1990.

Rabbani, Shoghi Effendi. *God Passes By*. 2d ed; Wilmette, Ill.:Bahá Publishing Trust, 1974.

Rabbani, Shoghi Effendi. *The World Order of Bahá'u'lláha*. 2d rev. ed; Wilmette, IL:Bahá Publishing Trust, 1974.

Radest, Howard B. *Toward Common Ground*. New York: Frederick Unger Publishing Co., 1969.

Radha, Sivananda. *Diary of a Woman's Search*. Port Hill, ID: Timeless Books, 1981.

Radha, Sivananda. *Hatha Yoga, Hidden Language*. Port Hill, ID: Timeless Books, 1987.

Rahula, Walpola. *What the Buddha Taught*. New York: Evergreen, 1974. 2nd, expanded edition (original edition, 1959).

Rajneesh, Bhagwan Shree. *Meditation: The Art of Ecstasy*. New York: Harper and Row, 1976.

Rajneesh, Bhagwan Shree. *Tantra, Spirituality, and Sex*. San Francisco: Rainbow Bridge, 1977.

Ram Dass, Baba. *Be Here Now*. San Christobal, New Mexico: Lama Foundation, 1971.

Ram Dass, Baba. *The Only Dance There Is.* New York: Aronson, 1976.

Rama, Swami. *Lectures on Yoga.* Arlington Heights, IL: Himalayan International Institute of Yoga Science and Philosophy, 1972.

Rama, Swami. *Life Here and Hereafter.* Glenview, IL: Himalayan International Institute of Yoga Science and Philosophy, 1976.

Ramaiah, Yogi S.A.A. *Shasta Ayyappa Swami Yoga Pilgrimage.* Imperial City, CA: Pan American Babaji Yoga Sangam, n.d.

Ramakrishna, Sri. *The Gospel of Ramakrishna.* Boston: Beacon Press, 1947.

Rand, Howard B. *Digest of Divine Law.* Haverhill, MA: Destiny Publishers, 1943.

Randall, E. *History of the Zoar Society,* n.p., 1904.

Randolph, Paschal Beverly. *P. B. Randolph...His Curious Life, Works, and Career.* Boston: The Author, 1872.

Ransom, Josephine, compiler. *A Short History of the Theosophical Society: 1875-1937.* Adyar, Madras: The Theosophical Publishing House, 1938.

Rausch, David A. *A Messianic Judaism.* New York: Edwin Mellon Press, 1982.

Rauscher, William V. *Arthur Ford: The Man Who Talked With the Dead.* New York: New American Library (1973); Arthur Ford, *Why We Survive.* New York: The Gutenberg Press, 1952.

Rawson, Philip. *Tantra: The Indian Cult of Ecstasy.* Thames & Hudson, 1974.

Ray, Sondra. *Drinking the Divine.* Berkeley, CA: Celestial Arts, 1984.

The Record of the Nephites. Independence, MO: Board of Publication, Church of Jesus Christ, "With the Elijah Message," Established Anew in 1929, 1970.

Reed, Rebecca Theresa. *Six Months in a Convent.* Boston: Russel, Odiorne & Metcalf, 1835.

Rees, Aylwin, and Brinsley Rees. *Celtic Heritage: Ancient Tradition in Ireland and Wales.* London: Thames & Hudson, 1961.

Regardie, Israel, ed. *Gems from the Equinox: Selected Writings of Aleister Crowley.* St. Paul, MN: Llewellyn Publications, 1974.

Regardie, Israel. *The Golden Dawn.* St. Paul, MN: Llewellyn Publications, 1969.

Regardie, Israel. *The Golden Dawn: An Account of the Teachings, Rites, and Ceremonies of the Order of the Golden Dawn. 1937-1940.* Hazel Hills, 2d ed., 1969.

Regardie, Israel. *What Every One Should Know About the Golden Dawn.* Phoenix, AZ: Falcon Press, 1983.

Renfrew, Sita Paulickpulle. *A Buddhist Guide for Laymen.* Cambridge, MA: Cambridge Buddhist Association, 1963.

Renn, Ruth E. *Study Aids for Part IV of The URANTIA Book, The Life and Teachings of Jesus.* Chicago, IL: URANTIA Foundation, 1975.

Report of a Meeting Between a Group of Shepherd's Rod Leaders and a Group of General Conference Ministers. Washington, DC:The Research Committee of the General Conference of Seventh-Day Adventists, 1960.

Resnick, Rosalind. "To one city it's cruelty. To cultists it's religion." *National Law Journal* (September 11, 1989).

Reston, James. *Our Father Who Art in Hell: The Life and Death of Jim Jones.* New York: Times Books, 1981.

Rettig, Lawrence. *Amana Today.* South Amana, IA: The Author, 1975.

The Revelations of James J. Strang. Church of Jesus Christ of Latter Day Saints, 1939.

Reyes, Benito F. *Christianizing Christians.* Ojai, CA: The Author, n.d.

Reyes, Benito F. *On World Peace.* Ojai, CA: World University, 1977.

Reyes, Benito F. *The Essence of All Religion.* Ojai, CA: The Author, 1983.

Reyes, Dominga L. *The Story of Two Souls.* Ojai, CA: The Author, 1984.

Rice, Charles S., and Rollin C. Steinmetz. *The Amish Year.* New Brunswick, NJ: Rutgers University Press, 1956.

Rich, Russell B. *Those Who Would Be Leaders.* Provo, UT: Brigham Young University, 1967.

Richards, Henry W. *A Reply to "The Church of the Firstborn of the Fullness of Times."* Salt Lake City: The Author, 1965.

Richards, M. C. *Toward Wholeness: Rudolf Steiner Education in America.* Middletown, CT: Wesleyan University Press, 1980.

Richardson, James C., Jr. *With Water and Spirit.* Martinsville, VA: The Author, n.d.

Richardson, James D., Jr. *With Water and Spirit: A History of Black Apostolic Denominations in the U.S.* Winston-Salem, NC: The Author, 1980.

Rijckenborgh, Jan Van. *Elementary Philosophy of the Modern Rosecross.* Haarlem, Netherlands: Rozekruis-Pers, 1961.

Rijckenborgh, Jan Van. *The Coming New Man.* Haarlem, Netherlands: Rozekruis-Pers, 1957.

Ring, Kenneth *Heading Toward Omega.* New York: William Morrow and Company, 1984.

Ring, Kenneth. *The Omega Project.* New York: William Morrow and Company, 1992.

Robbins, Thomas and Dick Anthony, eds. *In Gods We Trust: New Patterns of Religious Pluralism in America.* New Brunswick, NJ: Transaction, 1981.

Robert S. Fogarty, *The Righteous Remnant* Kent, OH: Kent State University Press (1981); Francis Thorpe, *House of David Victory and Legal Troubles Reviewed.* Benton Harbor, MI: Israelite House of David, n.d.

Roberts, Dana. *Understanding Watchman Nee.* Plainfield, NJ: Haven Books, 1980.

Roberts, David L. *The Angel Nephi Appears to David L. Roberts*. Independence, MO: The True Church of Jesus Christ Restored, 1974.

Roberts, Jane. *The Coming of Seth*. New York: Frederick Hall Publishers, 1966.

Roberts, Jane. *The Seth Material*. Englewood Cliffs, NJ: Prentice Hall, 1970, pp. 304.

Robertson, Constance Noyes. *Oneida Community, An Autobiography, 1851-1876*. Syracuse, NY: 1970.

Robertson, Constance Noyes. *The Strange Autobiography of Frank B. Robinson*. Moscow, ID: Psychiana, 1949.

Robinson, Elmo Arnold. *American Universalism*. New York: Exposition Press, 1970.

Robinson, Frank B. *Life Story of Frank B. Robinson*. Moscow, Idaho: Psychiana, 1934.

Robinson, James, ed. *The Nag Hammadi Library in English*. San Francisco: Harper, 3d ed., 1988.

Robinson, Louie. *"The Kingdom of King Narcisse."* Ebony 18. July 1963.

Robison, John, A.M. *Proofs of a Conspiracy*, 4th ed. NY: Geo. Forman, 1798. Belmont, MA: Western Islands, 1967.

Roerich, Nicolas. *The Banner of Peace*. Colombo, Ceylon: The Buddhist, 1933.

Rolland, Romain. *The Life of Vivekananda and the Universal Gospel*. Calcutta, India: Advaita Ashrama, 1970.

Root, Jean Christie. *Edward Irving, Man, Preacher, Poet*. Boston: 1912.

Rosenblum, Art. *Aquarian Age or Civil War?* Philadelphia: Aquarian Research Foundation, 1970.

Rosenblum, Art. *The Natural Birth Control Book*. Philadelphia: Aquarian Research Foundation, 1984.

Rosenblum, Art. *Unpopular Science*. Philadelphia: Running Press, 1974.

Rothenberg, Paula. *Racism and Sexism*. New York: St. Martins, 1988.

Rubin, Israel. *Satmar, An Island in the City*. Chicago: Quadrangle Books, 1972.

Rudolf Steiner, *An Autobiography*. Blauvelt, NY: Rudolf Steiner Publications, 1977.

Ruhnau, Helena Elizabeth. *Let There Be Light: Living Water of Life for the New Age*. Ava, MO: Lighting the Way Foundation, 1987.

Ruhnau, Helena Elizabeth. *Light on a Mountain*. Riverside, CA: The Author, 1966.

Ruhnau, Helena Elizabeth. *Reappearance [The Return?] of the Dove*. Colorado Springs, CO: Colleasius Press, 1978.

Russell, Jeffrey B. *A History of Witchcraft: Sorcerers, Heretics, and Pagans*. Thames and Hudson, 1980.

Ryerson, Kevin, and Stephanie Harolde. *Spirit Communication: The Soul's Path*. New York: Bantam Books, 1989.

Sachse, Julius F. *The German Pietists of Provincial Pennsylvania.* Philadelphia: 1895.

Saether, George W. "Oral Memoirs." 1975. Institute for Oral History, Baylor University, Waco, TX.

Sahn, Seung. *Ten Gates.* Cumberland, RI: Primary Point Press, 1987.

Sai Baba, Sathya. *Sathya Sai Speaks.* 7 vols. Bombay, India: Sri Sathya Sai Educational Foundation, 1970-71.

Saint Michael and the Angels. Compiled from Approved Sources. Rockford, IL: Tan Books and Publishers, 1983.

Saliba, John A., "Religious Dimensions of UFO Phenomena," in *The Gods Have Landed*, ed. by James R. Lewis. Albany, NY: SUNY, 1995, pp. 15-64.

Salmon, J. Warren, ed. *Alternative Medicine, Popular and Policy Perspectives.* New York: Tavistock Publications, 1984.

Samuels, Andrew, Bani Shorter and Fred Plaut, *A Critical Dictionary of Jungian Analysis.* London: Routledge & Kegan Paul, 1986.

Sananda, as recorded by sister Thedra. *I, the Lord God Say Unto Them.* Mt. Shasta, CA: Association of Sananda and Sanat Kumara, 1954.

Sandars, N.K., Transl. *The Epic of Gilgamesh,* rev. ed. New York: Penguin, 1972.

Sangharakshita, Maha Sthavira. *Flame in Darkness: The Life and Sayings of Anagarika Dharmapala.* Yerawada, Pune, Maharastra, India: Triratna Grantha Mala, 1980.

Sann, Paul. *Fads, Follies, and Delusions of the American People.* New York: Bonanza Books, 1967.

Sant Thakar Singh: A Brief Life Sketch, n.p., n.d.

Sappington, Roger E., ed. *The Brethren in the New Nation.* Elgin, IL: Brethren Press, 1976.

Sara, Lady [Cunningham]. *Questions and Answers on Wicca Craft.* Wolf Creek, OR: Stonehenge Farm, 1974.

Saradarian, Haroutiun. *The Magnet of Life.* Reseda, CA: Aquarian Educational Group, 1968.

Saradarian, Haroutiun. *The Science of Meditation.* Reseda, CA: Aquarian Educational Group, 1971.

Saraswati, Ma Yogashakti. *Prayers and Poems from Mother's Heart.* Melbourne, FL: Yogashakti Mission, 1976.

Saraswati, Swami Dayananda. *Meditation at Dawn.* The Author, n.d.

Saraswati, Swami Dayananda. *Purbamadah Purnamidam.* The Author, n.d.

Saraswati, Swami Dayananda. *The Sadhana and the Sadhya (The Means and the End).* Rishikish, India: Sri Gangadhareswar Trust, 1984.

Saraydarian, Torkom. *A Commentary on Psychic Energy.* West Hills, CA: T. S. G. Enterprises, 1989.

Saraydarian, Torkom. *Christ the Avatar of Sacrificial Love.* Agoura, CA: Aquarian Educational Group, 1974.

Saraydarian, Torkom. *Sex, Family, and the Woman in Society.* Sedona, AZ: Aquarian Educational Group, 1987.

Saraydarian, Torkom. *The Flame of Beauty, Culture, Love, Joy.* Agoura, CA: Aquarian Education Group, 1980.

Saraydarian, Torkom. *The Symphony of the Zodiac.* Agoura, CA: Aquarian Education Group, 1980.

Saraydarian, Torkom. *Woman: Torch of the Future.* Agoura, CA: Aquarian Educational Group, 1980.

Sarkar, P. R. *Idea and Ideology.* Calcutta: Acarya Pranavananda Avadhuta, 1978.

Sasaki, Joshu. *Buddha is the Center of Gravity.* San Cristobal, NM: Lama Foundation, 1974.

Sasaki, Ruth Fuller. *Zen, A Method for Religious Awakening.* Kyoto, Japan: First Zen Institute of America in Japan, 1959.

Saunders, Monroe R. *Book of Church Order and Discipline of the United Church of Jesus Christ (Apostolic).* Washington, 1965.

Saved to Serve. Portland, OR: Apostolic Faith Publishing House, 1967.

Scheuner, Gottlieb. *Inspirations - Histories.* 2 vols. Trans. by Janet W. Zuber. Amana, IA: Amana Church Society, 1976-77.

Schimmel, Annemarie. *Mystical Dimensions of Islam.* Chapel Hill: University of North Carolina Press, 1975.

Schmidt, Roger. *Exploring Religion.* Belmont, CA: Wadsworth, 1988.

Schneerson, M. M. *Letters by the Lubavitcher Rebbe.* Brooklyn, NY: Kehot Publication Society, 1979.

Schreiber, William I. *Our Amish Neighbors.* Chicago: University of Chicago Press, 1962.

Schroeder, Werner. *Man—His Origin, History and Destiny.* Mount Shasta, CA: Ascended Master Teaching Foundation, 1984.

Schwartz, Alan M., and Gail L. Gans. "The Identity Churches: a Theology of Hate." In *ADL Facts* 28, 1, Spring 1983.

Scientology, Church of. *L. Ron Hubbard: The Man and His Work.* Los Angeles: Church of Scientology, 1986.

Scott, Gini Graham. *Cult and Countercult.* Westport, CT: Greenwood Press, 1980.

Seale, Ervin. *Ten Words that Will Change Your Life.* New York: William Morrow & Company, 1954.

Sears, Julia Seton. *Fundamental Principles of the New Civilization, New Thought; Students Manual.* New York: E. J. Clode, 1916.

Sears, Julia Seton. *Methods of Obtaining Success.* New York: E. J. Clode, 1914.

Sebald, Hans. "New-Age Romanticism: The Quest for an Alternative Lifestyle as a Force of Social Change." *Humboldt Journal of Social Relations* 1984. 11:2.

Seivertson, Genevah D. *The Christ Highway.* Marina del Rey, CA: DeVorss & Company, 1981.

Sellers, Charles Coleman. *Lorenzo Dow, the Bearer of the Word.* New York: 1928.

Senzaki, Nyogen, and Ruth Stout McCandless, eds. *Buddhism and Zen.* New York: Philosophical Library, 1953.

Senzaki, Nyogen, and Salidin Reps, trans. *10 Bulls.* Los Angeles: DeVorss & Co., 1935.

Seton, Julia. *Fundamental Principles of the New Civilization.* New York: Edward J. Clode, 1916.

"Seton, Julia." In *National Cyclopedia of American Biography*, vol. 16, pp. 295-96. New York: James T. White & Co., 1931.

Seton, Julia. *The Key to Health, Wealth and Love.* New York: Edward J. Clode, 1917.

Seton, Julia. *The Mystic's Goal.* London: William Rider & Son, 1924.

Seton, Julia. *The Science of Success.* New York: Edward J. Clode, 1914.

Seton, Julia. *Western Symbology.* Chicago: New Publishing Company, 1929.

Seventh-Day Adventist Encyclopedia, Washington, D.C.: n.p., 1976.

Seymour, William J. *The Doctrine and Discipline of the Azusa Street Apostolic Faith Mission of Los Angeles.* Los Angeles: Apostolic Faith Mission, n.d.

Shabbos, Zmiros, and Yon Tov. *From the Rebbe's Table.* Brookline, MA: New England Chasidic Center, 1983.

Shah, Sayed Idries. *The Secret Lore of Magic: Books of the Sorcerors.* Muller, 1957; Citadel paperback, 1970.

Shaku, Soyen. *Sermons of a Zen Buddhist Abbot.* Chicago: Open Court Publishing Co., 1906. Reprinted as *Zen for Americans.* LaSalle, IL: Open Court Publishing Co., 1974.

Shambaugh, Bertha M. H. *Amana That Was and Amana That Is.* Iowa City, IA: State Historical Society of Iowa, 1932.

Sharma, Indrajit. *Sivananda: Twentieth Century Saint.* Rishikish, India: Yoga-Vedanta Forest Academy, 1954.

Shearman, Hugh. *Charles Webster Leadbeater, A Biography.* Sydney, Australia: St. Alban Press, 1982.

Sheehan, Edmund. *Teaching and Worship of the Liberal Catholic Church.* Los Angeles: St. Albans Press, 1925.

Sheng-Yen, Ch'an Master. *Faith in Mind: A Guide to Ch'an Practice.* Elmhurst, NY: Dharma Drum Publications, 1987.

Sheng-Yen, Ch'an Master. *Getting the Buddha Mind: On the Practice of Ch'an Retreat*. Elmhurst, NY: Ch'an Meditation Center, 1982.

Sheng-Yen, Ch'an Master. *Ox Herding at Morgan's Bay*. Elmhurst, NY: Institute of Chung-Hwa Buddhist Culture, 1988.

Shepard, Leslie A., ed. *Encyclopedia of Occultism & Parapsychology*. Detroit, MI: Gale Research, 1991.

Shepard, William; Donna Falk and Thelma Lewis, eds. *James J. Strang, Teaching of a Mormon Prophet*. Burlington, WI: Church of Jesus Christ of Latter Day Saints (Strangite), 1977.

Shepherd, A. P. *A Scientist of the Invisible*. New York: British Book Centre, 1959.

Shields, Steven L. *Divergent Paths of the Restoration*. Los Angeles: Restoration Research, 1990.

Shields, Steven L. *The Latter Day Saint Churches: An Annotated Bibliography*. New York: Garland Publishing, Inc., 1987.

Shih, Ching Hai Wu Shang. *The Key to Enlightenment*. Miaoli Sien, Taiwan, ROC: Meditation Association in China, 1990.

Shin Buddhist Handbook. Honolulu: Honpa Hongwanji Mission of Hawaii, 1972.

Shin, Gosung. *Zen Teachings of Emptiness*. Washington, DC: American Zen College Press, 1982.

Shirley, Eugene B., Jr. and Michael Rowe. *Candle in the Wind*. London: Ethics and Public Policy Center, 1989.

Short, Dennis R. *For Men Only*. Sandy, UT: The Author, 1977.

Sigstedt, Cyriel Odhner. *The Swedenborg Epic*. New York: Bookman Associates, 1952.

Silver, Ednah C. *Sketches of the New Church in America*. Boston: MA: New Church Union, 1920.

Silver, Stephen M. "Priesthood and Presidency, An Answer to Henry W. Richards." *Ensign* 2, no. 11 (January 1963): 1-127.

Simmons, John K. *The Ascension of Annie Rix Militz and the Home(s) of Truth: Perfection Meets Paradise in Early 19th Century Los Angeles*. Ph.D. diss., University of California, Santa Barbara, 1987.

Simonton, O. Carl, Stephanie Matthews-Simonton, and James Creighton. *Getting Well Again*. Los Angeles: J.P. Tarcher, 1978.

Simpson, Albert B. *The Four-fold Gospel*. Harrisburg, PA: Christian Publications, n.d.

Simpson, Albert B. *The Larger Christian Life*. Harrisburg, PA: Christian Pubcations, n.d.

Simpson, Charles. *A New Way to Live*. Greensburg, PA: Manna Christian Outreach, 1975.

Simpson, Patti. *Paulji: A Memoir*. Menlo Park, CA: ECKANKAR, 1985.

Sinclair, John R. *The Alice Bailey Inheritance*. Wellingsborough, Northamptonshire: Turnstone Press, 1984.

Singh, Darshan. *The Cry of the Soul*. Bowling Green, VA: Sawan Kirpal Publications, 1977.

Singh, Darshan. *The Secret of Secrets*. Bowling Green, VA: Sawan Kirpal Publications, 1978.

Singh, Gopal. *The Religion of the Sikhs*. Bombay: Asia Publishing House, 1971.

Singh, Huzur Maharaj Sawan. *Philosophy of the Masters*, 5 vols. Beas, India: Radhasoami Satsang, Beas, 1963-1967.

Singh, Kirpal. *A Brief Sketch of Hazur Baba Sawan Singh*. Delhi, India: Ruhani Satsang, 1949.

Singh, Kirpal. *Surat Shabd Yoga*. Berkeley, CA: Images Press, 1975.

Singh, Kirpal. *The Way of the Saints*. Sanbornton, NH: Sant Bani Ashram, 1976.

Singh, Sawan. *My Submission*, 2 vols. Beas, India: Radhasoami Satsang Beas, 1985.

Singh, Sawan. *Tales from the Mystic East*. Beas, India: Radha Soami Satsang Beas, 1961.

Singh, Thakar. *Good Stories Make Us Good*. Delhi, India: Ruhani Satsang, Sawan Ashram, 1983.

Singh, Thakar. *Gospel of Love*. Delhi, India: Ruhani Satsang, Sawan Ashram, 1984.

Sitchin, Zecharia. *The 12th Planet*. 1976; New York: Avon, 1978.

Sivananda, Swami. *Practical Lessons in Yoga*. Sivanandanagar, India: Divine Life Society, 1978.

Sivananda, Swami. *Science of Yoga*, 18 vols. Durban, South Africa: Sivananda Press, 1977.

Skir, Leo. "Shlomo Carlebach and the House of Love and Prayer." *Midstream* (February 1970).

Slater, Herman, ed. *The Magickal Formulary*. New York: Magickal Childe, 1981.

Slay, James L. *This We Believe*. Cleveland, TN: Pathway Press, 1963.

Smart, Ninian. *The World's Religions*. Englewood Cliffs, NJ: Prentice Hall, 1989.

Smith, Arthur M. *Temple Lot Deed*. Independence, MO: Board of Publication, Church of Christ (Temple Lot), 1967.

Smith, Bradford. *Meditation*. Philaelphia, PA: J.P. Lippencott Company, 1963.

Smith, Elmer Lewis. *The Amish People*. New York: Exposition Press, 1958.

Smith, Elmer Lewis. *The Amish*. Witmer, PA: Applied Arts, 1966.

Smith, Michael G. *Crystal Power*. St. Paul, MN: Llewellyn Publications, 1985.

Smith, Peter. *The Babi and Bahá" Religions:From Messianic Shi'ism to a World Religion.* Cambridge: Cambridge Univ. Press, 1987.

Smith, Timothy. *Called Unto Holiness.* Kansas City, MO: Nazarene Publishing House, 1962.

Smith, Willard J. *Fetting and His Messenger's Messages.* Port Huron, MI: The Author, 1936.

Snyder, Mark. "Self-Fulfilling Stereotypes." In Rothenberg, Paula. *Racism and Sexism.* NY: St. Martins, 1988:263-269.

Songs for the Old Religion. Oakland, CA: Nemeton, 1972.

Songs of Love and Pleasure, n.p.: Vanthi, 1977.

Sontag, Frederick. *Sun Myung Moon and the Unification Church.* Nashville, TN: Abingdon Press, 1977.

Sopa, Geshe Lhundub. *The Wheel of Time.* Madison, WI: Deer Park Books, 1985.

Sopa, Geshe Lhundup, and Jeffrey Hopkins. *Practice and Theory of Tibetan Buddhism.* New York: Grove Press, 1976.

Spalding, John Howard. *Introduction to Swedenborg's Religious Thought.* New York: Swedenborg Publishing Association, 1977.

Spangler, David, ed. *Conversations with John.* Elgin, IL: Lorian Press, 1980.

Spangler, David. *Emergence, the Rebirth of the Sacred.* New York: Delta, 1984.

Spangler, David. *Towards a Planetary Vision.* Forres, Scotland: Findhorn Publications, 1977.

Speak Shining Stranger. Austin, TX: Association for the Understanding of Man, 1975.

Special Report to the Readers of THE URANTIA BOOK: URANTIA Foundation Ends Its Relationship with the Former URANTIA Brotherhood. Chicago: URANTIA Foundation, 1990.

Speck, S. L., and H. M. Riggle. *Bible Readings for Bible Students.* Guthrie, OK: Faith Publishing House, 1975.

Speeth, Kathleen Riordan and Ira Friedlander. *Gurdjieff, Seeker of Truth.* New York: Harper & Row, 1980.

Speeth, Kathleen Riordan. *The Gurdjieff Work.* Berkeley, CA: And/Or Press, 1976.

The Spinner of Tales: A Collection of Stories as Told by Ramtha. Ed. by Deborah Kerins. Yelm, WA: New Horizon Publishing Co., 1991.

Spiritual Organization. New York: Integration Publishing Company, 1948.

The Spiritual Philosophy of Shrii Shrii Anandamurti. Denver, CO: Ananda Marga Publications, 1981.

Spiritual Unfoldment and Psychic Development Through Inner Light Consciousness. Atlanta, GA: Fellowship of the Inner Light, n.d.

Spraggett, Allen and William V. Rauscher. *Arthur Ford: The Man Who Talked with the Dead*. New York: New American Library, 1973.

Spretnak, Charlene, ed. *The Politics of Women's Spirituality*. Garden City, NY: Anchor Books, 1982.

Sproule, Terry. *A Prophet to the Gentiles*. Blaine, WA: Bible Believers, n.d.

Spruit, Herman A. *Constitution and Statement of Principles*. Mountain View, CA: Church of Antioch Press, 1978.

Spruit, Herman A. *The Sacramentarion*. Mountian View, CA: The Author, n.d.

Spruit, Mary, ed. *The Chalice of Antioch*. Mountian View, CA: Archbishop Herman Adrian Spruit, 1979.

Spurling, Richard, Jr. *The Lost Link*. Turtletown, TN: The Author, 1920.

Sri Nisargadatta Maharaj Presentation Volume: 1980. Bombay, India: Sri Nisargadatta Adhyatma Kendra, 1980.

Sridhara Deva Goswami, Srila Bhakti Raksaka. *The Golden Volcano of Divine Love*. San Jose, CA: Guardian of Devotion Press, 1984.

Sridhara Deva Goswami, Srila Bhakti Raksaka. *The Hidden Treasure of the Absolute*. West Bengal, India: Sri Chaitanya Saraswati Math, 1985.

Stam, Cornelius R. *Satan in Derision*. Chicago: Berean Bible Society, 1972.

Stam, Cornelius R. *The Controversy*. Chicago: Berean Bible Society, 1963.

Stam, Cornelius R. *Things That Differ*. Chicago: Berean Bible Society, 1951.

Stam, Cornelius R. *True Spirituality*. Chicago: Berean Bible Society, 1959.

Stanford, Ray. *Fatima Prophecy, Days of Darkness, Promise of Light*. Austin, TX: Association for the Understanding of Man, 1974.

Stanford, Ray. *The Spirit Unto the Churches*. Austin, TX: Association for the Understanding of Man, 1977.

Stanford, Ray. *What Your Aura Tells Me*. Garden City, NY: Doubleday, 1977.

Starhawk. *Dreaming the Dark*. Boston, MA: Beacon Press, 1982.

Starhawk. *The Spiral Dance*. New York: Harper & Row, 1979.

Starhawk. *The Spiral Dance: A Rebirth of the Ancient Religion of the Great Goddess*, 2d ed. San Francisco: Harper and Row, 1989.

Starry, David. "Dwight Goddard—The Yankee Buddhist." *Zen Notes* 27 (July 1980): 1-3.

Statement of Principles. San Diego, CA: Liberal Catholic Church, 1977.

Stearn, Jess. *Soul Mates*. New York: Bantam Books, 1984.

Stearn, Jess. *The Power of Alpha-Thinking; Miracle of the Mind*. New York: Morrow, 1976.

Stein, Diane. *The Women's Spirituality Book*. St. Paul, MN: Llewellyn Publications,

1987.

Steiner, Rudolf. *The Course of My Life*. New York: Anthroposophic Press, 1951.

Stelle, Robert D. *The Sun Rises*. Ramona, CA: Lemurian Fellowship, 1952.

Sterner, R. Eugene. *We Reach Our Hands in Fellowship*. Anderson, IN: Warner Press, 1960.

Stevens, John Robert. *Baptized in Fire*. North Hollywood, CA: Living Word Publications, 1977.

Stevens, John Robert. *Living Prophecies*. North Hollywood, CA: Living Word Publications, 1974.

Stevens, John Robert. *Present Priorities*. North Hollywood, CA: Living Word Publications, 1968.

Stevens, John Robert. *The Lordship of Jesus Christ*. North Hollywood, CA: Living Word Publications, 1969.

Stevenson, Ian. *Twenty Cases Suggestive of Reincarnation*, 2d ed. Charlottesville, VA: University Press of Virginia, 1974.

Stewart, Omer C. *Peyote Religion: A History*. Norman, OK: University of Oklahoma Press, 1987.

Stillings, Dennis. "I Walked on Fire." *Fate* 39:2. February 1986. Pp56-61.

Stocker, Clara T. *Realization through Concentrated Attention*. Pasadena, CA: Church of the Truth, n.d.

Stockman, Robert H. *The Bahá Faith in America: Origins, 1892-1900, Volume 1*. Wilmette, IL: Bahá Publishing Trust, 1985.

Stoes, K. D. *The Land of Shalam*. Evansville, Indiana: 1958.

Stokes, Keith. "Plane Searchers Seek More Help." *The Newport Daily Express* (Friday, August 6, 1993).

Stone, James. *The Church of God of Prophecy: History and Polity*. Cleveland, TN: White Wing Press, 1977.

Stone, Merlin. *When God Was a Woman*. New York: Harcourt Brace Javonovich, 1976.

Storey, Kenneth. *Worldwide Church of God in Prophecy*. Pasadena, CA: World Insight International, 1979.

The Story of the Aetherius Society. Hollywood, CA: Aetherius Society, n.d.

The Story of the Lotus Ashram. Miami, FL: Lotus Ashram, n.d.

The Story of the White Eagle Lodge. Liss, Hampshire, England: White Eagle Publishing Trust, 1986.

Stowes, K.D. *The Land of Shalam, Children's Land*. Evansville, IN: Frank Molinet Print Shop, n.d.

Strang, James J. *The Prophetic Controversy*. Lansing, MI: n.p., 1969.

Strang, Mark A., ed. *The Diary of James J. Strang*. East Lansing, MI: Michigan State University Press, 1961.

Straughn, R. A. *Black Woman's, Black Man's Guide to a Spiritual Union*. Bronx, NY: Maat Publishing Company, 1976.

Straughn, R. A. *Meditation Techniques of the Kabalists, Vedantins and Taoists*. Bronx, NY: Maat Publishing Company, 1976.

Straughn, R. A. *The Oracle of Thoth: The Kabalistical Tarot*. Bronx, NY: Oracle of Thoth Publishing Company, 1977.

Straughn, R. A. *The Realization of Neter Nu*. Brooklyn, NY: Maat Publishing Company, 1975.

Strieber, Whitley. *Communion*. New York: Morrow/Beech Tree Books, 1987.

Strong, Donald S. *Organized Anti-Semitism in America*. Washington: American Council of Public Affairs, 1941.

Stuart, David. *Alan Watts*. New York: Stein and Day, 1976.

Stupple, David W. *A Functional Approach to Social Movements with an Analysis of the I AM Religious Sect and the Congress of Racial Equality*. Kansas City, MO: Master's thesis, University of Missouri, 1965.

Sturdivant, Lori. "The People of Jacob Hutter." *The Minneapolis Tribune* (October 16, 1977).

Subuh, Muhammad. *Susila Budhi Dharma* ("A poem received in high Javanese and Kawi, and later rendered into Indonesian, with Javanese, Indonesian and English translations"). England: Subud Publications International, 1975.

The Sufic Path. Berkeley, CA: Privately printed, n.d.

Sugrue, Thomas. *There is a River*. New York: Henry Holt & Co., 1945.

Sujata, Anagarika. *Beginning to See*. Denver: Sasana Yeiktha Meditation Center, 1973.

Sukul, Sri Deva Ram. *Yoga and Self-Culture*. New York: Yoga Institute of America, 1947.

Sukul, Sri Deva Ram. *Yoga Navajivan*. New York: Yoga Institute of America, 1947.

Sullivan, Edward C. *A Short History fo the Church of Antioch and Its Apostolic Succession*. Bellingham, WA: Holy Order of the Rose and Cross, 1981.

Sullivan, Edward C. and Jeffrey A. Isbrandtsen. "An Interview with Abbot George Burke." Parts 1, 2. *AROHN* 3, no. 3 (1980): 26-29, 24-30.

Sullivan, Matthew. *Living Religion in Subud*. East Sussex, England: Humanus, Ltd., 1991.

Summum, Sealed Except to the Open Mind. Salt Lake City, UT: Summum Press, 1988.

Sun Bear. *At Home in the Wilderness*. Happy Camp, CA: Naturegraph Publishers, 1968.

Sun Bear. *Path of Power*. Spokane, WA: Bear Tribe Publishing, 1983.

Sunim, Mu Soeng. *Thousand Peaks, Koeran Zen—Tradition and Teachers*. Berkeley, CA: Parallax Press, 1987.

Susag, S. O. *Personal Experiences*. Guthrie, OK: Faith Publishing House, 1976.

Suster, Gerald. *Crowley's Apprentice*. London: Rider, 1989.

Suster, Gerald. *The Legacy of the Beast: The Life, Work and Influence of Aleister Crowley*. York Beach, ME: Samuel Wizer, 1989.

Sutphen, Dick. *Sedona: Psychic Energy Vortexes*. Malibu, CA: Valley of the Sun Publishing, 1986.

Sutphen, Dick. *You Were Born Again to Be Together*. New York: Pocket Books, 1976. Suzuki, Daisetz Teitaro. *On Indian Mahayana Buddhism*. New York: Harper & Row, 1968.

Sutphen, Dick. *Zen Buddhism and Its Influences on Japanese Culture*. Kyoto, Japan: 1938. Rept. as *Zen and Japanese Culture*. Princeton, NJ: Princeton University Press, 1959.

Suzuki, Daisetz T. *The Chain of Compassion*. Cambridge, MA: Cambridge Buddhist Association, 1966.

Suzuki, Shunryu. *Zen Mind, Beginner's Mind*. New York: Weatherhill, 1970.

Swainson, William P. *Thomas Lake Harris and His Occult Teaching*. London: William Rider & Son, 1922.

"Swami Dayananda Renounces Chinmaya Mission West: Changes and Challenges Ahead." *New Saivite World* (Fall 1983).

Swami Prem Paramahansa and His Message. Hawthorne, CA: Intergalactic Lovetrance Civilization Center, 1983.

Swami, Jyotir Maya Nanda. *Yoga Can Change Your Life*. Miami, FL: International Yoga Society, 1975.

Swami, Jyotir Maya Nanda. *Yoga Vasistha*. Miami, FL: Yoga Research Society, 1977.

Swami, Murti. "The Interfaith City of God in New Vrindaban, West Virginia: Communalism with God at the Center." Paper read before the National Historic Communal Society, Winston-Salem, NC: 1988.

Swami, Paramahamsa Krishna. *Conspiracy in West Virginia*. n.p. [New Vrindaban]: n.p. [League of Devotees International], n.d. [1991].

Swami, Paramahamsa Krishna. "The Trial of Swami Bhakipada." *New Vrindaban World*: April 26, 1991, 3-6.

Swamiji, Ganapati Sachchidananda. *Insight into Spiritual Music*. Mysore, India: The Author, n.d.

Swank, George. *Bishop Hill, Showcase of Swedish History*. Galva, IL: 1965.

Swedenborg, Emanuel. *The New Jerusalem and Its Heavenly Doctrine*. Bryn Athyn, PA: The Lord's New Church, 1997.

Swedenborg, Emanuel. *Words of Spirit and Life*. Charleston, SC: Arcana Books, 1997.

Swedenborg, Emanuel. *The World of Spirits and Man's State After Death*. New York: Swedenborg Foundation, 1940.

Swift, Wesley A. *God, Man, Nations, and the Races*. Hollywood, CA: New Christian Decade Church, n.d.

Swift, Wesley A. *Testimony of Tradition and the Origin of Races*. Hollywood, CA: New Christian Crusade Church, n.d.

Swihart, Altma K. *Since Mrs. Eddy*. New York: Henry Holt and Company, 1931.

Switzer, A. Irwin III. *D. T. Suzuki: A Biography*. London: The Buddhist Society, 1985.

Sykes, Egerton. *Who's Who: Non-Classical Mythology*. New York: Oxford, 1993.

Szekely, Edmond Bordeaux. *Talks*. San Diego, CA: Academy of Creative Living, 1972.

Szekely, Edmond Bordeaux. *The Essene Gospel of Peace*. San Diego, CA: Academy of Creative Living, 1971.

Szekely, Edmond Bordeaux. *The Essene Way, Biogenic Living*. Cartago, Costa Rica: International Biogenic Society, 1978.

Tadbhavananda Avadhuta, Acharya. *Glimpses of Prout Philosophy*. Copenhagen, Denmark: Central Proutist Publications, 1981.

Taizan, Maezumi Hakuyu, and Bernard Tetsugen Glassman, eds. *The Hazy Moon of Enlightenment*. Los Angeles: Zen Center of Los Angeles, 1977.

Taneyhill, R. H. *The Leatherwood God*. Cincinnati: 1870.

Tanner, Jerald and Sandra Tanner. *Mormonism: Shadow or Reality?* Salt Lake City: Utah Lighthouse Ministry, 1982.

Tapp, Robert B. et al. "Theology and the Frontiers of Learning." In *The Free Church in a Changing World*. Boston: Unitarian Universalist Association, 1963. Pp. 25-26.

Tarasoff, Koozma J. *A Pictorial History of the Doukhobors*. Saskatoon, SK: Modern Press, 1969.

Tart, Charles. *Altered States of Consciousness*. Anchor, 1969.

The Task Force on Brethren History and Doctrine. *The Brethren: Growth in Life and Thought*. Ashland, OH: Board of Christian Education, Brethren Church, 1975.

Tattwa Katha: A Tale of Truth. New York: Ajapa Yoga Foundation, 1976.

Tawker, K. A. *Sivananda, One World Teacher*. Rishikish, India: Yoga-Vedanta Forest

University, 1957.

Taylor, Anne. *Annie Besant: A Biography*. Oxford: Oxford University Press, 1992.

Taylor, R. James. *200 Years: Joanna Southcott-1792 through the City of David, 1992*. n.p., 1992.

Taylor, Wayne H. *Pillars of Light*. Columbus, NM: The Author, 1965.

Taylor, William G. L. *Katie Fox*. New York: G. P. Putnam's Sons, 1933.

Teachings of Babaji. Nainital, India: Haidakhan Ashram, 1983-84.

Teachings of Meishu-Sama, 2 vols. Atami, Japan: Church of World Messianity, 1967-68.

Teachings of Meishu-Sama, 2 vols. Atami, Japan: Church of World Messianity, 1967-68.

Teachings of the Temple, 3 vols. Halcyon, CA: Temple of the People, 1947-85.

Tebecis, A. K. *Mahikari, Thank God for the Answers at Last*. Tokyo: L. H. Yoko Shuppan, 1982.

Tebecis, A.K. *Thank God for the Answers at Last*. Tokyo: L.H. Yoko Shuppan, 1982.

Teish, Luisah. *Jambalaya: The Natural Woman's Book of Personal Charms and Practical Rituals*. San Francisco: Harper & Row, 1985.

Tenrikyo, Its History and Teachings. Tenri, Japan: Tenrikyo Overseas Mission Department, 1966.

Tepper, Muriel R. *Mechanisms of Personality through Personology*. Pacific Palisade, CA: Lighted Way, n.d.

Tepper, Muriel R. *The Lighted Way to Freedom*. Los Angeles: Lighted Way Press, n.d.

Thakar, Singh, *Gospel of Love*. Delhi: Ruhani Satsang, 1984.

Thakar, Vimala. *On an Eternal Voyage*. Ahmedabad, India: New Order Book Co., 1972.

Thakar, Vimala. *Why Meditation?* Dehli, India: Motilal Banarsidass, 1977.

Thakur, Srila Bhaktivedanta. *Sri Chaitanya Mahaprabhu: His Life and Precepts*. Brooklyn, NY: Gaudiya Press, 1987.

Thakura, Bhaktivedanta. *The Bhagavat; Its Philosophy, It Ethics, and Its Theology*. San Jose, CA: Guardians of Devotion Press, 1985.

Thedick, Eleanor. *Jewels of Truth and Rays of Color*. Oakland, CA: Christ Ministry Foundation, n.d.

Thedick, Eleanor. *Light on Your Problems*. Oakland, CA: Christ Ministry Foundation, n.d.

Thedick, Eleanor. *The Christ Highway*. Oakland, CA: Christ Ministry Foundation, n.d.

Thedra, Sister. *Mine Intercome Messages from the Realms of Light*. Sedona, AZ: Association of Sananda and Sanat Kumara, 1990.

Thedra. *Excerpts of Prophecies from Other Planets Concerning Our Earth*. Mt. Shasta, CA: Association of Sananda and Sanat Kumara, 1956.

The Theosophical Movement: 1875-1950. Los Angeles: The Cunningham Press, 1951.

The Theosophical Society: Constitution, as amended August 27, 1971.

"The Theosophical Society: Inaugural Address of the President Delivered Before the Society November 17th, 1875."

Theriault, Harry W. *Grass Roots of the New Song*. Millington, TN: Book University of the New Song, 1979.

Thieme, R. B. *Anti-Semitism*. Houston, TX: Berachah Tapes and Publications, 1979.

Thieme, R. B. *Blood of Christ*. Houston, TX: Berachah Tapes and Publications, 1979.

Thieme, R. B. *Freedom Through Military Victory*. Houston, TX: Berachah Tapes and Publications, 1973.

Thieme, R. B. *The Integrity of God*. Houston, TX: Berachah Tapes and Publications, 1979.

Thirty Years' Work. New York: Lucis Publishing Company, n.d.

This We Believe. Wheaton, IL: Independent Fundamental Churches of America, 1970.

Thomas, Lately. *The Vanishing Evangelist*. New York: Viking Press, 1959.

Thomas, Wendell. *Hinduism Invades America*. New York: Beacon Press, 1930.

Thompson, A. *The Life of A.B. Simpson*. New York: 1921.

Thompson, Charles Blanchard. *The Nachash Origin of the Black and Mixed Races*. St. Louis: George Knapp & Co., 1860.

Thompson, Keith. "Portrait of a Sorcerer: An Interview with Carolos Castaneda." *New Age Journal* (April 1994). Pp. 66-71; 152-156.

Thomsen, Harry. *The New Religions of Japan*. Rutland, VT: Charles E. Tuttled Co., 1963.

Thorpe, Francis. *House of David Victory and Legal Troubles Reviewed*. Benton Harbor, MI: The Author, n.d.

Thurman, Howard. *Disciplines of the Spirit*. New York: Harper & Row, 1963.

Thurman, Howard. *Illuminous Darkenss*. New York: Harper & Row, 1965.

Thurman, Howard. *The First Footsteps*. San Francisco, 1975.

Thurman, Howard. *The Inward Journey*. New York: Harper & Row, 1961.

Thurman, Howard. *With Heart and Head*. New York: Harcourt Brace Jovanovich, 1979.

Tillett, Gregory. *The Elder Brother: A Biography of Charles Webster Leadbeater*. London: Routledge & Kegan Paul, 1982.

Tims, Dana. "Azalea Sect Riles Region." *Oregonian* (April 7, 1988).

Tinney, James S. "William J. Seymour: Father of Modern-Day Pentecostalism." In Randall K. Burkett and Richard Newman, eds. *Black Apostles*. Boston: G. K. Hall, 1978.

Tirth, Shivam. *A Guide to Shaktipat*. Paige, TX: Devatma Shakti Society, 1985.

Tiryakian, Edward, ed. *On the Margin of the Visible*. New York: John Wiley and Sons, 1974.

Tkach, Joseph. *Transformed by Truth*. Sisters, OR: Multnomah Publishers, 1997.

Toksvig, Signe. *Emanuel Swedenborg, Scientist and Mystic*. New Haven, CT: Yale University Press, 1948.

Tolles, Frederick. *Meeting House and Counting House*. Chapel Hill, NC: University of North Carolina Press, 1948.

Tomlinson, A. J. *Diary*. 3 vols. Queens Village, NY: Church of God, World Headquarters, 1949.

Tomlinson, Homer A. *Miracles of Healing in the Ministry of Rev. Francisco Olazabal*. Queens Village, New York: The Author, 1939.

Tomlinson, Homer A. *The Shout of a King*. Queens Village, NY: Church of God, 1968.

Torre, Teofilo de la. *Psycho-Physical Regeneration, Rejuvenation and Longevity*. Milwaukee, WI: Lemurian Press, 1938.

Torres, Penny [Mafu]. *And What Be God?* Vacaville, CA: Mafu Seminars, 1989.

Torres, Penny [Mafu]. *Reflections on Yeshua Ben Joseph*. Vacaville, CA: 1989.

Towne, Elizabeth. "A Church of the New Thought." *The Nautilus* 10 (June 1908): 44.

Towne, Elizabeth. *Joy Philosophy*. Chicago: Psychic Research Co., 1903.

Towne, Elizabeth. *Practical Methods for Self-Development*. Holyoke, MA: E. Towne Co., 1904.

Traditions of Jodoshinshu Hongwanji-Ha. Los Angeles: Senshin Buddhist Temple, 1982.

Trafzer, Clifford E., ed. *American Indian Prophets*. Newcastle, CA: Sierra Oaks, 1986.

Traill, Stewart. *The Gospel of John in Colors*. Worcester, MA: Church of Bible Understanding, 1976.

A Treatise of the Faith and Practices of the Free Will Baptists. Nashville, TN: Executive Office of the National Association of Free Will Baptists, 1981.

Trine, Ralph Waldo. *The Greatest Thing Ever Known*. New York: Thomas Y. Crowell, 1899.

Triumph with Christ. Vancouver, BC: Bible Holiness Movement, 1984.

Trobridge, George. *Swedenborg, Life and Teachings*. New York: Swedenborg Foundation, 1907.

Troeger, Thomas H. *Meditation: Escape to Reality*. Philadelphia: Westminster Press, 1977.

Troxell, Hope. *From Matter to Light*. June Lake, CA: School of Thought, 1968.

Troxell, Hope. *The Mohada Teachings*. Independence, CA: School of Thought, 1963.

Troxell, Hope. *Through the Open Key*. El Monte, CA: Understanding Publishing Co., n.d.

Trungpa, Chögyam. *Born in Tibet*. Boulder, CO: Shambhala, 1976.

Trungpa, Chögyam. *Shambhala: Sacred Path of the Warrior*. Boulder, CO: Shambhala, 1985.

Trust, Josephine C. *Bible Mystery by Superet Light Science*. Los Angeles: Superet Press, 1950.

Trust, Josephine C. *Superet Light*. Los Angeles: Superet Light Center, 1953.

Tuella (Thelma B. Terrell). *Ashtar: A Tribute*. Durango, CO: Guardian Action Publication, 1985.

Tuella (Thelma B. Terrell). *Project World Evacuation*. Salt Lake City, UT: Guardian Action International, 1982.

Tumminia, Diana and R. George Kirkpatrick. "Unarius: Emergent Aspects of a Flying Saucer Group" In *The Gods Have Landed: New Religions from Other Worlds*. James R. Lewis, ed. Albany: SUNY Press, 1995.

Turiyasangitananda, A.C. *Endless Wisdom*. Los Angeles: Avatar Book Institute, 1981.

Turiyasangitananda, A.C. *Monument Eternal*. Los Angeles: Vedantic Book Press, 1977.

Turner, Alice K. *The History of Hell*. New York: Harcourt Brace & Co., 1993.

Turner, W. G. *John Nelson Darby*. London: C. A. Hammond, 1944.

Twitchell, Paul. *Difficulties of Becoming the Living ECK Master*. Menlo Park, CA: IWP Publishing, 1980.

Twitchell, Paul. *ECKANKAR: The Key to Secret Worlds*. Crystal, MN: Illuminated Way Press, 1969.

U.L.T. "Biochronology of Robert Crosbie." Unpublished.

U.L.T. "U.L.T. History: The United Lodge of Theosophists: 1909 to date." Unpublished.

Unitarian Universalist Association: 1992 Directory. Boston: Unitarian Universalist Association, 1992.

Universal Spiritualist Manual. N.p.: Universal Spiritual Church, n.d.

Update on the Reappearance of Christ. North Hollywood, CA: Tara Center, 1983.

The URANTIA Book. Chicago: URANTIA Foundation, 1955.

Valer, Nola Van. *My Meeting with the Masters on Mt. Shasta.* Mt. Shasta, CA: Radiant School, 1982.

Valiente, Doreen. *The Rebirth of Witchcraft.* London: Robert Hale, 1989.

Van Anderson, Helen. *The Illumined Life.* Chicago: A. C. McClurg & Co., 1912.

Van Anderson, Helen. *The Journal of a Live Woman.* Boston: Lee and Shepard, 1895.

Van Der Leeuw, G. *Religion in Essence and Manifestaton, Vol. I.* Gloucester, MA: Peter Smith, 1967. Transl. of first German edition, 1933.

Van Straelen, Henry. *The Religion of Divine Wisdom.* Kyoto, Japan: Veritas Shoin, 1957.

Van Tassel, George. *I Rode a Flying Saucer.* Los Angeles: New Age Publishing Co., 1956.

Van Tassel, George. *When Stars Look Down.* Los Angeles: Kruckeberg Press, 1976.

Varner, K.H. *Prevail.* Little Rock, AR: Revival Press, 1982.

Vasiliev, Leonid L. *Mysterious Phenomena of the Human Psyche.* New York: University Books, 1965.

Vasudevadas. *Running Out of Time and Who's Catching?* Bedford, VA: Prema Dharmasala, 1979.

Vasudevadas. *Vasudevadas Speaks to Your Heart.* Bedford, VA: Prema Dharmasala and Fellowship Association, 1976.

Verity. *The Going and the Glory.* Auckland, New Zealand: Heralds of the New Age, 1966.

Vethathiri, Yogiraj. *Sex and Spiritual Development.* Madras, India: Vethathiri Publications, 1982.

Vethathiri, Yogiraj. *The Story of My Life.* Madras, India: Vethathiri Publications, 1982.

Vimalananda, Dadaji. *Yogamritam (The Nectar of Yoga).* San Rafael, CA: Yoga Ashram House, 1977.

Vincent, T. G. *Black Power and the Garvey Movement.* Berkeley, CA: Ramparts Press, 1976.

Vintage Years. Mobile, AL: New Wine Magazine, 1980.

Visions of a Better World. London: Brahma Kumaris World Spiritual University, 1993.

Vivekananda, Swami. *The Complete Works of Swami Vivekananda.* 12 vols. Calcutta, India: Advaita Ashrama, 1965.

Volpe, Anthony, and Lynn Volpe. *Principles and Purposes of Delval UFO, Inc.* Ivyland, PA: The Authors, n.d.

Von Däniken, Erich. *Chariots of the Gods? Unsolved Mysteries of the Past*. New York: G.P. Putnam's Sons, 1970.

von Straelen, Henry. *The Religion of Divine Wisdom*. Kyoto, Japan: Veritas Shoin, 1957.

von Straelen, Henry. *The Religion of Divine Wisdom*. Kyoto, Japan: Veritas Shoin, 1957.

Vorilhon, Claude (1986) *Extraterrestrial Took Me to their Planet*. Brantome: l'Edition du Message.

Wachsmuth, Guenther. *The Life and Work of Rudolf Steiner*. New York: Whittier Books, 1955.

Wadia, B. P. *To All Fellow Theosophists and Members of the Theosophical Society*. Los Angeles, 1922.

Wagner, H. O., comp. *A Treasure Chest of Wisdom*. Denver, CO: H. O. Wagner, 1967.

Waite, Arthur Edward. *A New Encyclopaedia of Freemasonry*. 1898. New York: Weathervane Books, 1970.

Waite, Arthur Edward. *The Brotherhood of the Rosy Cross*. London: Rider, 1924.

Wakefield, Wesley H. *Bible Doctrine*, n.p., n.d.

Waldron, Caryline. "Bashar: an Extraterrestrial Among Us." *Life Times* 3.

Waley, Arthur. *The Way and Its Power*. New York: Grove Press, 1968.

Walker, Robert G. *The False Teachings of R. B. Thieme, Jr*. Collinwood, NJ: Bible for Today, 1972.

Walker, William J. *History of the Remnant of Israel*. Opportunity, WA: Remnant of Israel, n.d.

Wall, Joe Layton. *Bob Thieme's Teaching on Christian Living*. Houston, TX: Church Multiplication, 1978.

Wallis, Roy. "The Aetherius Society: A Case Study in the Formation of a Mystagogic Congregation." *Sociological Review* 22 1974: 27-44.

Walser, Allen H. *Who Are the Moravians*. Bethlehem, PA: The Author, 1966.

Walters, J. Donald. *Cities of Light*. Nevada City, CA: Crystal Clarity Publishers, 1987.

Walters, J. Donald. *The Path*. Nevada City, CA: Ananda Publications, 1977.

Wangyal, Geshe. *The Door of Liberation*. New York: Maurice Girodias Associates, 1973.

Wanted: The Answer to Abortion. Island Pond, VT: Island Pond Freepaper, 1987.

Ward, Gary L., Bertil Persson, and Alan Bain, eds. *Independent Bishops: An International Directory*. Detroit, MI: Apogee Books, 1990.

Ward, Gary L., ed., *Spiritualism I: Spiritualist Thought.* New York: Garland Publishing Co., 1990.

Warner, Daniel S. *The Church of God.* Guthrie, OK: Faith Publishing House, n.d.

Warshaw, Ma. *Tradition, Orthodox Jewish Life in America.* New York: Schrocken, 1976.

Waskow, Arthur I. *The Bush Is Burning.* New York: MacMillan Company, 1971.

Wassen, Ralph, ed. *Yada Speaks.* San Diego, CA: Kethra E'Da Foundation, 1985.

Watkins, Edward L. *The Teachings and the Liberation.* Mt. Shasta, CA: Association of Sananda and Sanat Kumara, 1977.

Watkins, Susan M. *Conversations with Seth.* 2 vols. Englewood Cliffs, NJ: Prentice-Hall, 1981.

Watson, Lyall. *Supernature.* Garden City, NY: Anchor Press, 1973.

Watts, Alan, and Chungliang Al Haing. *Tao: the Watercourse Way.* New York: Pantheon Books, 1975.

Watts, Alan. *In My Own Way.* New York: Pantheon Books, 1972.

The Way and Goal of Raja Yoga. Mount Abu, India: Prajapita Brahma Kumaris Ishwariya Vishwa Vidyalaya, 1975.

"We Believe." Hartford, CT: Christian Millennial Church, 1980.

We're Your Neighbor. Alma, AR: Holy Alamo Christian Church Consecrated, 1987.

Weaver, C. Douglas. *The Healer-Prophet, William Marrion Branham: A Study in the Prophetic in American Pentecostalism.* Macon, GA: Mercer University Press, 1987.

Weaver, Dusk, and Willow Weaver. *Sunburst, A People, A Path, A Purpose.* San Diego, CA: Avant Books, 1982.

Webb, Gisela. *"Subud."* *America's Alternative Religions,* Timothy Miller, ed. Albany: State University of New York Press, 1995.

Webb, Gisela. *"Sufism in America."* *America's Alternative Religions,* Timothy Miller, ed. Albany, NY: State University of New York Press, 1995.

Webb, James. *The Harmonious Circle.* New York: G. P. Putnam's Sons, 1980.

Webb, Lillian Ashcraft. *About My Father's Business.* Westport, CT: Greenwood Press, 1981.

Webber, Everett. *Escape to Utopia: The Communal Movement in America.* New York: Hastings House Publishers, 1959.

Weiner, Bob and Weiner, Rose. *Bible Studies for a Firm Foundation.* Gainesville, FL: Maranatha Publications, 1980.

Weiner, Bob and Weiner, Rose. *Bible Studies for the Life of Excellence.* Gainesville, FL: Maranatha Publications, 1981.

Weiner, Bob and Weiner, Rose. *Bible Studies for the Lovers of God.* Gainesville, FL: Maranatha Publications, 1980.

Weinlick, John R. *The Moravian Church Through the Ages*. Moravian Church in America, 1988.

Weisbrot, Robert. *Father Divine and the Struggle for Racial Equality*. Urbana, IL: University of Illinois Press, 1983.

Weiss, Jann. *Reflections by Anoah*. Austin, TX: Planetary Light Association, 1986.

Welch, Holmes. *Taoism, The Parting of the Way*. Boston: Beacon Press, 1965.

Weltmer, Sidney A. "Tenets of the Weltmer Philosophy." Weltmer's Magazine 1 (October 1901): 39.

Weltmer, Sidney A. *The Healing Hand*. Nevada, MO: Weltmer Institute of Suggestive Therapeutics, 1918.

Wentz, Abdel Ross. *A Basic History of Lutheranism in America*. Philadelphia: Muhlenberg Press, 1964.

Weor, Samuel Aun. *The Perfect Matrimony*. New York: Adonai Editorial, 1980.

West, Earl. *Search for the Ancient Order*. 4 vols. Nashville, Indianapolis, and Germantown, TN: Gospel Advocate Company and Religious Book Service, 1950-87.

What Is Arcana? Beverly Hills, CA: Arcana Workshops, n.d.

What Say the Scriptures About the Ransom, Sin Offering, Covenants, Mediator, Scapegoat? Melbourne, Australia: Covenant Publishing Company, 1920.

What the Writings Testify Concerning Themselves. Bryn Athyn, PA: General Church Publication Committee, 1961.

The What? Where? When? Why? and How? of the House of David. Benton Harbor, MI: Israelite House of David, 1931.

Wheatley, Richard. *The Life and Letters of Mrs. Phoebe Palmer*. New York: 1876.

Wheaton, Clarence L., and Angela Wheaton. *The Book of Commandments Controversy Reviewed*. Independence, MO: Church of Christ (Temple Lot), 1950.

When Pastor Russel Died. East Rutherford, NJ: Dawn Bible Students Association, 1946.

The Whirlwind of the Lord. War! Exeter, MO: Universal Publishing Association, 1987.

White, James. *Sketches of the Christian Life and Public Labors of William Miller*. Battle Creek, MI: Steam Press, 1875.

White, Joseph. *Musser Celestial or Plural Marriage*. Salt Lake City, UT: Truth Publishing Co., 1944.

White, Philip. "Island Pond Raid 10 Years Later: State Versus Church." *The Sunday Rutland Herald and the Sunday Times Argus*. (June 19, 1994).

Whitfield, Thomas. *From Night to Sunlight*. Nashville, TN: Broadman Press, 1980.

Whitney, Louise Goddard. *The Burning of the Convent*. New York: Arno Press, 1969;

rpt. of 1877.

Whitten, Ivah Bergh. *The Initial Course in Colour Awareness*. London: Amica, n.d.

Who Do You Worship? Abilene, TX: House of Yahweh, n.d.

Who Is Swami Prem Paramahansa Mahaprabho? Hawthorne, CA: Intergalactic Lovetrance Civilization Center, [1982].

Whorf, Raymond B. *The Tibetan's Teachings*. Ojai, CA: Meditation Groups Inc., n.d.

Wickland, Carl A. *Thirty Years Among the Dead*. North Hollywood, Calif.: Newcastle Publishing Co., 1974. First published 1924.

Widmar, Siegfried J. *The Political Kingdom of God*. El Paso, TX: The Author, 1975.

Wight, Lyman. *An Address by Way of an Abridged Account and Journal of My Life from February 1844 up to April 1848, with an Appeal to the Latter Day Saints, Scattered Abroad in the Earth*. Austin, TX: The Author, 1848.

Wilbur, Henry W. *The Life and Labours of Elias Hicks*. Philadelphia: 1910.

Wilcox, Hal. *Contact With the Master*. Hollywood, CA: Galaxy Press, 1984.

Wilcox, Hal. *Gateway to the Superconsciousness*. Hollywood, CA: The Author, n.d.

Wiley, Elnora. *Inside the Shalam Colony*, n.p., n.d.

Wilgus, Neal. *The Illuminoids*. New York: Pocket Books, 1978.

Wilk, Chester A. *Chiropractic Speaks Out*. Park Ridge, IL: Wilk Publishing Co., 1976.

Wilkerson, Clark L. *Celestial Wisdom*. Gardena, CA: Institute of Cosmic Wisdom, 1965.

Wilkerson, Clark L. *Hawaiian Magic*. Playa Del Rey, CA: Institute of Cosmic Wisdom, 1968.

Wilklson, David. "Dark Side to Palace: Krishnas See New Dawn Despite Shrine's Trouble." *Chicago Tribune*. Evening update: April 21, 1994, 8.

Williams, Cyrill G. *Tongues of the Spirit: A Study of Pentecostal Glossolalia and Related Phenomena*. Cardiff, 1981.

Williams, Gertrude M. *Priestess of the Occult*. New York: Alfred A. Knopf, 1946.

Williams, Raymond Brady. *A New Face of Hinduism: The Swaminarayan Religion*. Cambridge: Cambridge University Press, 1984.

Williams, Raymond Brady. *Religions of Immigrants from India and Pakistan: New Threads of the American Tapestry*. New York: Cambridge University Press, 1988.

Williams, Smallwood Edmond. *Significant Sermons*. Washington, DC: Bible Way Church Press, 1970.

Williams, Smallwood Edmond. *This Is My Story*. Washington, DC: Wm. Willoughby Publishers, 1981.

Williamson, George Hunt [Brother Philip]. *The Brotherhood of the Seven Rays*. Clarksburg, VA: Saucerian Books, 1961.

Williamson, George Hunt. *Road in the Sky*. London: Neville Spearman, 1959.

Williamson, George Hunt. *Secret Places of the Lion*. London: Neville Spearman, 1959.

Williamson, George Hunt. *The Saucers Speak*. London: Neville Spearman, 1963.

Wilmans, Helen. *A Search for Freedom*. Sea Breeze, FL: Freedom Publishing Co., 1898.

Wilmans, Helen. "Temple News." *Freedom* 9 (October 23, 1901): 9.

Wilson, Colin. *Afterlife*. London: Harrap, 1985.

Wilson, Ernest C. "Dr. H. Emilie Cady: Author with Authority." *Unity Magazine* (June 1979): 4-9.

Wilson, Robert Anton and Robert Shea. *The Illuminatus Trilogy*. New York: Pocket Books, 1973.

Wilson, Robert Anton. *Cosmic Trigger: The Final Secret of the Illuminati*. Berkeley, CA: And/Or Press, 1977.

Wilson, Robert Anton. *Masks of the Illuminati*. New York: Pocket Books, 1981.

Wilson, Robert Anton. *Schroedinger's Cat*. 3 vols. New York: Pocket Books, 1980-81.

Wilson, Robert Anton. *The Illuminati Papers*. Berkeley, CA: And/Or Press, 1980.

Wimber, John, with Kevin Springer. *Power Evangelism. Praise Offerings*. Anaheim, CA: Vineyard Christian Fellowship, 1977.

Winberg, Steven L., ed. *Ramtha*. Eastsound, WA: Sovereignty, 1986.

Wingo, E. Otha. *The Story of the Huna Work*. Cape Girardeau, MO: Huna Research, 1981.

Winkler, Arthur. *Hypnotherapy*. Valley, NB: Eastern Nebraska Christian College, 1972.

Winkler, Herbert E. *Congregational Cooperation of the Churches of Christ*. Nashville, TN: The author, 1961.

The Wisdom of White Eagle. Liss, Hampshire, England: White Eagle Publishing Trust, 1967.

Wisdom Workshop Lessons, Series 1. 12 vols. Los Angeles: Fellowship of Universal Guidance, n.d.

Witherspoon, Thomas E. *Myrtle Fillmore: Mother of Unity*. Unity Village, MO: Unity Books, 1977.

Wittek, Gabriele. *The Path of Love to God*. New Haven, CT: Christ State, 1984.

Wolff, William. *Healers, Gurus, and Spiritual Guides*. Los Angeles: Sherbourne Press, 1969.

Wood, Henry. *Ideal Suggestion Through Mental Photography*. Boston: Lee & Shepard, 1893.

Wood, Samuel. *The Infinite God*. Fresno, CA: The Author, 1934.

Woodcock, George, and Ivan Avakumovic. *The Doukhobors*. Toronto: Oxford University Press, 1968.

The Word of the Lord. Independence, MO: Church of Christ, 1935.

World Peace Gathering. San Francisco: Sino-American Buddhist Association, 1975.

Wright, Arthur F., ed. *The Confucian Persuasion*. Stanford, CA: Stanford University Press, 1960.

Wright, Conrad. *The Beginnings of Unitarianism in America*. Boston: Starr King Press. Distributed by Beacon Press, 1955.

Wroe, John. *The Life and Journal of John Wroe*. Ashton-under-Lyne, England: 1900.

Yahweh's Passover and Yahshua's Memorial. Abilene, TX: House of Yahweh, n.d.

Yanagawa, Keiichi. *Japanese Religions in California*. Tokyo: Department of Religious Studies, University of Tokyo, 1983.

Yeakley, Flavil R., ed. *The Discipling Dilemma: A Study of the Discipling Movement Among Churches of Christ*. Nashville, TN: Gospel Advocate Co., 1988.

Yehuda, Shaleak Ben. *Black Hebrew Israelites from America to the Promised Land*. New York: Vantage Press, 1975.

Yeshe, Thubten, and Thubten Zopa. *Wisdom Energy*. Honolulu, HI: Conch Press, 1976.

Yin, Heng, comp. *Records of the Life of the Venerable Master Hsuan Hua*, 2 vols. San Francisco: Committee for the Publication of the Biography of the Venerable Master Hsuan Hua, 1973-75.

Yinger, J. Milton. *Religion, Society, and the Individual*. New York: Macmillan, 1957.

Yoder, Elmer S. *The Beachy Amish Mennonite Fellowship Churches*. Hartville, OH: Diakonia Ministries, 1987.

Yogananda, Paramahansa. *Autobiography of a Yogi*. Los Angeles: Self-Realization Fellowship, 1946.

Yogananda, Swami Paramahansa. *Autobiography of a Yogi*, 11th ed. Los Angeles: Self-Realization Fellowship, 1971.

Yogananda, Swami Paramahansa. *The Science of Religion*. Los Angeles: Yogoda Sat-Sanga Society of America, 1928.

Young, Henry James, ed. *God and Human Freedom*. Richmond, IN: Friends United Press, 1983.

Yutang, Lin. *The Wisdom of Confucius*. New York: The Modern Library, Random House, Inc., 1938.

Zablocki, Benjamin. *The Joyful Community*. Baltimore, MD: Penguin Books, 1971.

Zacharias, Paul. *Death, Dying and Beyond*. Pasadena, CA: Dhyanyoga Centers, 1979.

Zacharias, Paul. *Insights into the Beyond*. New York: Swedenborg Publishing Association, n.d.

Zacharias, Paul. *Light on Meditation*. Los Angeles: 1978.

Zacharias, Paul. *Message to Disciples*. Bombay, India: Shri Dhyanyogi Mandal, 1968.

Zacharias, Paul. *Shakti, Hidden Treasure of Power*. Pasadena, CA: Dhyanhoga Centers, 1979.

Zahn, Michael. "Heaven City Dies with Founder" *Milwaukee Journal* (August 14, 1979).

Zalman, Aryeh Hilsenrad. *The Baal Shem Tov*. Brooklyn, NY: 1967.

Zell, Timothy [Otter]. *Cataclysm and Consciousness: From the Golden Age to the Age of Iron*. Redwood Valley, CA: The Author, 1977.

Zimmer, Heinrich. *Philosophies of India*. New York: Bollingen, 1951. Macmillan, 1987.

Zinsstag, Lou. *George Adamski, Their Man on Earth*. Tucson, AZ: UFO Photo Archives, 1990.

Zion's Echoes of Truth. Box 110, French Lick, IN 47432.

Zuber, Janet W., trans. *Barbara Heineman Landmann Biography/E. L. Gruber's Teaching on Divine Inspiration and Other Essays*. Lake Mills, IA: Graphic Publishing Company, 1981.

Zuromski, Paul. "A Conversation with Shirley MacLaine." *Psychic Guide* 2 (December 1983): 11-15.